SHORT ESSAYS
SEVENTH EDITION

GERALD LEVIN
PROFESSOR EMERITUS OF ENGLISH
University of Akron

Harcourt Brace College Publishers

Fort Worth   Philadelphia   San Diego   New York   Orlando   Austin   San Antonio
Toronto   Montreal   London   Sydney   Tokyo

Publisher   *Ted Buchholz*
Senior Acquisitions Editor   *Stephen Jordan*
Senior Developmental Editor   *Sarah Helyar Smith*
Project Editor   *John Haakenson*
Production Manager   *Tad Gaither*
Senior Art Director   *Don Fujimoto*

Cover Image: © Laurie Rubin / The Image Bank

Address for Editorial Correspondence: Harcourt Brace College Publishers, 301 Commerce Street, Suite 3700, Fort Worth, TX 76102.

Address for Orders: Harcourt Brace & Company, 6277 Sea Harbor Drive, Orlando, FL 32887-6777. 1-800-782-4479, or 1-800-433-0001 (in Florida).

ISBN: 0-15-501188-X

Library of Congress Catalog Card Number: 94-76300

Printed in the United States of America

4 5 6 7 8 9 0 1 2 3   066   9 8 7 6 5 4 3 2 1

Preface

Short Essays, Seventh Edition, emphasizes students' choices in the organization and development of ideas. Like the Sixth Edition, it covers the rhetorical modes and strategies important to the student writer, illustrating each with three- to five-page essays. The book gives equal attention to expository and argumentative writing, with discussion of inductive and deductive reasoning and paired essays on two important issues. Brief comments that follow each essay point to features that are the basis of the questions that follow. The essays by outstanding contemporary and older writers cover a broad range of interesting topics.

The range of subjects continues to be wide, including differences in how men and women converse, censorship, changing values in American life, the Nez Percé, the effect of stereotypes, liberal and conservative values, testing for drugs on the college campus, fighting ground fires, dialects, and the social life of dogs. Of the 76 essays, 21 are new to this edition.

As in the Sixth Edition, Part One discusses strategies for organizing and developing the essay, including example, process, comparison and contrast, cause and effect, definition, and classification and division. Narration and description are also discussed. Part Two discusses strategies for expressive writing, with a focus on autobiographical and reflective essays. Part Three discusses strategies for exposition—returning to example, process, and other methods discussed in Part One to show how they combine in various essays. Part Four discusses strategies of argument and persuasion and presents contrasting articles on two controversial issues. Finally, Part Five discusses sentence style and diction, at various levels of usage. Six topics are discussed: emphasis, parallelism and sentence variety, concreteness, figurative language, tone, and usage.

Each of the five parts of the book opens with an introductory discussion of the rhetorical or logical topic and an analysis of a representative essay in light of the specific topics. Part Four contains introductory analyses of an argumentative and a persuasive essay. Each essay in the book is followed by a comment on the rhetorical principles discussed in the section. The Questions for Study and Discussion explore the content and rhetoric of the essay, developing points in the general comment. The Vocabulary Study supplements these questions.

A thematic table of contents appears at the beginning of the book. Since each essay illustrates topics other than the one it illustrates in the book, instructors may want to switch essay and rhetorical topic or group essays on a single theme. Suggestions for Teaching and Suggestions for Writing in the Instructor's Manual often suggest alternatives for teaching.

Again, I wish to thank Andrea A. Lunsford, Ohio State University, and Anne Raimes, Hunter College of the City University of New York, for their advice on the first edition. Eben W. Ludlow originally suggested the book, helped to plan it, and gave me strong encouragement and support. Thanks also to former colleagues at the University of Akron for suggestions over many years. I owe thanks as well to those who have contributed their suggestions for the Seventh Edition and for the Instructor's Manual: Tonya Amankwatia, St. Petersburg Junior College; Roger Craik, Kent State University, Ashtabula; Godfrey Gattiker, Wilson College; Larry LaPointe, University of Maine; Debra Levy, Indiana Institute of Technology; Patrick McGuire, University of Wisconsin; and Shirley Sawdon, South Puget Sound Community College.

I owe special thanks to those who produced this book: to Stephen T. Jordan, senior editor; Sarah Helyar Smith, senior developmental editor; John Haakenson, project editor; Sheila Shutter, permissions editor; Don Fujimoto, senior art director; and Tad Gaither, production manager.

My debt to my wife, Lillian Levin, is a great one. Christopher, Daniel, and Sarah Rubin, and Matthew and Meredith Ziegler were always in mind. So, too, were Sylvia and David Rubin and Elizabeth and Bill Ziegler.

GERALD LEVIN

Contents

Thematic Table of Contents

Contemporary Social Issues

Animal Experimentation

Crime

Drug-Testing

The Environment

Gender

Multiculturalism

Introduction

This book is concerned with essays of personal expression, information or exposition, and persuasion, and it shows how they each serve particular purposes. The purposes for which we write are so numerous that no one classification can account for all of them, but one recent classification distinguishes four purposes: personal expression, reference or giving information, creating literary effect, and persuasion. These purposes are not exclusive of one another. Thus, an essay may express one's personal feelings or beliefs, and it may also give information about a particular subject, as in a textbook, or generate laughter or pathos as in a play or novel, or seek to change opinion on an issue as in a political speech. A piece of writing may have several purposes. For example, a satirical essay may amuse and inform us about a contemporary issue while it seeks to persuade us to change our minds about the issue.

Part One of this book presents various strategies for organizing and developing essays. One strategy is to develop a central impression or central idea or thesis for the essay as a whole. The individual paragraphs of the essay would also contain a topic sentence or statement of the subject or guiding idea. In turn, the paragraphs would have some kind of organization or order of ideas, held together by transitional words and phrases. Other strategies or means of development include narration and description. In writing home about your first week at college, you might use narration to give a chronological account of the events of the week and description to give details about your room, new friends, or classes. Still other means of developing the essay include example, process, comparison and contrast, cause and effect, definition, and classification and division. In your letter you might use the registration of classes as an example of why college life can be frustrating, give details of the registration process, compare and contrast a college class with a high school class, give reasons for differences you find, define a new interest or activity you have taken up, or classify the various friends or teachers encountered during the week.

Part Two of the book describes two important kinds of expressive writing—autobiography and reflection. Part Three shows how various methods of development such as definition and comparison and contrast work together to give information. Part Four describes strategies for developing arguments and making them persuasive. Persuasive essays use narration, description, and other means of development such as definition, classification, and comparison and contrast, but they chiefly use argument. Argument is concerned with establishing the truth of statements; persuasion, with getting readers to accept these statements and perhaps take action that the statements support. Part Five describes ways of making sentences and diction serve the various purposes of the essay.

The questions and suggestions for writing that follow each selection will give you practice in achieving various objectives through various means or strategies. Although an understanding of purposes and strategies alone will not make you a better writer, knowledge of how other writers develop their experiences and ideas will help in drafting and revising your own essays. You will become a better writer only through constant writing and revision. The essays presented here are examples of proven ways of organizing and developing essays. They show how a wide range of writers who differ in background and interest achieve their various purposes.

PART ONE

STRATEGIES FOR ORGANIZING AND DEVELOPING THE ESSAY

When I hear a phrase in Spanish in a Cincinnati restaurant, my head turns quickly. I listen, silently wishing to be part of that other conversation—if only for a few moments, to feel Spanish in my mouth.

Pat Mora

The word *essay* has various meanings. To many writers the word describes a short, carefully organized composition that develops a single idea or impression. To other writers the word describes a beginning or trial attempt, in which an idea is weighed or explored rather than developed or analyzed thoroughly. Thus Samuel Johnson, the great eighteenth-century essayist and dictionary writer, referred to the essay as "an irregular undigested piece."

Johnson's definition describes many essays that, like a first draft or an informal letter, state ideas and impressions without immediate concern for their organization or a central guiding idea or thesis. Like journal entries, trial essays help writers discover what they want to say. Of course, upon revision the trial essay may become, in the final draft, a carefully organized composition that focuses upon a central idea, proposition, observation, or impression.

Essays take different forms and have different purposes. An article in a newspaper or magazine may describe methods of energy conservation; a newspaper editorial may argue for energy conservation; a personal column, like those of Anna Quindlen, Russell Baker, and Art Buchwald, may describe amusing experiences with energy-saving devices or reflect upon the problems of conservation. The writer of the article seeks to inform; the editorial writer, to persuade; the columnist, to entertain or share feelings and thoughts. There are numerous ways to organize essays, and each writer seeks an organization that will best achieve the purpose of the essay, keeping in mind the knowledge and beliefs of the intended audience. The writer of the article on energy conservation, addressing readers unfamiliar with the subject, may begin with simple methods and build up to complex ones. The editorial writer, addressing the same general audience, may build up to the most important reasons for saving energy. The humorist may organize the description or narration in a way that best generates laughter.

As Barbara Ehrenreich's essay on busyness shows, the essayist may have more than one purpose in writing. Though Ehrenreich informs us about how men and women live and work today, her essay is mainly reflective and persuasive. Ehrenreich reflects upon her own busyness, contrasting it with that of a friend. She also wants us to consider our own busyness, though she does not make a direct appeal to us to change our attitudes and behavior.

Ehrenreich keeps her readers in mind in organizing her essay. Aware that her readers vary in knowledge of the subject and need to understand what she means by the "cult of conspicuous busy-ness," she gives an example in her opening paragraphs, then builds through additional examples to her central idea or *thesis*, stated in the opening sentence of paragraph 6:

> But if success is the goal, it seems clear to me that the fast track is headed the wrong way.

She develops her thesis by analyzing true success in life and giving more examples. In her concluding paragraph, she restates her thesis.

In writing your own essays, remember that few readers see the world exactly as you do. They may see different things and have different ideas and feelings about them. Whether your purpose is to give information about the world, to express your feelings or beliefs, or to persuade readers to take action or accept a belief, you must give sufficient details and examples that help them share your view and may persuade them to change their ideas and behavior. You must also help them follow the flow of your observations and thoughts. The sections that follow discuss ways of doing so.

Barbara Ehrenreich

THE CULT OF BUSYNESS

In her numerous essays and books Barbara Ehrenreich has written about social and political change in the United States. Her books include *The Hearts of Men: American Dreams and the Flight from Commitment* (1983) and *Fear of Falling: The Inner Life of the Middle Class* (1989), and with Deirdre English *For Her Own Good: 150 Years of Advice to Women* (1978). "Sometime in the eighties, Americans had a new set of 'traditional values' installed," Ehrenreich states in the introduction to *The Worst Years of Our Lives: Irreverent Notes from a Decade of Greed* (1990). She writes about one of these new values in her essay on the cult of busyness.

NOT TOO LONG AGO a former friend and soon-to-be acquaintance called me up to tell me how busy she was. A major report, upon which her professional future depended, was due in three days; her secretary was on

1

strike; her housekeeper had fallen into the hands of the Immigration Department; she had two hours to prepare a dinner party for eight; and she was late for her time-management class. Stress was taking its toll, she told me: her children resented the fact that she sometimes got their names mixed up, and she had taken to abusing white wine.

All this put me at a distinct disadvantage, since the   2 only thing I was doing at the time was holding the phone with one hand and attempting to touch the opposite toe with the other hand, a pastime that I had perfected during previous telephone monologues. Not that I'm not busy too: as I listened to her, I was on the alert for the moment the dryer would shut itself off and I would have to rush to fold the clothes before they settled into a mass of incorrigible wrinkles. But if I mentioned this little deadline of mine, she might think I wasn't busy enough to need a housekeeper, so I just kept on patiently saying "Hmm" until she got to her parting line: "Look, this isn't a good time for me to talk, I've got to go now."

I don't know when the cult of conspicuous busyness   3 began, but it has swept up almost all the upwardly mobile, professional women I know. Already, it is getting hard to recall the days when, for example "Let's have lunch" meant something other than "I've got more important things to do than talk to you right now." There was even a time when people used to get together without the excuse of needing something to eat—when, in fact, it was considered rude to talk with your mouth full. In the old days, hardly anybody had an appointment book, and when people wanted to know what the day held in store for them, they consulted a horoscope.

It's not only women, of course; for both sexes, busy-   4 ness has become an important insignia of upper-middle-class status. Nobody, these days, admits to having a hobby, although two or more careers—say, neurosurgery and an art dealership—is not uncommon, and I am sure we will soon be hearing more about the tribulations of the four-paycheck couple. Even those who can manage only one occupation at a time would be embarrassed to be caught doing only one *thing at* a time. Those young men who jog with their headsets on are not, as you might innocently guess, rocking out, but are absorbing the principles of international finance law or a lecture on one-minute management. Even eating, I read recently, is giving way to "grazing"—the conscious ingestion of unidentified foods while drafting a legal brief, cajoling a client on the phone, and, in ambitious cases, doing calf-toning exercises under the desk.

But for women, there's more at stake than conform- 5
ing to another upscale standard. If you want to attract men, for example, it no longer helps to be a bimbo with time on your hands. Upscale young men seem to go for the kind of woman who plays with a full deck of credit cards, who won't cry when she's knocked to the ground while trying to board the six o'clock Eastern shuttle, and whose schedule doesn't allow for a sexual encounter lasting more than twelve minutes. Then there is the economic reality: any woman who doesn't want to wind up a case study in the feminization of poverty has to be successful at something more demanding than fingernail maintenance or come-hither looks. Hence all the bustle, my busy friends would explain—they want to succeed.

But if success is the goal, it seems clear to me that 6
the fast track is headed the wrong way. Think of the people who are genuinely successful—path-breaking scientists, best-selling novelists, and designers of major new software. They are not, on the whole, the kind of people who keep glancing shiftily at their watches or making small lists entitled "To Do." On the contrary, many of these people appear to be in a daze, like the distinguished professor I once had who, in the middle of a lecture on electron spin, became so fascinated by the dispersion properties of chalk dust that he could not go on. These truly successful people are childlike, easily distractable, fey sorts, whose usual demeanor

resembles that of a recently fed hobo on a warm summer evening.

The secret of the truly successful, I believe, is that they learned very early in life how *not* to be busy. They saw through that adage, repeated to me so often in childhood, that anything worth doing is worth doing well. The truth is, many things are worth doing only in the most slovenly, halfhearted fashion possible, and many other things are not worth doing at all. Balancing a checkbook, for example. For some reason, in our culture, this dreary exercise is regarded as the supreme test of personal maturity, business acumen, and the ability to cope with math anxiety. Yet it is a form of busyness which is exceeded in futility only by going to the additional trouble of computerizing one's checking account—and that, in turn, is only slightly less silly than taking the time to discuss, with anyone, what brand of personal computer one owns, or is thinking of buying, or has heard of others using.

If the truly successful manage never to be busy, it is also true that many of the busiest people will never be successful. I know this firsthand from my experience, many years ago, as a waitress. Any executive who thinks the ultimate in busyness consists of having two important phone calls on hold and a major deadline in twenty minutes, should try facing six tablefuls of clients simultaneously demanding that you give them their checks, fresh coffee, a baby seat, and a warm, spontaneous smile. Even when she's not busy, a waitress has to look busy—refilling the salt shakers and polishing all the chrome in sight—but the only reward is the minimum wage and any change that gets left on the tables. Much the same is true of other high-stress jobs, like working as a telephone operator, or doing data entry on one of the new machines that monitors your speed as you work: "success" means surviving the shift.

Although busyness does not lead to success, I am willing to believe that success—especially when visited on the unprepared—can cause busyness. Anyone who has invented a better mousetrap, or the contemporary equivalent, can expect to be harassed by strangers demanding that you read their unpublished manuscripts or undergo the humiliation of public speaking, usually on remote Midwestern campuses. But if it is true that success leads to more busyness and less time for worthwhile activities—like talking (and listening) to friends, reading novels, or putting in some volunteer time for a good cause—then who needs it? It would be sad to have come so far—or at least to have run so hard—only to lose each other.

Questions for Study and Discussion

1. How does the episode described in paragraphs 1 and 2 illustrate the "cult of conspicuous busyness"? What additional illustrations does Ehrenreich provide in paragraphs 3-5?
2. What point is Ehrenreich making about her experience as a waitress in paragraph 8?
3. What is her thesis, and what does Ehrenreich gain by building up to it in paragraph 6 and restating it in paragraph 9?
4. What explanation does Ehrenreich give for the cult of busyness? Does she propose an alternate way of living and pursuing a career?
5. Do you agree with Ehrenreich's explanation? If so, why? If not, can you suggest another?

Vocabulary Study

Explain the difference between the words in each pair. Then explain why Ehrenreich chooses the first and not the second:
a. *conspicuous* (paragraph 3), *prominent*
b. *ingestion* (paragraph 4), *consumption*
c. *upscale* (paragraph 5), *ambitious*
d. *feminization* (paragraph 5), *feminizing*
e. *acumen* (paragraph 7), *wisdom*

Suggestions for Writing

1. Give your own examples of busyness in your own life or that of people you know. Then discuss whether Ehrenreich's explanation applies to your own experience and observations.
2. Ehrenreich states that "many things are worth doing only in the most slovenly, halfhearted fashion possible, and many other things are not worth doing at all." Give examples of your own and explain why you cite them.

Unity and Thesis

In a unified essay all ideas and details connect to the thesis or controlling idea, or sometimes to a controlling impression. The reader sees their connection at every point and experiences them as a unit. The central idea that organizes the many smaller ideas and details of an essay is called the *thesis*. Occasionally the thesis appears in the first sentence or close to the beginning, as in many newspaper articles and editorials. The effect is likely to be dramatic, as in these opening paragraphs of a newspaper article:

> "Don't you want to be one of the Now people?" asks an ad for a new soft drink, going on to urge, "Become one of the Now generation!"
>
> The only thing I can think of that is worse than being one of the Now people is being one of the Then people. As a member of civilization in good standing, I reject both the *nowness* and the *thenness* of the generations. I opt for the *alwaysness*.
> —Sydney J. Harris, "Now People and Then People"

In fact, the newspaper or magazine reader *expects* to find the main ideas or details of the editorial or column in the opening sentences.

Beginning an essay or article directly with the thesis can seem abrupt, however, and often the thesis may not be clear to the reader without background. So the essayist frequently builds up to the thesis, sometimes through details of a controversy or issue, as in the following opening paragraphs:

> Most Americans still carry with them, like a-well-loved picture in a frame, the idea of small-town life—as a way they themselves once lived, or wish they had lived, or hope one day to live. White houses on green lawns set not too far apart, lights in windows

at which shades are not pulled down, safety for one's children wherever they wander, everyone known by name and reputation. These are the values remembered by families living in city houses that stand, one just like the other, in bleak and deteriorated or jerry-built rows; in anonymous apartments; and in the vast, unbounded suburbs where the lawns must be kept green but everyone is a stranger. Older people complain and younger people wonder about the disappearance of this neighborly friendliness and trust. In modern American life each family has become, or is fast becoming, a small, self-contained unit in a world of strangers.   —Margaret Mead and Rhoda Metraux, "Neighbors vs. Neighborhoods"

Such introductory comments and details before the statement of the thesis help to place the reader in the world of the writer.

Sometimes the thesis is stated toward the end of the essay rather than toward the beginning. One reason for this delay is that the reader may not understand the thesis without examples and considerable explanation. Another reason is that the writer may need to make the reader receptive to a controversial thesis before stating it. Also, a thesis is highlighted when it appears toward the end, particularly if the writer builds up to it gradually.

In some essays—especially those that are mainly narration (that recount a series of events) or description—the thesis may be implied rather than explicitly stated, or the essay may contain a central impression rather than a thesis. In these instances, a carefully planned accumulation of details, rather than any single statement in the essay, conveys the main idea or impression the writer wishes to share with the reader. In the absence of a stated thesis, it is especially important that the writer maintain a clear sense of purpose and a consistent point of view in presenting the details.

You will find that you can produce unified, well-developed essays of your own if you take time to formulate a clear preliminary thesis statement after an initial draft. The act of writing is often an act of discovery—of finding meanings and ideas you could not anticipate at the start. In the course of writing, you may discover that your details and discussion suggest another thesis. When you do state a thesis that you find completely satisfactory, you need to review what you have written to be certain that the details develop it and not another idea. This review is particularly necessary if you decide not to state the thesis explicitly in the essay.

Susan Walton

THE CAUTIOUS AND OBEDIENT LIFE

Susan Walton received her B.A. in anthropology from Carleton College and an M.A. in journalism from the University of Wisconsin–Madison. Walton has done scientific and technical writing for the National Academies of Science and Engineering and various federal agencies, and she has written on science and education for numerous periodicals including *BioScience, Education Week*, and *Psychology Today*. Her essay on living an obedient life originally appeared in *The New York Times*.

Little herds of people mill around intersections in the   1
morning, waiting for the lights to change. Washington is full of traffic circles, so sometimes you have to wait through several lights, standing on narrow islands of concrete while traffic comes at you from unexpected directions.

Not everyone waits. Some people dash, even when   2
they see the No. 42 bus bearing down on them or some squirrel of a driver running every red light for blocks. The particularly daring ones make the cars stop for them.

I seldom walk until the light turns green. It is part   3
of being obedient, a manifestation of the misbegotten belief that you must do what people tell you to do, and if you do, you will be rewarded. This syndrome of behavior is characterized by a dedication to form at the expense of spontaneity and substance. It is turning papers in on time and expecting to receive better grades than those who turn them in late, even if theirs are superior. It is believing your mother—who probably didn't believe it herself—when she says that boys prefer nice girls. This toe-the-line mentality is not confined to women; men, too, lie awake wondering how things ended up so wrong when they so carefully did everything right. Which is exactly the problem.

Some people are born to follow instructions. They   4
are quiet children who always finish their homework,

are never caught being bad, never sneak off and do undetected wicked things. They never figure out that it is possible to ignore what others want you to do and do whatever you like. The consequences of deviation are usually minimal. Nobody really expects you to be that good. If you are born this way, you acquire a look of puzzlement. You are puzzled because you can't figure out how or why these other people are doing outrageous things when the rules have been so clearly stated. Nor do you understand why people are not impressed with your mastery of those rules.

Puzzlement may turn to smugness. At first, when people asked me whether I had completed an assignment, I was surprised: of course I had; didn't the teacher *tell* us to? After I realized that punctuality was not all that common, I became smug. Yes, of course I turned my paper in on time. I did not see that the people who got noticed were likely to be erratic and late, rushing in explaining that their thesis had not fallen into place until 4 a.m. of the third Monday after the paper was due. Us punctual types did not wait for theses to fall into place. Whatever could be knocked into shape in time was what got turned in. The thing was due, wasn't it?

The message did not sink in for years, during which I always showed up for work, double pneumonia and all. I wandered into a field—journalism—mined with deadlines and populated by more missed deadlines, per capita, than any other. I repeated the process—first the assumption that you had to make the deadline, or why did they call it a deadline? Then I realized that this behavior was not universal. By the time I began working for a weekly, I had deluded myself into thinking that reliability was the way to success.

And it was, sort of. At this job, however, I encountered one of those people apparently sent by life as an object lesson. For every deadline I made, he missed one. Stories that everyone was counting on failed to materialize for weeks, as he agonized, procrastinated and interviewed just one more person. Everyone was annoyed at the time, but when the work was completed, mass amnesia set in. Only the product mattered, and the product, however late it was, was generally acceptable.

We advanced together, but what I gained with pro- 8 motion was the opportunity to meet more deadlines per week and to hang around waiting to edit the copy of those who were late. What he got was the opportunity to linger over ever more significant stories. In my case, virtue was its own punishment. The moral of this story is that you should stop to think whether being good is getting you anywhere you want to go.

The most common and forgivable reason for the 9 cautious, obedient life is fear. It is true, something terrible could happen if you stray. Something terrible could also happen if you do not stray, which is that you might be bored to death. Some people are lucky; what they are supposed to do is also what they like to do. They do not need to muster their nerve. I do not consider myself a nervy person. Rather, I think of myself as a recovering coward. Cowardice, like alcoholism, is a lifelong condition.

The James boys, William and Henry, are instructive 10 on the subject of following too narrow a path. William James wrote in a letter to Thomas Ward in 1868 that the great mistake of his past life was an "impatience of results," which, he thought, should not be "too voluntarily aimed at or too busily thought of." What you must do, he believed, is to go on "in your own interesting way." Then the results will float along under their own steam. Henry left the classic record of the unlived life in "The Beast in the Jungle." It is the story of a man convinced that fate has something momentous in store for him, and he sits around carefully waiting for it to arrive. Consequently, his fate turns out to be that of a man to whom nothing ever happens. Better for him had he not listened quite so earnestly to the inner voice murmuring about fate. Better had he been distracted from his mission.

Be bold, my graduate school adviser, Mr. Ragsdale, 11
used to say—his only advice. I see now that he was right.
Think again of your future self: the little old lady sitting
on the porch of the old folks' home. When she thinks
back on opportunities, will she regret the ones that
passed unused?

Or find some other device. Myself, I keep a dumb 12
postcard in my desk drawer. It is light purple, with a
drawing of a cowering person standing on the edge of
a diving board. Beneath the drawing it says, "If you
don't do it, you won't know what would have happened
if you had done it." Think about the possible headline:
"Cautious Pedestrian Squashed by Bus While Waiting
on Traffic Island—Should Have Jaywalked, Police Say."
Then look both ways, and go.

Comment

Susan Walton echoes the advice given by the nineteenth-century
American writer Ralph Waldo Emerson in "Self-Reliance": "The
virtue in most request is conformity. Self-reliance is its aversion. It
loves not realities and creators, but names and customs." In his ser-
mon-like essay, Emerson advises us to be nonconformists; the advice
is unqualified—Emerson does not suggest exceptions. Like Emerson,
Walton ranges widely over the subject; but her essay is not a loosely
organized series of ideas. Walton states a thesis about the cautious
and obedient life early in the essay and supports it through her personal experience, observations of other people, and ideas of the
American philosopher William James and his brother Henry James,
the novelist and short-story writer.

Questions for Study and Discussion

1. What is Walton's thesis, and how does she introduce it?
    How does she keep the thesis before the reader as the
    essay proceeds?

2. Is Walton one of the people "born to follow instructions," or is she describing other people?
3. What did Walton learn from her experiences as a journalist?
4. Walton states that the commonest reason for the cautious and obedient life is fear. What other reasons does she give? In what order does she present these reasons?
5. Is Walton reflecting upon her character and that of others, or is she writing to persuade cautious and obedient readers to change their lives? How do you know?
6. Do you agree with Walton that the "most common and forgivable reason for the cautious, obedient life is fear"? If you disagree, what explanation seems a better one, and why?

Vocabulary Study

1. Would substitution of *groups* for *herds* change the meaning of Walton's statement that she sees "little herds of people mill around intersections in the morning"?
2. What does Walton mean by "a dedication to form at the expense of spontaneity and substance" (paragraph 3)? Is a "syndrome of behavior" the same thing as a "pattern" of behavior?
3. What is the dictionary meaning of "erratic" (paragraph 5)? What images or feelings does the word connote or bring to mind? Is an erratic person necessarily eccentric or odd?
4. Walton states in paragraph 8: "In my case, virtue was its own punishment." What does she mean by *virtue*? What dictionary meaning of the words are inapplicable to the sentence?
5. Explain the word *distracted* in the closing sentence of paragraph 10.

Suggestions for Writing

1. Discuss the extent to which you live "the cautious and obedient life." Then discuss why you do.
2. Discuss your agreement or disagreement with Walton on the issue of conduct, referring to your own habits and experiences.

3. Describe how you meet deadlines at school or at work. Then discuss what these habits reveal about your character, attitudes, or way of living.

Thomas Beller

A BIKER IN THE CITY

Thomas Beller, staff writer for *The New Yorker*, is a graduate of Vassar College and the Creative Writing Program at Columbia University. His stories and essays have appeared in *The New Yorker* and other periodicals and in *Best American Short Stories 1992*. Beller has held a variety of jobs in New York City. In the essay reprinted here, he describes one of his experiences as a bike messenger.

For some people, a bicycle is something taken out for a pleasant jaunt in the park on weekends, an opportunity to feel the breeze in their hair and to coast alongside novice roller bladers whose eyes are wide with terror. Then, there are the brave souls who use it to make a living—the bicycle messengers, a group I once belonged to. For others, however—including me, now— a bicycle is simply the best way to get around the city, and it's the best way to see the city as well. A bicycle can provide the ideal perspective on the quilt of neighborhoods pieced invisibly together. "Neighborhood" is not the right word, though: biking through the city is like moving through a series of moods.

And looking at people is different when you're on a bicycle. Whereas most New Yorkers shun anything more than fleeting eye contact while they're walking down the street, a pedestrian and a bike rider can engage in the sort of lengthy gaze that is usually reserved for people looking at each other through a pane of glass.

The downside is the way biking around town implicates you—suddenly and without warning—in the ugly confrontational energy that seems to rise up from our sidewalks like heat.

I was recently biking down Broadway, enjoying the 4 burst of speed that begins with the incline at Fifty-fourth Street, when a brand-new blue sports car pulled up beside me, its multiple antennas bristling. I was in the bicycle lane—more a formality than anything else, but a comforting one—and for a moment the car was right beside me. I was about to glance into the window, to see who was driving, but it suddenly jumped ahead and made a sharp left onto Forty-eighth Street, cutting me off; and sending me into a skid. For a second, I was outside the scene, watching myself from a distance as my brakes locked and the car's rear bumper brushed my leg. Then I was back in the moment, safe and undamaged.

Common sense, civility, and sheer survival instinct 5 should have dictated that I go on my way, but I was in the grip of something else, and the blue car was pulling up at a red light down the block. I headed after it. As I approached, an ambulance came up behind me, on its way to or from some other catastrophe, its sirens wailing at a volume designed to cut through the midtown din. It was an appropriately apocalyptic soundtrack, and as I came up next to the car, shimmering in its newness, I administered a violent kick to its side. The resulting sound resembled that of a crisp piece of paper being crumpled up, and that surprised me. I turned to find out what had come of my gesture, and saw the ambulance slowing beside the car, within which I could vaguely make out someone furiously bouncing up and down in the driver's seat. And then a voice emanated from the ambulance, tremendously amplified, yet conversational in tone, almost tender. It said, "I think he damaged your car."

Damaged! What had I done? I fled down Seventh 6 Avenue and then through side streets, like a fugitive, remorse building within me. Contemplating my unpleasant behavior in hindsight, I've concluded that biking in the city entails a kind of Faustian bargain with its streets: you can float above them, and see the city from the safe distance of the voyeur, but sooner or later the city becomes part of you.

Questions for Study and Discussion

1. Is Beller making a general comment about urban life, based on a typical experience on a city street? Or is he making a limited observation about himself or about the city, based on an experience on a particular day?
2. Does Beller state the idea explicitly, once or more in the essay, or let the reader infer it from the episode?
3. How do paragraphs 1-3 prepare the reader for the episode and the comments that follow? Do they provide details and commentary that help the reader understand Beller's point or thesis?
4. How does the central point or thesis unify the details Beller gives about himself, the sports car, the ambulance, and the city street?

Vocabulary Study

1. Why is "neighborhood" not the right word to describe the sections of the city the biker passes through?
2. What dictionary definition of *apocalyptic* best explains the use of the word in paragraph 5? Why were the ambulance sirens an "appropriately apocalyptic soundtrack" for the scene?
3. What is a "Faustian bargain" (paragraph 6)? In what sense does biking in the city entail such a bargain?
4. In what sense is a biker a "voyeur" (paragraph 6)? When does the biker cease to be a voyeur?

Suggestions for Writing

1. Beller comments that "looking at people is different when you're on a bicycle." Develop this idea or a similar one by

describing how people look to you when biking, walking, or driving a car.

2. Describe an episode in traffic that taught you something about yourself or your town or city. Connect the details of the episode to your central idea or thesis, and set the scene carefully. In the course of the essay, give enough information about yourself and the town or city to help the reader experience what you did.

Topic Sentence

The *topic sentence* is usually the main or central idea of the paragraph—the idea that organizes details and subordinate ideas. In many paragraphs it is the opening sentence:

> Viewed from the distance of the moon, the astonishing thing about the earth, catching the breath, is that it is alive [*topic sentence*]. The photographs show the dry, pounded surface of the moon in the foreground, dead as an old bone. Aloft, floating free beneath the moist, gleaming membrane of bright blue sky, is the rising earth, the only exuberant thing in this part of the cosmos. If you could look long enough, you would see the swirling of the great drifts of white cloud, covering and uncovering the half-hidden masses of land. If you had been looking for a very long geologic time, you could have seen the continents themselves in motion, drifting apart on their crustal plates, held aloft by the fire beneath. It has the organized, self-contained look of a live creature, full of information, marvelously skilled in handling the sun [*topic idea restated*]. —Lewis Thomas, "The World's Biggest Membrane"

In some paragraphs explanatory details and commentary lead into the central idea, as in the following opening sentences:

> Some of the changes made by wild creatures we would call beneficent: beavers are famous for making ponds that turn into fertile meadows; trees and prairie grasses build soil. But sometimes, too, we would call natural changes destructive [*topic sentence*]. . . . —Wendell Berry, "Getting Along with Nature"

Some paragraphs state a general idea, restrict or narrow the statement to an aspect of the subject, then explain and illustrate the restricted idea:

Members of the barrio describe the entire area as their home [*topic*]. It is a home, but it is more than this. The barrio is a refuge from the harshness and the coldness of the Anglo world [*restriction*]. It is a forced refuge. The leprous people are isolated from the rest of the community and contained in their section of town. The stoical pariahs of the barrio accept their fate, and from the angry seeds of rejection grow the flowers of closeness between outcasts, not the thorns of bitterness and the mad desire to flee. There is no want to escape, for the feeling of the barrio is known only to its inhabitants, and the material needs of life can also be found here [*illustration*]. —Robert Ramirez, "The Woolen Sarape"

Some paragraphs, by contrast, open with a series of details that build up to a statement of the central idea:

The first transcontinental New Year's excess occurred in 1894-95 when Amos Alonzo Stagg took his University of Chicago team to Los Angeles to play Stanford. The trip served as a multifaceted precedent for intercollegiate football. The distance travelled (6,200 miles), the duration (three weeks), and the trip's national publicity all served to demonstrate the possibilities of such intercollegiate games. When the teams from the two young universities met at the turn of the year far from either campus and for no discernible educational purpose, the modern bowl concept was established [*topic sentence*]. —Robin Lester, "The Bowl as Cathedral"

When a paragraph ends with the central idea, the succeeding paragraph may open with a transitional sentence that states the subject or topic:

Before coming to Bellevue, in the course of my medical school training, most of my meager experience had been with patients in private hospitals, well-to-do people who co-operated with us medical students at the request of their private doctor. It didn't take me long to see that there was an enormous sociological gap between Bellevue patients and private patients. Our Bellevue patients didn't think like private patients [*topic sentence*].

Take their attitude toward hospitalization [*transition*]. Most private patients have absolutely no desire to be hospitalized. They'd rather be in their nice, comfortable, warm homes, drinking martinis, eating steak, surrounded by their families. The most luxurious of hospitals can't offer the comforts of home [*topic sentence*].

But what if you have no home? [*transition*] What if you sleep in doorways in the warm weather and in a flophouse in the cold? What if you never know where your next meal is coming from and have no family to solace you? What, then, is your attitude toward hospitalization? [*topic sentence*]   —William A. Nolen, *The Making of a Surgeon*

As these examples show, the topic sentence may appear later in the paragraph—toward the middle or at the end. In such paragraphs the opening sentence still announces the subject—as in Lester's paragraph on the year's-end football bowl, "the first transcontinental New Year's excess." The reader knows from this opening phrase what the paragraph will discuss.

Beginning your paragraphs with the central idea, or with a statement of the subject, will help in organizing the details and ideas. In writing or in revising the paragraph, you may decide to restate the topic idea because new details and ideas may occur to you as you record your experiences and think about their meaning.

Anna Quindlen

MELTING POT

A journalist and essayist, Anna Quindlen wrote about herself, her family, and life in New York in a regular column for *The New York Times*, "Life in the 30's." Quindlen now writes a column on social and political issues for the *Times*. *Living Out Loud* (1988), and *Thinking Out Loud* (1993) are collections of her essays on a broad range of topics, including life in a multicultural world, the subject of the essay reprinted here. Quindlen is also author of a novel, *Object Lessons* (1991).

My children are upstairs in the house next door, hav- 1
ing dinner with the Ecuadorian family that lives on the top floor. The father speaks some English, the mother less than that. The two daughters are fluent in both their native and their adopted languages, but the youngest child, a son, a close friend of my two boys, speaks almost no Spanish. His parents thought it would be better that way.

This doesn't surprise me; it was the way my mother was raised, American among Italians. I always suspected, hearing my grandfather talk about the "No Irish Need Apply" signs outside factories, hearing my mother talk about the neighborhood kids, who called her greaseball, that the American fable of the melting pot was a myth. Here in our neighborhood it exists, but like so many other things, it exists only person-to-person.

The letters in the local weekly tabloid suggest that everybody hates everybody else here, and on a macro level they do. The old-timers are angry because they think the new moneyed professionals are taking over their town. The professionals are tired of being blamed for the neighborhood's rising rents, particularly since they are the ones paying them. The old immigrants are suspicious of the new ones. The new ones think the old ones are bigots. Nevertheless, on a micro level most of us get along. We are friendly with the Ecuadorian family, with the Yugoslavs across the street, and with the Italians next door, mainly by virtue of our children's sidewalk friendships. It took awhile. Eight years ago we were the new people on the block, filling dumpsters with old plaster and lath, drinking beer on the stoop with our demolition masks hanging around our necks like goiters. We thought we could feel people staring at us from behind the sheer curtains on their windows. We were right. 2

My first apartment in New York was in a gritty warehouse district, the kind of place that makes your parents wince. A lot of old Italians lived around me, which suited me just fine because I was the granddaughter of old Italians. Their own children and grandchildren had moved to Long Island and New Jersey. All they had was me. All I had was them. 3

I remember sitting on a corner with a group of half a dozen elderly men, men who had known one another since they were boys sitting together on this same corner, watching a glazier install a great spread of tiny glass panes 4 to make one wall of a restaurant in the ground floor of an old building across the street. The men laid bets on how long the panes, and the restaurant, would last. Two years later two of the men were dead, one had moved in with his married daughter in the suburbs, and the three remaining sat and watched dolefully as people waited each night for a table in the restaurant. "Twenty-two dollars for a piece of veal!" one of them would say, apropos of nothing. But when I ate in the restaurant they never blamed me. "You're not one of them," one of the men explained. "You're one of me." It's an argument familiar to members of almost any embattled race or class: I like you, therefore you aren't like the rest of your kind, whom I hate.

Change comes hard in America, but it comes constantly. The butcher whose old shop is now an antiques store sits day after day outside the pizzeria here like a lost child. The old people across the street cluster together and discuss what kind of money they might be offered if the person who bought their building wants to turn it into condominiums. The greengrocer stocks yellow peppers and fresh rosemary for the gourmands, plum tomatoes and broad-leaf parsley for the older Italians, mangoes for the Indians. He doesn't carry plantains, he says, because you can buy them in the bodega.

Sometimes the baby slips out with the bath water. I wanted to throw confetti the day that a family of rough types who propped their speakers on their station wagon and played heavy metal music at 3:00 a.m. moved out. I stood and smiled as the seedy bar at the corner was transformed into a slick Mexican restaurant. But I liked some of the people who moved out at the same time the rough types did. And I'm not sure I have that much in common with the singles who have made the restaurant their second home.

Yet somehow now we seem to have reached a nice mix. About a third of the people in the neighborhood think of squid as calamari, about a third think of it as sushi, and about a third think of it as bait. Lots of the single people who have moved in during the last year or two are easygoing and good-tempered about all the kids. The old Italians have become philosophical about the new Hispanics, although they still think more of them should know English. The firebrand community organizer with the storefront on the block, the one who is always talking about people like us as though we stole our houses out of the open purse of a ninety-year-old blind widow, is pleasant to my boys.

Drawn in broad strokes, we live in a pressure cooker: oil and water, us and them. But if you come around at exactly the right time, you'll find members of all these groups gathered around complaining about the condition of the streets, on which everyone can agree. We melt together, then draw apart. I am the granddaughter of immigrants, a young professional—either an interloper or a longtime resident, depending on your concept of time. I am one of them, and one of us.

Comment

Anna Quindlen introduces her thesis at the end of her opening paragraph and reminds us of it in succeeding paragraphs, often in her topic sentences. Mixing ideas with personal recollection, she uses these sentences also to unify the essay. Notice that Quindlen provides just enough detail to support her ideas; too much detail would have blurred the focus. Writing an essay is much like taking a photograph: author and photographer must find the proper distance from the subject if it is not to disappear into a mass of details. The photographer frames the picture by eliminating as much of the background as necessary to focus attention on the subject; the author does the same in reporting just those details that illuminate the subject or explain the idea and in eliminating needless details in the course of revision.

Questions for Study and Discussion

1. Quindlen uses the concluding topic sentence of paragraph 1 to state her thesis. How does she introduce the topic and build up to her thesis statement?
2. Each of the opening sentences in paragraphs 2-5 states the subject or topic of the paragraph. Which of these sentences also states an idea? How is that idea related to the thesis, stated in paragraph 1?
3. How do the details of paragraph 6 explain the opening statement, "Sometimes the baby slips out with the bath water"? How does paragraph 6 develop the idea introduced in paragraph 5? How do paragraphs 5 and 6 develop the thesis of the essay?
4. What are the topic sentences of paragraphs 7 and 8, and what is their function?
5. Does Quindlen conclude the essay with a restatement of her thesis or with final explanatory details or reflections?

Vocabulary Study

1. How do the details of paragraph 2 help you to understand the phrases "macro level" and "micro level"?
2. What is a goiter, and how is the word used in paragraph 2?
3. How does the context, or surrounding statements and details, help to explain the following words:
   a. *glazier, dolefully* (paragraph 4)
   b. *gourmands, bodega* (paragraph 5)
   c. *interloper* (paragraph 8)
4. In what sense do the people of the neighborhood think of squid as calamari, sushi, and bait?

Suggestions for Writing

1. Discuss the extent to which your own experiences in your college dormitory or in a neighborhood confirm the thesis that Quindlen develops in her essay.

2. Develop one of the following statements, or a related idea from your own experience, giving specific details:
   a. "Change comes hard in America, but it comes constantly."
   b. "Drawn in broad strokes, we live in a pressure cooker: oil and water, us and them."
   c. "We melt together, then draw apart."

Pat Mora

CONNECTED TO THE BORDER

A graduate of the University of Texas at El Paso, Pat Mora held several positions in the administration of that institution between 1981 and 1989, including director of the University Museum. Mora is the author of numerous children's stories and essays on Hispanic culture, as well as several collections of poetry. Awards for creative writing include the Harvey L. Johnson Award from the Southwest Council of Latin American Studies.

Last September, I moved away from the United States–Mexico border for the first time. Friends were sure I'd miss the visible evidence of Mexico's proximity found in cities like my native El Paso, Texas. Friends smiled that I'd soon be back for good Mexican food, for the delicate taste and smell of fresh cilantro, for fresh, soft tortillas. There was joking about the care packages that would be flying to the Midwest.

Although most of my adult home and work life had been spent speaking English, I was prepared to miss the sound of Spanish weaving in and out of my days like the warm aroma of a familiar bakery. I knew I'd miss the pleasure of moving back and forth between two languages—a pleasure that broadens one's human flexibility.

When I hear a phrase in Spanish in a Cincinnati restaurant, my head turns quickly. I listen, silently wishing to be part of that other conversation—if only for a few moments, to feel Spanish in my mouth. I think Hispanics

who become U.S. citizens need to speak English in order
to participate in public life, but I think it's equally
important to value native languages, to value the rich
range of options for communicating. In my apartment,
I'm reading more books in Spanish, sometimes reading
the sentences aloud to myself, enjoying sounds I don't
otherwise hear.

I smile when my children, who never had time for 4
learning Spanish when they were younger, now as young
adults inform me that when they visit they hope we'll
be speaking Spanish. They have discovered as I did once
that languages are channels, sometimes to other people,
sometimes to other views of the world, sometimes to
other aspects of ourselves. So we'll struggle with irregular verbs, laughing together which is such a part of
Mexican homes.

Is it my family that I miss in this land of leaves so 5
unlike my bare desert? Of course, but although they are
miles away, my family is with me daily. The huge telephone bills and the steady stream of letters and cards
are a long-distance version of the web of caring we
would create around kitchen tables. Our family web just
happens to stretch across these United States, a sturdy,
flexible web steadily maintained by each in his or her
own way.

I miss the meals seasoned with that phrase, "remem- 6
ber the time when. . . ." But I've learned through the
years to cherish our gatherings when I'm in the thick of
them, to sink into the faces and voices, to store the memories like the industrious squirrel outside my window.

I've enjoyed this furry, scurrying companion as I've 7
enjoyed the silence of bare tree limbs against an evening
sky, updrafts of snow outside our third floor window,
the ivory light of cherry blossoms. I feel fortunate to be
experiencing the part of this country which calls itself
the heartland. If I'm hearing the "heart," its steady,
predictable rhythms, what am I missing from its Southern border, its margin?

Is it other rhythms? I remember my mixed feelings 8
as a young girl whenever my father selected a Mexican
station on the radio, feelings my children now experience about me. I wanted so to *be* an American—which
to me, and perhaps to many on the border, meant (and
means) shunning anything from Mexico.

As I grew, though, I learned to like dancing to those 9
rhythms. I learned to value not only the rhythms but all
that they symbolized. As an adult, I associated such
music with celebrations and friends, with warmth and
the showing of emotions. I revel in a certain Mexican
passion not for life or about life, but *in* life, a certain
intensity in the daily living of it, a certain abandon in
such music, in the hugs, sometimes in the anger. I miss
the *chispas*, sparks which spring from the willingness,
the habit, of allowing the inner self to burst through
polite restraints. Sparks can be dangerous but, like risks,
are necessary.

I brought cassettes of Mexican music with us when 10
we drove to Ohio. I rolled my car window down and
turned the volume up, taking a certain delight in sending
such sounds across fields and into trees—broadcasting
my culture, if you will.

On my first return visit to Texas I stopped to hear 11
a group of mariachis playing their instruments with
proud gusto. I was surprised and probably embarrassed
when my eyes filled with tears not only at the music,
but at the sight of wonderful though often undervalued
Mexican faces. The musicians were playing for some
senior citizens. The sight of brown, knowing eyes which
quickly accepted me with a smile, and the stories in
those eyes were more delicious than any *fajitas* or *flan*.

When I lived on the border, I had the privilege of daily 12
seeing the native land of my grandparents. What I miss
about that land is its stern honesty. The fierce light of
that grand, wide Southwest sky not only filled me with
energy, it provided unsoftened viewing, a glare of truth.

The desert is harsh, hard as life, no carpet of leaves 13 to cushion a walk, no forest conceals the shacks on the other side of the Rio Grande. Although a Midwest winter is hard, it ends, melts into rich soil yielding the yellow trumpeting of daffodils. But the desert in any season can be as relentless as poverty and hunger. Oddly, I miss that clear view of the difference between my comfortable life as a U.S. citizen and the lives of my fellow human beings who also speak Spanish, value family, music, celebration. In a broader sense, I miss the visible reminder of the difference between my economically privileged life and the life of most of my fellow humans.

Comment

Pat Mora describes two worlds that she lives in daily. Topic sentences in the essay focus our attention on this central subject or topic. Some of these sentences state the central topic of the paragraph, sometimes in the form of a question; some state the central idea. At the end of the essay, Mora broadens her focus by introducing another topic or idea—one that she cannot explore within the limits of her short essay but one she can at least suggest to the reader.

Questions for Study and Discussion

1.   What are the two worlds that Mora describes in her essay? How many aspects of these worlds does she refer to or describe?
2.   What points does Mora make about these worlds?
3.   Which topic sentences state these points or ideas?
4.   What contrast does Mora develop in paragraph 13? How does this contrast pick up contrasting themes and details of earlier paragraphs?
5.   What new subject or theme does Mora introduce at the end of the essay? How is this subject or theme related to the point or thesis of the whole essay?

Vocabulary Study

Use an unabridged or Spanish dictionary to explain the following terms:
1. *cilantro, tortilla* (paragraph 1)
2. *mariachi, fajita* (paragraph 11)

Suggestions for Writing

1. Describe two worlds in which you live, and develop a point of your own about them, perhaps one related to different values or personal attitudes toward people or life.
2. Mora states that "languages are channels, sometimes to other people, sometimes to other views of the world, sometimes to other aspects of ourselves." Illustrate this statement, drawing on your own experience with a language other than English, perhaps one that you or your parents or friends speak, or a language you have studied.

✦
Order of Ideas

Ideas in the paragraph as well as in the whole essay can be presented or ordered in various ways. We saw in the previous section that paragraphs commonly open with a general idea, which is then developed through specific details. But, as in Robin Lester's paragraph on bowl games (p. 22), some paragraphs move from the *specific* to the *general*—building up to the central or topic idea.

Certain kinds of writing have their own order. Descriptions are *spatial*—perhaps moving from foreground to background or from earth to sky:

> Once we even saw a giraffe, but miles, miles away from us, alone under the clear sky among the thorn trees on the horizon, and we could see its silhouetted head and long neck turned to watch us; it seemed very lonely, very small, and very far away on the yellow flats; when the noise of our trucks reached it, it was frightened and began to run, heaving itself up and down. It ran away from us for a long time and got even smaller but never out of sight. At last it reached the horizon. —Elizabeth Marshall Thomas, *The Harmless People*

Narrative, in contrast, presents events chronologically—in the order of *time*. The paragraph just quoted combines spatial description with chronological narrative: the writer presents the sighting of the giraffe, the movement of the trucks, and the flight of the animal in their temporal order. In reporting an experience or explaining a process, the facts or steps are usually presented as they occur. To a person learning to drive, you would not explain how to turn corners until you explained how to brake and steer.

In expository and persuasive writing ideas may be presented in numerous ways. The author considers the reader's knowledge of the subject, the purpose of the paragraph or essay, and the subject itself in organizing the paragraph. For example, in describing the care of an automobile you would probably describe simple procedures before complex ones, especially if your readers are owners of new models. In training mechanics to repair a new kind of engine, you might proceed from the most common to the most unusual problems mechanics are likely to encounter.

In the following definition of the potlatch, a ceremony in which native Americans of the Northwest dispose of property, the author clearly has his readers in mind in presenting details of the ceremony in the order of *importance*:

> A proper potlatch involved prodigious displays of eating, since it was a point of honor with the host to provide much more food than his guests could consume. The eating would last for days, interspersed with singing, belching, speechmaking, dramatic performances and the ceremonial conferring of honorific names. But the vital part of the occasion was the bestowing of gifts—bowls, boxes, baskets, blankets, canoes, ornaments, sculptures—that the chief had collected among his people, from each according to his ability, and now distributed among his guests, to each according to his rank. —Frederic V. Grunfeld, "Indian Giving"

The greater the drama of the event, the greater our sense of *climax*—of increasing importance or intensity as the paragraph or essay moves to the end.

Some paragraphs (and essays) move from *question* to *answer*:

> How wide is the scope of physical law? Do life, thought, history fall within its orderly domain? Or does it describe only the inanimate, the remote and the very tiny? It is the claim of contemporary physics that its laws apply to all natural things, to atoms, stars and men. There are not two worlds: the cold, precise mechanical world of physics, and the surprising, disorderly and growing world of living things or of human existence. They are one. —Philip Morrison, "Cause, Chance and Creation"

A related order is the movement from *problem* to *solution*. The following paragraph states a problem in biology and then presents a tentative solution:

> How either whales or seals endure the tremendous pressure changes involved in dives of several hundred fathoms is not definitely known [*problem*]. They are warm-blooded mammals

like ourselves. Caisson disease, which is caused by the rapid accumulation of nitrogen bubbles in the blood with sudden release of pressure, kills human divers if they are brought up rapidly from depths of 200 feet or so. Yet, according to the testimony of whalers, a baleen whale, when harpooned, can dive straight down to a depth of half a mile, as measured by the amount of line carried out. From these depths where it has sustained a pressure of half a ton on every inch of body, it returns almost immediately to the surface. The most plausible explanation is that the whale, unlike the diver, does not have air pumped to him while he is under water, and therefore has in his body only the limited supply he carries down. Therefore he does not have enough nitrogen in his blood to do serious harm [*solution*]. The plain truth is, however, that we really do not know, since it is obviously impossible to confine a whale and experiment on him, and almost as difficult to dissect a dead one satisfactorily [*qualification*].
—Rachel Carson, *The Sea Around Us*

As Elizabeth Marshall Thomas's paragraph on giraffes shows, paragraphs can combine various orderings of ideas and details—in this case, the spatial arrangement of details with the chronological presentation of events. A paragraph may, in addition, show that the events increase in importance or intensity. In writing your own paragraphs and essays, you may discover better ways of presenting details and ideas as you see the paragraph or essay take shape.

Harold Krents

DARKNESS AT NOON

Harold Krents graduated from Harvard College and later studied law at Oxford University and Harvard Law School. He practiced law from 1971 until his death in 1986. Krents was the prototype for the blind boy in Leonard Gershe's play (and the later film) *Butterflies Are Free*. His experiences at Harvard are the basis of the film *Riding on the Wind*. Krents was long active in organizations and government agencies concerned with the employment of handicapped people.

Blind from birth, I have never had the opportunity [1] to see myself and have been completely dependent on the image I create in the eye of the observer. To date it has not been narcissistic.

There are those who assume that since I can't see, I obviously also cannot hear. Very often people will converse with me at the top of their lungs, enunciating each word very carefully. Conversely, people will also often whisper, assuming that since my eyes don't work, my ears don't either.

For example, when I go to the airport and ask the ticket agent for assistance to the plane, he or she will invariably pick up the phone, call a ground hostess and whisper: "Hi, Jane, we've got a 76 here." I have concluded that the word "blind" is not used for one of two reasons: Either they fear that if the dread word is spoken, the ticket agent's retina will immediately detach, or they are reluctant to inform me of my condition of which I may not have been previously aware.

On the other hand, others know that of course I can hear, but believe that I can't talk. Often, therefore, when my wife and I go out to dinner, a waiter or waitress will ask Kit if "*he* would like a drink" to which I respond that "indeed *he* would."

This point was graphically driven home to me while we were in England. I had been given a year's leave of absence from my Washington law firm to study for a diploma in law degree at Oxford University. During the year I became ill and was hospitalized. Immediately after admission, I was wheeled down to the X-ray room. Just at the door sat an elderly woman—elderly I would judge from the sound of her voice. "What is his name?" the woman asked the orderly who had been wheeling me.

"What's your name?" the orderly repeated to me.

"Harold Krents," I replied.

"Harold Krents," he repeated.

"When was he born?"

"When were you born?"

"November 5, 1944," I responded.

"November 5, 1944," the orderly intoned.

This procedure continued for approximately five 13
minutes at which point even my saint-like disposition
deserted me. "Look," I finally blurted out, "this is
absolutely ridiculous. Okay, granted I can't see, but it's
got to have become pretty clear to both of you that I
don't need an interpreter."

"He says he doesn't need an interpreter," the orderly 14
reported to the woman.

The toughest misconception of all is the view that 15
because I can't see, I can't work. I was turned down by
over forty law firms because of my blindness, even
though my qualifications included a cum laude degree
from Harvard College and a good ranking in my Harvard
Law School class.

The attempt to find employment, the continuous 16
frustration of being told that it was impossible for a
blind person to practice law, the rejection letters, not
based on my lack of ability but rather on my disability,
will always remain one of the most disillusioning experiences of my life.

Fortunately, this view of limitation and exclusion is 17
beginning to change. On April 16, [1978] the Department of Labor issued regulations that mandate equal-
employment opportunities for the handicapped. By and
large, the business community's response to offering
employment to the disabled has been enthusiastic.

I therefore look forward to the day, with the expec- 18
tation that it is certain to come, when employers will
view their handicapped workers as a little child did me
years ago when my family still lived in Scarsdale.

I was playing basketball with my father in our 19
backyard according to procedures we had developed.
My father would stand beneath the hoop, shout, and
I would shoot over his head at the basket attached to
our garage. Our next-door neighbor, aged five, wandered over into our yard with a playmate. "He's blind,"
our neighbor whispered to her friend in a voice that
could be heard distinctly by Dad and me. Dad shot and

missed; I did the same. Dad hit the rim: I missed entirely: Dad shot and missed the garage entirely. "Which one is blind?" whispered back the little friend.

I would hope that in the near future when a plant 20 manager is touring the factory with the foreman and comes upon a handicapped and nonhandicapped person working together, his comment after watching them work will be, "Which one is disabled?"

Comment

Krents states a problem and proceeds to a solution: this is the general organization of the essay. But Krents wishes to do more than state a solution; he wishes his readers to fully understand the difficulties of being blind. Krents organizes the three misconceptions about blindness with this purpose in mind. He might have presented these misconceptions in a different order; the order he chooses helps us appreciate the bizarre situation he describes. A notable quality of the essay is the proportion of examples to discussion—just enough are provided to illustrate each of the ideas. Krents selects his details carefully. Leonard Kriegel describes a different handicap and its effect on his life on pages 126-131.

Questions for Study and Discussion

1. In what paragraph does Krents state the basis for his ordering of the three misconceptions? How does this order help you to appreciate the bizarre situation created by blindness? How does the change in tone in paragraph 15 accord with the order of ideas?
2. What is his thesis? Does Krents state it directly, or is it implied?
3. What are the implied causes of the problems described? What is the solution? Does Krents state or imply this solution?
4. What attitudes and feelings does Krents express in the final anecdote?
5. Do you find the organization of ideas successful, or would you have organized them in a different way?

Vocabulary Study

Use your dictionary to distinguish the differences in meaning in the following series of words. Write a sentence using each of the words according to its dictionary meaning. The first word in each series is Krents's:

1. *narcissistic* (paragraph 1), vain, conceited, proud
2. *enunciating* (paragraph 2), pronouncing
3. *graphically* (paragraph 5), sharply, starkly, vividly
4. *disillusioning* (paragraph 16), disappointing, frustrating

Suggestions for Writing

1. Discuss the effect that a permanent or temporary handicap or disability has had on your life, or discuss problems you have observed in the life of a handicapped friend or relative. You may want to organize your essay as Krents does—working from a problem to a solution. Note that the solution need not be complete or permanent; you may want to discuss the extent to which the problems described can be solved.
2. Krents writes about his blindness with humor. Discuss how he achieves that humor and what it tells you about his view of himself and people in general.
3. Describe an embarrassing experience of your own—how it came about, the persons involved in it, its outcome. Then discuss its causes, focusing on the most important of them.

✧

Coherence

In a unified essay all of the details and ideas connect to a central idea or thesis and fit together into a whole. Pronoun reference and the repetition of key words and phrases help the reader see how these details and ideas cohere or hold together:

> *For six days of the week* we find it no trouble at all to drive a car about town. New York's traffic, however furious, is predictable; and her taxis, even in moments of great verve, are accurate. *For six days* driving is a pleasure, but on Sundays all is changed *[topic sentence]:* the town, we have discovered, fills up with *visiting motorists* who have come in from the Oranges and the Pelhams to see a movie. *They* make driving a hazard almost too great to take on. The minute a red light shows, *they* stop dead, imperiling everybody behind. The instant a taxi seems about to sideswipe them, *they* swerve desperately over and sideswipe somebody else, usually *us*. When *they* are confronted by *a mass of pedestrians* at the crossing, instead of charging boldly in and scattering *them* in the orthodox manner by sheer bluster (which is the only way), *they* creep timidly up blowing their horns, which lulls *the pedestrians* and ties up everything. *They* are easy to spot, *these visiting motorists*, and the only thing to do, we have found, is to nudge *them* frequently on the bumper, and chivy *them* about. —E. B. White, "Visiting Motorists" [emphasis added]

Another important means of achieving coherence is parallel structure—the arrangement of similar words, phrases, and clauses to highlight similar ideas:

> Though perhaps Brooklyn is not quite a refuge anymore where sheep may safely graze, *there are places* there where you can listen in the dark of winter to the wind attacking from the Atlantic as moon-whitened waves break against the beach. *There are neighborhoods* of nations so alien and incredible that crossing

into them mobilizes beyond any expectation both distance and time. *There are streets where, on January nights, fires burn on every floor of every house, sending fragrant smoke through the cold black trees. There are meadows and fields, long rows of oak trees, bridges that sparkle from afar, ships about to leave for Asia, lakes, horses and islands in the marsh.*   —Mark Helprin, "Brooklyn's Comforting Infinitude" [emphasis added]

Where the natural course of ideas is clear through pronoun reference, repetition of key words and phrases, and parallel structure, no helping words or formal connectives are necessary. Sometimes, however, you will need transitional words and phrases when the connection of ideas or details is not immediately clear. If the steps of a process are presented chronologically and each step requires explanation, you may introduce the words *first, second,* and *third* to keep the steps distinct. You may also add the phrases *less important, just as important,* or *more important* to show that you are presenting ideas in the order of importance. Connectives like *thus, therefore, however, moreover,* and *nevertheless* show the logical relation of ideas. *Thus* and *therefore* show that one idea is the consequence of another or that certain conclusions can be drawn from the evidence presented; *however* and *nevertheless* show that one idea qualifies or contradicts another; *moreover* shows addition. A question may also serve as a transition:

> We learn, as we say, by "trial and error." Why do we always say that? Why not "trial and rightness" or "trial and triumph"? The old phrase puts it that way because that is, in real life, the way it is done.   —Lewis Thomas, "To Err Is Human"

L. E. Sissman

THE OLD FARMER'S ALMANAC, 1872

The poet and essayist L. E. Sissman was born in Detroit, Michigan, in 1928. After graduating from Harvard University he worked in advertising. His poems are collected in *Hello, Darkness* (1978); his personal essays for *The Atlantic Monthly* are collected in *Inner Bystander* (1975). Sissman died in 1976. In the essay reprinted here, Sissman compares our world today with the world described in an issue of a nineteenth-century farmer's almanac.

The homely publications of a hundred years ago 1
have a message for us. The *Official Railway Guide* of
June, 1868, for example, tells me the disheartening news
that my regular twenty-seven-mile commute took ten
minutes less one hundred and four years ago than it does
today. And the 1872 *Old Farmer's Almanac,* which I
picked up in a New Hampshire secondhand store some
years ago, bears even odder tidings.

If you consult the *Almanac* today, you know that 2
behind its familiar yellow cover is a thick pack of
oddments—snippets of astrology, weather prognostications, old rhymes and jokes, a spate of small-space ads
for trusses, roach-killer, and fish lures, and on pages that
deal with the months of the year ahead, a series of
nostalgic, neatly written "Farmer's Calendars."

Things were different in 1872. The *Almanac* was 3
thin—a mere fifty-two pages—and the only ads inside
its peach covers (the original yellow was dropped for
a time in the middle of the nineteenth century) touted
Hallet & Davis pianos (endorsed by "F. Liszt, the First
Pianist in the World"), Webb & Twombly's Premium
Chocolates (which "have taken the highest award at
every Fair in which they have been exhibited"), Wheeler
& Wilson's Sewing Machines, Worcester's Quarto Dictionary (with a testimonial from Edward Everett), and
the wares of Henry C. Sawyer, whose Waltham Book
Store also sold stationery, wallpaper, silverplate, lug-
gage, desks, Bibles, brushes, combs, perfumery, soap,
pocket knives and scissors, fans for ladies, umbrellas,
picture frames, and, of course, the *Almanac.*

But it is the editorial matter of the old *Almanac* that 4
startles the modern reader. Beginning soberly with a
table of Meetings of Friends in New England and a list
of salaries of executive officers of the United States
("Ulysses S. Grant, Ill., Pres., $25,000; Hamilton Fish,
N.Y., Sec. State, $8,000"), it goes on through a page of
astronomical data and rosters of New England colleges
and registers in bankruptcy to an early crescendo: the

spreads for the months of the year. Each is laid out much as it is today: a table of astronomical calculations on the left, a rather sketchy forecast and the "Farmer's Calendar" on the right. But these "Farmer's Calendars" are nothing like the rather bland, pleasant little essays of today. Each of them preaches and rails at the farmer to keep a better farm and live a better life; the Protestant ethic rears its minatory head in January and harangues the reader through the waxing and the waning year. The nameless scourge of slothful husbandmen begins the cycle, after a terse New Year's greeting, well into his evangelical stride: "Make up your mind therefore to be better and to do better, to aim higher and to have nobler ends in view. . . . Let us sit down by the crackling fire and lay out plans for the year. I suppose you have done the chores, of course, fed the cattle and the pigs, and cleaned up the barn. No use to sit down till the chores are done. . . ." In February, he has progressed a step further in his righteous indignation at his captive parishioners; now he begins by berating them: "Snug up about the barn this winter. Shut the door and the windows. Cold won't make cattle tough. . . . I wouldn't give a fig for a man who can't turn his mind to little things. All your luck in farming hangs on the chores at this season."

In March, he is quick to turn on the hapless, snow-bound farmer who grouses about the weather. "No use to fret about the storm and the snow. Keep your temper is a good rule on the farm. This way of finding fault with heaven and earth won't do. . . . It's a pity you don't raise more roots. Hadn't you better look about for a spot to put in an acre of mangolds and another of swedes?"

The Old Farmer takes the offensive early and keeps the pressure up; the shiftless reader won't get a breather, even in springtime: "All plant life is on the spring now, and animal life too, as to that matter. And so you'd better spring around, John, if you want to see your barn well filled in the fall. Yoke up and go at it with your fine and sprightly team. . . . The fact is, there is no end to the work this month, and no time to lose in standing around or leaning over the wall with a gossiping neighbor." And: "It is of no use to find fault with work. We ought to thank our stars that we are able to work."

As the summer ends, the taskmaster's lips are thinner 7 than ever: "Now that the dog star rages, why don't you give the dog a bullet [presumably a pill of dog-days medicine], the boy a hoe, the girl the knitting needles. No work, no eating, is the rule, you know. Can't afford to keep drones on the farm." In September, to keep the enervated farmer on the qui vive, the *Almanac* lays out an impressive list of chores, including removing stones from fields to be tilled. "I hope you got out those rocks. . . . It is a shiftless way to lay down a lot with the bushes growing along the walls. Why don't you dig them out, and clean up the lot?" In October, he notes, with relish, that "there is enough to do to keep us on the jog all this month"; in November, after a peremptory reference to Thanksgiving, he's off again about stalling the cattle every night, fall sowing and plowing, and trimming the grapevines. Even in December—notably, there's no mention of Christmas—he's harping about the grapevines again, as well as pruning the fruit trees, making an inventory of stock and tools on the farm ("the sooner you set about it, the better you will be off"), and generally preparing for the worst: "Spruce up and get ready for a hard winter."

The rest of the *Almanac* is similarly grim; it dispels 8 a number of common notions among farmers about cabbage, kitchen gardens, grass for horses, and food for stock, calls attention to the adulteration of commercial fertilizers, cautions the reader about transplanting evergreens ("it is a mistake to suppose that the same rules apply to evergreens as to deciduous trees"), and sagely discusses the pitfalls of stockbreeding farms. Then a little light relief: three pages of poetry, anecdotes, and puzzles, most of them not so light, at that. One poem, a tearjerker, was "found under the pillow of a soldier who died in a hospital near Port Royal, South Carolina." "Selections" includes Scott's "O, what a tangled web we weave/When first we practise to deceive"; the jokes include this epitaph: "I was well—wished to be better—read medical books—took medicine—and died."

The 1872 *Almanac* ends there, with the exception of a few population tables (according to the census of 1870, there were 38,555,983 people in the United States, of whom 942,292 lived in New York City and 4,382,759 in New York State; California could boast a mere 560,247), weather tables, tide tables, and post office regulations (first-class letters, 3 cents per half ounce). It ends with a sort of a whimper and a curious feeling of oppression in the reader, as if he had just been through that exhausting year with the poor, bone-weary farmer. It ends, finally, with a question forming in the modern reader's mind: Were the good old days that bad? In an age when we are daily and sorely tried by all sorts of mind-boggling disasters and injustices, when we daily repair to the past for reassurance and refreshment, is it possible that we are really better off than our forebears, and that our carefully cultivated nostalgia is founded on a mirage? On the evidence of the 1872 *Almanac,* that could well be. The stern preachments of the anonymous author of the "Farmer's Calendar" are not mere mouthings; it seems clear that the struggling farmer of a century ago really needed these appeals to his pride and his sense of duty in order to get on with the backbreaking, dawn-to-dusk job of cultivating his garden. It was a savage life of imponderables—blizzards floods, crop failures, insect plagues, human and animal diseases for which there were no known cures—and only the most bitterly Calvinistic outlook could prepare one to compete in what had, eventually, to be a losing race. There was no social security in those days, no government price supports, no anesthesia, and above all no leisure. The farmer had literally nothing to look forward to except the fruits of a job well done and another day, week, month, and year of unremitting toil to keep ahead of a hostile nature.

To us, seated in our warm houses on our choreless 10 days off from work, knitted to all our friends by the telephone, possessed of cars to take us across the county or across the country as the whim strikes us, disposing of a hundred diversions to beguile our leisure, protected by effective medical care (for those, at least, who can afford it), assured of a cash competence in our retirement, this stark world of a hundred years ago is hard indeed to believe in—which is one of the reasons why we believe in a gilded age when all the world was young, when cares were few, when love was true, when, over the river and through the woods, grandmother's house was filled with goodwill, provender, and jollity. What a shame the truth was otherwise.

Comment

Sissman depends on a number of devices to hold together the various details and ideas. The opening sentences of some of the paragraphs make transitions to a new consideration or new stage of the analysis of the almanac. For example, the opening sentence of paragraph 4 marks the turn from advertisements to the editorial matter; the opening sentence of paragraph 6 shifts the discussion to the attitude of the Old Farmer toward his readers. The long paragraphs require careful transitions to mark turns of idea—for example, in the following transitional sentence in paragraph 4: "But these 'Farmer's Calendars' are nothing like the rather bland, pleasant little essays of today." Sissman is describing a publication and a world unfamiliar to his readers, and he keeps his many details in focus through his much longer paragraphs, each devoted to one idea or feature of the almanac.

Questions for Study and Discussion

1. How do the topic sentences of paragraphs 1-8 keep our attention focused on the central topic of the essay?
2. How late in the essay does Sissman state his thesis? What is gained by not stating it in the opening paragraph?
3. How are paragraphs 1-8 organized? Does Sissman describe the almanac cover to cover, or does he present the contents in a different order?
4. The "Protestant ethic" (paragraph 4) is the ideal of hard, unremitting work that exercises the virtues of the upright person. How is this ideal related to the "Calvinistic outlook," referred to in paragraph 9? How does the discussion of the farmer's life throughout the essay explain these phrases?
5. Do you agree with Sissman's explanation of our romantic view of the American past? What additional or different reason would you cite?

Vocabulary Study

Give the dictionary meanings of the following words. Then write an explanation of how the word is used in the particular sentence:
1. *homely, tidings* (paragraph 1)
2. *snippets, prognostications, spate, nostalgic* (paragraph 2)
3. *touted* (paragraph 3)
4. *bland, minatory, harangues, scourge, evangelical* (paragraph 4)
5. *enervated, qui vive, peremptory* (paragraph 7)
6. *anesthesia, unremitting* (paragraph 9)
7. *beguile, competence, provender* (paragraph 10)

Suggestions for Writing

1. Examine an issue of a magazine published in the 1940s or the 1950s, and describe some of its contents. Organize your description to develop a thesis—perhaps a conclusion about the world of your parents or grandparents based on the evidence of the magazine.

2. Discuss how true a recent movie or newspaper or magazine article describing teenagers is to your own experiences and observations. Restrict your discussion to one or two characters or episodes; don't try to discuss the whole movie or article. Use your discussion to state a general conclusion— a thesis suggested by the similarities or differences you have discussed.

Narration

You are familiar with narration through works of fiction that present a series of events chronologically or weave past and present events into complex narratives or plots that explore the connection of events. Narratives are also basic in expository, persuasive, and expressive essays. An essay tracing historical events may do so through narrative. The following paragraph describing the first landfall of Christopher Columbus in the Bahamas shows how narration serves historical exposition:

> As the sun set under a clear horizon October 11, the northeast trade breezed up to gale force, and the three ships tore along at 9 knots. But Columbus refused to shorten sail, since his promised time was running out. He signaled everyone to keep a particularly sharp watch, and offered extra rewards for first landfall in addition to the year's pay promised by the Sovereigns. That night of destiny was clear and beautiful with a late rising moon, but the sea was the roughest of the entire passage. The men were tense and expectant, the officers testy and anxious, the Captain General serene in the confidence that presently God would reveal to him the promised Indies. —Samuel Eliot Morison, "First Crossing of the Atlantic"

Narration is also important in persuasive writing. In the legal brief it is essential in providing the background of the case—the events at issue. A simple argument may contain a supporting narrative of an event. A plea for a change in public policy may trace the consequences of present policy through a narrative illustrating them. We will consider examples in a later section.

Narration is important, too, in expressive writing. Gloria Emerson's account of her parachute jump in Part Two is a simple narrative. Here, Sue Hubbell begins her essay on woodcutting with a narrative of her experiences:

This morning I finished sawing up a tree from the place where I had been cutting for the past week. In the process I lost my screwrench, part screwdriver, part wrench, that I use to make adjustments on my chain saw. I shouldn't carry it in my pocket, but the chain had been loose; I had tightened it and had not walked back to the truck to put the wrench away. Scolding myself for being so careless, I began looking for another tree to cut and found a big one that had recently died. —"Felling Trees"

In narration the amount of detail you present depends on the knowledge of your readers. Since you usually cannot know how much knowledge each reader possesses about a subject, you will do best to include essential facts about the world and the characters in your essay. It is important, however, not to give excessive or irrelevant detail that diverts the reader from the central event. In his paragraph on Columbus, Morison gives a necessary though brief description of the sailors and officers of the ship. To have described each of their reactions in detail would lessen the suspense and divert attention from Columbus himself, who is the actual focus of the narrative.

Edward Rivera

THE SOCIOLOGY FINAL

Born in Orocovia, Puerto Rico, Edward Rivera grew up in New York City, attending school in Spanish Harlem, and at nineteen entered evening school at City College. He returned to college after army service, graduating from City College in 1967 and later from Columbia University. Rivera describes the very different worlds of Puerto Rico and New York in his semi-autobiographical book *Family Installments: Memories of Growing Up Hispanic* (1982). The experience described in this excerpt—taking a final exam in a college course—will be familiar to many students. Selection title by editor.

I took a cab up to school, but I was still late. On the way there, I reviewed the "material" in my head: almost total confusion, a jumble of jargon, ordinary things passed off as profundities with the aid of "abstractionitis." ("The home then is the specific zone

of functional potency that grows about a live parent-
hood . . . an active interfacial membrane or surface
furthering exchange . . . a mutualizing membrane between the family and the society in which it lives. . . .")

The classroom was packed for the first time since the 2
opening day of classes, and filled with smoke. Over forty
students were bent over their examination booklets,
most of them looking confused by the questions. The
professor, puffing an immense pipe, was at his desk
(manufactured by Vulcan), reading Riesman on *The
Lonely Crowd,* casually, as if it were a murder mystery
whose ending he had figured out back on page one. He
didn't look pleased when I stepped up to his desk:
another pair of lungs in a roomful of carbon dioxide and
cigarette smoke.

"Yes?"   3

I asked him for a question sheet and an examination 4
booklet. They were on the desk, weighted down with
the eighth edition of his anthology.

"Are you registered in this course?" he asked.   5

Yes, I was. He wanted to know my name. I told him. 6
He looked me up in his roll book. Had I been coming
to class regularly? Every time. How come I never spoke
up in class? Because I sat in the back. It was hard to
be heard from back there. I might try sitting up front,
he said. I said I would. He said it was a little late for
that. For a moment I'd forgotten what day this was.
Dies irae, according to my paperback dictionary of
foreign phrases. Do-or-die day.

There were no empty chairs, so I walked to the back 7
of the room and squatted in a corner, keeping my coat
and scarf on.

"Answer one from Part A, one from Part B, and one 8
from Part C." I had no trouble understanding that
much. But my mind blanked out on the choices in Parts
A, B, and C. There was something about "group membership as the source of individual morality and social
health" (Durkheim? I couldn't remember). I must have

slept through that lecture, and I couldn't remember any mention of it in the eighth edition. Another one asked for something or other on Weber's contention that "minorities in 19th-century Europe—the Poles in Russia, the Huguenots in France, the Nonconformists in England, and the Jews in all countries—had offset their socio-political exclusion by engaging in economic activity whereas the Catholics had not." This one had to be explained in fifteen minutes. I got around it by drawing a blank.

The easiest choice in Part C asked for "a sociological autobiography, demonstrating your command of certain relevant aspects in this course, as well as the terminology of sociology." [9]

"Terminology of sociology." That wasn't even a good rhyme. It was also asking too much for fifteen minutes. It wasn't even enough time for my nerves to calm down. Too bad. I got up and left the room. No one noticed. [10]

I went down to the student cafeteria for a cup of coffee, and while I drank it, I read the opening chapter of Dr. A. Alonso's *El Gibaro*, a Puerto Rican classic which I'd brought with me to reread on the subway back home. "I am one of those," it went, "and this can't matter much to my readers, who are in the habit of not sleeping without first having read something"—another one, I thought, nineteenth-century version— "and this something must be of the sort that requires more than usual seclusion, order and meditation, since I think that at no time other than the night's silence can one withdraw from the real world, to elevate oneself into the imaginary; above all when the day has been spent without affliction, something that a young man achieves from time to time, before he becomes the head of a family, or while he does not have to govern, on his own, the vessel of his future." [11]

In the examination blue book, which I hadn't bothered returning, I translated some of these long, rhythmic sentences as best I could (no dictionary on me, for one [12] thing), just for practice, and then, when I'd finished a second cup of coffee, I shoved the Alonso and the blue book back inside my coat pocket and left for the subway.

Comment

"Let me tell you what the final was like," a friend says to you. The story she tells expresses various feelings—perhaps joy or anger or frustration. It may even develop a thesis—either an explicit or implicit point that your friend wants to make. You discover the implicit thesis largely through the tone of the narrative and the stress given particular details. Tone is an essential consideration, because it conveys the attitude of the narrator (see p. 519). These are matters to consider in Rivera's narrative of his sociology final.

The effectiveness of Rivera's narrative arises from the exactness of his detail. He does not tell us everything about the professor or the exam, but rather he selects the details that best convey the atmosphere of the classroom and that explain why he leaves without completing the exam. The episode is undramatic, but it tells us much about the feelings of the outsider—of a Puerto Rican youth facing numerous barriers.

Questions for Study and Discussion

1. What are Rivera's feelings in arriving for the exam, in talking to the professor, in reading the questions, and in leaving the building? To what aspects of the experience does Rivera give the most attention in his narrative?

2. How do the details of the episode help you to understand Rivera's feelings? What may be the significance of the title of the book the professor is reading?

3. What does the quotation from Alonso's *El Gibaro* tell you about Rivera's feeling at the moment? What is the general tone of paragraph 11?

4. Is Rivera merely expressing his feelings about the sociology exam, or is he in addition making a point? If so, what is that point?

Vocabulary Study

1. How do Rivera's examples explain the word *abstractionitis*?
2. The *Dies irae* ("Day of Wrath") is a hymn describing Judgment Day, sometimes included in masses for the dead. What is the point of the reference?
3. Read the entry on *Vulcan* in a dictionary of classical mythology. Then explain the reference to Vulcan in paragraph 2.

Suggestions for Writing

1. Describe an exam you took, or a similar experience, and convey your feelings through your details and the tone of your description. Remember that your tone need not be the same throughout the essay.
2. Rivera shows how language, like the jargon or the directions quoted, sometimes creates barriers or difficulties in everyday situations. Discuss a barrier or difficulty that jargon or unclear directions created for you.
3. Narrate an episode in your life in which you felt and acted like an outsider. Let the details of your narrative reveal why you did.

Description

Usually a narrative contains description of people and places—a drawing in words of what they look like. The narrator may pause to draw this picture, sometimes doing so in a few words and sometimes at greater length. Description is always spatial—the scene observed from a particular angle of vision. This angle may remain fixed or may change.

Earl Shorris describes a New York City Latino neighborhood as a visitor would see it on a hot summer night walking through it. Shorris first describes a restaurant and its customers, then the outside of a Latino grocery store on the next corner, where four men are playing dominoes, and, not far from the bodega, a social club:

> Two blocks away, next to the funeral home, down the street from the Pentecostal church, the neighborhood social club has opened for the night. Couples drift in. They are middle-aged and older. One man wears a cap to hide his baldness; another man shows his full head of white hair.

Shorris concludes his description by returning to the street where people are gathering after a rainstorm:

> Unadorned women and their children gather in front of the Pentecostal church; something is going on in the funeral home. Near the corner, in a doorway, a young man dressed in dark clothing and gold jewelry beckons. —*Latinos*

Shorris tells us from what vantage point the visitor observes the interior of the restaurant and afterward the domino players and the people in the social club and on the street outside the church. The visitor is close enough to see what the people look like. A description from the point of view of someone driving quickly down the street would not be as specific. Shorris is showing us the barrio as any observer would see it if sensitive to the special qualities of the barrio world.

Description is an essential part of every kind of writing. An expository essay on auto repair may include a description of some of the tools or the workplace. A persuasive essay may give us a picture of the people the writer wants us to help. The expressive essay centers on the writer primarily; a descriptive passage may therefore be colored by the writer's personal feelings. Not every student entering the classroom Edward Rivera describes would see it or describe the professor as Rivera does:

> The professor, puffing an immense pipe, was at his desk (manufactured by Vulcan), reading Riesman on *The Lonely Crowd*, casually, as if it were a murder mystery whose ending he had figured out back on page one. He didn't look pleased when I stepped up to his desk: another pair of lungs in a roomful of carbon dioxide and cigarette smoke.

Maya Angelou

PICKING COTTON

Maya Angelou was born Marguerite Johnson in 1928. When her parents separated, the three-year-old girl traveled with her brother from California to Stamps, Arkansas, to live with her grandmother. The woman Angelou called "Momma" owned the only black general store in town. Angelou and her brother later returned to California to live with their mother. During her long career, Angelou has worked in the theater and television as a dancer, an actress, and a producer. She served as northern coordinator of the Southern Christian Leadership Conference, traveled in Africa, and taught school and wrote for newspapers in Egypt and Ghana. On her return to the United States, she wrote for television. Angelou has written several autobiographies and several volumes of poetry, collected in *Maya Angelou: Poetry.* Her description of black cotton pickers in Stamps is a self-contained section from her first autobiography, *I Know Why the Caged Bird Sings* (1969). Selection title by editor.

Each year I watched the field across from the Store   1
turn caterpillar green, then gradually frosty white. I

knew exactly how long it would be before the big wagons would pull into the front yard and load on the cotton pickers at daybreak to carry them to the remains of slavery's plantations.

During the picking season my grandmother would ₂ get out of bed at four o'clock (she never used an alarm clock) and creak down to her knees and chant in a sleep-filled voice, "Our Father, thank you for letting me see this New Day. Thank you that you didn't allow the bed I lay on last night to be my cooling board, nor my blanket my winding sheet. Guide my feet this day along the straight and narrow, and help me to put a bridle on my tongue. Bless this house, and everybody in it. Thank you, in the name of your Son, Jesus Christ, Amen."

Before she had quite arisen, she called our names and ₃ issued orders, and pushed her large feet into homemade slippers and across the bare lye-washed wooden floor to light the coal-oil lamp.

The lamplight in the Store gave a soft make-believe ₄ feeling to our world which made me want to whisper and walk about on tiptoe. The odors of onions and oranges and kerosene had been mixing all night and wouldn't be disturbed until the wooded slat was removed from the door and the early morning air forced its way in with the bodies of people who had walked miles to reach the pickup place.

"Sister, I'll have two cans of sardines." ₅

"I'm gonna work so fast today I'm gonna make you ₆ look like you standing still."

"Lemme have a hunk uh cheese and some sody ₇ crackers."

"Just gimme a coupla them fat peanut paddies." ₈ That would be from a picker who was taking his lunch. The greasy brown paper sack was stuck behind the bib of his overalls. He'd use the candy as a snack before the noon sun called the workers to rest.

In those tender mornings the Store was full of laugh- ₉ ing, joking, boasting and bragging. One man was going to pick two hundred pounds of cotton, and another three hundred. Even the children were promising to bring home fo' bits and six bits. The champion picker of the day before was the hero of the dawn. If he prophesied that the cotton in today's field was going to be sparse and stick to the bolls like glue, every listener would grunt a hearty agreement. The sound of the empty cotton sacks dragging over the floor and the murmurs of waking people were sliced by the cash register as we rang up the five-cent sales.

If the morning sounds and smells were touched with the supernatural, the late afternoon had all the features of the normal Arkansas life. In the dying sunlight the people dragged, rather than carried their empty cotton sacks. Brought back to the Store, the pickers would step out of the backs of trucks and fold down, dirt-disappointed, to the ground. No matter how much they had picked, it wasn't enough. Their wages wouldn't even get them out of debt to my grandmother, not to mention the staggering bill that waited on them at the white commissary downtown.   10

The sounds of the new morning had been replaced with grumbles about cheating houses, weighted scales, snakes, skimpy cotton and dusty rows. In later years I was to confront the stereotyped picture of gay song-singing cotton pickers with such inordinate rage that I was told even by fellow Blacks that my paranoia was embarrassing. But I had seen the fingers cut by the mean little cotton bolls, and I had witnessed the backs and shoulders and arms and legs resisting any further demands.   11

Some of the workers would leave their sacks at the Store to be picked up the following morning, but a few had to take them home for repairs. I winced to picture them sewing the coarse material under a coal-oil lamp with fingers stiffening from the day's work. In too few hours they would have to walk back to Sister Henderson's Store, get vittles and load, again, onto the trucks. Then they would face another day of trying to earn enough   12 for the whole year with the heavy knowledge that they were going to end the season as they started it. Without the money or credit necessary to sustain a family for three months. In cotton-picking time the late afternoons revealed the harshness of Black Southern life, which in the early morning had been softened by nature's blessing of grogginess, forgetfulness and the soft lamplight.

Comment

Angelou combines narration with description, beginning with her grandmother's rising at four o'clock in the morning and ending with a picture of workers mending their sacks under coal-oil lamps at night. Descriptive details at the beginning suggest the "soft make-believe feeling": "The odors of onions and oranges and kerosene had been mixing all night and wouldn't be disturbed until the wooded slat was removed from the door"; the sounds and smells of morning "were touched with the supernatural," she tells us in a later passage. In contrast to the morning, the late afternoon is harsh and ordinary, and she gives details of that world in the remaining paragraphs. The concluding sentence of the essay combines these impressions.

Questions for Study and Discussion

1. What details in the essay suggest "nature's blessing of grogginess, forgetfulness and the soft lamplight"? Why are these a blessing? What other details suggest the "features of the normal Arkansas life"?
2. How does Angelou suggest the influence of that world on her feelings about her race?
3. How do the details contradict a stereotype of the Southern black? How does Angelou remind us of that stereotype? What other stereotypes is she possibly criticizing?
4. Is her main purpose in writing to challenge this stereotype?
5. What personal qualities does Angelou stress in her description of her grandmother? What does this description contribute to the picture of Southern black life?

6. What mistaken picture or stereotype of a group—perhaps teenagers or high-school athletes—could you correct through a similar description?

7. What impression do you get of Angelou as a person, judging from the qualities of people and the things in her world that catch her eye?

Vocabulary Study

1. What does Angelou mean by "tender mornings" (paragraph 9), "touched with the supernatural" (paragraph 10), and "dirt-disappointed" (paragraph 10)?

2. What is *paranoia*, and in what sense does Angelou use the word in paragraph 11?

Suggestions for Writing

1. Describe a scene from your childhood or adolescence that tells the reader something important about your upbringing. Build your details to a statement of your controlling idea as Angelou does.

2. Describe one of your childhood or adolescent experiences from two points of view—that of the child and that of the young adult remembering the experience. Then comment on the differences between what the child or adolescent remembers and what the young adult understands. Use these differences to state a thesis.

3. Discuss a stereotype that shaped your view of other people or of yourself. Explain how you came to hold the stereotype, and how you discovered its falseness.

Example

An example is a picture or illustration of an idea. In explaining ideas, we fit our examples to the knowledge and experience of our readers or listeners. In explaining to a child that points of light in the night sky are really very large distant objects, we first have to explain why large objects can appear small. An example suited to the child's experience might be a ball that seems to get smaller as it flies through the air. In explaining to college physics students why the space of the universe is said to be "curved," a professor draws on mathematical formulas and scientific observations, but for the person who knows little or nothing about science, the professor would look for comparisons or analogies in everyday experience.

The word *example* carries the meaning of typical: that is, the example represents the many occurrences or forms of the idea. Examples are essential in exposition, particularly to the explanation of complex ideas. For instance, it would be difficult to explain the following idea without an example:

> The attitude that produces the pseudo-technical tone is made up of a desire to dignify the subject and the writer, coupled with the belief that important matters require a special vocabulary.
> —Jacques Barzun, *Simple and Direct*

Barzun provides this example of pseudo-technical tone:

> I am sorry not to be able to accept the experience of more intensive interaction with your group and its constituency.

No amount of definition and descriptive detail can replace an effective example such as this. At the same time, many examples do require explanation or analysis, particularly when the idea is a complex one.

Tom Wicker

"COURT DAY" IN MOORE COUNTY, NORTH CAROLINA

Born and raised in Hamlet, North Carolina, Tom Wicker studied journalism at the University of North Carolina, graduating in 1946. He worked as a sports editor, feature editor, and correspondent for several Southern newspapers before beginning his long career with *The New York Times* in 1960. Until his retirement in 1991, Wicker worked as a reporter, Washington bureau chief (1964-68), associate editor, and columnist. Wicker's novels include *Facing the Lions* (1973) and *Unto This Hour* (1984). His nonfictional books include *JFK and LBJ: The Influence of Personality Upon Politics* (1968); *A Time to Die* (1975), on the Attica prison uprising; and *On Press* (1978), from which this essay on an early experience as a reporter for a North Carolina newspaper is reprinted. Selection title by editor.

Monday was "court day" in Moore County, North 1 Carolina, in 1949, and I regularly spent it at the county seat, Carthage, as correspondent for the *Sandhill Citizen*, of Aberdeen, North Carolina (population 1603). I reserved most of the afternoon for peddling ads—another of my duties—to the Carthage merchants, in keen competition with the county seat weekly, the *Moore County News*. On first arrival at the courthouse in the morning, I checked with the register of deeds, the clerk of court, the sheriff, and other officials for suits newly filed, big property transfers, scandalous foreclosures, heinous crimes, and the like; then I laboriously copied down births, deaths, and marriages of note. Later I hastened to the courtroom, where County Judge Leland McKeithen dispensed even-handed justice, or something as close to it as anything I've seen since.

That courtroom was rank with the enduring follies 2 and foibles of mankind. It was segregated still, and in the summer months sweltering in the harsh dry heat of the North Carolina Sandhills in the days before universal air conditioning. But it provided a generous education in

human nature, lawyers' tricks, oratory, and the law itself—in roughly that order. I witnessed court actions
involving murders, manslaughters, crimes of property too
numerous to define, vagrancies, seductions, desertions,
auto offenses of every variety, bitterly disputed wills,
breaches of promise and peace, recoveries of damage,
alienations of affection, assaults, rapes, batteries, break-
ins, reckless endangerments, ad infinitum. It seemed
natural enough to me in the South of the 1940s that
most defendants, and most victims, were black.

One divorce case—that of a white couple—had a   3
particular impact on me, although I scarcely recall its
details. They involved one party futilely chasing the other
with an ax. The story plaintively related from the witness stand by the complainant, a worn-out woman with
a ZaSu Pitts voice, haggard eyes, and hair just beginning
to go gray, was the human comedy at its most ribald and
perverse—Moore County transported to Chaucer's time
and *The Canterbury Tales*. The spectators scattered
around the courtroom, the press—another reporter and
I—at its privileged table, even occasionally Judge
McKeithen, rocked with laughter. The conclusion was
foregone—divorce granted, with a fine crack of the gravel.

That was Monday. That afternoon, I hawked the   4
Citizen's ad space, probably to no better effect than
usual. The next day, armed with copious notes, I turned
out a humorous account of the divorce case for my long
lead over the agate type that summed up the other court
cases ("Lonzo McNair, Star Route, Carthage, failure to
observe stop sign, costs of court"; "A. C. Overby,
Vermont Avenue, Southern Pines, aggravated assault,
continued to Superior Court") and sent it back to the
Citizen's ever-clacking Linotype machine (in a small
shop in the days before offset printing, it was mandatory
to keep "the machine" running, both to make the thing
pay and to keep the lead pot from "freezing").

On Thursday, putting on my editor's hat, I wrote a   5
two-column head for my court story and scheduled it

for page one, above the fold—top play in the *Citizen* as in any other newspaper. We went to press routinely that night, got the mail copies to the post office in the nick of time, and went off for a few late beers.

Working late justified sleeping late; and when I dragged myself into the *Citizen* office about noon the next day, I had a visitor: a worn-out looking woman with a ZaSu Pitts voice, but whose once-haggard eyes were blazing, whose fluttering hands were clenched into fists, and whose graying hair—I suddenly saw at range closer than that of the witness stand—was that of a woman not too many years older than I, who not too long before probably had been considered a peach by the boys in her high school class.

"Mr. Wicker," she said without preamble, "why did you think you had the right to make fun out of me in your paper?"

I have never forgotten that question—and I still can't answer it. In 1949 I doubt if I even tried. I remember thinking I had not bargained for such awful moments when I had landed my first reporter's job a few months before. Accurate though my story had been, and based on a public record, it had nevertheless exploited human unhappiness for the amusement or titillation of others. I had made the woman in my office something less than what she was—a human being possessed, despite her misfortunes, of real dignity.

Seeing that, I saw too that I had not only done her an injury but missed the story I should have written. This is one of the besetting sins of journalism—sensationalism at the expense of the dignity and truth of the common human experience. I have been fortunate to have worked mostly for publishers and editors who sought to avoid that sin—not always successfully. And reading some of the more lurid journals, I've often thought that sensationalism and gossip columns tend to be techniques employed mostly by big-circulation publications for an anonymous audience. Not many editors and reporters would be callous or unseeing enough to engage in them if they had to face the victims the next morning over a battered desk in an office not much bigger than a closet.

Comment

Our understanding of the concluding paragraph depends on the example Wicker develops: without it the "sensationalism" that he refers to would be a vague term. In developing his example, Wicker gives us the setting as well as some of the important details—enough of them to make his point. Had he given all of them, the focus would have shifted from his own experience as a young reporter to the woman and the divorce hearing.

Questions for Study and Discussion

1. What information about the divorce does Wicker include, and what details show why he found it funny? What other aspects of the case might he have included had he wished to focus on its humor?
2. How does the episode reveal the "sensationalism" that Wicker refers to in the final paragraph?
3. What personal qualities does Wicker reveal in his account of the episode? Which of these qualities does he want to stress?
4. Is Wicker saying that the divorce was not newsworthy and should not have been reported?

Vocabulary Study

Use your dictionary to explain how Wicker uses the following words:
1. *heinous, dispensed* (paragraph 1)
2. *foibles, sweltering, vagrancies* (paragraph 2)
3. *ribald, perverse* (paragraph 3)
4. *copious, Linotype* (paragraph 4)
5. *exploit, titillation* (paragraph 8)
6. *lurid, callous* (paragraph 9)

Suggestions for Writing

1.   The character of a newspaper is often revealed by its front page—by what news, what pictures, what headlines the front page includes. Analyze the front page of a paper you read regularly to define its character. Do not try to describe everything on the page. Focus on key details.

2.   We have all had experiences like Wicker's in which we made important discoveries about ourselves. Discuss one such experience of your own, giving enough details to let the reader discover what you did. Draw a conclusion from your example.

Process

Another important method of developing ideas is process analysis. A *process* is any activity or operation that contains steps usually performed in sequence. It may be a mechanical one, like changing a tire, or a natural one, like the circulation of the blood. The process referred to in the following statement is a natural one:

> Just as human individuals and populations undergo continual alteration in response to infectious disease, so also the various infectious organisms that provoke disease undergo a process of adaptation and adjustment to their environment.   —William H. McNeill, *Plagues and Peoples*

These are two common types of process analysis.

A third type deals with a historical process—one that occurred in the past, and can occur again, according to identifiable causes and effects:

> At all times famines have led to social disturbances. In mere self-preservation people took food wherever they could find it, or stole the money to buy it. Criminality, brigandage, and prostitution were well known symptoms of famines. Families were torn apart and children grew up without guidance, as in the Russian famine of 1921, when the hordes of vagrant children presented a serious problem. Exasperated by starvation, people were ready to rise against the authorities. The sight of rich families indulging in luxuries while they were deprived of the bare necessities made them acutely aware of class distinctions. Hunger was one factor that contributed to unleash revolutionary forces in France in 1789. The Roman emperors well knew that the best way to keep the masses quiet was to give them *panem et circenses*, food and entertainment—and usually, the more entertainment, the less food. In the 2nd century after Christ about 500,000

inhabitants of Rome lived on public charity. The emperors' example has been followed by all dictators.   —Henry E. Sigerist, *Civilization and Disease*

Whether mechanical, natural, or historical, the steps of a process are usually described chronologically. In mechanical processes, you may have a choice of procedures or tools, and you may decide to describe more than one of these—for example, you may discuss several kinds of tire jacks and how they work. In the course of explanation, you may have to define and illustrate key terms, make comparisons, and comment on the uses of the process.

Many processes are complex, containing several related processes, each of which must be carefully distinguished. For example, the instruction book that gives directions for wiring a stereo receiver and a tape deck to a turntable and speakers describes each process step by step. Assembling a receiver from a kit is even more complex a procedure.

Faith McNulty

HOW TO RAISE A WOODCHUCK

Faith McNulty has written about nature and wildlife in *The Whooping Crane* (Dutton Animal Book Award in 1966), *Must They Die?: The Strange Case of the Prairie Dog and the Black-Footed Ferret* (1971), *The Great Whales* (1974), and *Wildlife Stories* (1980). Many of her essays were first published in *The New Yorker*. The following essay on raising a woodchuck first appeared in *Audubon Magazine*, March 1977.

I have faith that for every piece of information there is someone somewhere who wishes to receive it. In that spirit I am putting down a few notes on the topic, "How to raise a woodchuck." Admittedly this is not a problem on everyone's mind: but if you live in woodchuck country, which in the East is almost anywhere, it is possible you will find yourself holding a baby woodchuck and wondering what to do with it.

This happened to me on a spring day at the end of ₂ May, and I haven't been sorry. It had been years since I had close contact with a wild animal. I wondered if possessing it would have any of the thrill it had when I was ten years old. Then, any creature I encountered was an individual, as distinct, for better or worse, and as irreplaceable as myself. Its death would be as final. This is a feeling that is often attacked as sentimental by those who see individual animals as interchangeable digits in a very large number and point out that while woodchucks come and go, only the existence of the species need concern us. This view has its validity, and I don't want anyone to think I have spent my adult years putting up tombstones for deceased pets or holding funeral rites over fallen sparrows, and yet I have never divorced myself from the idea that individual worth in the animal kingdom is not restricted to human beings.

On May 29th there was a heavy rain. Our farm near ₃ Wakefield, Rhode Island, is in the midst of rolling fields. They were thoroughly soaked, and the new grass turned even more brilliant green. There were puddles in the driveway and on the low spots in our neighbor's potato field. The next day the sun came out beautifully hot. Driving back from the village, I decided that instead of going on another errand I would go home and get my bathing suit. I turned in and pulled the car up short, because a small woodchuck was traveling along the road, its belly almost flat to the gravel. It was smaller than any I had ever seen except the one I had picked up after a similar rain, so many years ago, when I was ten years old.

I got out of the car, took off my sweater, threw it ₄ over the woodchuck and wrapped him in it, then put him on the floor of the car while I drove the short distance home. I surmised the rain had washed out his burrow and the young had wandered off in different directions. If I hadn't come along he would have gone on in a hopeless search until he died of starvation. Rescuing him, I felt as large as Fate. It also occurred to me that by picking him up I was letting myself in for quite a lot of bother. I wondered if I really wanted to do it at my age. But by the time I thought of this, the woodchuck was already wrapped in my sweater and it was too late to reconsider.

At home I put him in the bathtub, where he gamely 5 scrabbled against the unyielding porcelain. My husband found a large carton. I put cat litter in the bottom and straw on top of that. I put the chuck in it. He did not try to bite. He gratefully burrowed into the straw.

I put the carton in the bathroom. This is where I 6 always kept animals in my childhood. This also, I must admit, is where my first woodchuck met his end. He somehow climbed up and fell into the toilet, where he stayed for some time with his nose just above the surface. He died later, presumably of pneumonia. Now, faced with my new responsibility, I recalled that first woodchuck. At that time we had a litter of kittens. We brought the mother and kittens into the bathroom. The little chuck shared their bed. The old cat licked him, and the kittens warmed him, but he could get no milk. We fed him with a bottle. I recall that he sat on his haunches like a bear and held the bottle in his paws. I remember, too, that he followed me around making a sound like a tiny outboard motor. He also shared the cat's toilet pan, which was filled with sand. At the time I thought the mother cat had taught him, but I have since learned that this is innate in woodchucks.

In the old days there were doll nursing bottles with 7 real rubber nipples. Now the doll bottles are plastic and no use. Instead I tried a coarse medicine dropper. The chuck sucked noisily and greedily while I squeezed out a mixture of nonfat milk and baby cereal. He accepted me quickly. Within a day or two he was rushing into my hands and making a strange little noise when I came to feed him. Two ounces filled him to bulging. Then he slept, often on his back with legs flung out in an attitude of abandon. Awake, he began to play, rolling around and biting at the straw. If I put my hand in the carton, he nibbled my fingers and wrestled with them, kicking against my hand the way kittens do.

It became clear that I was imprinting the woodchuck 8 and vice versa. When I had first picked him up, I thought he was homely as a burlap bag. I felt sorry for him for being what he was—a mere woodchuck. He would never be graceful or very bright, never swift or surprising or beautiful. He would just be a chunky brown fellow with coarse fur and a taste for the depths of the earth. Now, as I held him, five or six times a day, I began to observe him closely.

I noticed his hands. They were black, with four very 9 long fingers ending in long curved nails. The thumb was only a small projection. He could close these fingers to grasp something—the medicine dropper or my finger. With these expressive hands he was almost as dexterous as a squirrel and, of course, a woodchuck is in the squirrel family. It is the largest of the family Sciuridae, which includes the prairie dog, the squirrel, and the chipmunk. His coat, coarse against my hands as I held him, was a mixture of grays and tans and consisted of a thick undercoat interspersed with long, bristly guard hairs, banded in black-and-white, giving a tweedy appearance. His front and hind legs were very short but stout and strong. His shoulders, upper arms, and lower flanks were covered with red fur. His tail wasn't much, neither long nor short, and only slightly bushy. His belly was round and babyish, with rather sparse dark hair the color of coffee beans. I noted his ears. They were small, round, squirrel ears, neat and pretty and appropriate to life spent partly in tunnels. His eyes were oval and set near the top of his skull to give good upward vision. They were dark as raisins and softly shiny. There were bristly whiskers by his nose and an additional set on his cheeks, I presume for checking the diameter of tunnels.

All of this, plus the energy and will emanating from 10 him as he struggled mightily in my grasp to get every drop of milk despite the odd shape of the new teat, added up to the statement, "I am a woodchuck, and I want to live." And, by holding him and feeding him, I was allowing myself to be imprinted with the added message, "I am *your* little brown woodchuck. My survival is up to you."

Very shortly the carton seemed too small. I let the 11 woodchuck loose in the bathroom and offered him a nest made of a covered box, bedded with straw and with a round doorway cut in the front. He knew instantly that a hole spells home, and he dashed inside. I put the cat litter in a dishpan nearby. In the wild, woodchucks are fastidious, burying their excrement in a special chamber of the burrow. The woodchuck immediately used the pan for this purpose.

Now that he was free, his extreme wariness became 12 evident. He was very sensitive to sound. Any sudden noise sent him flying into his house. At first the sight of me or my husband walking around scared him, too, but his fear wore off rapidly. He began to greet me by scrabbling at my ankles, trying to climb up my legs, a painful process. He often followed closely at my heels, making his funny, urgent little noise. If I offered my hand he nibbled it eagerly. He possessed four long, curved front teeth that could easily have punctured me, but his bite was always restrained. I guessed that wild woodchucks groom each other with these gentle bites. Together the nibbling and the chuckling sound were very expressive of emotion.

We have a dog, and a meeting was inevitable. The 13 first few times the woodchuck fled at sight of the dog. Then he stood his ground. The dog, filled with curiosity, extended her nose, and the woodchuck's nose came up to meet it. After one sniff the woodchuck turned, hissed as if he had tasted something disgusting, and withdrew. The dog's odor must advertise the meat-eater's lethal habits.

At this stage it occurred to me that I really knew little 14
about the lives of woodchucks, and I turned to the
library for some basic data. I found that there are
woodchucks practically everywhere in the United States—
including Alaska, but not in the Deep South—and in
Canada. The species that frequent the West and the high
mountains are known as the yellowbelly marmot and
the hoary marmot. The proper name of our woodchuck
is *Marmota monax,* and there are nine subspecies. My
particular woodchuck is *Marmota monax preblorum,*
and it must once have been a forest dweller, since before
our time dense forests covered the East. With the cultivation of open fields *monax* has found an improved
food supply and has prospered.

Woodchucks, the textbook says, have three white 15
nipple-like organs just inside the anus that emit a musky
odor when the animal is excited and whose purpose
probably is communication. (I have smelled no musky
odor on my woodchuck, however.) The woodchuck also
is said to whistle. I have not heard mine whistle, either,
but in addition to his chuckling plea for attention, I have
heard an indignant yip when I dipped his front paws in
water.

The life of the woodchuck revolves around its bur- 16
row. This is a complicated structure that may be from
25 to 30 feet long, with a front door that is obvious
because of the dirt heaped around it and a second plunge
hole dug from beneath and thus hard to see. Within the
hole there is a turnaround near the entrance, a nest
chamber lined with soft grass, and a toilet chamber used
exclusively for sanitary purposes. The nest chamber is
invariably 14 by 16 inches, which is so small that a full-
grown woodchuck must sleep curled up. The digging of
woodchucks improves the soil by its mixing action and
by letting in air and water. An average den requires the
moving of nearly 400 pounds of dirt. In New York State,
it has been estimated, woodchucks turn over 1.6 million
tons of earth each year.

An ability for deep hibernation is the woodchuck's [17] most famous characteristic, one it shares with ground squirrels, bats, and jumping mice. The older and fatter woodchucks go to earth first, sometimes before the first frost, followed by the yearlings and juveniles. They sleep in a tightly curled ball. A captive woodchuck was examined once a week during hibernation, and although it was handled its eyes did not open. It was cold to the touch. It took one breath every six minutes, and its heartbeat was equally slow. Its temperature had sunk from 96.8 degrees F. while awake to 50 degrees. Thin woodchucks emerge from hibernation first, sometimes even during winter. Wakening may be either slow or abrupt and accompanied by trembling. Woodchucks do not sleep in their summer dens but move to new dens in woods or brush, where leaves carpet the ground and the frost does not go deep. They prefer a slope safe from flooding. Their weight loss during hibernation ranges from one-third to one-half their body weight, but the newly awakened woodchucks are nonetheless in good condition. While they are asleep their teeth and toenails do not grow.

Woodchucks lead a relatively unsocial life. They [18] live together only briefly during mating, though yearlings not yet ready to mate sometimes consort together and even occupy the same den. Chucks place their dens at a distance from each other whenever they can. They compete for food, but there is no real territoriality. Bigger woodchucks chase off smaller ones, which do not defend their home range. A woodchuck threatens by arching its back, flipping its erect tail up and down, and approaching the adversary with open mouth, but actual fights are few. Woodchucks are notorious eaters, and this is their main occupation. They eat selected succulent plants, particularly clover, chickweed, alfalfa, and dandelion when these are abundant. They love fruit and vegetables, and it is to this that they owe the great hostility of most farmers. Fat woodchucks weigh

10 or 12 pounds, but a 15-pound specimen is not unheard of.

When the cycle of woodchuck life begins in the 19 spring, the males immediately begin to wander, searching for dens occupied by females. The females stay at home, waiting to be courted. Thus in the spring it is possible to tell the sex of a woodchuck at a distance— a wanderer is a male, a stay-at-home is a female. Females also are warier, especially when pregnant.

Tails wagging, the males check each den to see if it 20 is occupied by an agreeable female. If it is, and she accepts him, he usually moves in with her, though sometimes the two live in different burrows while the male visits his mate daily. During this period a mated pair is monogamous, something we tend to read of with approval, but the conjugal period is brief. The gestation of woodchucks is only about 30 days, and as the time of birth approaches, the female drives the male away. He is to be permitted no part in raising the young. It is one of nature's casual cruelties that the male remains sexually ardent after the female has rejected him, and so, for a while, the fields are full of frustrated males wandering lonesomely about. The arrangement, however, ensures that any female coming into heat later than the others will be mated nonetheless.

The young woodchucks are born in the early spring 21 in litters that average four but may be larger. The newborn woodchuck is tiny: blind and hairless, it is only about four inches long and weighs an ounce. At four weeks its eyes are open and it weighs six and one-half ounces. At six weeks young chucks are active, weigh half a pound, and follow their mother into the open, but they don't go far. They sun themselves at the edge of the burrow and wrestle and play. The mother grooms them affectionately. It is at this stage, I was interested to read, that she begins to wean them by going farther from the burrow than they dare to follow so they are forced to eat herbs to stay their hunger.

Sometime after the young are six weeks old their [22] increasing size crowds the nest, and the mother separates them, leading each one to a new den dug nearby. There it must learn to do without the emotional support of the family and prepare for the solitary life that lies ahead. This preparation is gradual. The mother visits each one daily and spends time with it, grooming it and continuing its opportunity to learn from her such survival lessons as wariness and the selection of the proper herbs as food. Young woodchucks sometimes take food from a mother's mouth, and it is thought this is part of learning what is good to eat. They follow her example when she shows alarm and learn to respond to the sight or sound or smell of danger with a quick dive to safety. As the young woodchucks become more prepared physically and psychologically to face life alone, the mother's visits taper off. Then, sometime in midsummer, the young will feel an urge to move off and explore the world. They may go a long way or only a few hundred yards before they find new homes, but now they are on their own.

Once I had acquainted myself with the scenario of [23] woodchuck life in the wild, it was clear how I must carry out my role as foster mother, but accomplishing it was not so easy. I brought my woodchuck all sorts of grasses and vegetables, but he merely tasted them and dropped them. I was happy when he consented to eat a cherry and a marigold, but he would go no further. I was also aware that life in my bathroom was not providing the proper lessons about growing plants, damp earth, and the sudden threat of a marauding dog, which would be the most important elements in his adult survival.

I took him outside and put him down on the lawn. [24] He showed sheer terror at the sight of the open sky. I brought his box outside. He dashed in and refused to leave it. There seemed nothing to do but bring him back to the bathroom. I continued to leave offerings of grass and flowers, but he allowed them to wilt and clambered into my lap as eagerly as ever for each feeding. He was getting quite big, and my husband remarked that if I didn't do something about it, I would be followed around for the rest of my days by a 15-pound woodchuck begging for milk.

At last I decided I must do what mother woodchucks 25 do: put him in a new burrow. I searched along the wall of our orchard and found a small hole. I wasn't sure of its origin, or if it was occupied, but decided I must take a chance. I put the chuck, housed in his box, near the hole and left him, knowing that eventually hunger would drive him out. A few hours later, when his next feeding time came, I went out. The box was empty. I called, and within seconds my woodchuck emerged from the hole and flung himself on my ankle, chuckling gladly. I sat down and fed him. When I finished he tried persistently to follow me back to the house, but I put him on the far side of the wall and escaped.

I continued to visit him several times a day with his milk. Each time he greeted me joyfully and drank greed- 26 ily, but I felt sure he must be finding food on his own. He also began to accept carrots and cherries and daisies. The final weaning came abruptly. Between breakfast and lunch he forgot how to suck. It was as if a switch had been flipped in his maturing nervous system. I offered milk a few more times, but he was quite unable to suck it in. Clearly, weaning had been accomplished.

Still the emotional ties persisted. I visited him every 27 day bringing carrots. Sometimes he was quite far away, but he would always come at the sound of my voice. He showed more emotion about nibbling my fingers and climbing up my legs and into my arms than he did about the carrots. It is an odd feeling to be desperately embraced by a lonesome woodchuck. I always left him with a slight sense of guilt at rejecting him, and I wondered if wild woodchucks tried as hard to keep their mother's waning interest.

The parting came unexpectedly. I went away on a   28
brief trip. When I came back there were days of rain and
I didn't visit the burrow. In truth it didn't seem as
important as it once had. When I remembered and went
out to call, no woodchuck came. In the past weeks I have
seen no sign of him, and I suppose he has moved away
as the textbook said young woodchucks do. I hope he
has found a safe, dry burrow. When autumn comes I will
wish him deep sleep and happy dreams. In the spring
when I see a large, handsome woodchuck ambling
through the new grass, I will hope that it is he.

Comment

Faith McNulty tells us how to raise a woodchuck and, in the course
of doing so, describes the habits and life cycle of woodchucks. Like
Rachel Carson, Annie Dillard, and other writers about nature in this
book, McNulty also tells us about herself—sometimes directly, sometimes indirectly. Specifically, she tells us about her rural life, her love
of animals, her view about nature. These details are not presented
casually, in a rambling, disconnected narrative; McNulty instead
weaves them together, each detail developing her central topic.

Questions for Study and Discussion

1. What aspects of raising a woodchuck does McNulty stress, and
    why does she? What aspects receive the least attention, and
    why do they?
2. How does McNulty connect the life cycle and habits of the
    woodchuck to the process of raising one? Why is it important
    to understand this life cycle and these habits?
3. Does McNulty make a point about raising a wild animal? Or
    is she concerned only with describing the process?
4. What does McNulty tell us about her interests, ideas, and life?
    What does she reveal to us indirectly?

Vocabulary Study

1. What does McNulty mean by the following words and phrases?
   a. *interchangeable digits* (paragraph 2)
   b. *imprinting the woodchuck* (paragraph 8)
   c. *dexterous as a squirrel; interspersed with long, bristly guard hairs* (paragraph 9)
   d. *fastidious* (paragraph 11)
   e. *nibbling and chuckling sound* (paragraph 12)
   f. *lethal habits* (paragraph 13)
   g. *deep hibernation* (paragraph 17)
   h. *no real territoriality; succulent plants* (paragraph 18)
   i. *gestation; casual cruelties* (paragraph 20)
   j. *ambling* (paragraph 28)
2. Explain the statement: "Rescuing him, I felt as large as Fate."
3. What does McNulty mean in paragraph 6 by "innate" behavior in woodchucks, and what other examples of innate behavior does she give?

Suggestions for Writing

1. Describe your own experience with a wild or domestic animal, perhaps your own attempt to raise it. In the course of your essay, give your reader details about yourself—your life, your interests, perhaps your own attitude toward animals and nature generally
2. Describe the pleasures and frustrations of building or repairing something. Give enough details about the process to let your readers experience what you did.
3. Describe the same process in enough detail that someone who has never performed it can do so. Assume that this person is unfamiliar with the tools required.

Comparison and Contrast

Like definition and division, comparison and contrast is an important method of developing ideas. *Comparison* deals with similarities, *contrast* with differences. In comparing, you show what two or more people or objects or places have in common; in contrasting, how they are unlike. There are many ways of organizing paragraphs or essays of comparison or contrast. One way is the block listing of the qualities of the first person or place, then the block listing of the qualities of the second—in the same order, as in this paragraph of comparison:

> Chicago, at the southern tip of Lake Michigan, is a port city and an important commercial and industrial center of the Middle West. It is also an important educational, cultural, and recreational center, drawing thousands to its concert halls, art museums, and sports arenas. Cleveland, on the south shore of Lake Erie, is also a port city and a commercial and industrial center important to its area. Like Chicago, it has several important colleges and universities, a distinguished symphony orchestra, one of the fine art museums of the world, and many recreational centers. The location of the two cities undoubtedly contributed to their growth, but this similarity is not sufficient to explain their wide social diversity.

A second way is an alternating comparison or contrast, point by point:

> Chicago is on the southern tip of Lake Michigan; Cleveland, on the south shore of Lake Erie. Both are important commercial and industrial centers of the Middle West, and both offer a wide range of educational, cultural, and recreational activities. . . .

In developing such paragraphs or essays, transitions like *similarly, likewise, by comparison,* and *by contrast* may be needed to clarify the organization. The purpose of comparison and contrast is usually to provide a relative estimate: we discover the qualities of the first person or object or place through the qualities of the second (or third), and the qualities of the second through the first. If Cleveland and Chicago share these characteristics and have the same history of growth, we are better able to understand the causes that shape cities. A contrast with Atlanta or Omaha—large inland cities—would clarify these causes further through a similar relative estimate.

Comparison and contrast provides a relative estimate: Carson tells us something about tropical regions through polar ones, and about polar regions through tropical ones:

> As between tropical and polar regions, the differences in the kinds and abundance of life are tremendous. The warm-water temperatures of the tropics speed up the processes of reproduction and growth, so that many generations are produced in the time required to bring one to maturity in cold seas. There is more opportunity for genetic mutations to be produced within a given time; hence the bewildering variety of tropical life. Yet in any species there are far fewer individuals than in the colder zones, and here we have no dense plankton swarms like the copepods of the Arctic. The pelagic forms of the tropics live deeper than those of the colder regions, so, with little surface life to feed on there are no seals in the tropics, and compared with the clouds of shearwaters, fulmars, auks, whalebirds, albatrosses, and other birds seen over far northern or southern fishing grounds, there are few birds.   —Rachel Carson, *The Sea Around Us*

Analogy is the comparison of two unlike things for the purpose of illustration. Comparison is possible because the two things resemble each other in a few ways:

> A number of analogies have been used to describe the breaking of waves. Some authors refer to the wave as "stubbing its toe" when the water gets shallower. A slightly more accurate image is that of the old vaudeville routine where one comedian is leaning on a cane and the other kicks the cane away, causing the first comedian to fall down. In just that way, the water in the crest finds its weight unsupported and comes crashing down.
> —James Trefil, *A Scientist at the Seashore*

We sometimes use analogy in arguing a point (see p. 282).

Sydney J. Harris

OPPOSING PRINCIPLES HELP
BALANCE SOCIETY

Sydney J. Harris attended the University of Chicago and later taught in its University College. From 1941 to 1978 he was a drama critic and columnist for the *Chicago Daily News*. His column "Strictly Personal" first appeared in the *Daily News* in 1944. Harris was one of the masters of the journalistic essay. Although his essays are brief (most are between 600 and 1,000 words), he deals with important social, political, and philosophical issues in simple, exact, and sometimes eloquent words. His essays are collected in *Majority of One* (1957), *For the Time Being* (1972), *Clearing the Ground* (1986), and other books. Harris died in 1986.

I devoutly wish we could get rid of two words in the 1
popular lexicon: *liberal* and *conservative.* Both are
beautiful and useful words in their origins, but now each
is used (and misused) as an epithet by its political enemies.

Liberal means liberating—it implies more freedom, 2
more openness, more flexibility, more humaneness, more
willingness to change when change is called for.

Conservative means conserving—it implies preserv- 3
ing what is best and most valuable from the past, a
decent respect for tradition, a reluctance to change merely
for its own sake.

Both attributes, in a fruitful tension, are necessary 4
for the welfare of any social order. Liberalism alone can
degenerate into mere permissiveness and anarchy. Conservatism alone is prone to harden into reaction and
repression. As Lord Acton brilliantly put it: "Every institution tends to fail by an excess of its own basic principle."

Yet, in the rhetoric of their opponents, both *liberal* 5
and *conservative* have turned into dirty words. Liberals
become "bleeding hearts"; conservatives want "to turn
the clock back." But sometimes hearts *should* bleed;

sometimes it would profit us to run the clock back if it is spinning too fast.

Radical, of course, has become the dirtiest of words, flung around carelessly and sometimes maliciously. Today it is usually applied to the left by the right—but the right is often as "radical" in its own way.   6

The word originally meant "going to the roots" and was a metaphor drawn from the radish, which grows underground. We still speak of "radical surgery," which is undertaken when lesser measures seem futile. The American Revolution, indeed, was a radical step taken to ensure a conservative government, when every other effort had failed.   7

Dorothy Thompson was right on target when she remarked that her ideal was to be "a radical as a thinker, a conservative as to program, and a liberal as to temper." In this way she hoped to combine the best and most productive in each attitude, while avoiding the pitfalls of each.   8

Society is like a pot of soup: It needs different, and contrasting, ingredients to give it body and flavor and lasting nourishment. It is compound, not simple; not like wine that drugs us, or caffeine that agitates us, but a blend to satisfy the most divergent palates.   9

Of course, this is an ideal, an impossible vision never to be fully realized in any given society. But it is what we should aim at, rather than promoting some brew that is to one taste alone. It may take another thousand years to get the recipe just right. The question is: Do we have the time?   10

Comment

Harris contrasts three words used widely in political discussion— *liberal,* *conservative,* and *radical.* Because those using these words seldom agree on their meaning, Harris is careful to define them. From his definition of them he leads into a discussion of his thesis. His series of short paragraphs are typical of newspaper articles, editorials, and journalistic essays that often devote each paragraph to a single idea and key supporting details. Harris uses his short paragraphs to contrast meanings and ideas.

Questions for Study and Discussion

1. Does Harris contrast *liberal* and *conservative* in blocks or point by point? Why does he introduce the word *radical* only after contrasting the first two words?
2. What essential differences in meaning between the three words does Harris stress? Why does he?
3. Why does Harris give us the etymology or origin of *radical?* What is a metaphor, and why is *radical* an example?
4. How early in the essay does Harris introduce his thesis? How does his discussion of the three words develop it?
5. Where does Harris finally restate his thesis?

Vocabulary Study

1. What did Lord Acton, the nineteenth-century British political writer, mean by the statement "Every institution tends to fail by an excess of its own basic principle"? What do the words *excess* and *principle* mean?
2. What did Dorothy Thompson, the American journalist, mean by the statement that she wished to be "a radical as a thinker, a conservative as to program, and a liberal as to temper"? What did she mean by *temper?*

Suggestion for Writing

Using the *Oxford English Dictionary*, *Dictionary of American English*, *Safire's Political Dictionary*, or other reference sources, trace the meanings of one of the following words or another word used in

politics. Then write a short essay explaining how the history of the word illuminates one or more of its current uses:
1. fascist
2. kingmaker
3. maverick
4. mossback
5. mugwump
6. radical
7. scalawag
8. Young Turk

✧

Cause and Effect

Reasoning about *cause and effect* is often a simple matter of connecting two events. When I get wet during a thunderstorm, I know that rain is the cause. But making other connections is usually not this simple. If I catch a cold the same day, I may blame it on the rain. However, I might have caught a cold even if I had stayed indoors; and if I had been in the rain, the rain alone may not have been the single cause or even a condition. A number of conditions together may have produced the cold: a run-down state arising from overwork or lack of sleep, poor eating habits, getting wet—these may have triggered a virus in the body.

The sum of these conditions is generally what we mean by *cause*. We often speak informally of one of these conditions as the cause. Except where an immediate action (exposure to the storm) produces a direct consequence (getting wet), reasoning about cause and effect is probable rather than certain. Having identified conditions that produced colds in the past, I cannot be sure that they *must* produce one. The identical conditions may be present, without producing a cold.

Paragraphs and essays may deal with causes only, or with effects, or with both, as in the following:

> Yet over the years, jet engines steadily become more complicated. Why? Commercial and military interests exert constant pressure to overcome limits imposed by extreme stresses and temperatures and to handle exceptional situations. Sometimes these improvements are achieved by using better materials, more often by adding a subsystem. And so, over time, jet designers achieve higher air pressures by using not one but an assembly of many compressors. They increase efficiency by a guide-vane control system that admits more air at higher altitudes and velocities

and prevents engine stalling. They increase combustion temperatures, then cool the white-hot turbine blades by a system that
circulates air inside them. They add bleed-valve systems, afterburner assemblies, fire-detection systems, fuel-control systems,
deicing assemblies.   —W. Brian Arthur, "Why Do Things Become
More Complex?"

All discussions of cause and effect, formal and informal, include
hidden or unstated assumptions or beliefs about people, society, the
ways things happen in nature—human beings are naturally aggressive, adolescents are naturally rebellious, the Irish have hot tempers,
the English are cold and reserved, opposites attract. Many who hold
these beliefs unquestioningly seldom think about them, nor do they
feel it necessary to test them through observation. In cause-and-
effect reasoning such assumptions are hidden in the explanation and
may be decisive.

Deborah Tannen

REPORT-TALK IN PRIVATE

Professor of linguistics at Georgetown University, Deborah Tannen
writes about the different conversational styles and "talking voices" of
men and women in *That's Not What I Meant* (1986) and *You Just
Don't Understand* (1990). Tannen distinguishes between public
speaking, or "report-talk," and private speaking, or "rapport-talk."
"For most women," she writes, "the language of conversation is
primarily a language of rapport: a way of establishing connections
and negotiating relationships. Emphasis is placed on displaying
similarities and matching experiences. . . . For most men, talk is
primarily a means to preserve independence and negotiate and
maintain status in a hierarchical social order. This is done by
exhibiting knowledge and skill, and by holding center stage through
verbal performance such as story-telling, joking, or imparting
information." In the following section from *You Just Don't
Understand*, Tannen illustrates this difference through the ways men
and women tell jokes.

Report-talk, or what I am calling public speaking,   1
does not arise only in the literally public situation of

formal speeches delivered to a listening audience. The more people there are in a conversation, the less well you know them, and the more status differences among them, the more a conversation is *like* public speaking or report-talk. The fewer the people, the more intimately you know them, and the more equal their status, the more it is like private speaking or rapport-talk. Furthermore, women feel a situation is more "public"—in the sense that they have to be on good behavior—if there are men present, except perhaps for family members. Yet even in families, the mother and children may feel their home to be "backstage" when Father is not home, "onstage" when he is: Many children are instructed to be on good behavior when Daddy is home. This may be because he is not home often, or because Mother—or Father—doesn't want the children to disturb him when he is.

The difference between public and private speaking 2 also explains the stereotype that women don't tell jokes. Although some women are great raconteurs who can keep a group spellbound by recounting jokes and funny stories, there are fewer such personalities among women than among men. Many women who do tell jokes to large groups of people come from ethnic backgrounds in which verbal performance is highly valued. For example, many of the great women stand-up comics, such as Fanny Brice and Joan Rivers, came from Jewish backgrounds.

Although it's not true that women don't tell jokes, 3 it is true that many women are less likely than men to tell jokes in large groups, especially groups including men. So it's not surprising that men get the impression that women never tell jokes at all. Folklorist Carol Mitchell studied joke telling on a college campus. She found that men told most of their jokes to other men, but they also told many jokes to mixed groups and to women. Women, however, told most of their jokes to other women, fewer to men, and very few to groups that included men as well as women. Men preferred and were more likely to tell jokes when they had an audience: at least two, often four or more. Women preferred a small audience of one or two, rarely more than three. Unlike men, they were reluctant to tell jokes in front of people they didn't know well. Many women flatly refused to tell jokes they knew if there were four or more in the group, promising to tell them later in private. Men never refused the invitation to tell jokes.

All of Mitchell's results fit in with the picture I have 4 been drawing of public and private speaking. In a situation in which there are more people in the audience, more men, or more strangers, joke telling, like any other form of verbal performance, requires speakers to claim center stage and prove their abilities. These are the situations in which many women are reluctant to talk. In a situation that is more private, because the audience is small, familiar, and perceived to be members of a community (for example, other women), they are more likely to talk.

The idea that telling jokes is a kind of self-display 5 does not imply that it is selfish or self-centered. The situation of joke telling illustrates that status and connection entail each other. Entertaining others is a way of establishing connections with them, and telling jokes can be a kind of gift giving, where the joke is a gift that brings pleasure to receivers. The key issue is asymmetry: One person is the teller and the others are the audience. If these roles are later exchanged—for example, if the joke telling becomes a round in which one person after another takes the role of teller—then there is symmetry on the broad scale, if not in the individual act. However, if women habitually take the role of appreciative audience and never take the role of joke teller, the asymmetry of the individual joke telling is diffused through the larger interaction as well. This is a hazard for women. A hazard for men is that continually telling jokes can be distancing. This is the effect felt by a man who complained that when he talks to his father on the phone, all his father does is tell him jokes. An extreme instance of a similar phenomenon is the class clown, who, according to teachers, is nearly always a boy.

Comment

Tannen shows that status and social relationships influence how women speak in public and in private. Men have a different view of what is public and private speaking. Tannen qualifies her statements to show that some behave in different ways in such situations; she does not claim to generalize about all women and men. In citing evidence from studies of public and private speaking, she allows readers to test her analysis and refer to their own experience.

Questions for Study and Discussion

1. Under what circumstances do women feel that they are speaking in public and speaking in private?
2. How true is the "stereotype" that women never tell jokes?
3. Why are the roles men and women play in joke telling sometimes hazardous?
4. Do you agree with Tannen that men are more likely to tell jokes in crowds than women are? Do you agree with her explanation of the cause?

Vocabulary Study

1. How do paragraph 5 and earlier paragraphs illustrate the statement, "The situation of joke telling illustrates that status and connection entail each other"?
2. How do the examples of *symmetry* and *asymmetry* in paragraph 5 help to explain these terms?

Suggestions for Writing

1. Discuss the extent to which your own experience with joke telling supports Tannen's statements about men or women, or both, as joke tellers. Like Tannen, limit your conclusions to what your personal experience and observations show.

2. Discuss the extent to which your personal experience and observation support one of the following statements:

    a. "For most women, the language of conversation is primarily a language of rapport: a way of establishing connections and negotiating relationships."

    b. "For most men, talk is primarily a means to preserve independence and negotiate and maintain status in a hierarchical social order."

✦
Definition

There are many ways to define a word, each depending on your purpose in writing and the knowledge of your readers. In defining a calf for a child, it may be enough to point to one in a pasture or picture book. For an older person you may point to a calf through words: first by relating it to the class *animal*, then stating the *specific differences* between the calf and all other animals: "the young of the domestic cow" (*Webster's Ninth New Collegiate Dictionary*). You could also explain that, as *Webster's Ninth* points out, the word may describe the young of animals related to the cow, like the bison and the water buffalo, and to the young of some large animals like the elephant.

These definitions are called *denotative* because they point to the object or single it out from all others in the same class. *Connotative* definitions by contrast refer to ideas and feelings associated with the word. Denotative definitions are the same for everyone; connotative definitions are not. To some people, the word *calf* refers to an "awkward or silly youth" (*Webster's Ninth*). The phrase *calf love* connotes awkwardness and silliness to some, mere youthfulness and inexperience to others.

If you want to explain the origin or derivation of a word, perhaps for the purpose of explaining current meanings, you may state its etymology. The word *coward* derives from the idea of an animal whose tail hangs between its legs. The etymology illuminates one or more connotations of the word. You may, if you wish, propose or stipulate a new word for an idea or discovery. In the thirties Congressman Maury Maverick proposed the word *gobbledygook* as a description for pretentious, involved official writing. Such definitions may gain general acceptance. Some definitions remain in use for years, only to fall into disuse as new discoveries are made and new ideas appear, and better terms are invented to describe them.

How complete the definition is depends on its purpose in the essay, as well as on the reader. For one kind of reader it may not be necessary to point to or single out an object: the writer will assume that the reader knows what the object is, and needs only to be told how it works. Parts of the object (the blade casing of a manual lawn mower) may be defined fully in the course of describing how to care for or fix it; other parts may not be defined because they are unimportant to the process. It may be enough to tell readers of novels written about the 1920s that the Pierce-Arrow is an expensive automobile, or you may give one or two distinctive qualities of the Pierce-Arrow to explain an allusion to it.

August Heckscher

DOING CHORES

August Heckscher worked for many years as a journalist. He later served as director of the Twentieth Century Fund, president of the Woodrow Wilson Foundation, and administrator of recreation and cultural affairs for New York City. His numerous writings on public affairs include *Alone in the City: Memoir of an Ex-Commissioner* (1974), *Open Spaces: The Life of American Cities* (1977), *When LaGuardia Was Mayor: New York's Legendary Years* (1978), and *Woodrow Wilson* (1991). His essay on chores is one of several essays in this book on work experiences.

I have been doing chores, being for a brief spell alone   1
in a house that recently was astir with bustle and echoed with the voices of a gathered family. For those who may be in some doubt as to the nature of chores, their variety, their pleasures and their drudgery, I am prepared to deliver a short disquisition.

The first point about chores is that they are repeti-   2
tive. They come every day or thereabouts, and once done they require after a certain time to be done again. In this regard a chore is the very opposite of a "happening"—

that strange sort of event which a few years back was so much in fashion. For a happening was in essence unrepeatable; it came about in ways no one could predict, taking form from vaporous imaginings or sudden impulse. Chores, by contrast, can be foreseen in advance; for better or worse, I know that tomorrow I must be re-enacting the same small round of ritualistic deeds; and they arise, moreover, from practical necessities, not from poetic flights.

A second point about chores is that they leave no 3 visible mark of improvement or progress behind them. When I am finished, things will be precisely as they were before—except that the fires will have been set, the garbage disposed of, and the garden weeded. In this, they are different from the works which optimistically I undertake. Ozymandias may have been presumptuous, but he was essentially right when he looked about him and said: "*See how my works endure!*" A work, once achieved, leaves a mark upon the world; nothing is ever quite the same again. The page of a book may have been printed or a page of manuscript written; a sketch, a poem, a song composed; or perhaps some happy achievement reached in one of the more evanescent art forms like the dance or cooking. All these have an existence of their own, outside of time, and at least for a little while live on in the mind of their creator and perhaps a few of his friends.

The well-meaning wife, seeing her husband about his 4 chores, will miss the character of his performance. "Henry loves to cut wood," she will say; "he positively dotes on controlling the flow of waste from dinner-table to compost heap." The wife is perhaps trying to appease an unnecessary sense of guilt at seeing her spouse engaged in mundane efforts. The fact is, he doesn't love doing chores. But neither does he feel humiliated or out of sorts for having to do them. The nature of a chore is that it is neither pleasant nor unpleasant in itself; it is entirely neutral—but it is obligatory.

Neutral—and yet I must confess that with their repe- 5
tition, and perhaps because of their very inconsequence,
chores can in the end evoke a mild sort of satisfaction.
Here, as in more heroic fields of endeavor, a certain
basic craft asserts itself. To do what must be done neatly,
efficiently, expeditiously—"without rest and without
haste"—lights a small fire deep in the interior being and
puts a man in good humor with the world. Santayana
described leisure as "being at home among manageable
things"; and if he was right we who are the chore-doers
of the world are the true leisure classes. At least one can
be sure that no chore will defeat us; none will raise
insuperable obstacles, or leave us deflated as when the
divine muse abandons her devotee.

A man I know became seduced by the minor pleasure 6
of doing chores—or at any rate by the absence of pain
which they involve—and could be seen from morning
till nightfall trotting about his small domain, putting
everything in order, setting everything to rights that the
slow process of time had disturbed. He was perhaps
going too far. To season chores with work, and to
intersperse them with a few happenings, is the secret of
a contented existence. Fortunate the man or woman
who achieves a just balance between these three types
of activity—as I have been able to do by good chance,
and for a little space of time.

Comment

Whereas Maya Angelou writes concretely about the experience of
work in an Arkansas community, Heckscher writes in general terms.
His purpose is to define one kind of happiness. That definition, coming in the final paragraph, takes the form of a general comment on
the three activities discussed in the essay—chores, work, and happenings: "To season chores with work, and to intersperse them with
a few happenings, is the secret of a contented existence." Heckscher
builds to this thesis instead of beginning with it, because his point

about these activities would not be clear without his having defined and illustrated them.

Questions for Study and Discussion

1. What are the differences between chores and work? Has Heckscher given a meaning to *work* different from your own? Do you ordinarily describe chores as work?
2. How does Heckscher introduce the essay? Does he merely state the subject—or does he also hint at his thesis?
3. Could the second point about chores (paragraph 3) have been discussed before the first?
4. Is Heckscher writing to a general audience or to a special one—perhaps husbands who perform weekend chores? What is his purpose in writing—to reflect on his personal experience, to inform his readers about work and chores, or to persuade them to change their thinking about work or their way of performing it?
5. Do you agree that chores can provide "a mild sort of satisfaction"?

Vocabulary Study

1. Read Shelley's poem "Ozymandias," and in a short paragraph discuss Heckscher's reference to it in his essay.
2. Compare the dictionary meaning of the italicized word with the word following it in parentheses. Be ready to explain how the parenthesized word changes the meaning of the sentence:
   a. *disquisition* (sermon) [paragraph 1]
   b. *ritualistic* (habitual) [paragraph 2]
   c. *presumptuous* (conceited) [paragraph 3]
   d. *evanescent* (changing) [paragraph 3]
   e. *dotes on* (enjoys) [paragraph 4]
   f. *mundane* (ordinary) [paragraph 4]
   g. *neutral* (uninteresting) [paragraph 4]
   h. *expeditiously* (speedily) [paragraph 5]
   i. *deflated* (tired); *devotee* (fan) [paragraph 5]
   j. *domain* (household) [paragraph 6]

Suggestions for Writing

1. Discuss how accurately Heckscher's definitions fit the various kinds of work you perform at home. In the course of your essay, discuss how closely your idea of happiness agrees with Heckscher's.
2. Discuss daily activities at home and at school that you do not consider chores, and explain why.
3. About chores, Heckscher states: "Here, as in more heroic fields of endeavor, a certain basic craft asserts itself." Discuss the "basic craft" of a chore that you perform regularly. Contrast this "craft" with work that you also perform regularly.
4. Write your own definition of a contented existence, comparing your ideas and experiences with Heckscher's if you wish.

Classification and Division

Classification and division are important methods of analysis in exposition. Repair manuals classify various tools into broad groups like drills, then explain the uses of individual drills. When you classify you arrange individual objects into broad groups or classes. Hardware stores, for example, shelve tools according to classes— hammers, drills, wrenches, pliers, and so on.

Division arranges the members of a general class into subclasses according to various principles. The division may be formal or scientific, as in the dictionary division of fleshy fruits like apples and oranges, drupaceous fruits (those with pits at the center) like cherries and peaches, and dry fruits like peas and nuts. The class to be divided may be as broad as *fruit* or as narrow as *apples* (a member of one of the subclasses of fruit).

The division of the class is made on a single basis or principle. For example, apples can be divided according to color, use, variety, or taste, to cite a few possible divisions:

by color: red apples, green apples, yellow apples, and so on
by use: eating apples, cooking apples, and so on
by variety: Golden Delicious, Jonathan, Winesap, and so on
by taste: sweet, tart, winy, and so on

If you divide apples in more than one way in the course of the essay (for example, dividing according to taste as well as variety), each division should be separate. The principle of division depends on the purpose of the analysis. In instructing people what apples to buy for baking pies, you would divide apples according to variety, then perhaps according to taste. The color of the skin would not be important. The division need be only as complete as your purpose requires: you might only distinguish tart from sweet and winy apples without naming the varieties. The division may be complete in naming all varieties. If it is not complete, it is sometimes important to note this fact. You might mention one or two varieties of tart apples like Jonathans and Granny Smiths, noting that other tart varieties are out of season.

Michele Huzicka

ON WAITING IN LINE

Michele Huzicka wrote the following essay in her first year at the University of Akron. She uses informal division simply and effectively, distinguishing types of students and experiences she encountered at various times of the day.

At one time or another, in the course of an average day, all of us must wait in some sort of line. In these lines we can learn much about ourselves and one another before we reach our destination. I wait in line often on campus—most often at meal time in the dining room.

As we all know, there are those who can be called "morning people" and there are those who cannot. Morning people don't mind getting up early. They are cheery, pleasant, organized, and attentive—all without a hair out of place or the least bit of sleep left in their eyes. The non-morning people loathe the morning people for these qualities. When the two come together in a line for breakfast, turbulent feelings may arise. For this reason the breakfast line is relatively quiet, compared to other lines. People would rather not run the risk of sparking ill-feelings so early in the morning. However, if the same people were to meet later in the day, the situation would probably be entirely different.

The lunch line is probably the most pleasant of all the lines we must cope with on campus. The majority of students are now fully awake. The non-morning people no longer feel muddled or groggy; they are now simply "people"—people waiting in line. Idle chatter about one's next class or one's hometown or mutual friends is a good distraction from what would otherwise be a very boring wait. It is here at lunch that we are forced to break away from our little cliques and explore the possibility that there are people different from ourselves. So we meet new people and learn about different classes on campus and about different towns and cities in Ohio. We even listen to trivial details just for the sake of having something to do.

In the dinner line I can see people once again return- 4 ing to the security of their friends as I join mine. It is always this line that seems to move the fastest as we recap the day's events, gossip about friends, analyze new boyfriends, and plan for the evening ahead. It is not surprising to look around and see other little groups doing very much the same thing. Talk of this sort is the most entertaining of the day.

Other lines, too, weave their way into our everyday 5 lives. Depending upon their location and the time of day, they can most definitely be quite uncomfortable and dull, or they can be adventurous discoveries about other people. Waiting in line at any time of day, we constantly learn new things about ourselves and other people. We are forced to be with masses of people who share one common goal—getting to the start of the line.

Comment

Michele Huzicka might have chosen another basis of division in her essay. Had she noticed differences in how students wait in different kinds of lines, for instance, she might have divided on that basis. Those waiting to register for classes perhaps behave differently from those waiting in a cafeteria. Huzicka began writing her essay with an observation that she wanted to develop and a sense of college life that she wanted to express. Her thesis occurred to her in the act of reporting that observation. At another time, she might have begun her essay with a general idea or thesis that she wished to illustrate and then searched her experience for examples.

Questions for Study and Discussion

1. How does Huzicka introduce her subject? How early in the essay does she state her thesis?
2. Huzicka writes both informatively and expressively. What does she reveal about her personality and interests in characterizing people and lines?
3. In what other ways might Huzicka have divided students standing in line? What other purposes might such divisions have?

Suggestions for Writing

1. Write an essay of your own on the same topic—on standing in line. Use classification or division at some point in the essay or throughout. Use your discussion to develop an idea as Huzicka does.
2. Write an essay characterizing people on another basis, drawing on your personal experience. Use classification or division to develop your essay.
3. Use classification or division to develop an essay on one of the following topics or another of your choosing:
   a. On writing essays
   b. On sitting in college classes
   c. On first living away from home
   d. On making repairs
   e. On studying for exams

PART TWO

STRATEGIES FOR EXPRESSIVE WRITING

*E*very day, writing. No matter how
bad. Something will come. I have
been spoiled to think it will come
too soon: without work and sweat.

Sylvia Plath

You have probably scribbled words or made designs in your notebook in an absent moment at home or at school. Perhaps you doodle on the edges of a newspaper or magazine as you listen to the stereo or watch television. Like this absent-minded scrawling, much writing has the purpose of personal expression, the play of the mind for its own sake. For instance, a rambling letter from a friend may jump from one experience to another without obvious transition. Your friend wrote the letter to share feelings and thoughts of the moment, and you may do the same in responding.

Other kinds of expressive writing are more organized. A journal entry, a statement of personal belief, an essay recalling a personal experience, a letter expressing pleasure or anger—these are different kinds of personal expression, and they may be organized in various ways for various purposes. For different audiences, you may choose a different order of ideas and details appropriate to a particular audience.

Expressive writing has many purposes. A journal entry, for example, is written for your own use, and that use determines the order in which you record impressions and ideas. You may keep the journal as a strictly chronological record of a trip or a loose compilation of facts collected for a paper. In contrast, a letter of protest is expressive in voicing anger at an unjust law; usually writing of this kind is also persuasive, urging a change in the law. The statement of personal belief may also be expressive and persuasive, and be shaped by the thoughts and feelings you want to stress as well as by considerations of audience. Writing to a familiar audience, you might include personal details that an unfamiliar audience might neither understand nor appreciate.

Expressive writing can also be informative. In the following essay, Gloria Emerson's purpose in describing her parachute jump is to share the pleasure and surprise of the experience: "Everyone at the center was pleased; in fact, I am sure they were surprised. Perhaps this is what I had in mind all the time." She presents enough details about the jump to allow us to imagine the experience. But these details are not presented separately from her description of her feelings. The essay focuses on these feelings throughout. Had Emerson wanted merely to give information about sky diving, the focus of her essay would have been different.

No doubt Emerson discovered new feelings and meanings as she wrote. In writing your own essays, you will probably make similar discoveries; indeed, you may discover a purpose you did not have in mind when you began writing. A piece of writing often changes in focus and organization as you put words on paper. Because expressive writing so often incorporates new discoveries and insights, this form of the essay is sometimes more open and organized more loosely than informative and persuasive essays. The writer of the expressive essay wishes to convey the openness of feeling and thought.

Gloria Emerson

TAKE THE PLUNGE . . .

Gloria Emerson worked as foreign correspondent for *The New York Times* from 1965 to 1972, reporting on Northern Ireland, on the Nigerian Civil War, and, from 1970 to 1972, on the Vietnam War. She received the 1971 George Polk Award for excellence in her reporting from Vietnam, and the 1978 National Book Award for her book on the war, *Winners and Losers*. Emerson is also the author of *Some American Men on Their Lives* (1985). In the essay reprinted here, she describes the experience of sky diving for the first time.

It was usually men who asked me why I did it. Some were amused, others puzzled. I didn't mind the jokes in the newspaper office where I worked about whether I left the building by window, roof or in the elevator. The truth is that I was an unlikely person to jump out of an airplane, being neither graceful, daring nor self-possessed. I had a bad back, uncertain ankles and could not drive with competence because of deficient depth perception and a fear of all buses coming toward me. A friend joked that if I broke any bones I would have to be shot because I would never mend.

I never knew why I did it. It was in May, a bright and dull May, the last May that made me want to feel reckless. But there was nothing to do then at the beginning of a decade that changed almost everything. I could not wait that May for the Sixties to unroll. I worked in women's news; my stories came out like little cookies. I wanted to be brave about something, not just about love, or a root canal, or writing that the shoes at Arnold Constable looked strangely sad.

Once I read of men who had to run so far it burned 3 their chests to breathe. But I could not run very far. Jumping from a plane, which required no talent or endurance, seemed perfect. I wanted to feel the big, puzzling lump on my back that they promised was a parachute, to take serious strides in the absurd black boots that I believed all generals wore.

I wanted all of it: the rising of a tiny plane with the 4 door off, the earth rushing away, the plunge, the slap of the wind, my hands on the back straps, the huge curve of white silk above me, the drift through the space we call sky.

It looked pale green that morning I fell into it, not 5 the baby blue I expected. I must have been crying; my cheeks were wet. Only the thumps of a wild heart made noise; I did not know how to keep it quiet.

That May, that May my mind was as clear as clay. 6 I did not have the imagination to perceive the risks, to understand that if the wind grew nasty I might be electro-cuted on high-tension wires, smashed on a roof, drowned in water, hanged in a tree. I was sure nothing would happen, because my intentions were so good, just as young soldiers start out certain of their safety because they know nothing.

Friends drove me to Orange, Massachusetts, seventy 7 miles west of Boston, for the opening of the first U.S. sports parachuting center, where I was to perform. It was the creation, the passion, of a Princetonian and ex-Marine named Jacques Istel, who organized the first U.S. jumping team in 1956. Parachuting was "as safe as swimming," he kept saying, calling it the "world's most stimulating and soul-satisfying sport." His center was for competitions and the teaching of skydiving. Instead of hurtling toward the earth, sky divers maintain a swan-dive position, using the air as a cushion to support them while they maneuver with leg and arm movements until the rip cord must be pulled.

None of that stuff was expected from any of us in   8 the little beginners class. We were only to jump, after brief but intense instruction, with Istel's newly designed parachute, to show that any dope could do it. It was a parachute with a thirty-two-foot canopy; a large cutout hole funneled escaping air. You steered with two wooden knobs instead of having to pull hard on the back straps, or risers. The new parachute increased lateral speed, slowed down the rate of descent, reduced oscillation. We were told we could even land standing up but that we should bend our knees and lean to one side. The beginners jumped at eight a.m., the expert sky divers performed their dazzling tricks later when a crowd came.

Two of us boarded a Cessna 180 that lovely morn-   9 ing, the wind no more than a tickle. I was not myself, no longer thin and no longer fast. The jump suit, the equipment, the helmet, the boots, had made me into someone thick and clumsy, moving as strangely as if they had put me underwater and said I must walk. It was hard to bend, to sit, to stand up. I did not like the man with me; he was eager and composed. I wanted to smoke, to go to the bathroom, but there were many straps around me that I did not understand. At twenty-three hundred feet, the hateful, happy man went out, making a dumb thumbs-up sign.

When my turn came, I suddenly felt a stab of pain   10 for all the forgotten soldiers who balked and were kicked out, perhaps shot, for their panic and for delaying the troops. I was hooked to a static line, an automatic opening device, which made it impossible to lie down or tie myself to something. The drillmaster could not hear all that I shouted at him. But he knew the signs of mutiny and removed my arms from his neck. He took me to the doorway, sat me down, and yelled "Go!" or "Now!" or "Out!" There was nothing to do but be punched by the wind, which knocked the spit from my mouth, reach for the wing strut, hold on hard, kick back the feet so weighted and helpless in those boots, and let go. The parachute opened with a plop, as Istel had sworn to me that it would. When my eyelids opened as well, I saw the white gloves on my hands were old ones from Saks Fifth Avenue, gloves I wore with summer dresses. There was dribble on my chin; my eyes and nose were leaking. I wiped everything with the gloves.

There was no noise; the racket of the plane and wind had gone away. The cold and sweet stillness seemed an astonishing, undreamed-of gift. Then I saw what I had never seen before, will never see again; endless sky and earth in colors and textures no one had ever described. Only then did the parachute become a most lovable and docile toy: this wooden knob to go left, this wooden knob to go right. The pleasure of being there, the drifting and the calm, rose to a fever; I wanted to stay pinned in the air and stop the ground from coming closer. The target was a huge arrow in a sandpit. I was cross to see it, afraid of nothing now, for even the wind was kind and the trees looked soft. I landed on my feet in the pit with a bump, then sat down for a bit. Later that day I was taken over to meet General James Gavin, who had led the 82nd Airborne in the D-day landing at Normandy. Perhaps it was to prove to him that the least promising pupil, the gawkiest, could jump. It did not matter that I stumbled and fell before him in those boots, which walked with a will of their own. Later, Mr. Istel's mother wrote a charming note of congratulations. Everyone at the center was pleased; in fact, I am sure they were surprised. Perhaps this is what I had in mind all the time.

Questions for Study and Discussion

1. What is Emerson's purpose in writing? Does she state her purpose directly, or do you discover it from her approach to the subject and her focus? What were her motives in making the jump?
2. What details does she provide about the operation of the parachute, the descent, and the landing? How are these details fitted to the discussion of her feelings at various stages in her experience? What are these stages?
3. How does she maintain the focus on her feelings throughout the essay? Do these feelings change?
4. Would you have reacted to the parachute jump as Emerson did? What comparable experience aroused similar expectations and feelings in you?

Vocabulary Study

Emerson uses a number of technical terms, among them *rip cord*, *static line*, and *wing strut*. See whether your dictionary—or an unabridged dictionary—contains these. If you do not find them listed, state how the essay clarifies their meaning. Notice that we do not always require a complete definition of a term to understand its purpose or role in the process. Is that true of these terms?

Suggestions for Writing

1. Describe an experience with a complex piece of equipment like a parachute. You might discuss the problems encountered in assembling it, or other difficulties it created for you.
2. Describe an experience comparable to the one Emerson describes. Explain your motives in undertaking the experience, and trace the stages of the experience as Emerson does, giving an account of your feelings at each stage.

Autobiography

In the autobiographical essay, the writer seeks to reach personal understanding by recalling vital experiences of the past. Virginia Woolf tells us that the nineteenth-century English writer Thomas De Quincey "understood by autobiography the history not only of the external life but of the deeper and more hidden emotions." Woolf uses this idea to define the art of the autobiographer:

> To tell the whole story of a life the autobiographer must devise some means by which the two levels of existence can be recorded—the rapid passage of events and actions; the slow opening up of single and solemn moments of concentrated emotion.
> —"De Quincey's Autobiography"

We see this art in the three autobiographical essays that follow. Mary E. Mebane re-creates the world of her North Carolina childhood through a description of daily chores and family life, Annie Dillard narrates girlhood experiences shared with her father, and Leonard Kriegel describes the effort to overcome crippling effects of polio. In the autobiographical essay, authors often reach insights about themselves in concentrating upon central experiences in their past.

The autobiographical essay may serve other purposes in addition to recalling the past and expressing personal feelings and insights. In re-creating the past, Mebane informs us about growing up black in America. Kriegel gives his essay an argumentative edge in questioning values that gave him strength to deal with physical handicaps.

Annie Dillard

MY FATHER

Annie Dillard describes her early life in Pittsburgh in *An American Childhood* (1987), in which the following chapter appears. Dillard later lived in the Roanoke Valley of Virginia, and she writes about her experiences there in *Pilgrim at Tinker Creek* (1974), awarded the Pulitzer Prize in 1975. A chapter from this book appears in Part Five. Dillard later lived in the Pacific Northwest and wrote about Puget Sound in a collection of essays, *Teaching a Stone to Talk* (1982). Her novel, *The Living*, was published in 1992. Selection title by editor.

Years before this, on long-ago summer Sundays, 1 before Father went down the Ohio and ended up selling his boat, he used to take me out with him on the water. It was a long drive to the Allegheny River; it was a long wait, collecting insects in the grass among the pebbles on shore, till Father got the old twenty-four-foot cabin cruiser ready to go. But the Allegheny River, once we got out on it, was grand. Its distant shores were mostly wooded on both sides; coal barges, sand barges, and shallow-draft oil tankers floated tied up at a scattering of docks. Father wore tennis shoes on his long feet, and a sun-bleached cotton captain-style hat. He always squinted outside, hat or no hat, because his eyes were such a pale blue; the sun got in them. He was so tall he had to lean under the house-top to man the wheel.

We stopped at islands and swam. There were wooded 2 islands in the river—like Smoky Island at Pittsburgh's point, where Indians had tortured their English and Scotch-Irish captives by night. The Indians had tied the soldiers and settlers to trees, heaped hot coals on their feet, and let their small boys practice archery on them. Indian women heated rifle barrels and ramrods over fires till they glowed, then drove them through prisoners' nostrils or ears. The screams of the tortured settlers on Smoky Island reached French soldiers at Fort Duquesne, who had handed them over to the Indians reluctantly, they said. "Humanity groans at being forced to use such monsters."

Father and I tied up at Nine-Mile Island, upstream ₃ from Smoky Island, and I jumped from a high rope-swing into the water, after poor Father told me all about those boaters' children who'd been killed or maimed dropping from this very swing. He could not bear to watch; he shut his eyes. From the tree branch at the top of the ladder I jumped onto the swing; when I let go over the water, momentum shot me forward like a slung stone. I swam up to find the water's surface again, and called to Father onshore, "It's okay now."

Our boat carved through the glossy water. Pittsburgh's ₄ summer skies are pale, as they are in many river valleys. The blinding haze spread overhead and glittered up from the river. It was the biggest sky in town.

We rode up in the locks and down in the locks. The ₅ locks scared me, for the huge doors that locked out the river leaked, and loud tons of water squirted in, and we sat helpless below the river with nothing to do but wait for the doors to give way. Enormous whirlpools dragged at the boat; we held on to the lock walls, clawed, with a single hand line and a boat hook. Once I dropped the boat hook, a new one with a teak handle, and the whirlpools sucked it down. To where? Where did the whirlpools put the water they took, and where would they put you, all ground up, if you fell in?

Oh, the river was grand. Outside the lock and back ₆ on the go, I sang wild songs at the top of my voice out over the roaring boat's stern. We raced under old steel bridges set on stone pilings in the river. How do people build bridges? How did anyone set those pilings, pile those stones, under the water?

Whenever I was on the river, I seemed to be visiting ₇ a fascinating place I had forgotten all about, where physical causes had physical effects, and great things got done, slowly, heavily, because people understood materials and forces.

Father on these boat outings answered my questions 8 at length. He explained that people built coffer dams to set bridge pilings in a river. They lowered a kind of big pipe, or tight set of walls, to the bottom, and pumped all the water out of it; then the men could work there. I imagined the men piling and mortaring stones, with the unhurried ease of stone masons; they stood on gasping catfish and stinky silt. They were working under the river, at the bottom of a well of air. Just a few inches away, outside their coffer dam, a complete river of water was sliding downhill from western New York to the Gulf of Mexico. Above the workers' heads, boats and barges went by, their engines probably buzzing the coffer-dam walls. What a life. Father said that some drowned in accidents, or got crushed; it was dangerous work. He said, answering my question, that these workers made less money than the men I knew, men I privately considered wholly unskilled. The bridge pilings obsessed me; I thought and thought about the brave men who built them in the rivers. I tried to imagine their families, their lunches, their boots. I tried to imagine what it would feel like to accomplish something so useful as building a bridge. What a queer world was the river, where I admired everything and knew nothing.

Father explained how to make glass from sand. He 9 explained, over and over, because I was usually too frightened to hear right, how the river locks worked; they ran our boat up or down beside the terrible dams. The concrete navigation dams made slick spillways like waterfalls across the river. From upstream it was hard to see the drop's smooth line. Drunks forgot about the dams from time to time, and drove their boats straight over, killing themselves and everyone else on board. How did the drunks feel, while they were up loose in the air at the wheels of their boats for a split second, when they remembered all of a sudden the dam? "Oh yes, the dam." It seemed like a familiar feeling.

On the back of a chart—a real nautical chart, with shoals and soundings, just as in *Life on the Mississippi*—Father drew a diagram of a water system. The diagram made clear something I'd always wondered about: how water got up to the top floors of houses. The water tower was higher than the highest sinks, that was all; through all those labyrinthine pipes, the water sought its own level, seeming to climb up, but really still trickling down. He explained how steam engines worked, and suspension bridges, and pumps.

Father explained so much technology to me that for a long time I confused it with American culture. If pressed, I would have claimed that an American invented the irrigation ditch. Certainly the coffer dam was American, I thought, and the water tower, the highway tunnel— these engineering feats—and everything motorized, and everything electrical, and in short, everything I saw about me newer than fishnets, sailboats, and spoons.

Technology depended on waterworks. The land of the forty-eight states was an extended and mighty system of controlled slopes, a combination Grand Coulee Dam and Niagara Falls. The water fell and the turbines spun and the lights came on, so steel mills could run all night. Then the steel made cars, millions of cars, and workers bought the cars, because Henry Ford in 1910 had come up with the idea of paying them enough to buy things. So the water rolled down the continent— just plain fell—and everyone got rich.

Now, years later, Father had picked Amy and me up after church. When we got out of the car in the garage, we could hear Dixieland, all rambling brasses and drums, coming from the house. We hightailed it inside through the snow on the back walk and kicked off our icy dress shoes. I was in stockings. I could eat something, and go to my room. I had my own room now, and when I was home I stayed there and read or sulked.

While we were making sandwiches, though, Father 14 started explaining the world to us once again. I stuck around. There in the kitchen, Father embarked upon an explanation of American economics. I don't know what prompted it. His voice took on urgency; he paced. Money worked like water, he said.

We were all listening, even little Molly. Molly, at 15 four, had an open expression, smooth and quick, and fine blond hair; she was eating on the hoof, like the rest of us, and looking up, a pale face at thigh level, following the conversation. Mother futzed around the kitchen in camel-colored wool slacks; she rarely ate.

Did we know how water got up to our attic bath- 16 room? Money worked the same way, he said, worked the way locks on the river worked, worked the way water flowed down from high water towers into our attic bathroom, the way the Allegheny and the Monongahela flowed into the Ohio, and the Ohio flowed into the Mississippi and out into the Gulf of Mexico at New Orleans. The money, once you got enough of it high enough, would flow by gravitation, all over everybody.

"It doesn't work that way," our mother said. She 17 offered Molly tidbits: a drumstick, a beet slice, cheese. "Remember those shacks we see in Georgia? Those barefoot little children who have to quit school to work in the fields, their poor mothers not able to feed them enough"—we could all hear in her voice that she was beginning to cry—"not even able to keep them dressed?" Molly was looking at her, wide-eyed; she was bent over looking at Molly, wide-eyed.

"They shouldn't have so many kids," Father said. 18 "They must be crazy."

The trouble was, I no longer believed him. It was 19 beginning to strike me that Father, who knew the real world so well, got some of it wrong. Not much; just some.

Comment

The writer of autobiography may narrate a personal history to make a point or argue a thesis. Other writers give us an account of their lives without developing a thesis, though they usually interpret events and may make comparisons with present-day life. Benjamin Franklin wrote his famous autobiography as a lesson on how to succeed in the world, his "having emerged from the poverty and obscurity in which I was born and bred to a state of affluence and some degree of reputation in the world." By contrast, Mark Twain, in his autobiographical *Life on the Mississippi*, had no intention of making his own life a model for others; he wanted instead to re-create the Missouri river town of his youth and recall his experiences as a cub pilot on the Mississippi. Like Twain, Annie Dillard also describes the river town of her youth and experiences that shaped her life. And like Twain, she is not presenting her life as exemplary; but she does make discoveries that tell us something about family relationships and the world in general.

Questions for Study and Discussion

1. Why does Dillard give us the history of Smoky Island? Does she wish to tell us something about her father, or the Pittsburgh of her youth, or her experiences on the Allegheny River? Or does this history serve another purpose?
2. What do her experiences on Nine-Mile Island and the conversations with her father tell you about their relationship?
3. What does the final episode reveal about her mother and family relationships?
4. What did her father get right about the world, and what did he get wrong? Is Dillard referring to the information he gave about dam building, water systems, and other technical matters, or to something else?

Vocabulary Study

1. How do the details of paragraph 4 explain the description of the river as *glossy?*
2. How do the details of paragraph 8 help to explain the term *coffer dam?*
3. What are *shoals* and *soundings* (paragraph 10)?
4. Explain the statement "His voice took on urgency; he paced" (paragraph 14).

Suggestions for Writing

1. Write an essay about a discovery you made about someone, giving details of the experience. Let your details reveal the discovery to your readers. Interpret the details as little as possible.
2. Describe a place—a river, an island, a neighborhood street, a city building—that has been important in your life. Let your details about the place reveal why it has been important.

Mary E. Mebane

THE RHYTHM OF LIFE

Born in Durham, North Carolina, in 1933, Mary E. Mebane grew up in a segregated world in which her parents struggled to make a living. Her mother worked in a tobacco factory and did housework; her father farmed and sold junk. Mebane tells us at the end of her autobiography, *Mary:* "I made it the main aim of my life to find someone who was understanding and sensitive, and to find an environment in which I could develop and flourish. Beyond me lay the great world, the white world, the world that I had been taught was my implacable enemy. I didn't know how I was going to get out, but I was going to try. I had to." Encouraged by her aunt, Mebane entered college in Durham, receiving a B.A. from North Carolina College. She later received an M.A. and Ph.D. from the University of North Carolina at Chapel Hill. She has taught at various universities in the United States. In this self-contained section from her autobiography, Mebane describes some of the happy experiences of her childhood. Jesse is her older brother, Ruf Junior her younger brother. Selection title by editor.

Life had a natural, inexorable rhythm. On weekdays, Mama went to work at a tobacco factory. On
Saturdays, early in the morning, we washed clothes. We
washed clothes outdoors. First Mama and Jesse drew
buckets of water from the well and poured it into the
washpot. It was a big iron pot that stood on three legs
and was very black from soot. Mama put paper and
twigs under it and poured kerosene on them. They
blazed up and soon there was blue smoke curling all
around the pot. She put all the "white" things in the
pot—sheets and pillowcases and underwear—and put
Oxydol in with the clothes. I was puzzled because most
of the things she put in with the "white" clothes were
colored. Our sheets were made from flour sacks and had
red or green or blue patterns on them. Some of the
underwear was colored, too.

My job was to stand over the pot and "chunk" the
clothes down to keep the water from boiling over and
putting out the fire. I loved my job. I had a big stick,
and sometimes I stood there and "dobbed and dobbed"
the clothes up and down all the morning.

Then Mama and Jesse drew water and filled up two
large tin tubs. One was to wash clothes in; the other was
the first rinse. Then there was a foot tub that was for
the second rinse, the one with the bluing in it. Sometimes
Mama let me melt the bluing, which came in a long, flat
cake.

Then there was an even smaller pot, full of starch—
cooked flour and water—with a heavy translucent skim
on it. It was my job to skim it and throw the heavy part
away. I loved that job, too.

After the clothes boiled and boiled, Mama would get
a big stick and carry them a few at a time from the
washpot to the washing and rinsing tubs. Then she
would put more clothes in the washpot, add water and
more Oxydol, and I would dob some more. Sometimes
instead of dobbing I "jugged" the clothes—that is, dobbed
from side to side.

While the second pot of clothes was boiling, I helped 6
Mama with the wash. There was a big washboard in
the first tub and a smaller one in the second tub (that
was the first rinse). Mama washed with a big cake of
lye soap that she had made, rubbing up and down the
washboard. The lye soap sometimes made tiny holes in
her fingers. Then I rubbed the clothes up and down in
the first rinse, which got the suds out; next I stirred them
around and pulled them up and down in the bluing
water. Then Mama wrung them out. Some things she
starched. She hung them up high on the clothesline. By
that time the second pot of boiling clothes was ready
and we started all over again. Later in the morning she
put in the "heavy things" to boil—overalls and her blue
factory uniforms and the blankets. While they boiled,
we ate dinner, the noon meal.

For dinner, Mama would send me to the field with 7
a basket over my arm to get a dozen ears of corn, some
cucumbers, and tomatoes. I would shuck the corn, pulling
the long green hard leaves off, next the lighter green
inner leaves, then the silk in long yellow strands. Ruf
Junior helped to silk it; then Mama would go over it
again. She would let me slice the tomatoes and put
mayonnaise on them, and slice the cucumbers and put
vinegar, salt, and black pepper on them. But I didn't
want to slice the onions because they made me cry, so
Mama would slice them in with the cucumbers herself.
She sliced the corn off the cob into a big frying pan, full
of hot grease. Then we ate the fried corn with tomatoes
and cucumber and onions, and a hunk of corn bread,
and a big mayonnaise jar full of buttermilk, and a piece
of pork.

Sometimes Mama put on a "pot." It cooked a long 8
time on the back of the wood stove. Sometimes it cooked
all day. It cooked all the while we were washing, and
when we came in we had a steaming plate of turnip
greens with tomatoes and cucumbers and onions. Sometimes it was cabbage, yellow from having cooked so

long. (I didn't like the yellowish cabbage or the orangey rutabagas.) Sometimes it was string beans. If we didn't have a pot, we had something quick, like fried squash with onions. Mama put on a pot of meat to go with the pot of vegetables. Often it was neck bones or pig feet or pig ears. Sometimes we had pork slices, swimming in red gravy. She would put on a pie at dinner, blackberry or apple, so it would be ready at suppertime; we had lemon meringue pie only on Sunday. We sometimes had sweet–potato custard through the week, also.

After dinner we went back out in the yard. By then 9 the heavy things had boiled, and Mama took them on a large stick to the washtub. The water in the tub was gray now, with a high meringue of foam on it. But she rubbed and I rinsed, and she hung out the clothes high, but now she gave me the socks and sweaters to hang on the bushes. She sent me to see if any of the clothes were "hard," and I went to the line and lowered the stick that was holding it up. I took down the clothes that had been in the sun so long that they were dry and stiff. I took them in the house and put them on the bed. Then Mama went over to the field to look at her crop, leaving me to churn.

I put the gallon jars of sweet milk into the tall churn, 10 using a stick shaped funny at the bottom. Then I jugged it up and down, up and down, looking every few minutes to see if the butter had come. If it hadn't, I jugged some more. Mama would be over in the field a long time and then she would come and say, "The butter come yet?" And I'd look up and say, "No, ma'am," and churn some more. When the butter came, she scooped it up and shaped it into a cake.

For supper we had what was left in the pot from 11 dinner, along with a pie Mama had put on then, and a glass of buttermilk, and corn bread.

Before supper, Mama would get out two heavy irons 12 and put them on the hot part of the stove. Then she'd tell me to go sprinkle the clothes. I would take some water and wet the clothes down and then roll them into a ball. That would soften them up some and make the wrinkles come out easier. After supper, Mama would start to iron on a big ironing board that had burned places at the end where the iron stood. I couldn't lift the real heavy iron, but she would let me have the small iron and I would push it up and down a handkerchief or a pair of socks, glad to be a woman like Mama.

She would fold the clothes and put them in a drawer and put the sheets and pillowcases on the beds. By that time the flies and mosquitoes would be buzzing the lamp. When she finished she would go out on the porch and sit in the cool, with the basket of butter beans to be shelled for Sunday dinner. I would take a newspaper and shell right along with her, pausing occasionally to protest when Ruf Junior got a pod that I wanted. 13

After we finished shelling the beans, my eyes would have sand in them and Mama would tell me to go to bed. I would go into the house and fall asleep while I heard her still moving around. 14

I helped Mama pick the green tomatoes for chow-chow. She cut up the green tomatoes, then a hill of onions while tears ran down her face. She put in green peppers and cup after cup of sugar and a bag of spice. Then she pushed the chowchow far back on the stove and let it cook. In a little while the kitchen and back porch smelled good. It was the chowchow cooking. Mama let it cook and cook until it "cooked down." By nightfall she was ready to put it in the jars that Ruf Junior and I had washed. 15

She canned vegetables after she came home from work. There were tomatoes, which she put in hot water and scalded, then peeled; peas and corn; corn and okra; and butter beans and string beans. She put down cucumbers in a large stone jar and filled it with brine for pickles. And after we finished eating watermelon, I peeled the rinds, front and back, and Mama cooked them with sugar and we had watermelon preserve. 16

I washed jars and Ruf Junior washed tops; and row 17
after row of canned goods, looking just like pictures,
formed on the shelves, around the sides of the back
porch, and under the house.

When the truck came with the peaches, we stopped 18
everything. If it was Saturday, we didn't wash anymore
or gather vegetables; if it was during the week we worked
until late at night. Everybody had to help because peaches
spoiled so fast. Daddy and Jesse and even Aunt Jo helped.
The grown folks and Jesse had big knives. Ruf Junior
and I had small paring knives. Mama didn't like Ruf Junior
and me to peel because she said we left more of the peach
in the peel than we put in the pot. But she let us peel, too,
because if she didn't we'd holler so loud and beg so hard
that she wouldn't have any peace. She picked out the soft
ones, near the bottom, that had bad places on them and
let us peel those. We peeled and ate and peeled and ate
and went to bed full of peaches, sometimes sick.

Slopping the hogs was Jesse's job when Daddy didn't 19
do it. But sometimes if Jesse heard them squealing over
in the pigpen before it was time, he'd let Ruf Junior and
me take them something. We'd get water buckets; I'd
take a full one and Ruf Junior would have half a one,
and we'd carry slops—discarded vegetables cooked with
"ship stuff," a coarse thickening substance about the
consistency of sawdust. We'd pour it through the big
spaces between the railings into the trough and watch
them eat. There would always be four or five, and we'd
beat the big ones away with sticks so the little ones could
eat. We were careful not to make too much noise because Daddy would wonder what was happening to the
hogs if he heard them squealing too much.

Sometimes Mama would get after Ruf Junior and me 20
when she'd hear a chicken squawking and would look
out to see a hen flying across the yard with Ruf Junior
and me running after it. We didn't want to hurt her; we
wanted to play with her; but she didn't understand that
and went running for her life.

Daddy and Jesse plowed in the Bottom in the to- 21
bacco and cotton. Mama and Aunt Jo hoed in the
vegetables. I hoed until I started chopping up too many
plants and Mama protested; then I joined Ruf Junior in
running up and down the rows, feeling the hot sun on
the dry dirt under my feet and the cool wet where the
plow had just been. If Ruf Junior and I were good, we
could go to the house and get cold water and bring it
to the fields in half-gallon jars.

Comment

Autobiographical writing usually expresses the writer's feelings about
the past. In this section from her autobiography, Mary E. Mebane
seeks to give us a sense of herself through the details of her world
and also through the experiences of growing up. Like Maya Angelou,
Mebane gives us the details of the everyday world so exactly that we
are not likely to forget them. Most of her readers probably never
washed clothes in a pot or cooked chowchow. She is careful, therefore, to give necessary details, at the same time using these details to
evoke the qualities and feelings of Southern life in the 1930s. Description and narrative combine in the essay, as they do in Angelou's.

Questions for Study and Discussion

1. What are the qualities and feelings that Mebane evokes in her
    description of her childhood world? What is her attitude
    toward that world?
2. How does her description of washing, preparing food, and
    other activities illustrate the "natural, inexorable rhythm" of
    life? How does Mebane show that these activities are inexo-
    rable?
3. How different is the impression of Southern black life in
    Mebane's essay from that in Angelou's? Are there significant
    similarities?
4. How different from Mebane's was your participation in every-
    day family activities such as preparing food? Did life have
    the same "natural, inexorable rhythm" in your growing up?

Vocabulary Study

1. Be ready to explain how Mebane helps us to discover the meaning of the following words:
   a. *"chunk,"* *"dobbed"* (paragraph 2)
   b. *"bluing"* (paragraph 3)
   c. *"jugged"* (paragraph 5)
   d. *"shuck"* (paragraph 7)
   e. *"pot"* (paragraph 8)
   f. *"hard"* (paragraph 9)
   g. *"chowchow"* (paragraph 15)
2. Examine the following reference books to find out how many of the above words are listed with the meaning they have in the essay:
   a. an unabridged dictionary
   b. *Dictionary of Americanisms on Historical Principles*
   c. *Dictionary of American Slang*
   d. *Dictionary of American English*

Suggestions for Writing

1. Write your own essay on the statement "Life had a natural, inexorable rhythm," drawing on your own childhood experiences. Make all of your details relate to this idea, and give your discussion unity by dealing with one experience at a time.
2. Like Angelou, Mebane tells us much about Southern life in general by focusing on a segment of that life and describing it in detail. Do the same with the world in which you grew up, focusing on a segment of it that you can describe fully in several pages. Define those terms and activities that your audience may not be familiar with.
3. Mebane describes the effect books, magazines, and radio programs had on her in high school: "I lived so intensely what I read in books and what I heard on the radio that even though I knew that it wasn't everyday, it was more real than everyday." Discuss reading and television experiences that had an intense effect on you during high school, and draw a conclusion from these experiences.

Leonard Kriegel

TAKING IT

Born in the Bronx, in 1933, Leonard Kriegel contracted polio at the age of eleven and spent two years in a hospital recovering from its effects; he later completed grade school and four years of high school through home instruction. In his book *Working Through* (1972), Kriegel states that, upon entering college, "I was far hungrier for education than [my friends]; I was both more expectant and less skeptical of the college experience. I very much wanted to learn, to read whatever was worth reading. It was obvious to me that I knew very little. I was fortunate since, having survived as a cripple, I suspect that I possessed a stronger sense of self and perhaps a better-developed sense of competitiveness than most of my fellow students." Kriegel relates these experiences in the following essay from his book *Falling into Life* (1991).

After I took sick with polio in the summer of 1944, 1 even geography changed. A city boy, I spent the next two years of my life in an upstate orthopedic hospital that was surrounded by trees and fronted by the Hudson River. The New York State Reconstruction Home was the hospital's remarkably appropriate name. Two years later, when I returned to the streets in which I had grown up, I had been reconstructed only to the point where I could walk very haltingly on steel braces and crutches.

But polio had managed to teach me a number of 2 other lessons as well. If it fed me a rich fantasy life, it also forced me to focus on survival. And it taught me that if I were to survive, I would have to become a man—and quickly. "Be a man!" my immigrant father would urge. I suspect that what he meant by that was, "Become an American. Do what you have to do to live." The year 1946 was a comparatively innocent time in this nation's psychological history. For better or worse, the country had very specific expectations of men. And of manhood. A man was expected to face adversity with courage, endurance, determination, and stoicism. With these, and with a touch of defiance, he might right the balance with his fate, however unjust and arbitrary that fate might appear.

"I couldn't take it, and I took it," says the wheel- 3 chair-doomed poolroom entrepreneur William Einhorn in Saul Bellow's *The Adventures of Augie March*. "And I can't take it, yet I do take it." I remember how thrilled I was when I first read those words in 1953. I was twenty years old by then. But I read them with the same shock of recognition Melville speaks of experiencing when he first read Hawthorne. I knew that Einhorn spoke for me, that he had given voice to the way I had learned to live my life and to make that life my own. And I knew that Einhorn spoke for scores of other men in this country who had confronted the legacy of a crippling disease or accident by risking whatever they possessed of substance in a nation that claimed to believe such risks were a man's wagers with his fate.

However unfashionable it may be to write this today, 4 I use the word "men" intentionally. Like so much else in American life during the 1940s and 1950s, how one faced adversity was in part a question of gender. The memory of such cultural beliefs is embarrassing, but that embarrassment doesn't change the way our beliefs had been structured. Simply put, a woman endured, whereas a man fought back. You will get no argument from me if you label such thinking sexist. But I believed, and everyone I knew believed with me, that you were better off struggling with the effects of disease as a man than as a woman. Polio, for example, was a disease battled by being tough, aggressive, and decisive. And by assuming that all limitations could be overcome, beaten, conquered. In short, triumph over polio's effects lay in "being a man." One was expected to "beat" polio by outmuscling the disease.

By the time I was eighteen and had lived with the 5 effects of polio for seven years, I felt I was a "better man" than my friends because I had managed to "overcome a handicap." And in the process of overcoming, I had shown that I could "take it." In the world inhabited by American men, to take it was a sign of being among the elect. Curiously enough, that was an assumption my "normal" friends shared. "You, you're lucky," my closest friend said to me during an intensely painful crisis in his own life. "You had polio." Strange to say, he meant it. And I believed it, too.

Obviously, though, I wasn't lucky. By the age of 6 nineteen, I was already beginning to understand that no one ever "conquers" disease and no one ever "overcomes" its legacy. And yet I managed to look upon resistance to what my virus had made of me as the very essence of who I was as a person. I had reduced questions of manhood to a simple—I am tempted to write "simplistic"—syllogism: A man stands his ground, because not to do so is to reduce his presence. I insisted on self-reliance. No doubt I was structuring my life around what psychologists used to call overcompensation. But I believed that I could create my own possibilities from the very limitations of my crippled body. And so I walked mile after mile on my braces and crutches. I did hundreds of push-ups every day to build up my arms, shoulders, and chest. At night I would walk up the hill to the deserted children's playground in the dredged reservoir that the WPA had turned into the neighborhood's magnificent recreation area. Alone, I would do dips on the monkey bars for hours to create triceps strong enough to carry me endlessly through the days and nights of my need. At home, I would work out to the point of collapse, lying exhausted but pleased with my performance on the linoleum-covered floor of my bedroom in the Bronx. And through it all, my desire to create a "normal" life for myself—whatever I might have had in mind by "normal"—was strengthened into a curious insistence on meeting the virus on its own terms. I would become the man my disease had decreed I should be. I would take whatever it offered, and in taking it I would teach myself to draw strength from whatever it might do to me. If disease was a liability, it was also, I discovered, a gesture of promise. Long before I read Emerson, I knew a good deal about his doctrine of compensation.

I enlisted a hungry imagination in my service, and 7 I took my heroes where I found them. A strange, disparate company of men were always at my call: Hemingway, whom I would write of years later as "my nurse" and whose tragic sense of loss seemed carved out of the continuing sense of absence the virus had insisted I live with; Pete Reiser, whom I had once dreamed of replacing in Ebbets Field's green pastures and whose remarkable penchant for crashing into outfield walls somehow fused in my mind with my own struggle against the virus; Franklin Delano Roosevelt, who had scornfully faced his own war with a virus with aristocratic disdain and patrician distance (years later, at a conference on the problems of the disabled in America, I would meet a historian who would disabuse me of that myth, a myth perpetuated, let me add, by almost all of Roosevelt's biographers); Henry Fonda and Gary Cooper, in whose resolute Anglo-Saxon faces Hollywood had blended the determination and strength and courage a man needed to survive as a man; and any number of boxers in whom heart, discipline, and training combined to stave off the defeats the body's limitations ultimately made inevitable.

These were the "manly" images I conjured up as I 8 walked mile after mile through those quiet Bronx streets, as I relentlessly did series after series of dips on the deserted monkey bars in the children's playground at night, as I taught myself to go up and down one subway staircase after another by fantasizing that those concrete stairs were a collective insult thrust at me by the virus and that with each step I took I was crushing the virus beneath my crippled, brace-bound feet. Whatever else my life might have lacked, it certainly didn't lack focus.

And they were still the "manly" images that flooded my mind when, fifteen years later, a Fulbright professor, married, the father of two boys of my own, I would muscle my brace-bound body onto a train in The Hague, grabbing hold of the vertical poles and swinging across the dead space between platform and carriage, filled with a self-congratulatory adolescent vanity as I watched amazement spread across the features of the Dutch train conductor.

Ambition needs to see itself reflected in the world. [9] And resistance to fate is never abstract. It mirrors precisely those aspects of the emerging self we keep hidden from others but secretly cherish for ourselves. Time and time again, I had to remind myself of how men handled their diseases and their pain, or of how, at least, they were supposed to handle them. I realized even when I was in college that it was not the idea of manhood alone that had helped me fashion a life out of what the virus had done to me. I might think of Hemingway as "my nurse," but it had not been Hemingway but an immigrant Jewish mother—already transformed into a cliché by scores of male Jewish writers—who had serviced my crippled body's needs and who fed me—what I am embarrassed to write about even today—love and patience and care, while I fed her the rhetoric of my adolescent rage and "toughness."

Still, I did take it. And it was ultimately the need to [10] prove myself an American man, tough, resilient, independent, and able to take it, that pulled me through my war with the virus. I have been, as every American man of my generation has been, reminded again and again of the price exacted for such ideas about manhood. At this point, I am quite willing to admit that my two sons will probably be better off in a country in which "manhood" will mean little more than, say, a name for an after-shave lotion. It has been more than forty years since my war with the virus began. Mortality creates its own bargains. And it is evident even to me that if mortality is the only legacy, defeat is the only guarantee. At fifty-one, my legs are still encased in braces and crutches are still cradled beneath my shoulders. My elbows are increasingly arthritic from the burden of all those streets walked and weights lifted and dips dipped and stairs climbed. My shoulders now burn with pain when I even remember the dips and the push-ups that would bring me vengeance upon my virus. And pain is no longer a source of resistance. It merely bores—and hurts.

But I remain an American man. If I know where I'm   11
going, I know even better precisely where I've been. Best of all, I know the price I have paid for being there. A man endures the disease that has shaped him, until he one day recognizes in it the source of his vanity. He can't take it, but he takes it. There was a time when I relished my ability to take it. I'm tired of that now. And I find myself wishing that taking it were easier. In such quiet surrenders do we American men call it quits with the diseases that have shaped us.

Comment

Kriegel gives us a few details about the onset of his polio and the physical effects of the disease. However, the focus of the essay is on the means by which he learned to cope with the physical effects. Had he given a full account of the onset of the disease and its effects, he would have blurred this focus. Kriegel's style is notable for its vigor and directness. His sentences are often colloquial, but he turns to metaphor in stating important ideas in the final paragraph: "A man endures the disease that has shaped him, until he one day recognizes in it the source of his vanity." We hear Kriegel speaking to us, but we also get the sense of a person thinking.

Questions for Study and Discussion

1. What ideal of manhood helped Kriegel survive the effects of polio? Does he tell us how he acquired this ideal?

2. How does Kriegel illustrate the effect that this ideal has had upon his character and behavior? What is his attitude toward the ideal? Would a different ideal have also helped him survive?
3. What does Kriegel mean by the final sentence, "In such quiet surrenders do we American men call it quits with the diseases that have shaped us"?
4. What is Kriegel's thesis? What is Kriegel's purpose in writing this essay, and how do you know?

Vocabulary Study

Explain the following words and phrases:
1. *orthopedic hospital* (paragraph 1)
2. *stoicism* (paragraph 2)
3. *poolroom entrepreneur* (paragraph 3)
4. *question of gender* (paragraph 4)
5. *transformed into a cliché* (paragraph 9)

Suggestions for Writing

1. Kriegel states that when he was growing up the way a man and a woman faced adversity was "like most of American life, a question of gender." Drawing on experiences at home and at school, discuss how you were taught to face adversity and how you do so. State whether your experience suggests that attitudes toward facing adversity have changed from those Kriegel discusses.
2. Discuss your own ideal of manhood or womanhood and how you reached it. Then discuss the effect of this ideal on your relationship with people—perhaps with friends or fellow workers.
3. Write your own essay on the topic, "Taking It." You might focus your essay on experiences at home, at school, or at work. In working out a thesis, you need not draw general conclusions about people or social attitudes. You might draw a specific conclusion about your own ideal of conduct or social attitudes.

✧

Reflection

The reflective essay is more open in its structure than essays bound by the requirements of narration or exposition. For example, it occasionally follows the wanderings of the writer's thought, concluding without tying ideas and details together. This kind of essay comes closest to the journal entry, like those from Sylvia Plath's journal (p. 134), and to the trial essay described in the introduction—the loosely organized essay that explores ideas without necessarily bringing the exploration to completion. The sixteenth-century French essayist Michel Montaigne defended these wanderings and unrevised thoughts in his essays, pointing out that his "understanding does not always advance, it also goes backwards. I do not distrust my thoughts less because they are the second or third, than because they are the first, or my present less than my past thoughts. Besides, we often correct ourselves as foolishly as we correct others."

Sometimes the reflective essay is tightly constructed, its ideas built carefully, without continuous restatement. The structure and language of the essay depend on the writer's personality and characteristic manner of thinking. Montaigne describes his own. Writers like Montaigne think as they put words on paper; they revise and correct as they compose. Other writers choose to revise the whole essay and present only their finished thoughts. The reflective essay, more so than other kinds, takes the shape of the writer's thought and feeling.

Sylvia Plath

JOURNAL, JULY 17, 1957

The American poet Sylvia Plath graduated from Smith College in 1955 and the same year began a Fulbright Fellowship at Cambridge University in England. In 1956 she married the poet Ted Hughes and the following year returned to the United States with Hughes, teaching for a year at Smith and writing before returning to England in 1959. Her collection of poems *The Colossus* was published in 1960; her novel *The Bell Jar*—a fictionalized account of mental illness during her college years—in 1963, a month before her death. *Ariel* and other collections of her poetry were published later. Plath kept a journal from childhood to close to the end of her life. "This is her autobiography," Hughes writes, "far from complete, but complex and accurate, where she strove to see herself honestly and fought her way through the unmaking and remaking of herself." In this entry during the second year of her marriage, Plath records her thoughts about the act of writing and, in passing, about Virginia Woolf's novel *The Waves*, which she had just finished reading. Mrs. Spaulding was an acquaintance who designed and built cottages on Cape Cod.

Cape Cod

Wednesday, July 17. No skipping after today: a page 1
diary to warm up, All joy for me: love, fame, life work, and, I assume, children, depends on the central need of my nature: to be articulate, to hammer out the great surges of experience jammed, dammed, crammed in me over the last five years, and before that, although before that it wasn't so desperate, for there was a slower flow of experience, digestible enough to be written out in short stories and poems, when I had a certain slickness that is enviable now, although that slickness would now never enclose and present the experience welling up in me full and rich as fruit on a blue and white pottery platter. Anyway, if I am not writing, as I haven't been this last half year, my imagination stops, blocks up, chokes me, until all reading mocks me (others wrote it, I didn't), cooking and eating disgusts me (mere physical

activity without any mind in it) and the only thing that sustains me, yet is not enjoyed fully, is the endless deep love I live in. . . . Without that, I would rush about, seeking solace, never finding it, and not keeping the steady quiet deadly determined center I have even now at the end of one of my greatest droughts: It Will Come. If I Work.

Poems are bad to begin with: elaborate ones espe- 2 cially: they freeze me too soon on too little. Better, little exercise poems in description that don't demand philosophic bear traps of logical development. Like small poems about the skate, the cow by moonlight, à la the Sow. Very physical in the sense that the worlds are bodied forth in my words, not stated in abstractions, or denotative wit on three clear levels. Small descriptions where the words have an aura of mystic power: of Naming the name of a quality: spindly, prickling, sleek, splayed, wan, luminous, bellied. Say them aloud always. Make them irrefutable.

Then: the magazine story: written seriously, but easily, 3 because it is easier to manipulate strictly limited characters, almost caricatures, some of them, than the diary "I" of the novel, who must also become, in her way limited, but only so that she can grow to the vision I have now of life, which tomorrow will be a fuller vision, and tomorrow.

Yesterday was the first day of work: a bad day. Spent 4 time on a very desperately elaborate psychological idea and wrote maybe one good image (the boy with the whole ocean bottled in his head) to a raft of brittle, stilted artificial stuff. Not touching on my deep self. This bad beginning depressed me inordinately. It made me not hungry nor want to cook, because of the bestialness of eating and cooking without keen thought and creation. The beach: too late, after a hot walk along a gravelly, sunny sidewalk on Route 6, the deathly pink, yellow and pistachio colored cars shooting by like killer instruments from the mechanical tempo of another planet.

Broken glass, then the scrub pine shadowing Bracket Road, the whisk of bird and squirrel in underbrush, green berried shrubs, and the rough tar. A great blue span of Atlantic under the cliff at Nauset Light, and a swim in the warmish green seaweeded water, rising and falling with the tall waves at tide turn. Lay in sun far up beach, but the sun was cold, and the wind colder. The boom, boom of great guns throbbing in the throat, then the ride back, bad-tempered. Making mayonnaise, and it coming out well. Fine. Then, grubbing over supper, with the badly begun poem like an albatross round the neck of the day, nothing else. And the tables and chairs insulting the way they are when a human being tries to live their merely phenomenal life and miserably doesn't succeed. They go smug, I-told-you-so. Now it is near ten, and the morning yet untried, unbroken. The feeling one must get up earlier and earlier to get ahead of the day, which by one o'clock is determined. Last night: finished *The Waves,* which disturbed; almost angered by the endless sun, waves, birds, and the strange uneven-ness of description—a heavy, ungainly ugly sentence next to a fluent, pure running one. But then the hair-raising fineness of the last 50 pages: Bernard's summary, an essay on life, on the problem: the deadness of a being to whom nothing can happen, who no longer creates, creates, against the casting down. That moment of il-lumination, fusion, creation: We made this: against the whole falling apart, away, and the coming again to make and make in the face of the flux: making of the moment something of permanence. That is the lifework. I under-lined & underlined: reread that. I shall go better than she. *No children until I have done it.* My health is making stories, poems, novels, of experience: that is why, or, rather, that is why it is good, that I have suffered & been to hell, although not to all the hells. I cannot live for life itself: but for the words which stay the flux. My life, I feel, will not be lived until there are books and stories which relive it perpetually in time. I forget too easily how it was, and shrink to the horror of the here and now, with no past and no future. *Writing breaks open the vaults of the dead and the skies behind which the prophesying angels hide.* The mind makes and makes, spinning its web.

Write down the passing thought, the passing obser- 5 vation. How Mrs. Spaulding, with her heavy-lidded blue eyes, her long braid of gray hair, wants her life written: so much happened. The San Francisco earthquake and fire, with her mother giving away the baked beans and bread to refugees, and she crying and wanting to keep the beans; hearing a sound like railway trains jamming into each other on a siding, seeing her doll cradle rock, grabbing the doll, her mother grabbing her into the bed. Her husband dropping dead. Her having an operation, coming out of the hospital to dry her hair at her friend's house, and have it set. Her second husband walks in the door, sees her long hair hanging: what a beautiful sight. The little child getting sick and missing him. His wife dying on the same day her husband did. All this: raw, material. To be useful. Also, images of life: like Woolf found. But she: too ephemeral, needing the earth. I will be stronger: I will write until I begin to speak my deep self, and then have children, and speak still deeper. The life of the creative mind first, then the creative body. For the latter is nothing to me without the first, and the first thrives on the rich earth roots of the latter. Every day, writing. No matter how bad. Something will come. I have been spoiled to think it will come too soon: without work & sweat. Well, now for 40 days I work & sweat. Write, read, sun & swim. Oh, to live like this. We will work. And he sets the sea of my life steady, flooding it with the deep rich color of his mind and his love and constant amaze at his perfect being: as if I had conjured, at last, a god from the slack tides, coming up with his spear shining, and the cockleshells and rare fish trailing in his wake, and he trailing the world: for my earth goddess, he the sun, the sea, the black complement power: yang to yin. The sky is clear blue, and the needles of the pine shine white and steely. The ground is orange-red with fallen pine needles, and the robins and chipmunks steal their color from this red earth.

Comment

The personal diary or journal is a record of events, impressions, chance thoughts, observations—the diarist often "writing to the moment" as they occur. The novelist Virginia Woolf valued this method, noting in her diary entry for January 20, 1919, "the rapid haphazard gallop at which it swings along." Woolf adds: "Still if it were not written rather faster than the fastest typewriting, if I stopped and took thought, it would never be written at all; and the advantage of the method is that it sweeps up accidentally several stray matters which I should exclude if I hesitated, but which are the diamonds of the dustheap." Sylvia Plath also writes to the moment in her journal, in this entry joining ideas and impressions as she explores her life as a writer. "Write down the passing thought, the passing observation." Diary entries often remain unfinished, for people and places look different when observed later, and there is always more to say about a topic. Writers sometimes revise or complete an entry, and often draw on the diary or journal in writing an autobiography or memoir.

Questions for Study and Discussion

1. What statements and features of the July 17 entry suggest that Plath is making discoveries about herself and the act of writing in "writing to the moment"?
2. Why does Plath consider writing essential to her life? Why is it necessary to write each day, "no matter how bad"?
3. Bernard says in the concluding monologue of Virginia Woolf's novel *The Waves*: "The trees scattered, put in order; the thick

green of the leaves thinned itself to a dancing light. I netted them under with a sudden phrase. I retrieved them from formlessness with words." Would Plath agree with Bernard that words rescue the things of the world from "formlessness"?

4. Why does Plath record the details of Mrs. Spaulding's appearance and life in paragraph 5?

Vocabulary Study

1. How does the magazine story described in paragraph 3 illustrate the "slickness" referred to in paragraph 1?
2. What does Plath mean by *flux* in paragraph 4?
3. How does Plath's comment on *The Waves* in paragraph 4 help to explain why she considers Virginia Woolf "too ephemeral" (paragraph 5)?
4. What does Plath mean by *yang* to *yin* in paragraph 5?

Suggestions for Writing

1. Explain why some kinds of writing are easier to perform than others, and give examples.
2. Plath records personal observations, "images of life." Write down a series of images that you connect with a particular person or place. Then comment on why these images made an impression on you and what they reveal.
3. For a week or two, record in a notebook daily impressions, thoughts, and observations relating to one or more of your classes or other experiences. At the end of this period, use one or more of these as a basis for an essay. Think of your notebook as a discovery draft, a basis for exploring ideas and observations that you will later refine into a longer, coherent piece of writing.

Henry Beetle Hough

ON SMALL THINGS

Henry Beetle Hough (1896-1985) was for more than forty years editor and co-publisher, with his wife, of the *Vineyard Gazette,* in Edgartown, Massachusetts. An early book, *History of Services Rendered by the American Press,* won the Pulitzer Prize in 1917. Hough was also the author of novels and nonfiction including his autobiography, *Mostly on Martha's Vineyard.* The essay reprinted here is an example of the reflective essay in which Hough excelled.

August 7

Dear Jack,

When I dressed this morning I inadvertently put on 1 an old green shirt and the bright blue slacks I bought a few weeks ago at Dave Golart's because my waistline now rebels at the long-familiar Size 36, and because bright blue was about as modest a shade as I could find in this pigment-passionate age. My investment in Size 36 pants is dropping faster and I fear more permanently than the value of the stock portfolios of my betters.

I say this morning's color combination was inadvert- 2 ent because I think it was, and in that case it was a small thing. If it was not inadvertent, it was probably a big thing, dictate of some enormous reason I shall never learn. Green and bright blue look odd, I know, but they feel all right, and I shall not change until time for the bank directors' meeting this afternoon. The require-ments for that are obviously severe.

Assuming my vagary in costume to be a small thing, 3 I remembered on my morning walk with Lochinvar something I had not thought of for years. I quote:

> Neglect of small things is the rock on which the great majority of the human race has split.

I learned this, and the rest of the moral passage, now   4
forgotten, in the Mary B. White School, a red brick
building in a graveled yard which stood at the corner
of Maxfield and Pleasant streets in New Bedford long
ago. It was popularly but incorrectly known as the
Maxfield Street School. There were four rooms, two
downstairs and two upstairs, and I had a year's schooling in each room. The principal's office was in the turret
which surmounted the outside stairs. All public buildings built of brick had turrets. I saw the principal's office
only once, and I have forgotten the occasion.

The janitor was Mr. Cochrane. He had a red beard   5
and so far as I can remember always wore a business
suit and a derby hat. The boys' urinal in the basement
smelled so strong and frightful that I have hardly escaped from it yet, but I suppose Mr. Cochrane considered this normal and acceptable. I tried to hold my
breath as I went through, but my lung capacity was
usually insufficient.

Once we were let out of school to watch the circus   6
parade pass by on Purchase Street, a block downhill
from Pleasant. Across from the school an elderly woman
sat on an uncommonly high porch platform attached to
the front of a dun-colored house, and just as we were
crossing the graveled yard the planks gave way and
dropped the elderly woman and her chair ten or twelve
feet to the ground. As I remember it, she landed upright,
still sitting in the chair. Mr. Cochrane set out on a dead
run. I wondered what he was so excited about.

I have forgotten the circus parade in particular; I   7
remember it only in an amalgamated succession of these
wonders, mixed up with seeing the circus come in of an
early morning at the Pearl Street railroad yards near the
Wamsutta Mills. My brother and I used to see the stakes
driven and the big tents raised in a lot at the North End
near Brooklawn where Daniel Ricketson lived and where
he entertained Henry Thoreau. Later the circus went to

the West End or the South End, and I lost interest. When something is completely right and wonderful, it shouldn't be changed.

I remember that in my class at the Mary B. White 8 School there were two boys with the given name of Byron.

These various details I supply because if one is going 9 to write of the importance of little things, he had best show he is himself really attentive to them. Maybe the things I have drawn from memory, though small, may not be small enough to make the desired point. I can't tell. Everything one remembers long enough tends to become fascinating, though not to a wide public.

The passage I was required to learn, the first sentence 10 of which I have quoted, was written by Dr. Samuel Smiles. He has seven lines and a fraction in the *Columbia Encyclopedia,* and I learn for the first time that he was Scottish, a physician, and that his books were mostly devoted to moral education. I think he is one of the writers of the past century (1812-1904) who has gone out, and I doubt if he will be back. There is no use whatever in putting the usual placard on the door, BACK IN TWENTY MINUTES or even BACK IN A HUNDRED YEARS.

I suppose the small things Dr. Smiles regarded as important were of an order now outdated: picking up 11 odds and ends of string, washing behind the ears, painting the length of fence behind the lilac bush even though no one will see it, lifting one's hat clear from the scalp instead of merely tipping the brim, sweeping out the corners with conscience rather than haste, and so on. It was Dr. Smiles who wrote, "A place for everything and everything in its place," but I never had to learn that. It was in Chapter 5 of a piece called *Thrift.*

This is all I shall say about Dr. Smiles, and it seems an odd beginning for the defense of small things I have 12 set out to make. He was so moral—so stuffy, I say— that I can hardly expect to lean upon him or his lavendered philosophy. I must start out for myself and may as well do so abruptly. I object to my life being portentous, and especially to the requirement that I pretend it to be.

Whatever comes up in the matter of ideas or enterprise, someone says, "Let's broaden it." I don't want to 13 broaden it. I prefer to narrow it. I can't paint, except for porches, walls, and things like that, but if I could I would not choose to paint on a large canvas. I probably wouldn't be able to reach the top or the sides, and I would only be an overblown, pretending artist, not a real one. Another thing—I don't want to be in the mainstream. The water is muddy, the pollution great, the vision limited, and too many people are trying to swim at once, each hitting another over the head.

I suppose what I am getting at principally is what I hope is the small integrity of my point of view. It has 14 to be small, because it is mine, and because I don't want to look out from way up there or way out yonder. I want to look out from here, and "here" happens to be an uncrowded place. Besides, if the ground on which I stand is too large or high I will surely be pushed over.

I think the small things now being importantly 15 neglected, that it is so much the fashion to neglect as routine and perfunctory, are the things generally that make life itself and in the end give it the meaning out of which new, fresh, or even grand ideas may spring. Information comes by radio, television, newspaper, magazine, and book, but these are not the country's thinking or the people's thinking. They may be stimulating and they may also be conforming. A man still needs his walking or hammering nails or chopping wood or bowling or shooting pool if he is really to find out what he thinks. The sweeping concept is often not much by itself; it's like the wind that blew over last night, leaving a scatter of debris.

Thoreau said that a man was not born into the world 16 to do everything, but to do something. The opportunities of modern times, puffed and inflated by so many prophets, some real, some false, are over-appreciated; the limitations are undervalued a hundredfold, though they are the intimate companionship of our days and nights, our Sundays and our weekdays.

I suppose, too, that although limitations are generally what they seem and no more, there is always a chance that they may nourish some particular fertility. Most great things nowadays are abstractions, and did not Dr. J. Robert Oppenheimer suggest that some of their puzzling relationships might be brought into understandable order through a small specific? 17

I argue that we, as ordinary people, ought to neglect great things, even at the cost of appearing presumptuous. I am aware that Dr. Samuel Smiles (there he is again), if he could rise up from his serene bit of God's acre among the yews and willows beside the ivy-mantled church, would be bound to insist that this was not what he had in mind. Maybe, though, he could be persuaded. 18

I remember how David Copperfield, after his life with Dora, declared that trifles make the sum of life. This is not what Dr. Smiles meant, either; his small things were not trifles. Not to him. But I am of David Copperfield's way of thinking. Life's trifles and trifling are not only its sum but its essence. 19

One small matter of doubt remains, rising from our experience in the newspaper profession. I remember Betty's intent pursuit of trifles: to keep Mrs. Duble's name from appearing in the *Gazette* as Mrs. Deeble, or vice versa; to defeat at all costs that persecuting vulgarity, "Rev. Smith"; to put the apostrophe in exactly and not approximately the correct place. So much of the good health of the paper lay here that, looking backward, I can almost accept the view that there are no minutiae. 20

As a last word in trying for an understanding or even for a compromise with Dr. Smiles, I suggest that if the great majority of the human race is going to split on the 21 rock of neglect of small things, it will at least be too bad for so many of us to split on the rock of the wrong ones.

Yours, as ever,

Comment

Hough's letter has the openness and loose structure typical of much expressive writing. The miscellany of details that leads into paragraph 9 seems to illustrate Samuel Johnson's definition of the essay as an "irregular undigested piece." But the details have a purpose related to the statement of Samuel Smiles—first quoted in paragraph 3. Throughout the essay Hough gives us a sense of the reflective writer turning over the experiences and sayings that have mattered over a lifetime; Hough discovers a special meaning in writing about them. Out of seemingly small details and ideas concerned with everyday experiences come ideas about life itself.

Questions for Study and Discussion

1. What is the purpose of the miscellany of details that leads into paragraph 9?
2. What is the meaning of the quotation from Samuel Smiles in paragraph 3? How does Hough explain the statement in later paragraphs?
3. Hough discusses how people can live meaningful lives. What paragraphs introduce and develop these ideas?
4. Hough addresses his letter to "Jack"—a particular friend and reader of his newspaper. What features of the essay suggest that Hough has a larger audience in mind?
5. What impression do you get of Hough through his letter? What personal qualities most stand out? What kind of sense of humor does he have?

Vocabulary Study

1. Look up the following words and be ready to discuss how Hough uses them:
    a. *inadvertently, inadvertent* (paragraphs 1-2)
    b. *vagary* (paragraph 3)
    c. *amalgamated* (paragraph 7)
    d. *attentive* (paragraph 9)
    e. *portentous* (paragraph 12)
    f. *integrity* (paragraph 14)
    g. *routine, perfunctory, concept* (paragraph 15)
    h. *intimate* (paragraph 16)
    i. *presumptuous* (paragraph 18)
    j. *trifles* (paragraph 19)
    k. *minutiae* (paragraph 20)
2. The following words and phrases call a picture or smell to mind. What is that picture, and what does the word or phrase contribute to the meaning of the sentence?
    a. *lavendered* (paragraph 12)
    b. *scatter of debris* (paragraph 15)
    c. *puffed, inflated* (paragraph 16)
    d. *split, rock of neglect* (paragraph 21)
3. The words and phrases in question 2 above are metaphors— implied comparisons that attribute the qualities of one thing to another. In paragraph 13 Hough uses another metaphor, *mainstream,* and describes it: "The water is muddy, the pollution great, the vision limited, and too many people are trying to swim at once, each hitting another over the head." What is the implied comparison in *mainstream,* and what other comparisons is Hough making in the sentence?

Suggestions for Writing

Hough gives us a picture of himself through a miscellany of details. He draws no conclusion other than to say that he has paid attention to small details in his life:

1. Write down quickly a scattering of details that give the reader a picture of your life and interests.

2. Look carefully at the details, then write down one or two patterns that they suggest. Discuss one of these patterns in a paragraph.
3. Your paragraph probably contains several ideas. Use one of these ideas as the thesis of an essay that incorporates some or all of the details you recorded. You may wish to add others. Remember that a thesis organizes the details of the essay, giving them direction and purpose.

Phyllis Rose

NEVER SAY GOODBYE

Phyllis Rose is professor of English at Wesleyan University, in Middletown, Connecticut. Her books on the lives of women include *Woman of Letters: A Life of Virginia Woolf* (1978), *Parallel Lives: Five Victorian Marriages* (1983), and *Jazz Cleopatra: Josephine Baker in Her Time* (1989). Her essay on an unusual country store, in southeastern Connecticut, appears in her collection of essays *Never Say Goodbye* (1991).

Two miles outside Higganum, Connecticut, on rural 1 Route 81, is a store named Never Say Goodbye. To call it an antique shop would give the wrong impression entirely. There is some furniture for sale, but furniture is not the store's strength. Hanging from the ceiling, hanging over doors, hanging on racks, are old dresses, trousers, blouses, nightgowns, capes, stoles, bathrobes, furs. There are racks of shoes, racks of hats, cases of jewelry, tables full of handbags, fur muffs, sheet music, vases, tableware, tablecloths, and lace. What makes the place extraordinary is not so much the variety as the depth in any area. A whole section is devoted to wedding dresses, another to tuxedoes, another to bed jackets. The alligator shoes alone would fill a closet. Hats frame two doorways and spill over to a bookcase; lace collars are tacked on a wall in rows. Each section constitutes a collection. There is so much of everything that one feels in the presence of a passion rather than a cool and reasoned attempt to sell.

I, for one, share the passion. I go to Never Say 2 Goodbye to try on—and sometimes buy—vintage clothing. My favorites are chiffon dresses of the 1920s, but I also like 1920s lace and crêpe de Chine from the 1930s. Some days, trying on flowered peach chiffon, I'm Zelda Fitzgerald, spoiled, talented, doomed. Other days, in navy blue crêpe, I'm Eleanor Roosevelt, elegantly dowdy, doing good. It's like being let loose in a film company's costume department. The store is a playland for grownups, and shopping there is a way of giving rein to fantasies that adult life usually inhibits.

My sister finds distasteful the idea of having against 3 her skin clothes that someone else has worn. She would no more put on a chiffon beaded dress that an unknown woman bought at an unknown store in the twenties than she would wear her neighbor's underwear. This difference between us could be attributed to the fact that she is older than I am and did not have the training I did in wearing hand-me-downs. But I prefer to think it's because she has spent her adult life in New York, whereas I have spent mine in New England. She looks to the new for value; I look to the old.

Sifting the past for value is a New England obses- 4 sion, pursued in colleges and universities but equally at tag sales, antiques fairs, and junk shops (never called that), which seem to be more profuse here than in other parts of the country.

The first thing one learns from this exercise is how 5 relative value is. One summer day, at a tag sale held by the United Methodist Ladies of Oak Bluffs on Martha's Vineyard, just outside the nineteenth-century gingerbread enclave on the meeting grounds, I spotted a gold candelabra I had to have. It held three candles and was covered in gilded roses. I made myself put a figure to how much I wanted it before I started bargaining. I decided I would pay $5.00 happily and would even go up to $8.00. But when I asked the frail, white-haired lady behind the table how much she was asking for the piece, she said, "Ten." I was surprised. I thought that was high. "Can you do any better?" I asked. It was her turn to look surprised. "Better than ten cents?"

One dreams of the opposite—finding certified trea- 6 sure amid dross, the East Coast version of prospecting. A friend and I attended a tag sale at the Connecticut Valley home of some people who had belonged to a print club in the 1930s. Their heirs were selling their collection at a dollar a print. My friend bought a Segonzac, which he took to a dealer the next day and sold for $200. His purchase, which ensured that something wonderful would not be thrown out with the garbage, was as much an act of conservation as of acquisition. The day my friend found his Segonzac, I found a Martin Lewis, which I won't sell until I'm in the Home for the Aged and need the money for medicine. Whenever I make another bad investment on the stock market, I console myself by thinking of my great investments in "junk."

It seems to me typical of New England to think that 7 good things will only get better in time, that in fact time is necessary to prove whether they are good. Remember that once-hallowed concept "the test of time"? I do not feel alone here believing in it. I have an image of time battering against an object to reveal its essential quality, as vivid as that of a solution, to which a precipitate has been added, turning green to indicate copper. A New York editor once described some of my work, disparagingly, as "timeless." She encouraged me to write something "timely" for a change. But I was educated in New England. For me, "timeless" is the highest praise there is.

There are Bostonians, I know, who do not consider 8 Connecticut part of New England, but it is, very much so. This is proved by the fact that a Connecticut governor, the late, beloved Ella Grasso, held a tag sale when

she wanted to clear out her house. Both buyers and
sellers at tag sales are demonstrating another trait I
associate with New England—thrift. This is not to be
confused with bargain hunting. The bargain hunter takes
a taxi from one side of New York to the other to save
a few dollars at a stocking sale or buys a fur coat that
she doesn't really want simply because it's a good buy.
Far different the practitioner of thrift! She may replace
her electric juicer with an old-fashioned kind because
she prefers its feel, but she will be sure to sell the electric
one at her next tag sale. She will wear a tag sale belt
with expensive clothes if the belt holds up her pants as
she wants them held.

I use as my typing table a hospital table, the kind 9
they place over beds for food trays. Mine is wood and
hence outmoded. I bought it for a dollar and, lapped
over my desk, it supports a typewriter perfectly. I consider that thrift. Hanging on my walls and lying on my
floors are quilts and rugs I bought during many sum-
mers in different parts of New England when I was
finished working for the day and wanted something else
to do. On my bed is a rag rug I bought at an antiques
fair in Deerfield, Massachusetts. The colors are still
good, the rug still covers. It was cheaper than a custom
bedspread. That, too, is thrift.

I no longer buy quilts. They have been discovered. 10
Even at tag sales, their prices are high. The same thing
has happened to photographs—visiting cards, stereopticon cards, tintypes, daguerr[e]otypes, which the careful shopper used to be able to pick up for virtually
nothing. People have caught on. It requires intelligence
and a bit of prescience to stay ahead of the crowd, to
figure out what is undervalued and to buy it while one
can still afford it. Now I buy rag rugs and vintage clothes.

Sometimes I get tired, staying ahead of the game like 11
that. I wish I could walk into a store on Newbury Street
or Madison Avenue and extravagantly buy, let us say,

a fur coat or an oriental rug or designer clothes without putting in all the time that's necessary to do things the thrifty way. But then I remind myself of something I've believed for a long time that is the playful side of thrift: anyone can live well on lots of money. The trick is to do it on little.

I take people I love to Never Say Goodbye, but not all of them see its charm. My mother said, "The lighting is terrible. How do they expect you to see the goods?" It's true. The lighting is warm and atmospheric but on the dark side. There are so many dresses squeezed together on a rack that to see any one dress involves exerting major force to push aside the others. Never mind that on the fall day I was there with my mother, a pot of mulled cider scented the store and browsers were invited to help themselves. That doesn't help one see "the goods." My mother, you see, is a New Yorker. Her idea of a good store is Bloomingdale's, Bergdorf's, or Bendel's.

Comment

Phyllis Rose states that New Englanders are thrifty and are obsessed with "sifting the past for value," and she reflects on how to measure value. These ideas are loosely related to other ideas and experiences, and to comments on her interests and habits. Rose passes from idea to idea, giving her impression of an unusual store and, in doing so, shares her thoughts about the experience and her recollection of visits to other places in New England.

Questions for Study and Discussion

1. The opening description of "Never Say Goodbye" and the concluding comment on the store frame the various reflections and details. How does Rose connect these?

2. What quality makes the store extraordinary? How does Rose illustrate this quality?
3. How are New Yorkers like her sister and her mother different from New Englanders, and how does Rose illustrate this difference? Why does she discuss this difference?
4. What discoveries does she make in visiting New England stores and tag sales?

Vocabulary Study

1. In using the word *dowdy* in paragraph 2, does Rose mean shabby or sloppy, or does she have another meaning in mind? How do you know?
2. Is Rose using *dross* in the sense of trash in paragraph 6?
3. Would the word *critically* convey the same meaning as *disparagingly* in paragraph 7?
4. What is the difference between a tintype and a daguerr[e]otype? What is a stereopticon card?

Suggestions for Writing

1. Describe a store that you find extraordinary, and show why it is. Like Rose, make your detail specific enough so that your readers experience what you do in visiting the store. In the course of the essay, present thoughts or ideas that writing about the store suggests.
2. Rose comments that a visit to tag sales, fairs, and junk shops shows "how relative value is." Develop this idea from your own experience and observation.

William Raspberry

LESSONS OF THE WHALES

Born in northeastern Mississippi, William Raspberry after college began his career as a journalist. In 1962 he joined the staff of the *Washington Post*, first as a reporter and editor, then as a columnist on urban and national affairs. Raspberry has written much about Afro-American life and education and on a wide range of other subjects—including American values and goals. His column on the California gray whales appeared in the *Washington Post* on September 10, 1990.

For three dramatic weeks, the world was able to rise   1
above its divisions of culture, competition, political ideology and even the pursuit of money and join in noble common cause.

The effort paid off. Two California gray whales have   2
been rescued from their arctic prison and are (presumably) on their way to the open sea and freedom.

It was, as President Reagan said, "an inspiring en-   3
deavor," involving cooperation from people often at odds with one another: scientists, environmentalists, oil developers, Eskimo whale hunters, American officials, Soviet sailors. And while hundreds of workers participated directly in the tricky—and extremely dangerous— rescue effort, millions of us were involved vicariously, cheering them and wishing them luck.

But I confess that for the whole of the three weeks,   4
I found myself asking a number of rude questions for which I still don't have answers.

The main question is: Why? Why is it that three   5
trapped whales—in a far off place where local residents routinely hunt and kill whales—should evoke such universal sympathy? If they had been bullheads (or whatever species the Eskimos prefer) they would have wound up as dinner, with no more tears than accompany the

slaughter of innocent chickens at Frank Perdue's Eastern Shore establishment.

The Eskimos participated in the rescue only because 6 they don't, except in dire circumstances, eat California grays.

Is it because California grays are an endangered 7 species? Because they were innocent victims of circumstance? Because they are huge? Because they seemed so determined to live? Because they are benign animals of above-average intelligence? Because they are fellow mammals?

Certainly it is difficult to imagine a similar effort on 8 behalf of other animals. Dolphins or porpoises or apes or koalas, yes, but not menhaden or snail darters or timber wolves or warthogs.

Even human tragedy often fails to inspire the sort of 9 international response evoked by the trapped whales. The recent slaughter of some 5,000 Hutu in Burundi inspired nothing like the media coverage, or the public response, sparked by three whales.

Where is the concerted outpouring on behalf of America's homeless families or AIDS victims? Where was the 10 international ideology-be-damned response to the Southeast Asian boat people? How can a few whales inspire us to action while hungry children and members of the desperate inner-city underclass elicit only helpless shrugs?

Maybe a part of the answer is in the particularity 11 of the whales. Millions who remain unmoved by a generalized Save the Whales campaign were genuinely concerned about these specific whales—just as millions who seem indifferent to the Children's Defense Fund's urgings on behalf of poverty-stricken and hungry children were willing to do whatever was necessary to rescue Jessica McClure from that Texas well a year ago.

Another part of it may be the clear-cut nature, no 12 matter how difficult, of what needed to be done for the whales. Hard work and technology saved the whales; charity can save the victims of an African drought. But no similarly simple action can save Africans from the encroachment of the Sahara, or the Hutu from tribal war, or ghetto youth from drug-induced violence and despair.

And surely part of it is just plain drama. For the 13 Hutu thousands (and a fair number of Burundi's ruling Tutsis), the outcome is not at issue; they are dead already. But with the whales, as with little Jessica McClure, the outcome was very much in doubt. Will they last until the rescue can be consummated? Will the icebreakers arrive in time? Will the well collapse? Tune in tomorrow.

The point is not that the whale rescue effort was silly, 14 or a waste of resources; I'm as glad as the next one that there were people willing to undertake the effort, and that it succeeded.

The point is whether there are lessons in the Arctic 15 rescue that could teach us how to generate concerted action on behalf of the other victims we know about but who seem to hover beyond the reach of our empathy.

Can we learn to respond to the nameless victims of 16 multifaceted problems as generously as we respond to particular victims of specific tragedies? I don't know the answer, but it's a whale of a question.

Comment

The reflective essay sometimes opens with a question that the writer answers in the remainder of the essay. This answer often consists of a series of thoughts or speculations rather than the formal thesis or proposition typical of persuasive essays. As in the expository and the persuasive essay, the writer usually takes account of the readers' knowledge and opinions in organizing the essay, particularly where the essay also has an argumentative edge. Raspberry wishes to generate interest in the particular issue discussed and also concern about mass slaughter like that in Burundi, about homelessness, and about AIDS victims. In organizing his essay, he has his readers' knowledge in mind; he also has in mind the fact that his readers hold different opinions on the issue, or perhaps hold no opinion at all.

Questions for Study and Discussion

1. How much knowledge does Raspberry assume his readers possess on the gray whales, the Burundi deaths, Jessica McClure, and other events and situations he refers to? How much detail on these does Raspberry provide?
2. How does Raspberry keep the attention of the reader directed to this central issue and not to important but peripheral matters to this essay, such as homelessness and AIDS?
3. Does Raspberry give a definitive answer to the question of inaction, or instead give a tentative, qualified one?
4. Do you agree with the answer that Raspberry gives to the question? Why or why not?

Vocabulary Study

State the meaning of the following words as Raspberry uses them. Then explain how the word immediately following would change the meaning of the sentence:

1. *vicariously* (paragraph 3), indirectly
2. *rude* (paragraph 4), simple
3. *evoke* (paragraph 5), awaken
4. *dire* (paragraph 6), serious
5. *benign* (paragraph 7), gentle
6. *ideology* (paragraph 10), opinion
7. *particularity* (paragraph 11), individuality
8. *generalized* (paragraph 11), general
9. *technology* (paragraph 12), equipment
10. *consummated* (paragraph 13), accomplished
11. *empathy* (paragraph 15), sympathy
12. *multifaceted* (paragraph 16), complex

Suggestions for Writing

1. State your own thoughts on the question discussed. You may wish to state a tentative thesis—that is, a qualified opinion rather than a definitive idea. You might introduce your thesis early in your essay or build up to it, as Raspberry does.
2. State your ideas on a question or issue related to that discussed by Raspberry. Again, you might introduce your thesis early or build up to it.

PART THREE

STRATEGIES
FOR
EXPOSITION

*O*ur ideas are like clan totems or old
school ties. We tend to think that our
ideas make us decent.

John Garvey

Much writing that you do is for the purpose of giving information. A recipe, directions on how to repair a tire, an explanation of how mules differ from horses, a definition of a molecule, analysis of how the United States became engaged in Vietnam—all these give information. The word *exposition,* meaning explanation or the unfolding or setting forth of an idea, describes this kind of writing.

Exposition may use one or more of the methods of analysis illustrated in Part One. These include narration, description, example, process, comparison and contrast, cause and effect, definition, and classification and division. In explaining how to repair a tire, you may describe the tire rim and the tire and define and classify the tools needed to do the repair. In explaining Vietnam, you may narrate the events leading to the American engagement, compare the policies of President Kennedy and President Johnson, and trace their effects. Most of the essays in this section illustrate more than one method of exposition.

Exposition, in turn, may serve other kinds of writing. Expressive writing often contains information of various kinds; a veteran's personal account of Vietnam probably may include informative details on weapons, terrain, and jungle warfare. Persuasive writing—for example, an essay arguing for or against America's involvement in Vietnam—probably would include details of that involvement as well as an analysis of causes and effects.

The purposes of giving information are obviously many. In the following essay on the need of error in human life, Lewis Thomas is defining the word *human.* Thomas might have developed an abstract definition that a special audience would understand without the observations and details he provides in the essay. Instead, he compares humans with computers and thus draws on experiences most readers have had. The technique of proceeding gradually from known experiences to complex and difficult ideas is a common method in exposition. Many essays do begin with abstract statements, but many essayists prefer to lead into abstract ideas gradually through concrete details. These generate interest in the subject, sometimes through historical background unfamiliar to most readers.

Thomas bases his exposition on comparison with computers, using the similarities between computers and humans (in particular the programmed error in computers) to define the kind of error that makes human life possible. And he uses analogy, or a point-by-point comparison between unlike things—here a good laboratory and a good computer—to illustrate why error promotes increased inefficiency and thinking. He also uses contrast between humans and lower animals, which lack the "splendid freedom" of error, to explain why error is essential to human development. Throughout the essay Thomas is concerned with cause and effect—the cause of human progress, the effect of error.

Thomas introduces his thesis early in the essay, following his discussion of computers:

> Mistakes are at the very base of human thought, embedded there, feeding the structure like root nodules. If we were not provided with the knack of being wrong, we could never get anything useful done.

He restates his thesis in the course of his illustration and discussion:

> The capacity to leap across mountains of information to land lightly on the wrong side represents the highest of human endowments.

> What we need, then, for moving ahead, is a set of wrong alternatives much longer and more interesting than the short list of mistaken courses that any of us can think up right now.

In this concluding restatement, Thomas moves from information to persuasion. But he stops short of developing proposals—ways to encourage acceptance of error, the "splendid freedom" that he earlier suggested animals lack.

Thomas organizes the essay according to his judgment of his audience. He is writing as you would converse with a friend—pausing to explain and illustrate ideas when you see that you are not being understood. You repeat your main point to give your explanation a frame but also to be persuasive even when your main purpose is informative. In writing, you must make a judgment about an audience and assess the kind of explanation and information needed to understand your main point or thesis.

Lewis Thomas

TO ERR IS HUMAN

Lewis Thomas (1913-1993) served in a number of medical posts, including chairman of pathology and medicine and dean of New York University-Bellevue Medical Center; chairman of pathology and dean of Yale School of Medicine; president and later chancellor of Sloan-Kettering Cancer Center in New York City; and professor of medicine and pathology at Cornell Medical School in New York. He described his medical career in *The Youngest Science: Notes of a Medicine Watcher* (1983). His essays, most of which first appeared in the *New England Journal of Medicine*, have been collected in *Lives of a Cell* (1974), *The Medusa and the Snail* (1979), *Late Night Thoughts on Listening to Mahler's Ninth Symphony* (1983), *Et Cetera, Et Cetera: Notes of a Word-Watcher* (1990), and *The Fragile Species: Notes of an Earth Watcher* (1992). Thomas wrote on science and medicine for the specialist as well as the general reader.

Everyone must have had at least one personal experience with a computer error by this time. Bank balances are suddenly reported to have jumped from $379 into the millions, appeals for charitable contributions are mailed over and over to people with crazy-sounding names at your address, department stores send the wrong bills, utility companies write that they're turning everything off, that sort of thing. If you manage to get in touch with someone and complain, you then get instantaneously typed, guilty letters from the same computer, saying, "Our computer was in error, and an adjustment is being made in your account."

These are supposed to be the sheerest, blindest accidents. Mistakes are not believed to be part of the normal behavior of a good machine. If things go wrong, it must be a personal, human error, the result of fingering, tampering, a button getting stuck, someone hitting the wrong key. The computer, at its normal best, is infallible.

I wonder whether this can be true. After all, the whole point of computers is that they represent an extension of the human brain, vastly improved upon but nonetheless human, superhuman maybe. A good computer can think clearly and quickly enough to beat you at chess, and some of them have even been programmed to write obscure verse. They can do anything we can do, and more besides.

It is not yet known whether a computer has its own 4 consciousness, and it would be hard to find out about this. When you walk into one of those great halls now built for the huge machines, and stand listening, it is easy to imagine that the faint, distant noises are the sound of thinking, and the turning of the spools gives them the look of wild creatures rolling their eyes in the effort to concentrate, choking with information. But real thinking, and dreaming, are other matters.

On the other hand, the evidences of something like 5 an *unconscious,* equivalent to ours, are all around, in every mail. As extensions of the human brain, they have been constructed with the same property of error, spontaneous, uncontrolled, and rich in possibilities.

Mistakes are at the very base of human thought, 6 embedded there, feeding the structure like root nodules. If we were not provided with the knack of being wrong, we could never get anything useful done. We think our way along by choosing between right and wrong alternatives, and the wrong choices have to be made as frequently as the right ones. We get along in life this way. We are built to make mistakes, coded for error.

We learn, as we say, by "trial and error." Why do 7 we always say that? Why not "trial and rightness" or "trial and triumph"? The old phrase puts it that way because that is, in real life, the way it is done.

A good laboratory, like a good bank or a corpora- 8 tion or government, has to run like a computer. Almost everything is done flawlessly, by the book, and all the numbers add up to the predicted sums. The days go by. And then, if it is a lucky day, and a lucky laboratory, somebody makes a mistake: the wrong buffer, something in one of the blanks, a decimal misplaced in reading counts, the warm room off by a degree and a half, a mouse out of his box, or just a misreading of the day's protocol. Whatever, when the results come in, something is obviously screwed up, and then the action can begin.

The misreading is not the important error; it opens 9 the way. The next step is the crucial one. If the investigator can bring himself to say, "But even so, look at that!" then the new finding, whatever it is, is ready for snatching. What is needed, for progress to be made, is the move based on error.

Whenever new kinds of thinking are about to be 10 accomplished, or new varieties of music, there has to be an argument beforehand. With two sides debating in the same mind, haranguing, there is an amiable understanding that one is right and the other wrong. Sooner or later the thing is settled, but there can be no action at all if there are not the two sides, and the argument. The hope is in the faculty of wrongness, the tendency toward error. The capacity to leap across mountains of information to land lightly on the wrong side represents the highest of human endowments.

It may be that this is a uniquely human gift, perhaps 11 even stipulated in our genetic instructions. Other creatures do not seem to have DNA sequences for making mistakes as a routine part of daily living, certainly not for programmed error as a guide for action.

We are at our human finest, dancing with our minds, 12 when there are more choices than two. Sometimes there are ten, even twenty different ways to go, all but one bound to be wrong, and the richness of selection in such situations can lift us onto totally new ground. This process is called exploration and is based on human fallibility. If we had only a single center in our brains, capable of responding only when a correct decision was to be made, instead of the jumble of different, credulous, easily conned clusters of neurones that provide for being flung off into blind alleys, up trees, down dead ends, out into blue sky, along wrong turnings, around bends, we could only stay the way we are today, stuck fast.

The lower animals do not have this splendid freedom. They are limited, most of them, to absolute infallibility. Cats, for all their good side, never make mistakes. I have never seen a maladroit, clumsy, or blundering cat. Dogs are sometimes fallible, occasionally able to make charming minor mistakes, but they get this way by trying to mimic their masters. Fish are flawless in everything they do. Individual cells in a tissue are mindless machines, perfect in their performance, as absolutely inhuman as bees. 13

We should have this in mind as we become dependent on more complex computers for the arrangement of our affairs. Give the computers their heads, I say; let them go their way. If we can learn to do this, turning our heads to one side and wincing while the work proceeds, the possibilities for the future of mankind, and computerkind, are limitless. Your average good computer can make calculations in an instant which would take a lifetime of slide rules for any of us. Think of what we could gain from the near infinity of precise, machine-made miscomputation which is now so easily within our grasp. We would begin the solving of some of our hardest problems. How, for instance, should we go about organizing ourselves for social living on a planetary scale, now that we have become, as a plain fact of life, a single community? We can assume, as a working hypothesis, that all the right ways of doing this are unworkable. What we need, then, for moving ahead, is a set of wrong alternatives much longer and more interesting than the short list of mistaken courses that any of us can think up right now. We need, in fact, an infinite list, and when it is printed out we need the computer to turn on itself and select, at random, the next way to go. If it is a big enough mistake, we could find ourselves on a new level, stunned, out in the clear, ready to move again. 14

Questions for Study and Discussion

1. To what extent do computers resemble human beings? How does Thomas distinguish the reasoning of each?
2. What is gained in the exposition by the comparison with computers?
3. What consequences of human reasoning does Thomas explore?
4. What is the thesis of the essay, and where is it stated?
5. Does Thomas explicitly say that nonhuman beings or things cannot possess the human faculty of reasoning?

Vocabulary Study

1. Explain how the italicized words are used in each sentence. Then explain how the word in brackets changes or modifies the meaning:
   a. "The computer, at its *normal* [average] best, is *infallible* [reliable]."
   b. "After all, the whole point of computers is that they represent an *extension* [development] of the human brain. . . ."
   c. "With two sides debating in the same mind, *haranguing* [arguing], there is an *amiable* [mutual] understanding that one is right and the other wrong."
   d. "It may be that this is a uniquely human gift, perhaps even *stipulated* [arranged for] in our *genetic instructions* [brains]."
   e. "[The lower animals] are limited, most of them, to absolute *infallibility* [predictability]."
   f. "I have never seen a *maladroit* [awkward], clumsy, or *blundering* [muddling] cat."
   g. "Think of what we could gain from the near *infinity* [immensity] of *precise* [exact], machine-made *miscomputation* [misconception] which is now so easily within our grasp."
2. Write a paraphrase of paragraph 12, giving particular attention to the metaphors of the final sentence.

Suggestions for Writing

1. Describe an experience of your own with a computer error. Use your description to develop your own conclusions about the impact of machines on our lives or about some other idea.
2. Discuss an important change that occurred in your life as a result of a mistake you made in thinking about people or about action you intended to take.
3. Discuss the extent to which your own experience with dogs and cats supports the statements Thomas makes about them.

Louis Inturrisi

ON NOT GETTING THERE FROM HERE

Louis Inturrisi describes the Italian way of giving instructions from a special point of view. An American, he gained knowledge of Italian life from experiences in Italy, including teaching English at the University of Rome. Through a series of examples, Inturrisi brings humor and insight to the situation of the traveler in a strange city.

Before my first trip to Europe, my grandfather, who was then a very confident 82 and is now a very opinionated 100, poured me a glass of wine and gave me the following instructions: Over there, don't believe anything until three people have told you the same thing. I not only found this advice invaluable for getting around Europe that summer, it has proven useful for traveling in other parts of the world as well. Nowhere, however, has my grandfather's advice been more useful than in his native Italy, where a remarkable enthusiasm to assist foreigners is sometimes overshadowed by a lack of reliable information.

One must start by realizing that in Italy the phrases used when giving directions—such as "go straight," "turn right," "follow this road"—are not to be taken literally. Most of the time they are only suggestions. For example, if you inquire about the location of a museum and are told to go straight—"sempre dritto"—the phrase usually means "go straight *and then ask again.*" Your informant may or may not add the second part, assuming that you are already aware of this vital additional step and will not be dumbfounded or, worse, upset if the museum doesn't appear in front of you in the next ten minutes.

The trouble comes from thinking that "sempre dritto" 3 means that by trudging ahead you will see what you are looking for. What it really means is that you are probably on the right track, and there is a very good chance that you might find the museum somewhere in this area.

Likewise, the phrase "segua questa strada"—"fol- 4 low this road"—must be interpreted to mean: "It's around here somewhere, and if you follow this road, you should see it." But do not think that just because you've understood you are within minutes of locating the museum and can start thinking about lunch. You have asked someone who thinks you are on the right track, but it is time to follow my grandfather's advice and ask someone else. If you still don't find the museum, either it is in the other direction or you are standing in front of it.

Another sign of unreliability is the phrase "mi pare"— 5 "I think"—or "it seems." A good general rule is to be suspicious of anything starting with the words "mi pare" because what follows will inevitably be too vague to be trusted.

Don't waste time with people who respond to your 6 question by asking *you* a question. This is a strange linguistic habit some Romans have. As a reply to a request for information, some people respond by inquiring, "Is it really around here?" or "Do you know if it's in this area?" These people aren't being perfidious; they're buying time. It's best to say "Grazie. Buona giornata," and move on.

It is important to remember that giving accurate 7 directions is much easier in Manhattan than in Mantua.

Many Italian cities are composed of a myriad of tiny streets, many of which are named after people no one has ever heard of. Moreover, the numbering systems change from place to place. In some cities, the numbers, instead of alternating, proceed up one side of the street and then down the other. Piazzas often have an official name and another by which they are popularly known. Often the best any native can do is give an approximation of where you want to go.

What Americans must avoid is a certain Anglo-Saxon 8 rigidity that manifests itself by taking words (especially words in foreign languages) too literally. For example, "laggiù in fondo" literally means "at the end of the street," but it hardly ever means that the building you are looking for is smack dab at the end of the street you are on. It may, in fact, mean that by walking straight on this street you will see what you are looking for. Or that by going straight *in the direction of* the end of the street you will see a sign directing you to your destination.

I have witnessed innocents abroad rush off happily 9 in the direction of a "laggiù in fondo," only to return minutes later more confused than ever. They didn't realize that just before the literal end of the street, they were supposed to make a turn that their informant never mentioned because he never expected to be taken quite so literally.

Gestures are another source of misunderstanding. In 10 this culture, gestures have the weight of words, a situation that can cause confusion. For example, there is often a confusing discrepancy between gestures and words, especially as regards the words "destra" ("right") and "sinistra" ("left").

Furthermore, Italians don't indicate directions by 11 pointing with their index fingers. Straight ahead, for example, is rendered by a vertical slicing gesture with the open palm outstretched in front of the speaker. But if the person you have asked raises his palm over his head and wiggles it back and forth in the air, it means that you are in big trouble. His reassuring "si si's" may encourage you to continue in the same direction, but his gesture is saying something entirely different. It means something like, "My God! You are nowhere near where you want to go," or "That street is way over on the other side of the city!" If the person should drop both palms to his sides, raise his eyebrows and exhale deeply, you're in the wrong city.

There is, of course, always the question of who to   12
ask for instructions. Police officers and taxi drivers are a good choice; newspaper and magazine vendors at sidewalk kiosks are even better. A general rule to follow is to put your trust in whoever answers by mentioning a specific place or landmark, such as, "It's behind Piazza Navona," or "It's next to St. John's Church." Be more than a little suspicious of replies such as, "Over there," or "Two or three streets in that direction."

When asking directions in Italy, an inquiry to one   13
individual very soon erupts into a group effort, with everyone in earshot joining in to offer an opinion. It takes some skill to extract reliable information from the middle of a heated debate in dialect, but when such a debate erupts, I tend to put my faith in the person who seems to be arguing the *least* vehemently. A fact is a fact to this signora, and she sees no merit in wasting time or energy proving the existence of the moon. Or you might wait out the debate until one participant offers to guide you to your destination to prove to herself and the others she knows what she is talking about.

I once saw a woman on a bus in Naples rescue a   14
Scandinavian tourist from a very loud discussion over the best stop for getting the funicular. Silently, and with mounting anger the woman listened to the debate, which involved most of the passengers as well as the driver, until the bus arrived at what she knew was the right stop. Abruptly, she stood up, grabbed the Scandinavian by the arm and gently eased her off the bus, while her fellow passengers continued to discuss the issue.

None of this should discourage you from asking ₁₅ questions in your high school or Berlitz Italian. Italians have one of the healthiest attitudes toward their language of any Europeans. They do not expect you to speak their language fluently nor are they ecstatic if you mouth a few words correctly. Rarely do they waste time by making you submit to a grammar lesson in the middle of the street. When they do correct you, it is more of a conditioned response than an admonition.

Armed with this advice, as well as your dictionary ₁₆ and a large-scale map, forge forward with a strong sense of adventure, a keen appreciation of the flexibility of words—and always with my grandfather's advice clearly in the back of your mind.

Comment

Writing for the travel section of *The New York Times,* Louis Inturrisi tells travelers to Italy what to expect when they ask directions in the street. Inturrisi shows that cultural differences play a role in everyday situations. In illustrating these differences, he gives us numerous insights into Italians and Italian culture, and into American habits and culture too. Inturrisi also shows that definition often depends on an unspoken contract between people. Asked to define a word, few of us give as much information as the dictionary provides; we usually begin our definition believing that those asking for information possess some knowledge about the word.

Questions for Study and Discussion

1. What mistaken assumptions do Americans hold in receiving directions from Italians? What assumptions do Italians hold in giving directions?
2. What do these differences reveal about the Italian character and Italian life?
3. What do these differences reveal about American character and habits?

4. How does Inturrisi organize his essay? Is he proceeding from less interesting to more interesting facts about Italians, or does he organize the essay in another way?
5. Does Inturrisi describe your own assumptions in asking directions in a strange city? Do you find that age, gender, or ethnic background affects how a person gives directions or receives them?

Vocabulary Study

Explain how each word is used within the sentence:
1. *opinionated* (paragraph 1)
2. *dumbfounded* (paragraph 2)
3. *linguistic, perfidious* (paragraph 5)
4. *myriad, piazza* (paragraph 6)
5. *rigidity* (paragraph 7)
6. *literally* (paragraph 8)
7. *gesture, discrepancy* (paragraph 9)
8. *landmark* (paragraph 11)
9. *dialect, vehemently, signora* (paragraph 12)
10. *fluently, admonition* (paragraph 14)
11. *flexibility* (paragraph 15)

Suggestions for Writing

1. Describe an experience in which confusion resulted after giving or receiving instructions. Then explain what attitudes or assumptions caused the confusion.
2. Characterize a professional class of people or an age group by how they behave in a social situation similar to the one presented by Inturrisi. In the course of your discussion, contrast this class with another, as Inturrisi does in comparing Italians with Americans.
3. Show how a lack of information about local customs can lead to confusion or misunderstanding between people. Be as specific as you can in illustrating the causes.

Sue Hubbell

FELLING TREES

Born in 1935 in Kalamazoo, Michigan, Sue Hubbell worked for many years as a librarian in New Jersey and Rhode Island. Since 1973, she has lived in the Ozark Mountains of southern Missouri, where she is a commercial beekeeper. She has written about her experiences in Missouri in *A Country Life: Living the Questions* (1986), *A Book of Bees* (1988), and *Broadsides from the Other Orders: A Book of Bugs* (1993). In describing the process of woodcutting, Hubbell tells us much about day-to-day country life and the chores at which everyone must be competent. Selection title by editor.

I was out in the woods early in the morning cutting 1 firewood for the winter. I do that every day this time of year. For an hour or two I cut wood, load it into the pickup and carry it back to my cabin and stack it. It isn't such a tiring job when I do a bit of it each day, before it gets hot, and I like being out there at that hour, when the woods are fresh and fragrant.

This morning I finished sawing up a tree from the 2 place where I had been cutting for the past week. In the process I lost my screwrench, part screwdriver, part wrench, that I use to make adjustments on my chain saw. I shouldn't carry it in my pocket, but the chain had been loose; I had tightened it and had not walked back to the truck to put the wrench away. Scolding myself for being so careless, I began looking for another tree to cut and found a big one that had recently died.

I like to cut the dead trees from my woodlot, leaving 3 the ones still alive to flourish, but this one was bigger than I feel comfortable about felling. I've been running a chain saw and cutting my own firewood for six years now, but I am still awed by the size and weight of a tree as it crashes to the ground. I have to nerve myself to cut the really big ones. I wanted this tree to fall onto a stretch of open ground that was free of other trees and brush, so I cut a wedge-shaped notch on that side of it. The theory is that the tree, thus weakened, will fall slowly on the side of the notch when the serious cut, slightly above the notch on the other side, is made. The trouble is that trees, particularly dead ones that may have rot on the inside, do not know the theory and may fall in an unexpected direction. That is the way accidents happen.

I was aware of that and was scared, besides, to be 4 cutting down such a big tree; as a result, perhaps, I cut too timid a wedge. I started sawing through on the other side, keeping an eye on the treetop to detect the characteristic tremble of a tree about to fall. I did not have time to jam the plastic wedge in my back pocket into the cut to hold it open because the tree began to sway and started to fall in my direction. I killed the engine on the saw and jumped out of the way.

There was no danger, however. Directly in back of 5 where I had been standing were a number of other trees, which was why I had wanted to have the dead one fall the other way, and as it started down, its top branches snagged. I had sawed completely through the tree, but now the butt end had trapped the saw against the stump. I had cut what is descriptively called a widow maker. If I had been cutting with someone else, we could have used the second saw to free mine and perhaps brought the tree down, but it is dangerous and I don't like to do it. I couldn't even free my saw by taking it apart, for I had lost my screwrench, so I drove back to the barn, gathered up the tools I needed, a socket wrench, chains and a portable winch known as a come-along.

The day was warming and I was sweating by the 6 time I got back to the woods, but I was determined to repair the botch I had made. Using the socket wrench, I removed the bar and chain from the saw and set the saw body aside. The weight of the saw gone, I worked the bar and chain free from under the butt of the tree. Then I spat and drank ice water from my thermos and figured out how I was going to pull down the tree with chain and winch.

The come-along is a cheery, sensible tool for a woman.   7
It has a big hook at one end and a hook connected to a steel cable at the other. The cable is wound around a ratchet gear operated by a long handle to give leverage. It divides a heavy job into small, manageable bits that require no more than female strength, and I have used it many times to pull my pickup free from a mudhole. I decided that if I wound a chain around the butt of the widow maker and another chain around a nearby standing tree and connected the two with a come-along, I might be able to winch the felled tree to the ground. I attached the chains and come-along appropriately and began. Slowly, with each pump of the handle against the ratchet gear, the tree sank to the ground. The sun was high, the heat oppressive, and my sweatshirt was soaked with sweat, so I decided to leave the job of cutting up the tree to firewood lengths until tomorrow. I gathered up my tools and, in the process, found the screwrench almost hidden in leaf mold.

I am good friends with a woman who lives across   8
the hollow. She and her husband sell cordwood to the charcoal factory in town. Her husband cuts the logs because a chain saw, in the Ozarks, is regarded as a man's tool, and she helps him load and unload the logs. Even though the wood is going to be turned into charcoal, it is traditional to cut it to four-foot lengths. A four-foot oak log is heavy; a strong man can lift it, but a woman has to use all her strength to do her part. My friend returns from her mornings sick with exhaustion, her head throbbing. She and I talk sometimes about how it would be if women were the woodcutters: the length would be less than four feet. Having to do work beyond her strength makes my friend feel weak, ineffectual, dependent and cross.

My friend, and other Ozark women, often ask me   9
curiously about my chain saw. Most people out here

heat with wood, and if families in the suburbs quarrel about taking out the garbage, here the source of squabbles is getting enough firewood cut early in the year so that it can season. Women usually help by carrying the cut wood to the truck, but it is the men who cut the wood, and since the women think they cannot cut it, they frequently worry and sometimes nag about it.

My female Ozark friends envy me having my fire- 10 wood supply under my own control, and they are interested when I tell them that they have had the hardest part of the job anyway, carrying the wood to the trucks. Cutting the wood into lengths with the chain saw is not hard work, although it does require some skill. So far, however, my friends have not taken up my offer to come over so that I can give them a lesson in using a chain saw. Forty years ago chain saws were heavy and certainly beyond the strength of a woman to use; today they are much improved and light. My saw is a small, light one, but with its 16-inch bar it is big enough to cut any tree I want to fell.

I know that feeling of helplessness and irritation that 11 my friends have, for that is the way I used to be. Like many women my age, I would stand back and let a man change a flat tire. I could press a button on a washing machine but not fix the machine if something failed. I felt uneasy with tools other than a needle, a typewriter or kitchen utensils.

When I began living here alone I had to learn how 12 to break down work into parcels that I could perform with my strength and I had to learn to use tools that I had never used and use them easily. Either that, or I would have had to leave. It was the hardest schooling I've ever taken but the most exhilarating. When there were Things in the world too heavy to move where I wanted them to be and too mysterious to be kept doing what I wanted them to do, I was filled with dissatisfaction and petulance. Those Things controlled me.

I prefer it the other way around. 13

Comment

The personal truth to which Hubbell builds her essay will have no meaning for the reader without the extended example of cutting firewood. To make her experiences clear to the reader who knows nothing about woodcutting, she combines several kinds of exposition: she defines the "come-along," describes the process of cutting down a tree, analyzes why trees fall in unexpected directions, and compares her woodcutting with that of the woman who lives nearby. For the reader experienced in woodcutting, she might have chosen another order of ideas.

Questions for Study and Discussion

1. What is the idea or truth that Hubbell illustrates through the felling of trees? How do the details of the essay illustrate this idea?
2. How different would the effect of the essay be if Hubbell had stated her purpose and central idea at the beginning?
3. Were the essay directed to readers experienced in woodcutting, what might Hubbell have omitted and how might she have reorganized the essay?
4. What personal qualities emerge in the course of the essay—particularly in the description of the tree cuttings? Which of these qualities stand out most?
5. Is Hubbell arguing for a change in attitude toward women like herself, or is she merely contrasting her own life with that of her female neighbors?

Vocabulary Study

Be ready to discuss how the details of the essay or the dictionary help you understand the following terms:
1. *widow maker*
2. *come-along*
3. *screw wrench*

Suggestions for Writing

1. Develop the central idea of Hubbell's essay through an extended example of your own. You might build to the idea through your example as Hubbell does or begin the essay with a statement of the idea.
2. Develop one of the following through examples drawn from personal experience:
   a. I have known people to stop and buy an apple on the corner and then walk away as if they had solved the whole unemployment problem.—Heywood Broun
   b. If you have to keep reminding yourself of a thing, perhaps it isn't so.—Christopher Morley
   c. There is no substitute for talent. Industry and all the virtues are of no avail.—Aldous Huxley

Diane Ackerman

WHY LEAVES TURN COLOR IN THE FALL

Diane Ackerman writes on animal life and the world of nature in *The Moon by Whale Light* (1991) and *A Natural History of the Senses* (1990), from which the essay reprinted here is taken. Her other books include *On Extended Wings* (1985), on air pilots in the United States, and *Wife of Light* (1978), *Lady Faustus* (1983), and *Reverse Thunder* (1988)—books of poetry. Ackerman writes in another essay about how "much of life can drift into the vague background of our attention. . . . Both science and art have a habit of waking us up, turning on all the lights, grabbing us by the collar and saying *Would you please pay attention!*"

The stealth of autumn catches one unaware. Was that a goldfinch perching in the early September woods, or just the first turning leaf? A red-winged blackbird or a sugar maple closing up shop for the winter? Keen-eyed as leopards, we stand still and squint hard, looking for signs of movement. Early-morning frost sits heavily on the grass, and turns barbed wire into a string of stars.

On a distant hill, a small square of yellow appears to be a lighted stage. At last the truth dawns on us: Fall is staggering in, right on schedule, with its baggage of chilly nights, macabre holidays, and spectacular, heart-stoppingly beautiful leaves. Soon the leaves will start cringing on the trees, and roll up in clenched fists before they actually fall off. Dry seedpods will rattle like tiny gourds. But first there will be weeks of gushing color so bright, so pastel, so confettilike, that people will travel up and down the East Coast just to stare at it— a whole season of leaves.

Where do the colors come from? Sunlight rules most living things with its golden edicts. When the days begin to shorten, soon after the summer solstice on June 21, a tree reconsiders its leaves. All summer it feeds them so they can process sunlight, but in the dog days of summer the tree begins pulling nutrients back into its trunk and roots, pares down, and gradually chokes off its leaves. A corky layer of cells forms at the leaves' slender petioles, then scars over. Undernourished, the leaves stop producing the pigment chlorophyll, and photosynthesis ceases. Animals can migrate, hibernate, or store food to prepare for winter. But where can a tree go? It survives by dropping its leaves, and by the end of autumn only a few fragile threads of fluid-carrying xylem hold leaves to their stems.

A turning leaf stays partly green at first, then reveals splotches of yellow and red as the chlorophyll gradually breaks down. Dark green seems to stay longest in the veins, outlining and defining them. During the summer, chlorophyll dissolves in the heat and light, but it is also being steadily replaced. In the fall, on the other hand, no new pigment is produced, and so we notice the other colors that were always there, right in the leaf, although chlorophyll's shocking green hid them from view. With their camouflage gone, we see these colors for the first time all year, and marvel, but they were always there, hidden like a vivid secret beneath the hot glowing greens of summer.

The most spectacular range of fall foliage occurs in 4
the northeastern United States and in eastern China,
where the leaves are robustly colored, thanks in part to
a rich climate. European maples don't achieve the same
flaming reds as their American relatives, which thrive
on cold nights and sunny days. In Europe, the warm,
humid weather turns the leaves brown or mildly yellow.
Anthocyanin, the pigment that gives apples their red and
turns leaves red or red-violet, is produced by sugars that
remain in the leaf after the supply of nutrients dwindles.
Unlike the carotenoids, which color carrots, squash, and
corn, and turn leaves orange and yellow, anthocyanin
varies from year to year, depending on the temperature
and amount of sunlight. The fiercest colors occur in
years when the fall sunlight is strongest and the nights
are cool and dry (a state of grace scientists find vexing
to forecast). This is also why leaves appear dizzyingly
bright and clear on a sunny fall day: The anthocyanin
flashes like a marquee.

Not all leaves turn the same colors. Elms, weeping 5
willows, and the ancient ginkgo all grow radiant yellow,
along with hickories, aspens, bottlebrush buckeyes,
cottonweeds, and tall, keening poplars. Basswood turns
bronze, birches bright gold. Water-loving maples put on
a symphonic display of scarlets. Sumacs turn red, too,
as do flowering dogwoods, black gums, and sweet gums.
Though some oaks yellow, most turn a pinkish brown.
The farmlands also change color, as tepees of cornstalks
and bales of shredded-wheat-textured hay stand drying
in the fields. In some spots, one slope of a hill may be
green and the other already in bright color, because the
hillside facing south gets more sun and heat than the
northern one.

An odd feature of the colors is that they don't seem 6
to have any special purpose. We are predisposed to
respond to their beauty, of course. They shimmer with
the colors of sunset, spring flowers, the tawny buff of
a colt's pretty rump, the shuddering pink of a blush.
Animals and flowers color for a reason—adaptation to

their environment—but there is no adaptive reason for leaves to color so beautifully in the fall any more than there is for the sky or ocean to be blue. It's just one of the haphazard marvels the planet bestows every year. We find the sizzling colors thrilling, and in a sense they dupe us. Colored like living things, they signal death and disintegration. In time, they will become fragile and, like the body, return to dust. They are as we hope our own fate will be when we die: Not to vanish, just to sublime from one beautiful state into another. Though leaves lose their green life, they bloom with urgent colors, as the woods grow mummified day by day, and Nature becomes more carnal, mute, and radiant.

We call the season "fall," from the Old English 7
feallan, to fall, which leads back through time to the Indo-European *phol*, which also means to fall. So the word and the idea are both extremely ancient, and haven't really changed since the first of our kind needed a name for fall's leafy abundance. As we say the word, we're reminded of that other Fall, in the garden of Eden, when fig leaves never withered and scales fell from our eyes. Fall is the time when leaves fall from the trees, just as spring is when flowers spring up, summer is when we simmer, and winter is when we whine from the cold.

Children love to play in piles of leaves, hurling them 8
into the air like confetti, leaping into soft unruly mattresses of them. For children, leaf fall is just one of the odder figments of Nature, like hailstones or snowflakes. Walk down a lane overhung with trees in the never-never land of autumn, and you will forget about time and death, lost in the sheer delicious spill of color. Adam and Eve concealed their nakedness with leaves, remember? Leaves have always hidden our awkward secrets.

But how do the colored leaves fall? As a leaf ages, the 9
growth hormone, auxin, fades, and cells at the base of the petiole divide. Two or three rows of small cells, lying at right angles to the axis of the petiole, react with water, then come apart, leaving the petioles hanging on by only

a few threads of xylem. A light breeze, and the leaves are airborne. They glide and swoop, rocking in invisible cradles. They are all wing and may flutter from yard to yard on small whirlwinds or updrafts, swiveling as they go. Firmly tethered to earth, we love to see things rise up and fly—soap bubbles, balloons, birds, fall leaves. They remind us that the end of a season is capricious, as is the end of life. We especially like the way leaves rock, careen, and swoop as they fall. Everyone knows the motion. Pilots sometimes do a maneuver called a "falling leaf," in which the plane loses altitude quickly and on purpose, by slipping first to the right, then to the left. The machine weighs a ton or more, but in one pilot's mind it is a weightless thing, a falling leaf. She has seen the motion before, in the Vermont woods where she played as a child. Below her the trees radiate gold, copper, and red. Leaves are falling, although she can't see them fall, as she falls, swooping down for a closer view.

At last the leaves leave. But first they turn color and   10
thrill us for weeks on end. Then they crunch and crackle underfoot. They *shush,* as children drag their small feet through leaves heaped along the curb. Dark, slimy mats of leaves cling to one's heels after a rain. A damp, stuccolike mortar of semidecayed leaves protects the tender shoots with a roof until spring, and makes a rich humus. An occasional bulge or ripple in the leafy mounds signals a shrew or a field mouse tunneling out of sight. Sometimes one finds in fossil stones the imprint of a leaf, long since disintegrated, whose outlines remind us how detailed, vibrant, and alive are the things of this earth that perish.

Comment

Ackerman gives a detailed explanation of why leaves change color, and at the same time expresses the feelings and thoughts aroused by the fall colors, allowing us to experience the sights of fall by describing them in exact and evocative detail. The essay combines process analysis with causal analysis and definition and description in a highly effective way to achieve these purposes.

Questions for Study and Discussion

1. How does the opening paragraph prepare us for the exposition that follows? What other purpose does the paragraph serve?
2. Does Ackerman develop a central point or thesis, or does she instead make a series of random observations on how leaves change color?
3. What is the main order of ideas in the essay, and how do you discover it?
4. Does the definition in paragraph 7 help to explain how leaves change color, and does it have another purpose?
5. What is the purpose of paragraph 8?

Vocabulary Study

Using your college dictionary, define *photosynthesis* and other key terms essential to understanding why leaves change color.

Suggestions for Writing

1. In an initial draft for an essay similar to Ackerman's, explain a process you are familiar with, for example, fishing for trout or preparing for an athletic event. In the course of your explanation, record the feelings and thoughts that occur as you write about the process.
2. In your final draft, organize the expository and expressive parts of your essay so they form a unified whole. Use your topic sentences to focus attention on the process and to alert your reader to departures from it.

Richard Selzer

MY BROTHER SHAMAN

A former surgeon and teacher at the Yale School of Medicine, Richard Selzer has written numerous essays on the physician and the art of surgery. Selzer grew up in Troy, New York, the son of a doctor who inspired his interest in literature and medicine. Selzer describes his father and early experiences in *Down from Troy: A Doctor Comes of Age* (1992). His fiction and essays are collected in *Rituals of Surgery* (1974), *Mortal Lessons: Notes on the Art of Surgery* (1976), *Confessions of a Knife* (1979), *Letters to a Young Doctor* (1982), *Taking the World in for Repairs* (1986), *Imagine a Woman and Other Tales* (1990), and *Raising the Dead* (1994). In his fiction and essays, Selzer describes the special qualities of mind and spirit needed by the doctor. In this essay on the doctor and the shaman, he compares two kinds of healers in the world of medicine.

In the cult of the Bhagavati, as it has been practiced   1
in southern India, there is a ritual in which two entranced shamans dressed in feathered costumes and massive headgear enter a circle of witnesses. All night long in the courtyard off a temple they lunge and thrust at each other, give shouts of defiance, make challenging gestures. It is all done to the sound of drums, conches and horns. Come daybreak, the goddess Kali "slays" the demon Darika, then plunges her hands into the very bowels of Darika, drinking of and smearing herself with blood. At last Kali withdraws from the field of battle having adorned herself with the intestines of the vanquished.

It is a far cry from the bloody trances of shamans   2
to the bloody acts of surgery. Or is it? Take away from Kali and Darika the disciplinary beat of tautened hide and the moaning of flutes, and you have . . . an emergency intestinal resection. The technique is there, the bravado, the zeal. Only lacking in surgery is the ecstasy.

In both surgery and shamanism the business is done   3
largely by the hands of the operator. The surgeon holds

his scalpel, hemostat, forceps; the shaman, his amulet
of bone, wood, metal. For each there is the hieratic
honoring of ritual objects. The handling of these objects
induces a feeling of tranquillity and power. One's mind
is nudged from the path of self-awareness into the pathless
glade of the imagination. The nun, too, knows this. She
tells her beads, and her heart is enkindled. Surely it is
true that the handling of instruments is conducive to the
kind of possession or devotion that is the mark of all
three—nun, surgeon, shaman. The surgeon and the
shaman understand that one must honor, revere and
entreat one's tools. Both do their handiwork with a
controlled vehemence most dramatically seen in those
offshoots of Buddhism wherein the shaman ties his fingers in "knots," giving them a strange distorted appearance. These priests have an uncanny flexibility of their
finger joints, each of which has a special name. During
these maneuvers the shaman is possessed by finger spirits.
He invokes the good spirits and repels the evil ones.
Such hand poses, or mudras, seen in Buddhist iconography, are used in trancelike rituals to call down the
gods to possess the shaman. In like manner the surgeon
restrains his knife even as he gives it rein. He, too, is
the medium between man and God.

The shaman has his drum which is the river of sound   4
through which he can descend to the Kingdom of Shad-
ows to retrieve the soul of his tribesfellow. The surgeon
listens to the electronic beep of the cardiac monitor, the
regulated respiration of anesthesia, and he is comforted
or warned. Even the operating table has somewhat the
shape and size of the pagan altars I saw in a tiny sixth-
century baptistry in the Provençal village of Vénasque.
Upon these slabs beasts and, in certain instances, humans were laid open to appease the gods. Should one
of these ancient pagans undergo resurrection and be
brought to a modern operating room with its blazing
lamps and opulence of linen and gleaming gadgetry,
where masked and gowned figures dip their hands in

and out of the body of someone who has been plunged into magical sleep, what else would he think but that he has happened upon a ritual sacrifice?

Nor is the toilet of decoration less elaborate for surgeon than for shaman. Take the Washing of the Hands: Behold the surgeon at his ablutions. His lavabo is a deep sink, often of white porcelain, with a central faucet controlled by the knee. The soap he uses is thick and red as iodine. It is held in a nozzled bottle on the wall. The surgeon depresses a pedal on the floor. Once, twice, three times and collects in his cupped palm a puddle of the soap. There it would sit, lifeless, if he did not add a little water from the faucet and begin to brush. Self-containment is part of the nature of soap. Now, all at once, suds break as air and water are incorporated. Here and there in the play of the bristles, bubbles, first one, then another and another, lift from the froth and achieve levitation. For a moment each globule sways in front of the surgeon's dazzled eyes, but only long enough to give him its blessing before winking out. Meanwhile, the stern brush travels back and forth through the slush of forearms, raising wakes of gauze, scratching the skin . . . Oh, not to hurt or abrade, but tenderly, as one scratches the ears of a dog. At last the surgeon thrusts his hands into the stream of water. A dusky foam darkens the porcelain and fades like smoke. A moment later the sink is calm and white. The surgeon too is calm. And purified.

The washing of the hands, then, is at once a rational step in the achievement of sterile technique and a ritual act carried out under the glance of God by which one is made ready to behold, to perform. It is not wholly unlike the whirling of dervishes, or the to and fro rocking of the orthodox Jew at his prayers. The mask, cap, gown and gloves that the surgeon puts on prior to surgery echo, do they not, the phylacteries of this same Jew? Prophetic wisdom, if it will come at all, is most likely to come to one so sacredly trussed. By these simple acts of bathing and adorning, both surgeon and shaman are made receptacular.

Time was when, in order to become a shaman, one 7 had to undergo an initiatory death and resurrection. The aspirant had to be taken to the sky or the netherworld; often he would be dismembered by spirits, cooked in a pot and eaten by them. Only then could he be born again as a shaman. No such rite of passage goes into the making of a surgeon, it is true, but there is something about the process of surgical training that is reminiscent of the sacred ur-drama after all. The modern surgical intern must undergo a long and arduous novitiate during which the subjugation of the will and spirit to the craft is virtually complete. After a number of years of abasement and humiliation he or she is led to a room where no one else is permitted. There is the donning of special raiment, the washing of the hands and, at last, the performance of secret rites before the open ark of the body. In this, surgery remains a hieratic pantomime marked by exorcism, propitiation and invocation. God dwells in operating rooms as He does everywhere. More than once I have surmised a presence . . . something between hearing and feeling. . . .

In the selection of students to enter medical school, 8 I wonder whether the present weight given to academic excellence in organic chemistry is justified. At least as valid a selection would be based upon the presence of a bat-shaped mole on the inner aspect of the thigh of the aspirant, or a specific conjunction of the planets on his birthday. Neither seems more prophetic than the other in the matter of intuition, compassion and ingenuity which form the trinity of doctorhood.

The shaman's journey through disorder and illness 9 to health has parallels to the surgeon's journey into the body. Both are like Jason setting out in the Argos, weathering many storms to return at last with the Golden Fleece. Or Galahad with the Holy Grail. The extirpated gallbladder, then, becomes the talisman of the surgeon's journey, the symbol of his hard-won manhood. What is different is that the surgeon practices inherited rites, while the shaman is susceptible to visions. Still, they both perform acts bent upon making chaos into cosmos.

Saint John of the Cross alludes to the mystic as a 10 solitary bird who must seek the heights, admit of no companionship even with its own kind, stretch out its beak into the air, and sing sweetly. I think of such a shaman soaring, plummeting, riding ecstatic thermals to the stars, tumbling head over heels, and at last descending among the fog of dreams. If, as it seems, the mark of the shaman was his ability to take flight, soaring to the sky or plummeting to the earth in search of his quarry, only the astronaut or the poet would now qualify.

Ever since Nietzsche delivered his stunning pro- 11 nouncement—"Dead are all the gods"—man has been forced to assume the burden of heroism without divine assistance. All the connections to the ancestral past have been severed. It is our rashest act. For no good can come to a race that refuses to acknowledge the living spirit of ancient kingdoms. Ritual has receded from the act of surgery. Only the flavor of it is left, giving, if not to the performers, then to the patients and to those forbidden to witness these events, a shiver of mysticism. Few and far between are the surgeons who consider what they do an encounter with the unknown. When all is said and done, I am left with the suspicion that we have gone too far in our arrogant drift from the priestly forebears of surgery. It is pleasing to imagine surgeons bending over their incisions with love, infusing them with the impalpable. Only then would the surgeon, like the shaman, turn himself into a small god and re-create the world.

Comment

"The machine does not exist that can take the place of the divining physician," Selzer writes in another of his essays, "Textbook." "The physical examination affords the opportunity to touch your patient. It gives the patient the opportunity to be touched by you. In this exchange, messages are sent from one to the other that, if your examination is performed with honesty and humility, will cause the divining powers of the Augurs to be passed on to you—their last heir." The Augurs were the official soothsayers of ancient Rome, prophets or diviners who depended on intuitive powers. In this essay on the doctor and the shaman, Selzer compares the medical doctor and another of his ancestors who drew on special powers of mind and spirit to heal.

Questions for Study and Discussion

1. What details in the ritual described in paragraph 1 suggest to Selzer that the goddess Kali is performing an act of healing by slaying the demon Darika?
2. What similarities in the use of hands lead Selzer to the conclusion that the surgeon and the shaman act as a "medium between man and God"? What additional support does Selzer find for this conclusion in the washing of hands?
3. What other similarities between the surgeon and the shaman does Selzer discuss? Does he draw the same conclusion from these similarities, or does he draw other conclusions?
4. Does Selzer stress any differences between the surgeon and the shaman? Or is he concerned only with similarities?
5. What is Selzer's purpose in making comparisons between the surgeon and the shaman and between the surgeon, the nun, and the orthodox Jew?
6. What is the thesis of the essay and where does it appear? Does Selzer restate the thesis in the course of the essay?
7. Is the comparison developed point by point or in blocks—that is, the characteristics of the doctor presented first and then those of the shaman?

Vocabulary Study

1. Does the definition of *shaman* in your college dictionary mention qualities that Selzer does not discuss? Does Selzer define the

word formally, or instead assume that his readers know its meaning?

2. Be ready to define the following words:
   a. *resection* (paragraph 2)
   b. *hemostat, forceps, amulet* (paragraph 3)
   c. *cardiac monitor, baptistry* (paragraph 4)
   d. *ablutions, lavabo, levitation, abrade* (paragraph 5)
   e. *phylacteries, trussed* (paragraph 6)
   f. *netherworld, novitiate, exorcism, surmised* (paragraph 7)
   g. *extirpated* (paragraph 9)
   h. *thermals* (paragraph 10)

3. Selzer refers to the "hieratic honoring of ritual objects" (paragraph 3). What do the words *hieratic* and *ritual* mean? What is the "Buddhist iconography" that is referred to in the same paragraph?

4. Use a classical dictionary and other special dictionaries to explain the references to Jason and the Golden Fleece (paragraph 9), Saint John of the Cross (paragraph 10), and Friedrich Nietzsche (paragraph 11).

Suggestions for Writing

1. Selzer defines other qualities of the medical doctor and surgeon in various essays: *Mortal Lessons: Notes on the Art of Surgery, Confessions of a Knife,* and *Taking the World in for Repairs.* Discuss the insight an essay in one of these collections gives into Selzer's ideal doctor or surgeon.

2. Discuss significant similarities and differences between one of the following pairs. Use your comparison to develop a thesis:
   a. learning to swim and learning to drive
   b. the experienced and the inexperienced driver
   c. reading a newspaper and reading a novel
   d. listening to a recording and attending a concert
   e. high school and college friends

Arthur L. Campa

ANGLO VS. CHICANO: WHY?

Arthur L. Campa was chairman of the Department of Modern
Languages at the University of Denver and the director of the Center
of Latin American Studies from 1946 to 1978. He served in the U.S.
Air Force and the Peace Corps. His several books on Hispanic-
American culture include *Treasure of the Sangre de Cristos* (1963) and
Hispanic Culture in the Southwest (1979). Campa depends chiefly on
contrast to develop his exposition.

The cultural differences between Hispanic and Anglo-   1
American people have been dwelt upon by so many
writers that we should all be well informed about the
values of both. But audiences are usually of the same
persuasion as the speakers, and those who consult
published works are for the most part specialists looking
for affirmation of what they believe. So, let us consider
the same subject, exploring briefly some of the basic
cultural differences that cause conflict in the Southwest,
where Hispanic and Anglo-American cultures meet.

Cultural differences are implicit in the conceptual   2
content of the languages of these two civilizations, and
their value systems stem from a long series of historical
circumstances. Therefore, it may be well to consider
some of the English and Spanish cultural configurations
before these Europeans set foot on American soil. English culture was basically insular, geographically and
ideologically; was more integrated on the whole, except
for some strong theological differences; and was particularly zealous of its racial purity. Spanish culture was
peninsular, a geographical circumstance that made it a
catchall of Mediterranean, central European and north
African peoples. The composite nature of the population produced a marked regionalism that prevented close
integration, except for religion, and led to a strong sense
of individualism. These differences were reflected in the

colonizing enterprise of the two cultures. The English isolated themselves from the Indians physically and culturally; the Spanish, who had strong notions about *pureza de sangre* [purity of blood] among the nobility, were not collectively averse to adding one more strain to their racial cocktail. Cortés led the way by siring the first *mestizo* in North America, and the rest of the conquistadores followed suit. The ultimate products of these two orientations meet today in the Southwest.

Anglo-American culture was absolutist at the onset; [3] that is, all the dominant values were considered identical for all, regardless of time and place. Such values as justice, charity, honesty were considered the superior social order for all men and were later embodied in the American Constitution. The Spaniard brought with him a relativistic viewpoint and saw fewer moral implications in man's actions. Values were looked upon as the result of social and economic conditions.

The motives that brought Spaniards and Englishmen [4] to America also differed. The former came on an enterprise of discovery, searching for a new route to India initially, and later for new lands to conquer, the fountain of youth, minerals, the Seven Cities of Cíbola and, in the case of the missionaries, new souls to win for the Kingdom of Heaven. The English came to escape religious persecution, and once having found a haven, they settled down to cultivate the soil and establish their homes. Since the Spaniards were not seeking a refuge or running away from anything, they continued their explorations and circled the globe twenty-five years after the discovery of the New World.

This peripatetic tendency of the Spaniard may be [5] accounted for in part by the fact that he was the product of an equestrian culture. Men on foot do not venture far into the unknown. It was almost a century after the landing on Plymouth Rock that Governor Alexander Spotswood of Virginia crossed the Blue Ridge Mountains, and it was not until the nineteenth century that the Anglo-Americans began to move west of the Mississippi.

The Spaniard's equestrian role meant that he was not 6
close to the soil, as was the Anglo-American pioneer,
who tilled the land and built the greatest agricultural
industry in history. The Spaniard cultivated the land
only when he had Indians available to do it for him. The
uses to which the horse was put also varied. The Spanish
horse was essentially a mount, while the more robust
English horse was used in cultivating the soil. It is therefore not surprising that the viewpoints of these two
cultures should differ when we consider that the pioneer
is looking at the world at the level of his eyes while the
caballero [horseman] is looking beyond and down at the
rest of the world.

One of the most commonly quoted, and often mis- 7
interpreted, characteristics of Hispanic peoples is the
deeply ingrained individualism in all walks of life. Hispanic individualism is a revolt against the incursion of
collectivity, strongly asserted when it is felt that the ego
is being fenced in. This attitude leads to a deficiency in
those social qualities based on collective standards, an
attitude that Hispanos do not consider negative because
it manifests a measure of resistance to standardization
in order to achieve a measure of individual freedom.
Naturally, such an attitude has no *reglas fijas* [fixed
rules].

Anglo-Americans who achieve a measure of success 8
and security through institutional guidance not only do
not mind a few fixed rules but demand them. The lack
of a concerted plan of action, whether in business or
in politics, appears unreasonable to Anglo-Americans.
They have a sense of individualism, but they achieve it
through action and self-determination. Spanish individualism is based on feeling, on something that is the result
not of rules and collective standards but of a person's
momentary, emotional reaction. And it is subject to
change when the mood changes. In contrast to Spanish

emotional individualism, the Anglo-American strives for objectivity when choosing a course of action or making a decision.

The Southwestern Hispanos voiced strong objec- 9 tions to the lack of courtesy of the Anglo-Americans when they first met them in the early days of the Santa Fe trade. The same accusation is leveled at the *Americanos* today in many quarters of the Hispanic world. Some of this results from their different conceptions of polite behavior. Here too one can say that the Spanish have no *reglas fijas* because for them courtesy is simply an expression of the way one person feels toward another. To some they extend the hand, to some they bow and for the more *intimos* there is the well-known *abrazo*. The concepts of "good or bad" or "right and wrong" in polite behavior are moral considerations of an absolutist culture.

Another cultural contrast appears in the way both 10 cultures share part of their material substance with others. The pragmatic Anglo-American contributes regularly to such institutions as the Red Cross, the United Fund and a myriad of associations. He also establishes foundations and quite often leaves millions to such institutions. The Hispano prefers to give his contribution directly to the recipient so he can see the person he is helping.

A century of association has inevitably acculturated 11 both Hispanos and Anglo-Americans to some extent, but there still persist a number of culture traits that neither group has relinquished altogether. Nothing is more disquieting to an Anglo-American who believes that time is money than the time perspective of Hispanos. They usually refer to this attitude as the "*mañana* psychology." Actually, it is more of a "today psychology," because Hispanos cultivate the present to the exclusion of the future; because the latter has not arrived yet, it is not a reality. They are reluctant to relinquish the present, so they hold on to it until it becomes the past. To an Hispano, nine is nine until it is ten, so when he arrives at nine-thirty, he jubilantly exclaims: *"¡Justo!"* [right on time]. This may be why the clock is slowed down to a walk in Spanish while in English it runs. In the United States, our future-oriented civilization plans our lives so far in advance that the present loses its meaning. January magazine issues are out in December; 1973 cars have been out since October; cemetery plots and even funeral arrangements are bought on the installment plan. To a person engrossed in living today the very idea of planning his funeral sounds like the tolling of the bells.

It is a natural corollary that a person who is present 12 oriented should be compensated by being good at improvising. An Anglo-American is told in advance to prepare for an "impromptu speech," but an Hispano usually can improvise a speech because *"Nosotros lo improvisamos todo"* [we improvise everything].

Another source of cultural conflict arises from the 13 difference between *being* and *doing*. Even when trying to be individualistic, the Anglo-American achieves it by what he does. Today's young generation decided to be themselves, to get away from standardization, so they let their hair grow, wore ragged clothes and even went barefoot in order to be different from the Establishment. As a result they all ended up doing the same things and created another stereotype. The freedom enjoyed by the individuality of *being* makes it unnecessary for Hispanos to strive to be different.

In 1963 a team of psychologists from the University 14 of Guadalajara in Mexico and the University of Michigan compared 74 upper-middle-class students from each university. Individualism and personalism were found to be central values for the Mexican students. This was explained by saying that a Mexican's value as a person lies in his *being* rather than, as is the case of the Anglo-Americans, in concrete accomplishments. Efficiency and accomplishments are derived characteristics that do not affect worthiness in the Mexican, whereas in the American it is equated with success, a value of highest priority in the American culture. Hispanic people disassociate themselves from material things or from actions that may impugn a person's sense of being, but the Anglo-American shows great concern for material things and assumes responsibility for his actions. This is expressed in the language of each culture. In Spanish one says, *"Se me cayó la taza"* [the cup fell away from me] instead of "I dropped the cup."

In English, one speaks of money, cash and all related 15 transactions with frankness because material things of this high order do not trouble Anglo-Americans. In Spanish such materialistic concepts are circumvented by referring to cash as *efectivo* [effective] and when buying or selling as something *al contado* [counted out], and when without it by saying *No tengo fondos* [I have no funds]. This disassociation from material things is what produces *sobriedad* [sobriety] in the Spaniard according to Miguel de Unamuno, but in the Southwest the disassociation from materialism leads to *dejadez* [lassitude] and *desprendimiento* [disinterestedness]. A man may lose his life defending his honor but is unconcerned about the lack of material things. *Desprendimiento* causes a man to spend his last cent on a friend, which when added to lack of concern for the future may mean that tomorrow he will eat beans as a result of today's binge.

The implicit differences in words that appear to be 16 identical in meaning are astonishing. *Versatile* is a compliment in English and an insult in Spanish. An Hispano student who is told to apologize cannot do it, because the word doesn't exist in Spanish. *Apologia* means words in praise of a person. The Anglo-American either apologizes, which is a form of retraction abhorrent in Spanish, or compromises, another concept foreign to Hispanic culture. *Compromiso* means a date, not a compromise. In colonial Mexico City, two hidalgos once entered a narrow street from opposite sides, and when they could not go around, they sat in their coaches for three days

until the viceroy ordered them to back out. All this
because they could not work out a compromise.

It was that way then and to some extent now. Many   17
of today's conflicts in the Southwest have their roots in
polarized cultural differences, which need not be irreconcilable when approached with mutual respect and
understanding.

Comment

Campa states the subject of his essay in his opening paragraph—
the "basic cultural differences that cause conflict in the Southwest."
And he states his thesis at the start of his second: "Cultural differences are implicit in the conceptual content of the languages of
these two civilizations, and their value systems stem from a long
series of historical circumstances." Paragraphs 2 through 6 deal
with the second part of this statement, identifying important Hispanic and Anglo-American values and historical circumstances.
Paragraphs 7 through 17 explore related values and connect these
values to the conceptual content of Hispanic and Anglo-American
words and phrases. Campa uses the opening sentences of his paragraphs to show the major turns in his analysis:

> A century of association has inevitably acculturated both Hispanos
> and Anglo-Americans to some extent, but there still persist a
> number of culture traits that neither group has relinquished
> altogether. (paragraph 11)

The topic sentence of the paragraph immediately follows:

> Nothing is more disquieting to an Anglo-American who believes
> that time is money than the time perspective of Hispanos.

Both the transitional and the topic sentences here mark the contrasts
Campa is developing. Campa gives emphasis to these contrasts in
the opening sentences of most of the paragraphs.

Questions for Study and Discussion

1. What topic does Campa begin his analysis with in paragraph
    2? What topic does he turn to in paragraph 3?

2. Campa turns in paragraph 4 to the first of several historical circumstances. Which circumstance does he begin with? How are the circumstances discussed in paragraphs 5 and 6 related to that of paragraph 4?

3. How is Hispanic individualism—introduced in paragraph 7 and explored by contrast in paragraph 8—suggested by the Hispanic equestrian role discussed in paragraph 6?

4. Paragraph 9, which illustrates the differences in Hispanic and Anglo-American individualism, introduces differences in the conceptual content of Spanish and English. What are these concepts?

5. What different values does Campa explore in paragraph 10? How are the different values discussed in paragraph 11 related to these? How does Campa illustrate the differences in these paragraphs? How does paragraph 12 develop the difference discussed in paragraph 11?

6. How do previous differences help to explain those discussed and illustrated in paragraphs 13 through 15?

7. What is the function of paragraphs 13 through 15?

8. Campa develops his essay chiefly by contrast. Which paragraphs open with transitional sentences that mark major turns in the analysis?

9. Are any of the values Campa discusses your own? Is your ethnic background chiefly responsible for them?

Vocabulary Study

1. Find synonyms for the following words. Be ready to discuss what the etymology of the word contributes to your understanding of its use in the paragraph:
   a. *conceptual, configurations, insular, peninsular, conquistadores* (paragraph 2)
   b. *peripatetic, equestrian* (paragraph 5)
   c. *incursion* (paragraph 7)
   d. *pragmatic, myriad* (paragraph 10)
   e. *corollary, improvising, impromptu* (paragraph 12)
   f. *circumvented, lassitude, disinterestedness* (paragraph 15)
   g. *abhorrent* (paragraph 16)

2. What are the meanings of the words *absolutist* and *relativistic* in paragraphs 3 and 9? What dictionary meanings do these words not have in the essay?

Suggestions for Writing

1. Contrast values of your own with those of a friend, perhaps referring to some of the values identified by Campa. Then discuss the possible causes of these differences—upbringing, ethnic background, friends, school. Refer to ideas of Campa if these help explain the differences.
2. Campa states: "Even when trying to be individualistic, the Anglo-American achieves it by what he does." Discuss the extent to which this statement describes your way of being an individual. Compare or contrast your individualism with that of one or more friends. Use your analysis to verify or challenge Campa's analysis of American values.

Sydney J. Harris

CLIMBING THE MOUNTAIN OF SUCCESS

Sydney J. Harris (p. 82) here explores a popular idea by looking closely at its supporting analogy. As in his essay on the words *liberal, conservative,* and *radical,* Harris writes with the extreme concision and clarity required of a newspaper columnist, yet without a sacrifice of depth.

It has long struck me that the familiar metaphor of   1
"climbing the ladder" for describing the ascent to success or fulfillment in any field is inappropriate and misleading. There are no ladders that lead to success, although there may be some escalators for those lucky enough to follow in a family's fortunes.

A ladder proceeds vertically, rung by rung, with each   2
rung evenly spaced, and with the whole apparatus leaning against a relatively flat and even surface. A child can

climb a ladder as easily as an adult, and perhaps with a surer footing.

Making the ascent in one's vocation or profession is far less like ladder climbing than mountain climbing, and here the analogy is a very real one. Going up a mountain requires a variety of skills, and includes a diversity of dangers, that are in no way involved in mounting a ladder.

Young people starting out should be told this, both to dampen their expectations and to allay their disappointments. A mountain is rough and precipitous, with uncertain footing and a predictable number of falls and scrapes, and sometimes one has to take the long way around to reach the shortest distance.

One needs different tools and the knowledge and skill to use them most effectively—as well as knowing when not to employ them. Most of all, a peculiar combination of daring and prudence is called for, which not all persons possess.

The art of rappelling is important, because sometimes one has to go down a little in order to go up. And the higher one gets, the greater the risk and the greater the fall; there is much exhilaration—but little security and less oxygen—in altitude. As many stars and standouts and company presidents have found to their regret, it is often harder to stay there than to get there.

Then, too, one must learn that there is no necessary relationship between public success and private satisfaction. The top of the ladder is shaky unless the base is firmly implanted and the whole structure is well defended against the winds of envy and greed and duplicity and the demands of one's own ego. The peak of the mountain is even more exposed to a chilling wind, as well as to a pervasive sense of loneliness. Many may have admired the ascent, but many more, eager to make the same endeavor, are waiting at the foot of the slope to witness an ignominious fall. It is easier to extend good will to those who do not threaten our own sense of worth.

People who are not prepared for failure are not 8
prepared for success; if not for failure, at least for set-
backs and slides and frustrations, and the acceptance of
the deficits that so often accompany the assets. Ambition untempered by realism will never see the missing
rung it falls through on that mythical ladder.

Comment

Analogy—a special kind of comparison—is an important method
of exposition and, as Harris points out, a difficult method because
of the precision required. The writer who uses analogy must be
careful that the differences between the things being compared are
not significant enough to weaken the point being made. Harris
begins by criticizing a weak analogy—climbing the ladder of success. He then develops an analogy of his own—with mountain
climbing—to argue a thesis. He develops each point of similarity
and, at the end of the essay, compares the weak analogy with which
he began his own.

Questions for Study and Discussion

1. Why is the analogy between climbing the ladder and trying to
   succeed in one's vocation or profession a weak one? Why
   does mountain climbing provide a stronger analogy?
2. What similarities between mountain climbing and trying to
   succeed does Harris discuss? Are these similarities of equal
   importance, or does Harris stress some more than others?
3. What is the thesis of the essay and where does it appear?
4. Why does Harris return at the end of the essay to the weak
   analogy criticized at the beginning?
5. Are there other similarities between mountain climbing and
   trying to succeed that Harris might have discussed? Are there
   differences that he might have noted? Do these differences
   weaken the analogy and therefore the thesis of the essay, in
   your opinion, or are they insignificant?

Vocabulary Study

Define each of the following words, and explain how each differs in meaning from the word immediately following it:
1. *metaphor* (paragraph 1), *simile*
2. *precipitous* (paragraph 4), *steep*
3. *prudence* (paragraph 5), *caution*
4. *rappelling* (paragraph 6), *ascending*
5. *duplicity* (paragraph 7), *cunning*
6. *deficits* (paragraph 8), *hazards*

Suggestions for Writing

Develop a topic of your own by analogy, noting similarities as well as differences between the things being compared. In the course of your discussion, explain why these differences do not weaken the analogy. Here are a few possible topics:
1. making an enduring friendship
2. losing a friend
3. winning an argument fairly
4. winning an argument unfairly
5. asking for a raise in salary and getting it

John Garvey

THINKING IN PACKAGES

John Garvey, a columnist for *Commonweal* for many years, attended Notre Dame University and later taught high school and worked as an editor. In his columns Garvey writes about social and religious issues. "There are true and false things," he has written, "and choices which align you with or against the universe." The column reprinted here appeared in *Commonweal* on November 6, 1981. In it Garvey discusses how we think about these things and the dangers of thinking too narrowly. Garvey uses exposition for a persuasive end.

There is a grave problem which faces those of us who care about ideas. (Notice how I have gathered us all

together in a noble little bunch.) It is something I have
been paying attention to in a half-conscious way ever
since I first started arguing with people, but it has only
recently surfaced in all its silly array, probably because
Ronald Reagan was elected president. It has to do not
so much with ideas as with the way we relate to them.
What I have noticed at long last, after years of doing
all the wrong things, is embarrassing. It makes me think
that everyone—every anarchist, libertarian, conservative, radical, and socialist—ought to take a vow of
emotional poverty where ideas are concerned.

We have an investment in our ideas which has nothing   2
to do with the particular worth of our ideas. Our ideas
are like clan totems or old school ties. We tend to think
that our ideas make us decent. If we have the right
opinion about something, it means that we ourselves
must be basically good folks; and the other side of this
is that those who do not share our feelings on any
particular subject are indecent, even perverse. Our ideas
become tokens which we shove across the table at one
another during conversations to show who we are. They
are signals to people we often don't know very well,
which we send through the space between us to let them
know what to expect of us, and we are delighted when
their response is approving: it means they are our sort.
If they bat our tokens back at us with a cool stare or,
more politely, through careful disagreement, our first
impulse is often to assume that their motive for doing
so must be base.

I believe, for example, that the arms race is suicidal   3
and that it is almost certainly bound to end in such
destruction as the world has never seen. I am putting
this as mildly as I can. I also believe that to accept it
as a tactical necessity means assuming something which
is morally indefensible: the military use of civilian populations, and the willingness to hold them hostage to
possible annihilation. I have noticed that people who
disagree with me assume all sorts of things I not only

have not said, but which I definitely do not believe. They assume that I believe the Soviet Union to be basically trustworthy and decent, not at all bad politically; they assume that I do not object to totalitarianism, and in fact have some sneaky attachment to it, and that I think of America as the world's greatest evil.

The problem is that people on my side of this life 4 and death question do the same sort of thing. Because I agree with them, I tend to forgive them more easily for the moves which, coming from the other side, properly infuriate me. One problem I have always had with *Dr. Strangelove,* much as I enjoyed it, was the sickly consolation it gave to liberals with all of its easy targets. The assumption was that those crazy hawks enjoyed destruction, that they had a romance going with Armageddon. They—our ideological opponents—couldn't honestly believe that unless we met and overtook the Soviets weapon for weapon, we would be faced with a situation in which we might really be forced to accept the domination of a group of people who believe that the Gulag is the proper answer to dissent. They must have a darker reason, something to do with their being anal sorts. They must have had a dreadful relationship with their fathers, or they must have been sexually confused. They couldn't have an honestly different view of the world, a different reading of the same facts.

I disagree with a view of the world which can en- 5 vision a situation in which our superior strength will force our enemies to back down; we wouldn't be cowed so easily, and it seems naive to suppose that they are that much unlike us. I not only disagree with that view. I think that if it does not kill me off, it will kill my children or grandchildren. Or it may keep them from being killed—at the expense of other people's children and grandchildren. Even if those who defend the arms race as a necessary evil were right in their predictions, I would have to oppose them.

But it is too easy, too self-satisfying, to assume that ₆
our own motives in this argument are pure while our
opponents are indecent. They are wrong, I think; but
to think that they are simply base (or even complicatedly
base) involves us in doing several false things. We assume an ulterior motive, which handily keeps us from
having to consider seriously the possibility that our
opponents could be right. We assume that no other
vision of the world could possibly have anything to
recommend it, which keeps us from having to examine
our own assumptions very closely. And we assume that
our having the right idea, which is usually projected at
people who already agree with us anyway, ought to gain
us support, applause, and moral approval. We do this
whether we are on the left or right. And by offering
package deals we make it all easier for ourselves. A
woman who knew that I opposed the war in Vietnam
was shocked to learn that I opposed abortion, because
in her package-deal way of thinking a person who
opposed war must be in favor of abortion. The left is
assumed by its enemies to be predictable, and so is the
right. Both sides are right too often. Left and right *are*
both pretty predictable, nearly tribal, and ideas and
opinions are frequently waved around as signs of respectability within the tribe, as if language had nothing
to do with exploring, or with moving towards a truth
in a tentative way, or with being doubtful, or with taking
a chance at the edge—which means being willing not
only to be wrong, because the only thing at stake here
is not whether an opinion falls into the true or false
column, but also takes into account the possibility that
your opponent is a human being as richly complicated
and oddly formed as you are.

That does not make your opponent right. One must ₇
firmly believe that there are ideas beyond decent debate.
Genocide and child molestation are closed issues, I think.
It is wrong not to be passionate about the things we care

for deeply. I feel as strongly about nuclear war as I do about abortion, and find it difficult to have much sympathy with defenders of capital punishment. If Matthew 25 is right and what is done to the least human being is done to Christ, then capital punishment, abortion, the notion of a war in which whole populations may be destroyed, and the idea that hunger is in some circumstances acceptable, are all under a terrible judgment. But to think of those whose disagreements with us are deep as indecent or base is to put ourselves under the same judgment. An idea must bear fruit; a Christian perception is meant to go out from itself. If we see it as a personal possession we are on the wrong track. As a possession it is something we have to get rid of.

The Quaker saint John Woolman opposed slave- 8 holders and the men who were about to make the Revolutionary War. He thought that their decisions were profoundly wrong, and he let them know that. His life was a lived disagreement—but he always assumed that he was talking to a human being, one loved by God. Even where we believe that there is no room for debate, we must have compassion—which means *suffering with,* which means understanding how a person could arrive at the place where he is—and we must realize that we share the disease of the heart which allows people to wound one another in the name of truth. Erasmus once wrote about one aspect of this universal problem: "There is great obscurity in many matters, and man suffers from this almost congenital disease, that he will not give in once a controversy is started, and after he is warmed up he regards as absolutely true that which he began to sponsor quite casually."

The point is not to become less committed, or to 9 assume that all ideas are of equal merit, but to be as clear as we can about our own motives, and to approach those who disagree with us the way Woolman did. We should not allow ourselves the luxury of thinking that our ideas have anything at all to do with our decency. We should realize that Matthew 25 applies to our judgments: the least of the brethren includes our opponents.

Comment

Garvey discusses the causes and effects of "thinking in packages." He begins with causes, as in these sentences of paragraph 2: "Our ideas are like clan totems or old school ties. We tend to think that our ideas make us decent." The transition to the effects occurs in paragraph 6: "but to think that they are simply base (or even complicatedly base) involves us in doing several false things." The concluding paragraphs present a solution to the problem.

Garvey analyzes causes and effects informally, as we would in ordinary conversation. Indeed, that is how he addresses the reader—as a friend with whom he might on another occasion engage in argument. He talks to the reader casually, amiably, without heat, and without such a narrow focus on the issues that understanding or honest concession becomes impossible.

Questions for Study and Discussion

1. In what ways are "our ideas . . . like clan totems or old school ties"? How does Garvey develop these similes?
2. How does he illustrate the causes identified in paragraphs 4 through 6?
3. What are the effects—the "several false things"—that result from "thinking in packages"?
4. Garvey refers in paragraph 6 to the need of examining our assumptions closely. What is an assumption in thinking, and how does Garvey explain and illustrate the term?
5. If there are "ideas beyond decent debate," how can and should they be discussed with those who hold opposite opinions? How does the statement of Erasmus help Garvey to deal with this question? And what use does he make of Matthew 25?

Vocabulary Study

1. Explain the difference between the following words:
    a. *investment* (paragraph 2), *interest*
    b. *tactical* (paragraph 3), *diplomatic*
    c. *totalitarianism* (paragraph 3), *dictatorship*
    d. *hawks* (paragraph 4), *fanatics*
    e. *ulterior* (paragraph 6), *deceitful*
    f. *opponents* (paragraph 6), *enemies*
    g. *genocide* (paragraph 7), *murder*
    h. *obscurity* (paragraph 8), *misunderstanding*
    i. *congenital* (paragraph 8), *inborn*
2. Be ready to distinguish between the following words in paragraph 1: *anarchist, libertarian, conservative, radical, socialist.*

Suggestions for Writing

1. Analyze an editorial in a newspaper or newsmagazine, or a letter to the editor, to determine whether the writer is "thinking in packages." In the course of your analysis, explain what Garvey means by this term and what his ideas on thinking are as a whole.
2. Develop one of the following statements from your own experience and point of view. If you disagree with the statement, explain why you do:
    a. "We have an investment in our ideas which has nothing to do with the particular worth of our ideas."
    b. "Our ideas are like clan totems or old school ties. We tend to think that our ideas make us decent."
    c. "And by offering package deals we make it all easier for ourselves."
    d. "It is wrong not to be passionate about the things we care for deeply. . . . But to think of those whose disagreements with us are deep as indecent or base is to put ourselves under the same judgment."

K.C. Cole

WOMEN AND PHYSICS

K.C. Cole has written on science and on women today for *The New York Times, Washington Post,* and other periodicals. Her books include *Facets of Light* (1980), *Order in the Universe* (1982), and *Sympathetic Vibrations: Reflections on Physics as a Way of Life* (1984). In the preface to her collection of essays *Between the Lines* (1982), Cole states that "what I find both so rich and so confusing about women's roles today is that so often what seem to be irreconcilable opposites are just two different aspects of the same thing—two different windows on the same rapidly changing world." She adds that "there's more to the many sides of today's woman than meets the eye—and more common ground on many 'women's issues' than most people think." Cole deals with the important issue of women and science in this essay, published in *The New York Times* on December 3, 1981.

I know few other women who do what I do. What 1
I do is write about science, mainly physics. And to do that, I spend a lot of time reading about science, talking to scientists and struggling to understand physics. In fact, most of the women (and men) I know think me quite queer for actually liking physics. "How can you write about that stuff?" they ask, always somewhat askance. "I could never understand that in a million years." Or more simply, "I hate science."

I didn't realize what an odd creature a woman in- 2
terested in physics was until a few years ago when a science magazine sent me to Johns Hopkins University in Baltimore for a conference on an electrical phenomenon known as the Hall effect. We sat in a huge lecture hall and listened as physicists talked about things engineers didn't understand, and engineers talked about things physicists didn't understand. What I didn't understand was why, out of several hundred young students of physics and engineering in the room, less than a handful were women.

Some time later, I found myself at the California 3
Institute of Technology reporting on the search for the
origins of the universe. I interviewed physicist after
physicist, man after man. I asked one young administrator why none of the physicists were women. And he
answered: "I don't know, but I suppose it must be
something innate. My 7-year-old daughter doesn't seem
to be much interested in science."

It was with that experience fresh in my mind that 4
I attended a conference in Cambridge, Massachusetts,
on science literacy, or rather the worrisome lack of it
in this country today. We three women—a science teacher,
a young chemist and myself—sat surrounded by a company of august men. The chemist, I think, first tentatively raised the issue of science illiteracy in women. It
seemed like an obvious point. After all, everyone had
agreed over and over again that scientific knowledge
these days was a key factor in economic power. But as
soon as she made the point, it became clear that we
women had committed a grievous social error. Our
genders were suddenly showing; we had interrupted the
serious talk with a subject unforgivably silly.

For the first time, I stopped being puzzled about why 5
there weren't any women in science and began to be
angry. Because if science is a search for answers to
fundamental questions then it hardly seems frivolous to
find out why women are excluded. Never mind the
economic consequences.

A lot of the reasons why women are excluded are 6
spelled out by the Massachusetts Institute of Technology
experimental physicist Vera Kistiakowsky in a recent article in *Physics Today* called "Women in Physics: Unnecessary, Injurious and Out of Place?" The title was taken
from a 19th century essay written in opposition to the
appointment of a female mathematician to a professor-
ship at the University of Stockholm. "As decidedly as
two and two make four," a woman in mathematics is a
"monstrosity," concluded the writer of the essay.

Dr. Kistiakowsky went on to discuss the factors that 7
make women in science today, if not monstrosities, at
least oddities. Contrary to much popular opinion, one of
those is *not* an innate difference in the scientific ability of
boys and girls. But early conditioning does play a stubborn and subtle role. A recent Nova program, "The
Pinks and the Blues," documented how girls and boys
are treated differently from birth—the boys always encouraged in more physical kinds of play, more active
explorations of their environments. Sheila Tobias, in her
book, *Math Anxiety,* showed how the games boys play
help them to develop an intuitive understanding of speed,
motion and mass. The main sorting out of the girls from
the boys in science seems to happen in junior high
school. As a friend who teaches in a science museum
said, "By the time we get to electricity, the boys already
have had some experience with it. But it's unfamiliar to
the girls." Science books draw on boys' experiences.
"The examples are all about throwing a baseball at such
and such a speed," said my stepdaughter, who barely
escaped being a science drop-out.

The most obvious reason there are not many more 8
women in science is that women are discriminated against
as a class, in promotions, salaries and hirings, a conclusion reached by a recent analysis by the National Academy of Sciences.

Finally, said Dr. Kistiakowsky, women are simply 9
made to feel out of place in science. Her conclusion was
supported by a Ford Foundation study by Lynn H. Fox
on the problems of women in mathematics. When students were asked to choose among six reasons accounting for girls' lack of interest in math, the girls rated this
statement second: "Men do not want girls in the mathematical occupations."

A friend of mine remembers winning a Bronxwide 10
mathematics competition in the second grade. Her
friends—both boys and girls—warned her that she
shouldn't be good at math: "You'll never find a boy who

likes you." My friend continued nevertheless to excel in math and science, won many awards during her years at the Bronx High School of Science, and then earned a full scholarship to Harvard. After one year of Harvard science, she decided to major in English.

When I asked her why, she mentioned what she   11 called the "macho mores" of science. "It would have been O.K. if I'd had someone to talk to," she said. "But the rules of comportment were such that you never admitted you didn't understand. I later realized that even the boys didn't get everything clearly right away. You had to stick with it until it had time to sink in. But for the boys, there was a payoff in suffering through the hard times, and a kind of punishment—a shame—if they didn't. For the girls it was O.K. not to get it, and the only payoff for sticking it out was that you'd be considered a freak."

Science is undeniably hard. Often, it can seem quite   12 boring. It is unfortunately too often presented as laws to be memorized instead of mysteries to be explored. It is too often kept a secret that science, like art, takes a well developed esthetic sense. Women aren't the only ones who say, "I hate science." That's why everyone who goes into science needs a little help from friends. For the past ten years, I have been getting more than a little help from a friend who is a physicist. But my stepdaughter—who earned the highest grades ever recorded in her California high school on the math Scholastic Aptitude Test—flunked calculus in her first year at Harvard. When my friend the physicist heard about it, he said, "Harvard should be ashamed of itself."

What he meant was that she needed that little extra   13 encouragement that makes all the difference. Instead, she got that little extra discouragement that makes all the difference. "In the first place all the math teachers are men," she explained. "In the second place, when I met a boy I liked and told him I was taking chemistry, he immediately said: 'Oh, you're one of those science types.' In the third place, it's just a kind of social thing. The math clubs are full of boys and you don't feel comfortable joining."

In other words, she was made to feel unnecessary, [14] and out of place.

A few months ago, I accompanied a male colleague [15] from the science museum where I sometimes work to a lunch of the history of science faculty at the University of California. I was the only woman there, and my presence for the most part was obviously and rudely ignored. I was so surprised and hurt by this that I made an extra effort to speak knowledgeably and well. At the end of the lunch, one of the professors turned to me in all seriousness and said: "Well, K. C., what do the women think of Carl Sagan?" I replied that I had no idea what "the women" thought about anything. But now I know what I should have said: I should have told him that his comment was unnecessary, injurious and out of place.

Comment

The issue that Cole explores—whether women lack ability in science and mathematics—is related to a broader issue considered briefly in paragraphs 6 and 7. This is whether males and females differ innately in scientific ability. Cole reviews some recent evidence, then presents personal experiences that support the view that social conditioning plays a decisive role in discouraging girls from excelling in science and mathematics. The evidence she presents from various sources is not, and cannot be, conclusive; but it is strong enough to give a highly probable answer to the question she poses at the beginning of the essay—"why, out of several hundred young students of physics and engineering in the room, less than a handful were women."

Questions for Study and Discussion

1. How various is the evidence Cole presents for the conclusion she reaches? Where does she state that conclusion?
2. How many causes does she distinguish for the failure of many women to excel in science and mathematics?
3. Does Cole say that innate differences in scientific ability do not exist between males and females, or does she reach a limited or qualified conclusion?
4. What other kind of evidence might be presented in consideration of the issue of innate scientific ability? For what kind of audience would this evidence have to be presented? For what audience is Cole writing?
5. Does your personal experience support the idea that ability in science and mathematics depends on encouragement and social conditions? Or do you have reason to believe that such ability is inborn?
6. How persuasive do you find the evidence Cole presents in support of her ideas?

Vocabulary Study

Explain the specific use Cole makes of the italicized words:
1. *genders, silly* (paragraph 4)
2. *factors, monstrosities, oddities* (paragraph 7)
3. *macho mores* (paragraph 11)
4. *comportment* (paragraph 11)

Suggestions for Writing

1. Discuss your own experiences in learning science and mathematics, giving attention to the conditioning and encouragement you received, and in general the reasons for your performance in them. Use your discussion to reach a limited conclusion or opinion on the issue Cole discusses.

2.   Discuss the extent to which your personal experience supports
     one of the following statements:
     a.   "The games boys play help them to develop an intuitive
          understanding of speed, motion and mass."
     b.   "The main sorting out of the girls from the boys in science
          seems to happen in junior high school."
     c.   "But the rules of comportment were such that you never
          admitted you didn't understand."
     d.   "Science is undeniably hard. Often, it can seem quite
          boring. It is unfortunately too often presented as laws
          to be memorized instead of mysteries to be explored."

Irving Lewis Allen

MAIN STREET

Irving Lewis Allen is professor of sociology at the University of
Connecticut. In the preface to *The City in Slang: New York and
Popular Speech* (1993), Allen writes that "nearly every form of human
expression in word and image—save language itself—has been used to
explore the historical city of the mind. . . . Popular images of the
modern city have been viewed through the selective and coloring
filters of the mass media in old newspapers, magazines, popular
fiction, popular music, and movies. Reconstructions of past urban
culture and society with these materials have increased our
understanding of the thoughtways of the people who made the images
and, though with more caution, of the people who consumed them.
The body of popular speech about the experience of social life in the
city adds to this story." In this section Allen discusses the American
image of Main Street, described later in the book as "the moral center
of the community." Selection title by editor.

Social stratification is a universal in modern societies   1
and the systems are in many ways encoded in culture
and language. Relative to traditional emblems, such as
clothing, and personal reputations of rank, exactly where
one lived in the modern city became more important as
a marker of class and status. A *good address* was near
the center of a settlement, especially on the main street,

and lesser status was measured roughly on a gradient with declining distance from the center. In New York, a city of many "urban villages" and other symbolic areas, the generic *main street* often has been used to denote a chief thoroughfare and social center. Streets and avenues such as Broadway, Fifth Avenue, or Seventh Avenue, in sequential periods and for different social sets, were the "main streets," the centers of fashionable New York life. Manhattan offers an especially well-developed, richly illustrated symbolic system based on the grid, always with one of its main streets at its center.

The story of the elaborate symbolic relationship 2 between the grid of city streets and social status begins in the early villages and small towns of America, not in the big cities. Main Street in American towns and cities had—and still has—a special significance in the symbolic life of the community, one that sets it apart from main streets in the urban histories of other countries. The High Streets of Britain and of certain Commonwealth nations are not quite the same thing; their chief social meaning is that of the focus of commerce and shopping, and the American connotations are generally lacking. Almost every American town seems to have its Main Street, though it may not bear that exact name. The main street is sometimes called Center Street, Broad Street—or for that matter Broadway—or some other name that denoted its status as the principal thoroughfare. When the town faced on a river or other water front, the main street was often called Front Street, which connoted that the street was not only at the front, but was the face of the town. Yet it is striking how often the main thoroughfare is actually named Main Street. Whatever its name, Main Street was, and to some extent remains, an American institution.

Carole Rifkind, an architectural historian, found the 3 origins of the American Main Street in the colonial villages of New England in the seventeenth century and traced the spread of the spatial form to New Jersey and

New York in the eighteenth century.[1] By the second half of the nineteenth century, the physical and cultural model of Main Street as the axis of the town was stamped on nearly every town and city in the country. Early in this century the epitome of Main Street in popular imagery was seen in the small towns of the great Middle West. Sinclair Lewis's 1920 novel *Main Street* commented on the physical as well as the moral drabness of many midwestern Main Streets.[2] The title of Lewis's novel thrust the name *Main Street,* with all these connotations, into popular speech, much as other of his fictional placenames and personal names (e.g., *Babbitt)* entered slang in the 1920s as popular labels of their types.

Main Street, as it was ideally conceived, built, and lived, signified an established way of doing things that articulated the social order, reflected the hierarchy of values, and had moral significance for the social life of the community. Main Street typically intersected the settlement and was the political, economic, and social center of the town. The edifices and monuments that reflected the official and usually prevailing values of local society were usually located about midway along the length of Main Street and at the center of the community. These symbolic structures expressed the town's integration with the regional and national societies. The courthouse square or the town square, the successor to the green in colonial villages, was the symbolic heart of the community and the site of such collective representations as monuments, public observances, recognitions, and other celebrations of common values.

Main Street was further the center of social prestige in the settlement. The largest and most prestigious residences traditionally were closest to the center and the

---

[1] *Main Street: The Face of Urban America* (New York: Harper & Row, 1977), pp. 17-23.

[2] Richard R. Lingeman, *Small Town America: A Narrative History, 1620–The Present* (New York: G. P. Putnam's Sons, 1980), pp. 293-98.

lesser dwellings at a farther distance or on cross, side, or back streets. In the ideal arrangement, the placement of buildings and institutions descended from the center in a predictable order of values: institutions of law at the center, flanked by a zone of commerce, all buttressed by the large houses of the middle classes, mostly merchants and the professionals. Other, lesser streets bore equally agreed-upon and predictable relations to Main Street and extended the spatial metaphor. Some towns, keeping certain activities in their place, relegated saloons and brothels to side streets and back streets; worse things were tolerated or escaped notice in alleys. The middle-class dominance of Main Street and the social meaning of all these arrangements caused Main Street to become the popular symbol of public scrutiny, social approval, and middle-class respectability. Mrs. Grundy, had she lived in America, would certainly have lived on and overseen the affairs of Main Street.

The corners of Main Street, significantly the intersec- 6 tions of cross streets and side streets, attracted socially marginal elements in the town and gave the language several new expressions. Street corners, often furnished with a lamp post that could be leaned against, became a favored hangout for *corner boys,* a term used since about 1855. An ethnographic tradition in sociology, beginning significantly with William Foote Whyte's *Street Corner Society* (1943), studied the social world of working-class corner boys in large cities. In this century corner boys who met on street corners, gossiped, and ogled women became known as *corner cowboys* and sometimes *corner wolves,* a low variety of street masher. By about 1925 *drugstore cowboys* were young men who loafed in and outside the corner soda fountains. Big-city street corners in cartoon images are also associated with tuxedoed drunks hanging onto lamp posts or with ladies of the night basking in circles of light cast by street lamps.

By the 1890s, when street paving and lighting had 7 become common across the country, *Main Street* had become a metaphor for the dominant social order of the community; in syntax, other streets and their corners stood for variance from it. Popular speech came to express the social understanding embodied in this spatial metaphor for social standing in the community and used the syntactic relation of streets in the grid as a signified idea. This was the beginning of a much more elaborate development about the meaning of city streets.

Comment

Allen gives both a denotative and connotative definition of *main street,* discussing both in detail. Supporting his definition is a brief causal analysis, a discussion of origin of the American main street in the colonial village. Allen also depends on comparison and example—in noting the difference between the American Main Street and the British High Street, and in illustrating the class divisions or social stratification reflected in the corners of main street and the side and back streets of towns and cities. In later sections Allen discusses the evolving symbolism of city streets, referred to in the concluding paragraph.

Questions for Study and Discussion

1. What denotative definition of *main street* does Allen give in paragraph 1? How does he develop this definition in paragraphs 2-4? What is the purpose of the comparison with the British High Street in paragraph 2?
2. What social attitudes do the alternate names discussed in paragraph 2 connote? How does Allen illustrate these attitudes in the course of the essay?
3. How did social attitudes in colonial America influence town planning? How did the main street evolve from colonial times to the present?
4. How do the popular terms discussed in paragraph 6 reflect the changing world of Main Street?

Vocabulary Study

1. Why does Allen refer to arrangement of streets as a "grid" as a "symbolic system"?
2. In what sense is *main street* a "generic" term (paragraph 1)?
3. In what sense is *main street* a "spatial metaphor"?
4. Who was Mrs. Grundy, and why would she have lived on Main Street if she had lived in America?

Suggestions for Writing

1. Discuss Allen's definition of *main street*—its denotation and connotations—in relation to your own town or city. You may wish to comment on changes that have occurred in the importance and social significance of your main street.
2. The arrangement of desks, chairs, and other furniture in a classroom tells something about the values of the school. Describe the classroom you are sitting in and discuss what it reveals about the school, the teachers who use the classroom, and the students.

Norman Maclean

CONTROLLING A GROUND FIRE

Norman Maclean (1902-90) grew up in Missoula, Montana, and as a young man worked as a logger and for the United States Forest Service. He was later a professor of English at the University of Chicago. In *A River Runs Through It and Other Stories* (1979), Maclean describes his early years in Montana. *Young Men and Fire* (1992) is an account of a fire in the remote Mann Gulch of Montana on August 5, 1949, and the death of thirteen young firefighters. Twelve of the dead had parachuted into the gulch with three other jumpers, who survived the fire. "Among other things, it was important to me, as an exercise for old age, to enlarge my knowledge and spirit so I could accompany young men whose lives I might have lived on their way to death. I have climbed where they climbed, and in my time I have fought fire and inquired into its nature." In the section of *Young Men and Fire* reprinted here, Maclean defines two kinds of forest fire and describes the process of controlling a ground fire. Selection title by editor.

The primary purpose of the first Smokejumpers, 1
then, was still primary to the Smokejumpers of 1949—
to land on a forest fire in difficult or otherwise inaccessible country before suddenly the universe tried to reduce its own frame of things to ashes and charred grouse. When the Mann Gulch fire was first spotted from the plane, the pilot, the crew foreman, and the spotter sized it up as a fairly ordinary fire—they reported it was just a "ground fire" that had "crowned" in one place where it had already burned out. None of the three saw any "spot fires" around its edges, and that meant the fire had been advancing slowly on the ground and was not playing leapfrog by throwing small fires ahead of the fire's main front.

The words in quotation marks above and undoubt- 2
edly some that are not are those of firefighters, and we had better be sure of the meaning of these key words in the Basic English of firefighters so that when the tragic race between the firefighters and the fire begins it won't have to be stopped for definitions. It is not enough to know the word for this or that kind of fire; to know one fire is to see how what was dropping live ashes from a dead tree at the end of one afternoon by next afternoon had become one kind of fire after another kind of fire until it had become a monster in flames from which there was no escape.

Of the two main kinds of forest fires distinguished 3
by their causes, man and nature itself, the Mann Gulch fire was a lightning fire, as 75 percent of the forest fires in the West are. Lightning fires usually start where lightning gets its first chance to strike—high up near the top of a ridge but slightly down its side where the first clump of dead trees stands, and the start of the Mann Gulch fire fits this description. The fire in the dead snag may drop live ashes for several days before starting a fire on the ground, for the ground near a mountaintop is likely to be mostly rocks with at best only a light covering of dead leaves, needles, or grass. But the lightning storm

that started the Mann Gulch fire passed over the gulch on August 4, and by the end of the next afternoon on the hottest day ever recorded in nearby Helena thirteen Smokejumpers were dead.

Once started on the ground the lightning fire became 4 simply a "ground fire," a term that includes most fires, and so ground fires are of many sizes, shapes, and intensities, and practically all man-made fires such as campfires and fires set to burn slash or brush but allowed to get away at least start as ground fires. A ground fire may become dangerous, even murderous, but most often it is just a lot of hard work to get under control. Until an hour before the end, that is what the Smokejumpers expected the Mann Gulch fire to be— hard work all night but easing up by morning.

The job of controlling most ground fires starts with 5 the job of scraping a "fire trench" or fire-line around it or its flanks so as to force it onto rocks or open meadows. A fire trench or fire-line is some two to three feet wide, is made with a Pulaski and shovel, and is nothing more than the surface of the ground scraped down to mineral soil. Nothing flammable, such as fallen trees or hanging branches, can be left across it.

The chief danger from a ground fire is that it will 6 become a "crown fire," that is, get into the branches or "crowns" of trees especially where the trees are close together and the branches interlace. So a crew has to be careful that a ground fire doesn't burn into a jack-pine thicket where the branches are close to the ground and can be set afire by low flames. But there is still a very different way for an ordinary-looking fire to explode. A fire doesn't always need flames to advance. A fire may seem under control, burning harmlessly under tall trees with branches too high to be touched by ground flames, but the fire is burning with such intensity that most of the oxygen has been burned out of the air near it, which is heated above the point of ignition. If the wind suddenly changes and fresh air is blown in loaded with oxygen, then the three elements necessary for a fire are suddenly present in the lower branches—flammable material, temperature above the point of ignition, and oxygen. An old-timer knows that, when a ground fire explodes into a crown fire with nothing he can see to cause it, he has not witnessed spontaneous combustion but the outer appearance of the invisible pressure of a "fire triangle" suddenly in proper proportions for an explosion.

The crown fire is the one that sounds like a train 7 coming too fast around a curve and may get so high-keyed the crew cannot understand what their foreman is trying to do to save them. Sometimes, when the timber thins out, it sounds as if the train were clicking across a bridge, sometimes it hits an open clearing and becomes hushed as if going through a tunnel, but when the burning cones swirl through the air and fall on the other side of the clearing, starting spot fires there, the new fire sounds as if it were the train coming out of the tunnel, belching black unburned smoke. The unburned smoke boils up until it reaches oxygen, then bursts into gigantic flames on top of its cloud of smoke in the sky. The new firefighter, seeing black smoke rise from the ground and then at the top of the sky turn into flames, thinks that natural law has been reversed. The flames should come first and the smoke from them. The new firefighter doesn't know how his fire got way up there. He is frightened and should be.

A fire-line, unless a river or a wide right-of-way on 8 a trail is being used as a line, is not much good when a crown fire is off and running. It usually takes a "backfire" to stop a big crown fire, and the conditions are seldom right for the foreman to start one. He has to build piles of fast-burning twigs, shavings, or dried bunch grass in front of the main fire and, before starting his backfire, must wait until the wind blows back toward the main fire, and often it never does. When you fool with a backfire, you are really fooling with fire—

you are counting on the wind to continue to blow your backfire toward the main fire. If the wind changes again and blows toward you, your backfire may only have given the main fire a fatal jump on you.

It's perhaps even more unpredictable if there isn't ⁹ much of a wind to begin with, because a big crown fire can make its own wind. The hot, lighter air rises, the cold, heavier air rushes down to replace it in what is called a "convection effect," and soon a great "fire whirl" is started and fills the air with burning cones and branches which drop in advance of the main fire like the Fourth of July and start spot fires. The separate spot fires soon burn together, and life is trapped between the main fire coming from behind and the new line of fire now burning back toward it.

Then something terrible can happen. The space ¹⁰ between the converged spot fires as they burn close to the main fire can become hotter than the point of ignition. If the convection effect or a change in the wind blows fresh oxygen between the two fires, suddenly replenishing the burned-out air, there can be a "blowup," although a blowup can be caused in still other ways. Not many have seen a blowup, even fewer have seen one and lived, and fewer still have tried afterwards to recover and record out of their scared memories exactly what happened. Later on in Mann Gulch we shall try to recreate a blowup seen by almost no one who lived to record it, and it might help as preparation if we turn briefly to the great pioneer in the science of fire behavior Harry T. Gisborne who was one of the first to observe and describe a blowup accurately.

In 1929 Gisborne was on what was up to then ¹¹ Montana's largest man-caused fire, the ninety-thousand-acre Half Moon fire in Glacier National Park (640 acres being a section or a square mile). As he says, measured "runs" show that even a big crown fire advances not much faster than a half-mile to a mile an hour. The blowup that Gisborne witnessed demolished over two square miles in possibly two minutes, although probably in a minute flat.

Returning two days later, he found the perfectly [12] balanced body of a young grouse, neck and head "still alertly erect in fear and wonder," the beak, feathers, and feet seared away. Within a few yards was a squirrel, stretched out at full length. "The burned-off stubs of his little hands were reaching out as far ahead as possible, the back legs were extended to the full in one final, hopeless push, trying, like any human, to crawl just one painful inch further to escape this unnecessary death."

Although young men died like squirrels in Mann [13] Gulch, the Mann Gulch fire should not end there, smoke drifting away and leaving terror without consolation of explanation, and controversy without lasting settlement. Probably most catastrophes end this way without an ending, the dead not even knowing how they died but "still alertly erect in fear and wonder," those who loved them forever questioning "this unnecessary death," and the rest of us tiring of this inconsolable catastrophe and turning to the next one. This is a catastrophe that we hope will not end where it began; it might go on and become a story. It will not have to be made up—that is all-important to us—but we do have to know in what odd places to look for missing parts of a story about a wildfire and of course have to know a story and a wildfire when we see one. So this story is a test of its own belief—that in this cockeyed world there are shapes and designs, if only we have some curiosity, training, and compassion and take care not to lie or be senti- mental. It would be a start to a story if this catastrophe were found to have circled around out there somewhere until it could return to itself with explanations of its own mysteries and with the grief it left behind, not removed, because grief has its own place at or near the end of things, but altered somewhat by the addition of some- thing like wonder—wonder, for example, because now we can say that the fire whirl which destroyed was caused by three winds on a river. If we could say something like this and be speaking both accurately and somewhat like Shelley when he spoke of clouds and winds, then what we would be talking about would start to change from catastrophe without a filled-in story to what could be called the story of a tragedy, but tragedy would be only a part of it, as it is of life.

Comment

In his introductory chapter, Maclean defines two main kinds of forest fire, giving most attention to the catastrophic blowup that led to the death of the thirteen firefighters at Mann Gulch. Later in the book he describes a blowup as "a dust kitten that has become a raging monster, but its basic mechanism is that of a swirl of dust that seemingly comes from nowhere and may pick up a loose newspaper and give it a toss." One theory is that a blowup originates as a thunderhead that creates a violent wind through a circular spinning. Another theory is that a wind strikes and shears off a rocky promontory or other obstacle and then begins to spin. "Any fire caught in these circles will throw off sparks and even burning branches which, if the conditions are right, will start spot fires, and these, when the conditions continue to be favorable, will swell into fire swirls . . . ." In describing the Mann Gulch fire, Maclean shows that the conditions present favored this second theory.

Questions for Study and Discussion

1. On what basis does Maclean divide the two main kinds of forest fire? Which kind of fire does he discuss in detail?
2. What are the first steps in controlling a ground fire? What elements are needed to produce a crown fire? What precautions must be taken to prevent a crown fire from occurring?
3. What images and comparisons does Maclean present to convey the force of the crown fire?
4. What are the risks of using a backfire to control a crown fire? What is the greatest risk?

5.   What is Maclean's purpose in telling the story? Why is it
     necessary to present all the facts?

Suggestions for Writing

1.   Maclean provides enough detail to understand the hazards of
     controlling ground fires. Write an account of how to perform
     another outdoor activity that requires a number of steps, for
     example, making a campfire in a windy area. Define essential
     terms, as Maclean does, and discuss possible hazards and
     how to avoid them.
2.   Maclean states that filling in the story of a catastrophe changes
     it to "the story of a tragedy, but tragedy would be only a part
     of it, as it is of life." Explain the statement, then illustrate
     it from a catastrophe reported fully in a newspaper or
     newsmagazine.

Robert Coles

SETTLING IN

Robert Coles is professor of psychiatry and medical humanities at
Harvard University. A psychiatrist concerned with children, he has
served on various boards, commissions, and foundations devoted to
the education and welfare of children. Coles has written a series of
books on American children under the general title *Children of Crisis,*
the first of these appearing in 1967; the second and third volumes—
Migrants, Sharecroppers, Mountaineers and *The South Goes North*—
were awarded the Pulitzer Prize in 1973. With Jane Hallowell Coles,
he wrote another series under the general title *Women of Crisis.* Coles
is also the author of books on American Eskimos; children of migrant
farm workers; the moral, spiritual, and political life of children; and
the fiction and poetry of some American and English writers. The
essay reprinted here is taken from *The South Goes North,* a study of
Southern rural people living in Northern cities.

Automobiles are hardly anything new to America's   1
youth. Up the remotest hollows one can find them, often

enough broken down and abandoned. But they are used too—and in the course of my work with young Appalachian men I have often wondered what we would have talked about had there not been an automobile to mention, then discuss at some length, then go over and look at, and finally drive in. I suppose before there were cars, men talked about horses. When one first begins to spend time in Kentucky or West Virginia the roads seem thoroughly dangerous. If one is like me, possessed of and sometimes victimized by a particular vocabulary, thoughts begin to assert themselves: am I crazy or suicidal to be on these roads with these drivers, or are *they* all crazy or suicidal—or "aggressive" or "antisocial"? The roads are narrow and winding and at times tortuous beyond all others in the nation. Asphalt can without warning turn into sand or mud. And the drivers: they seem so casual and vigorous; they move along as though lanes and lanes of road were on either side of them, and no cars were in sight for miles ahead—even when only a few inches separate them from the steepest of hills, or a curve approaches around which totally unseen, a car or huge coal truck may be coming in the opposite direction. Yet throughout the years of my work in Appalachia, I have never seen an accident—which is not to say accidents don't occur, but simply to suggest that my fearfulness must have had something to do with the limitations of my own experience: as a driver I took for granted certain road conditions, consequently I was made nervous when I found them lacking.

By the same token a youth from, say, Leslie County, 2 Kentucky, can find superhighways and most especially city traffic puzzling if not terrifying. All that space and all those cars and all those traffic lights and traffic signs! So many distractions: horns blowing, stores with things in the window and pictures of wine and women! And the turnoffs, the constant intersections, the warnings which insist this highway has now become something else, or is about to join with yet another road—all of that is confusing, as are those constant reminders that one is so-and-so miles from such-and-such a town or city, not to mention from some state line. Then, there are the restaurants and gas stations: how can they all stay open? How can there be so many people eager to use such places? How can there be so many people at all?

For Larry Walker, age seventeen and a half, who is   3
originally from a creek near Thousand-Sticks, Leslie County, Kentucky, but now lives in Dayton, Ohio, those questions are not openly asked. They are very much on his mind, though; and after a beer or two they come to expression. Larry has been in Dayton for five years, but he is not *from* Dayton. His little brother and sister may have the notion at times that they are from Ohio, that Dayton is their home, that their future is to be found in a growing city, but not Larry: "I'm from Leslie County, and I'll always say that's where my home is. When I turn eighteen I'll probably go into the Army. I hurt my arm once, broke it, but I don't think they will hold that against me. They'd be fools to; I'd make a good soldier, I believe. I've always dreamed I might one day go into the service and maybe stay there for a while. If you stay in twenty years, you can retire, and you have a good pension, and then you can go back to Leslie County and there's no ache over money. We only left the county because we had to leave. My father's brother left first, my Uncle Jim. He got a job here in a factory, and he came back with all those green bills in his hand and told my father he had to come up to Ohio, too; so here we are. My mother says it's like in the stories you see on television: people go away for a while, but then they come home, and they're glad. She means they go on vacation. Like my dad says: it's a vacation having a job and money; you don't have to stand around all the time and worry if you're going to survive the winter.

"If I had my choice, I'd go into the Navy. I know   4
it's strange, because I've never seen the ocean, only a lake or two in Kentucky. But I saw a movie once about

the Navy when I was real little, maybe seven, I'd say. I've wanted ever since to join the Navy. The Navy people might decide I'm no good, being from the mountains. I'd probably get seasick. I'm going to wait to be drafted; I'll have a chance to go back to Leslie County then and take my physical. The government will pay for my travel home, I believe. The Army can tell me where they want me to go, and I'll be glad to serve my country—even if it means Vietnam. There's too many people these days who don't salute the flag the way they should. This is the greatest country in the world, and if there's going to be a great country, there has to be a great Army.

"Until we moved to Ohio I never realized how *big* ₅ the country is, and how you can go from one place to another, and it all changes. I knew we had these cities, these big cities, but like I tell my friends when we go back home and I can talk with them: seeing is believing. If I'd stayed there and seen pictures of Dayton on the television, I wouldn't know much, not compared to what I know now. I mean, you have to drive in a city to know it. You can't believe it's like it is until you try to drive from one place to another, one street to another; then you find out. The guys back home, kids I grew up with, they say a road is a road, and that's all there is to it. I tell them they don't know what they're talking about. I have my car, and I've got to keep my foot on the brake more than on the gas—that's what it means to live in the city. Living in the city for a guy like me is learning to brake the car all the time, and wearing the clutch out, and using gas like it's water that's come down the mountain and is waiting to be picked up in buckets and poured into the tank. Living in the city means you have to turn your head every other minute you're driving and keep your eye out for almost anything—when all you want to do is push that gas pedal to the floor and take off.

"I love my car. She's a beauty. She's a Chevy, the best ₆ car there is. The motor is good. The tires are good. I think there's no use driving a car if you can't have good tires. Have you ever had a flat on a city street? That's no fun. I'd rather have to fix a flat right in the middle of a curve up one of those hills; there I could hear the car coming and flag it down. Here in Dayton no one pays any attention to the next guy driving, and it is so noisy you can't hear your own voice speaking. They tell me it's even worse in Cleveland. I can get around here, though; now I can. And if my car goes bad, I can take it off the road and fix it myself. I've learned everything I can about car engines. I like new cars and I like old cars. Don't you love the old Thunderbirds? They were some car—1955 or 1956, I believe. I was only a baby then. When I was a little older and just beginning to go to school I remember a big shot, someone from Hazard, coming up to the little schoolhouse we had; and it was a Thunderbird he drove. I think they were talking about closing down the school and sending us someplace else. I think a mine company bought the hill nearby, and they were going to tear it up for coal. I recall telling my friend Carl—he was my best friend—that I hoped one day I could drive a car like that, a Thunderbird; then I'd have everything I wanted. I still don't have a Thunderbird, but now I don't think I'd buy one even if I had a huge bankroll on me. I'd buy a Mustang or a Cougar, maybe. But for a beginner like me, this old Chevy is a good car to have.

"I've taken the motor apart three times. I painted the car myself. I know how. I know how to spray the right way. If I go into the Army, I hope I can be near some of those jeeps and trucks. I wouldn't mind driving them; I hear they're something to drive all right! I'd rather work on the motors, though; that way I could learn more about the different kinds and how they all work. If I could only get a job back home working in a garage or a gas station! But it's not easy to do. I don't know anyone who owns a gas station, and if I did he'd want to use his own son, I'm sure. Jobs are scarce back home. That's why we drove here, and that's why my car is going to spend most of its life in Ohio. The poor car will suffer plenty on that account, but that's just how it works out. I'll be driving—and stopping and starting and stopping and starting—and I can hear the motor saying: stop it, and get me out of here, fast. So, I just talk back to it. I say: motor, take it easy and just keep going, because there's not a thing in the world you or I can do anyway, except keep going. Then I baby her a bit; I go easy on the brakes and try not to shift more times than I have to—and the old motor seems happier.

"I get nervous when I'm in a crowd of cars; that's 8 when I guess I keep shifting the gears back and forth, and it's not good to do. But how are you supposed to live with all those other cars? I never knew there were so many real, live, honest-to-goodness people in America until we came up here. To this day I can hardly believe it. In school they taught us that it was New York City that was most crowded, and next Chicago. But I asked the teacher if it could get much more crowded than Dayton, Ohio, when the factories were letting out, and she said no, she was sure it couldn't, because there are hundreds and hundreds of cars all over the road, and they're coming in and turning off and switching from one lane to the other, and the horns are going, and you get the meanest looks, and all you're trying to do is mind your own business and not get yourself in a giant of a wreck.

"I've had two accidents. If I'd have been driving only 9 in Kentucky I'm sure I wouldn't have any accidents to my name. They weren't big accidents, just small ones, a fender each time. I fixed them myself, did the straightening and sanding and painting. I knew how to do that from watching my dad. He learned as a boy himself. He'd hit the car into a tree going up or down the creek sometimes. Mostly he's a good driver, though. He never had an accident in Leslie County, but he's had one up here, and that makes three in the family—two for me and one for him. It's different, driving in Kentucky. There aren't all the other cars. There aren't a lot of signs every mile or so, confusing you, always confusing you. They'll drive me to wearing glasses, those signs will, I do believe. And I don't mean to say anything against the people up here, but I think it's friendlier back in Leslie County, and it comes out on the road, because at home people will be more helpful to each other.

"I'll drive out away from Dayton sometimes. I'm not   10 going anyplace special. I'm not going to see someone. I just want to give my Chevy a rest from the city. I want to give her a good time. I want to take her on a road and let her roll along, and not stop and start. I don't want to have to clutch her and shift her and brake her and idle her and get her so tired and hot she's ready to explode or go dead on me. Out in the country I can bring her up to sixty or seventy pretty fast. She holds the road good. She's no new racing car. She's no big new car. She's light and six years old. But she's got pep in her, a lot of life in her. I hope I'll be like her when I'm that old. A car is like a dog, you know. Each year is six or seven. I figure my car is getting on to forty-five, and that's old.

"My dad says it is not old, forty-five, but to me that's   11 a long way off. I can't picture what it's like to be twenty-five, never mind forty or forty-five. You must begin to feel real tired. I get tired myself. I'll be in the stockroom, handling all those crates, from eight in the morning to five in the afternoon. When I punch my card, and it says five minutes after five, I ask myself where the day has gone to, and my muscles answer that they can tell me, they surely can. Then I come home and have my supper, and I go and drive around. I rest that way. I'm sitting in my car, and I have a good, soft blanket on the seat, and that rests my back. I have some friends I take for a ride—a few of the guys I know up here. And I have two girls I take out. I switch to one, then I switch to the other; they're both from Ohio, born here, and I don't know if I want to get serious with a girl who isn't from Kentucky. I don't have to marry a girl from Leslie County, but Kentucky is my home state, and I want to be going back there someday, so I don't see why I should get myself married to a girl who has other ideas in her head, you know. I've heard them talk, the girls from around here. A lot of them are spoiled. They want everything. They *expect* everything.

"I went to school until last year, until I was sixteen. 12 I didn't graduate from high school, but I went there, and you get taught a lot. My friends back home, a lot of them never bothered going beyond sixth or seventh grade. They said: what's the reason to? I can see how they think that way. I wish I'd gone and finished high school. It's just that I had this chance for a job, and I couldn't turn a good job down. The job means money for all of us, and I save some for a new car. In school that's all the girls wanted, a guy with a new car; they didn't care much what the guy himself was like. I always thought it showed something about the girls, the way they looked at you for your car and not yourself. I don't believe a girl in Leslie County would be like that, though my mother and dad say they would, because it's only natural. I guess a girl is going to like a car, just like a toy, and that's why they ask you right away: what are you driving?

"They want to know your *plans,* the girls do. I tell 13 them I don't have any. I tell them I may one day get into my car and drive and drive and fill the tank and empty it, until the road ends, and I'm somewhere, but I don't know where. Then, wherever it is I stop, I'll settle down. I'll get settled in, settled into a house, and there'll be a garage for my Chevy, and another garage in case I decide to get a second car, and I'll work in a job—I don't know what kind. The girl will be waiting for me to mention her. They don't know how much they tell about what's on their mind by the way they look. I try to keep myself from laughing, and I keep talking—but I never mention getting married. They always ask me why I may get myself a second car, and I tell them it's nice to give one car a rest and use the other, and then switch back again. You can get attached to a car. You have driven it so long and worked on it all that time, so it's yours, and you don't want to lose what's yours. The nice thing about living in Dayton is you stand a chance of making money, all the money you need. Then you can treat your car right!"

He thinks about it more than he talks about it, the money Dayton, Ohio, permits him to make, the money he cannot make in Leslie County, Kentucky. With each year he is more and more a city dweller, an owner of property, a worker—hence, less likely to return for very long to his home in the mountains, unless things should drastically change there, which is highly unlikely. He is no longer a child, yet not quite a grown-up. Almost half his childhood has been spent in Ohio, but with each month the balance changes, and he feels increasingly "settled in." He often uses that term "settled in," uses it as he did just above, in connection with what I suppose can be called a daydream or a fantasy—or an utterly exact way of describing what is on his mind and what he at least presently intends to do. He cannot really go back home, he knows that, yet he is not very happy living in even a medium-sized city like Dayton. He dreams of the West, the open and endless West, perhaps in the way his ancestors dreamed of what stretched ahead as they left the eastern seaboard. But he may actually spend the rest of his life in Ohio.

As one talks with him it becomes quite apparent that he finds a life without automobiles inconceivable, and a life without a decent home and a garage and suitable clothes and enough food also impossible to contemplate. He very much enjoys buying himself a sporty new jacket, unworn by someone else, not handed down to him to be used for a while and then in turn handed over to a brother or a cousin. And he likes to do other things that in sum reassure him how well he is coming along, how able he is to take care of himself, put away a little cash, and feel like what he calls "a going business." His father always had wished he could raise the money to have just that, a gas station or a garage, "a going business," he also puts it when he reminisces. The son now has those same dreams, but of course knows that if his business is going to grow, or even survive, Dayton will have to be the address and not some very small town in Leslie County.

So, step by step, innocently but decisively, the young man thinks things and dreams things and says things and decides things that commit him more and more to the life of a northern city, or maybe a far western one— and commit him, perhaps, to a girl who does not come from home, from the mountain country of eastern Kentucky. He does not say out and out what I have just written. How many of us at seventeen (maybe at any age) want to say exactly what we will be doing, come five or ten years? But we do at all times have certain assumptions, silent but influential, and during his five or so years in the city Larry Walker has become a different youth than he would be had he not been brought to Ohio as a child by his parents. He especially notices those various differences when he goes back home on a visit, and when he returns to Dayton he is most likely to talk about such matters. He is most likely to observe what he does in the day, and contrast all of his activities with those of his friends he knew as a small child. He is most likely to notice the way he dresses and the way others who live near Thousand-Sticks, Kentucky, dress. And yes, he is most likely to look at those girls he once knew and had crushes on and fought with and felt close to, and then think of the girls he met when he went to school in Dayton, three or four of whom he has courted in an offhand fashion, then forsaken, then gone back to, then again withdrawn from.

What distinguishes those girls from the girls in   17
Kentucky, what distinguishes him from the boys in
Kentucky, is something he finds hard to find words for,
yet very much wants to clarify in his mind—hence the
effort of language: "It's my home, my folks' home, Leslie
County is. When I go back there I feel like I'm back
where I belong. I can sit back and enjoy myself with the
best people the Lord ever made. But after a few days
I don't mind it too much if I have to leave. I begin to
hear myself saying: it's near time to go, Larry, it's near
time. There will even be a time when I start having a
talk with myself. I say I'm ready to leave. Then I say
why on earth are you actually looking forward to going,
when you know full well how you'll soon be complaining about Dayton?

"I guess that the more you live in a place, the more   18
it grows on you. I don't mean to say I like living here
in the city rather than up in the hills, but a man has to
earn a living, like my dad says. And if I'm going to get
married and have kids, I can't see being so down and
out, the way a lot of people in Kentucky are. I don't
want my son to see me just sitting on a porch and
carving wood and maybe picking on my guitar. My dad
said he'd never have stayed alive, if he had kept on
spending his days like that. He came up here, instead,
and he was lucky to get a job for himself and hold on
to it, and I've been lucky to get a job for myself and
hold on to it—and that's why I don't think either of us
can go back to Leslie County for more than a few days.
There's no work, compared to the work you get here.

"But I do admit work isn't the only thing good up   19
here. I talk a lot about my job, because I'm grateful to
have it, and the money is good; it's sweet, real sweet,
that money. I like Dayton, though. There are the movies,
all of them; I've never seen the number of movie houses
we have here in all of Kentucky I've been through, not
just Leslie County. There are restaurants, good ones.
You can live it up here. You can take a girl out on the

town. You can have a good supper, any kind you want, then go to a movie, almost any kind you want. You can go bowling and you can go play pool and you can hear a good singer in a club and have a few drinks. It's not bad living in a city. There's a lot you miss, but there's a lot you have, too. I guess it's a matter of what your philosophy is, and where you can get the money.

"I'm not sure I could bring a girl up here from 20 Kentucky, though. It might be real hard on someone to live here—a person who hasn't grown into the place, like I have. I think the kids I grew up with, they'd have a hard time coming up here now. The reason I don't mind a lot of things, and like living here, at times, anyway, is that I was brought up here when I was much younger. I wasn't a baby. I was over twelve. I was growing fast. I was outgrowing everything, I can recall my mother saying. But I was still a kid, and I wasn't set in my ways. I'm getting set now; my dad says so, and he's right. I might want to get married soon, except that I may go into the service in a few months. Sometimes I think I'd be smarter to come back to Dayton after two years in the Army, rather than make a career of it, go regular. I'll have to wait and see.

"If I meet a real nice, pretty girl from here in Dayton, 21 I might just marry her, if she'd have me. I once asked my favorite girl in Leslie County, Sylvia is her name, if she'd think of coming back with me, just for a week or so. I told her she could stay with us, and she knows my folks. She's distant kin to us, I believe. No, she said; she didn't want to leave the county. I asked her why. She said she didn't have anything against me or my folks, no sir; she'd love to stay with us, she said, and for longer than a week, she said. But to go all the way up to Dayton, out of the county and out of the state, that was too much for her, she said. She gave me a long look, right into my eyes, and I could see she really wanted me to propose marriage to her then and there, but I believe she knew, like I did, that I had to go back up North, and there wasn't any two ways about it. I said to her: Sylvia, just come and give it a try; come and travel through Kentucky and cross the river, the Ohio River, and look at Cincinnati, and then go up into the state of Ohio and get to know Dayton a little. But she kept on shaking her head. She didn't answer me. She just turned her head to the left and to the right, and I knew what she was telling me. Maybe the reason she couldn't speak her thoughts out loud was that she really did want to go with me, and she couldn't bear hearing herself say she wouldn't.

"I came home and told my folks what I'd said to 22
Sylvia and what her answer had been. I never mentioned the word *marriage*, or anything like that, but my mother said she thought that since we all are settling in, me included, and we're not going to leave Dayton for a long time, then I might have better luck if I chose a girl from Dayton, provided she's a good girl, for my wife than someone like Sylvia from back home. I was mad as I've ever been. I told my mother she was talking out of her head, because I wasn't thinking of getting married now, and when I did think of marriage, that would be the time I would go home to Kentucky and by God I'd stay there until I found a wife, and if my wife wanted to stay there and never leave, I'd stay that long myself and be glad to do it. Then my mother told me to cool myself down, and she said the way I was talking, she was sure I wasn't going to get married in a long, long time, not if I meant every word I'd said to her. Well, I had to smile then. I saw what she meant."

He not only saw what his mother meant; he knew 23
it in his bones, her message. He is glad in so many ways to be in Dayton, bothersome as its traffic is, hard as his car finds the going, crowded and anonymous and noisy as the city, any city, can always be. He is glad that he is not living in a cabin up a hollow or creek. He is glad he does not live in a small town whose "unemployment problem" is severe and chronic and to a youth like him

discouraging beyond the power of words to convey. Still, he does straddle two worlds, does go back and forth, feel divided loyalties, dream of one place while he lives in another. At seventeen nostalgia can be as powerful and summoning as at any other age, but at seventeen the meaning of a job and money is no less influential. What an observer like me has to watch very closely is the temptation to take a young man like Larry Walker too seriously *at any one moment in his life*. One day he can sound utterly convinced that he will soon, very soon, be a mountaineer again—a real one, not a distant, would-be one. The next time we talk, all of that seems not gone or buried or forgotten or "repressed" or denied or contradicted, but gently and tactfully put aside.

It is in such moments of "adjustment" to Dayton 24 that a youth like Larry feels most alert, most challenged, most sure of himself—and most at loose ends. What indeed will he do and where—now that he has ("sort of") decided that his destiny is to be found in Ohio's industrial cities, or perhaps in Illinois, or (who knows?) California, to which the Army might one day order him? And will he, therefore, slowly lose contact with Leslie County? Will he less and less think of those hills and valleys, those waterfalls and high trees and soaring birds, those clever animals and those dumb animals, those innocent but ever so swift and elusive fish? Will his car lose forever the feel of a narrow mountain road, with the sharp rises and the sudden falls, with the exciting twists and turns and curves? Will traveling by car become a bore, a nuisance, a tedious necessity? Will he one day say good-bye to that Chevy and good-bye to the notion that motors are wonderful, demanding, endlessly stimulating puzzles—objects of interest, exploration, and passion? Will he instead find his woman, his wife; find his job that lasts and lasts; find his nice, comfortable home, near others, near dozens and dozens of others? And for his two cars will he have no proud old two-door

Chevy, no Mustang or Cougar, but a station wagon and perhaps a brand new Chevy four-door sedan? At seventeen one often doesn't *ask* such questions; instead, one does things—and so Larry's actions gradually will supply the answers to those questions.

Comment

Coles might have summarized his interview with the young man from a Kentucky mountain community to give one example of the process of adjustment to Northern urban life. Coles chooses instead to let us hear Larry Walker talk about his life in Dayton, Ohio, and his much different life in Leslie County, Kentucky. Verbatim testimony helps us discover the conflict in attitudes and values that a witness like Larry is experiencing. For Coles, Larry is typical of many young Southerners who do not want to lose contact with the rural world they grew up in; Coles might therefore have stated his conflict in the abstract language of the sociologist or social psychologist. But Larry is an individual and his conflict is a personal one. Coles does not want us to forget that although people belong to classes, they are also individuals.

Questions for Study and Discussion

1. What is the personal conflict that Larry is experiencing? How does Larry express that conflict?
2. What point does Coles make through Larry about Southern-born people who live in Northern cities? Why does he title his essay "Settling In"?
3. What personal qualities emerge in Larry's account of his life? What most distinguishes him as a person?
4. Is Larry's love of his Chevy typical only of the American teenager's love of cars? Or does Coles want us to see something more than this general attitude?
5. For Coles, is Sylvia typical of young Southern women? Or does she represent one set of attitudes only?

Suggestions for Writing

1. Describe the experience of living in two different worlds—
    perhaps a small town and a large city. Then discuss an
    important change in attitude or values, or a conflict in at-
    titudes, that resulted from this experience. Use your discus-
    sion to develop a thesis.

2. Coles says the following about Larry Walker and people gen-
    erally:

    > How many of us at seventeen (maybe at any age) want to say
    > exactly what we will be doing, come five or ten years? But we
    > do at all times have certain assumptions, silent but influential,
    > and during his five or so years in the city Larry Walker has
    > become a different youth than he would be had he not been
    > brought to Ohio as a child by his parents. (paragraph 16)

    Discuss one or two assumptions that shape your own attitudes
    and life at the present time. Discuss the possible origin of
    these assumptions. In the course of your discussion, compare
    them with the assumptions of Larry or Sylvia.

William Safire

LIBERAL AND CONSERVATIVE

William Safire began his career in journalism as a reporter for the
New York Herald Tribune. A senior speechwriter for President
Richard M. Nixon from 1968 to 1972, he describes his White House
experience in *Before the Fall: An Inside View of the Pre-Watergate
White House.* A political columnist for *The New York Times* since
1973, Safire was awarded the Pulitzer Prize for Commentary in 1978.
He is also a novelist and the author of books on English words and
phrases, including *Words of Wisdom: More Good Advice* (1989) and
Coming to Terms (1991). His short essays on the words *liberal* and
conservative reprinted here are from *Safire's Political Dictionary,* first
published in 1968—a book showing that the "new, old, and
constantly changing language of politics is a lexicon of conflict and
drama, of ridicule and reproach, of pleading and persuasion." Sydney
J. Harris also discusses the meaning of *liberal* and *conservative* in his
essay on pages 82-83. Selection title by editor.

LIBERAL currently one who believes in more gov-   1
ernment action to meet individual needs; originally one
who resisted government encroachment on individual
liberties.

In the original sense the word described those of the   2
emerging middle classes in France and Great Britain
who wanted to throw off the rules the dominant aris-
tocracy had made to cement its own control.

During the 1920s the meaning changed to describe   3
those who believed a certain amount of governmental
action was necessary to protect the people's "real" freedoms as opposed to their purely legal—and not necessarily existent—freedoms.

This philosophical about-face led former New York   4
Governor Thomas Dewey to say, after using the original
definition, "Two hundred years later, the transmutation
of the word, as the alchemist would say, has become one
of the wonders of our time."

In U.S. politics the word was used by George Wash-   5
ington to indicate a person of generosity or broad-
mindedness, as he expressed distaste for those who would
deprive Catholics and Jews of their rights.

The word became part of the American vocabulary   6
in its earlier meaning during a rump convention of
Republicans dissatisfied with the presidency of Ulysses
S. Grant, at Cincinnati in 1872. German-born Carl
Schurz, who chaired the convention, used the word
often. So did the leading journalist-thinker of the rebellion, Edwin L. Godkin of *The Nation*, who began
his career in England. The short-lived party born of
the convention was called "The Liberal Republican"
party.

In its present usage, the word acquired significance   7
during the presidency of Franklin D. Roosevelt, who
defined it this way during the campaign for his first
term: "Say that civilization is a tree which, as it grows,
continually produces rot and dead wood. The radical
says: 'Cut it down.' The conservative says: 'Don't touch

it.' The liberal compromises: 'Let's prune, so that we lose neither the old trunk nor the new branches.'"

Liberalism takes criticism from both right and left, 8 leading to various terms of opprobrium. Herbert Hoover in a magazine article referred to "fuzzy-minded totalitarian liberals who believe that their creeping collectivism can be adopted without destroying personal liberty and representative government."

To its opponents, liberalism and liberals seem to call 9 out for qualifying adjectives expressing contempt. Barry Goldwater, trying to combat the popularity of President Johnson with businessmen, told a U.S. Chamber of Commerce conference, "If you think President Johnson is going to give you any better attention than you have got, you're very, very mistaken. If he's a conservative," said the senator, "I'm a screaming liberal."

Sometimes even liberals cannot avoid the temptation 10 to assault the term. Adlai Stevenson, quoting an uncertain source, once described a liberal as "one who has both feet firmly planted in the air." And columnist Heywood Broun, who came to consider himself a radical, wrote: "A liberal is a man who leaves a room when a fight begins," a definition adopted by militant Saul Alinsky.

The word has fallen on hard times. In the 1976 11 presidential primaries, Representative Morris Udall told columnist David Broder: "When a word takes on connotations you don't like, it's time to change the label." Henceforth, Udall said—though he would think of himself as a liberal—he would use the word "progressive" instead because the word "liberal" was "associated with abortion, drugs, busing and big-spending wasteful government."

Liberals are variously described as limousine, double- 12 domed, screaming, knee jerk, professional, bleeding heart.

CONSERVATIVE a defender of the status quo who, 13 when change becomes necessary in tested institutions or practices, prefers that it come slowly, and in moderation.

In modern U.S. politics, as in the past, "conservative" is a term of opprobrium to some, and veneration to others. Edmund Burke, the early defender and articulator of the conservative philosophy, argued that the only way to preserve political stability was by carefully controlling change and seeking a slow, careful integration of new forces into venerable institutions. In his *Reflections on the Revolution in France,* he wrote: "It is with infinite caution that any man ought to venture upon pulling down an edifice which has answered in any tolerable degree for ages the common purposes of society, or on building it up again without having models and patterns of approved utility before his eyes." Abraham Lincoln called it "adherence to the old and tried, against the new and untried."   14

The philosophy has had some famous detractors as well. Disraeli, who was to become a Tory Prime Minister, wrote in his sprightly novel *Coningsby:* "Conservatism discards Prescription, shrinks from Principle, disavows Progress; having rejected all respect for antiquity, it offers no redress for the present, and makes no preparation for the future." Lord Bryce was of two minds about it in *The American Commonwealth:* "This conservative spirit, jealously watchful even in small matters, sometimes prevents reforms, but it assures the people an easy mind, and a trust in their future which they feel to be not only a present satisfaction but a reservoir of strength."   15

The political origin of the word can be traced to the *Sénat Conservateur* in the 1795 French Constitution, and was used in its present English sense by British statesman, later Prime Minister, George Canning in 1820. J. Wilson Croker, in the *Quarterly Review* of January 1830, made the concrete proposal: "We have always been conscientiously attached to what is called the Tory, and which might with more propriety be called the   16

Conservative party." It was soon applied in America to the Whigs, amid some derision: *"The Pennsylvania Reporter,"* wrote the *Ohio Statesman* in 1837, "speaking of a probable change in the name of the opposition, from Whig to 'Conservative,' says the best cognomen they could adopt would be the 'Fast and Loose' party."

Today the more rigid conservative generally opposes virtually all governmental regulation of the economy. He favors local and state action over federal action, and emphasizes fiscal responsibility, most notably in the form of balanced budgets. William Allen White, the Kansas editor, described this type of conservative when he wrote of Charles Evans Hughes as "a businessman's candidate, hovering around the status quo like a sick kitten around a hot brick." 17

But there exists a less doctrinaire conservative who admits the need for government action in some fields and for steady change in many areas. Instead of fighting a rear-guard action, he seeks to achieve such change within the framework of existing institutions, occasionally changing the institutions when they show need of it. 18

Comment

Safire states in the introduction to the first edition (1968) that his dictionary records "words and phrases that have misled millions, blackened reputations, held out false hopes, oversimplified ideas to appeal to the lowest common denominator, shouted down inquiry, and replaced searching debate with stereotypes that trigger approval or hatred." His dictionary also shows "how the choice of a word or metaphor can reveal sensitivity and genius, crystallize a mood and turn it to action; some political language captures the essence of an abstraction and makes it understandable to millions." Safire shows that the words *liberal* and *conservative* have had some of these effects.

Questions for Study and Discussion

1. How do the historical and political backgrounds of *liberal* and *conservative* help you to understand their contemporary meanings?
2. What is gained by knowing the various meanings, past and present, of terms like *liberal* and *conservative?*
3. Is Safire writing to suggest how we should use these words, or is he merely describing their past and present meanings?
4. How does Safire's purpose in writing differ from Sydney J. Harris's, in his discussion of *liberal, conservative,* and *radical* (pages 82-83)?

Vocabulary Study

The *Oxford English Dictionary* (or *New English Dictionary*) and *Dictionary of American English,* and other historical dictionaries, trace the history and use of words like *liberal* and *conservative.* Unabridged dictionaries of contemporary usage like *Webster's Third New International Dictionary* and *The Random House Dictionary of the English Language,* and abridged dictionaries like *Webster's Tenth New Collegiate Dictionary* and *Webster's New World Dictionary of The English Language* give current meanings but also cite obsolete and rare uses of words. Special dictionaries and reference works like the *Dictionary of American Biography* and *Encyclopedia of American History,* as well as special studies of British and American history, give additional information and background. Examine a historical, an unabridged, and an abridged dictionary in the reference section of your library to determine the differences in the information they provide about *liberal, conservative,* or *radical.*

Suggestion for Writing

Use historical dictionaries and other sources to write a history of one of the following words. Give enough details about the word to distinguish it from similar ones, and discuss the special qualities or effects associated with it. Include information about its etymology:

1. *anarchism*
2. *appeasement*
3. *apartheid*
4. *nihilism*
5. *toryism*

Philip H. Ennis

ELVIS IN MEMPHIS

Philip H. Ennis, emeritus professor of sociology at Wesleyan University, Middleton, Connecticut, has made a study of the social and legal aspects of the arts, including conditions of employment of actors and the structure and workings of popular music industries. Ennis was part of a research project in the 1950s that investigated the influence of disk jockeys on musical taste. "In the first report," Ennis tells us in his history of rock and roll, *The Seventh Stream: The Emergence of Rocknroll in American Popular Music* (1992), "we had established what everyone in the industry already knew—that the disk jockey was 'king,' that collectively disk jockeys made the hits. The second report announced what everybody also knew as a fact—that the 'fad' was bigger than the 'king.'" The section reprinted here describes the rapid rise of Elvis Presley as a popular singer, as well as the influence of disk jockeys on rock and roll. "It is only in the external, objective story of its formation and development," Ennis states, "that its complexity and wider contexts are revealed."

The familiar story about Elvis is that this poor country   1
boy with a heart full of music and mother love came out of the South to bring together country music, rhythm and blues, and pop and to form a new thing. Rocknroll, the story continues, was its name, and it carried off the nation's teenagers in exactly the same way and for the same reasons the Pied Piper took away the children of Hamelin; that is, the greed and violence of the adults was so ferocious that the children sought out each other and Elvis to conquer their fears (of the bomb), to repair their abandonment (by the family), and to escape their oppression (by the school). This origin story is true in

the sense that all myths eschew the particularities of historical fact in order to state unchallengeably an intolerable contradictory situation that exists on the ground, and then to solve those contradictions in the air.

The facts are interesting, though, and perhaps more 2 sustaining than the myth. Other cities were very much like Memphis, and each would have its own rocknroll moment within a short span of years; but it was in Memphis that youth rebellion found its musical voicing in the merging of black, country, and pop. That city's unique constellation of contemporary musical resources and its history made it a predisposed point of confluence for the pop, country, and rhythm and blues streams.

Memphis is a major river port connecting the agri- 3 cultural delta of the Mississippi River states to the industrial urban cultures of the deep South and to the mountains of Appalachia. Its cultural life, reflecting the diversity of the great Mississippi River port cities, was concentrated in its colorful, if shabby, downtown sprawl. Radiating out of Beale Street was every show business technology and organization that could nurture the city's entertainment richness. Its theaters, saloons, and nightclubs presented a full and continuing parade of local and national black entertainment.[1] The city was also part of the more egalitarian but invisible "League of Rhythm and Blues Cities," with the new station WDIA (1948) bringing in black popular music in all its varieties.

Memphis had an equally rich country music tradi- 4 tion, which was carried to the smallest rural community via the radio stations. The country disk jockeys carried on the entrepreneurial traditions of organizing local shows and contributing to the major tours headed by the top stars. Country music had expanded its presence dramatically in the city after the war and in the expansion

---

[1]This discussion draws upon Margaret McKee and Fred Chisenhall's *Beale Black and Blue: Life and Music on Black America's Main Street* (Baton Rouge: Louisiana State University Press, 1981).

days following World War II. The four radio stations founded in the 1920s were augmented by five more, along with two TV stations. Memphis had a huge, multistate radio audience, but only a small number of country disk jockeys. It was a relatively small stop far from the peak of the pyramidal hierarchy of country music.

Popular music was also thoroughly covered by both 5 the network stations and the independents. The three major music markets were therefore all present and thoroughly interconnected in the city, though none of the three dominated the others. Its disk jockeys were similar to those in all the other urban centers but with far less emphasis on the high-pressure, hit-making procedures. The city was located, in short, at just the right place to bring together the reservoirs of all three musics. It had a rich, unharvested pool of artists and responsive audiences in a low-pressure atmosphere. The scene invited experiments across those boundary zones protecting each of the musics from the overbearing presence of the others.

Memphis is also a southern city. From 1909, the first 6 elected mayor, E. H. Crump, virtually ruled the city via his control of the Democratic machine of Shelby County. He was a strict segregationist, yet the black voters supported him at the polls in spite of the principled opposition of local black elites. "Boss" Crump finally fell in 1954, the year the Supreme Court struck down school segregation, though the Memphis schools did not begin to integrate until 1961.

Sam C. Phillips, Alabama born, was sidetracked from 7 an anticipated legal career by the death of his father and the coming of World War II in the year of his graduation from high school.[2] He began his radio career as a disk jockey at WLAY, Muscle Shoals, Alabama, in 1942. He

---

[2]See Colin Escott and Martin Hawkins, *Catalyst: The Sun Records Story* (London: Aquarius Books, 1975).

then moved to WHSL, Decatur, Georgia, then to WLAC, Nashville, and reached WREC, Memphis, in 1946, where he remained as record spinner and talent agent. By 1950 he had opened the Memphis Recording Service and secured enough capital to begin Sun Records on the model of hundreds of other small enterprises living at the edges of the rapidly growing music scene in the South.

In spite of a lack of local expertise and enterprise in 8 recording, Phillips saw that he had a good purchase on a growing market. In the radio environment of that time, the race issue was at maximum alert. The struggles over how the hit-making disk jockey used his crucial exposure and exploitation machinery often had a racial dimension that sometimes reached the surface. A self-imposed censorship was a common device. In the words of a disk jockey in Louisville, Kentucky (about four hundred miles northeast of Memphis but not a mile beyond its thinking), who was replying to a question about why he didn't play rhythm and blues records,

> Not because the person is colored, but it's the rhythm and tone of the things. It's not melodic. Our audience doesn't like this sort of thing. They would be ashamed if they thought that their friends knew they were listening to it. The quality of the music is poor, it really is. It brings out the . . . well . . . the savage in people.[3]

Phillips did not hold to such racial views. In fact, he 9 was looking for exactly that kind of music. He became involved with one of the more successful incubations of a music that could be acceptably simple and savage. He got his appetite whetted by recording Jackie Brenston's "Rocket 88," sending it to Chess in Chicago. He saw it top the R&B charts, not realizing that he had participated in making what some have called the first rocknroll record. He continued recording sides by local black and

---

[3]William N. McPhee, Philip H. Ennis, and Rolf Meyersohn, *The Disk Jockey: A Study of the Emergence of a New Occupation and Its Influence on Popular Music on America*, Bureau of Applied Social Research, Columbia University, July, 1953.

white artists, including B. B. King and Rufus Thomas, which he sold or leased to independents in the North. In 1954, *Billboard* reviewed his recording of Harmonica Frank's "Rockin Chair Daddy" as "an unusual mixture of r&b and country music. The singer is a country artist, instrumentation is the type used for down-home blues wax."[4] This success intensified Phillips' search of the clubs and radio stations in the Memphis region for white performers working the small roadhouses and cocktail lounges. There was a surprisingly diverse range of styles in the regional "country boogie," basically soloists and small combos playing a danceable blues rhythm out of a stripped-down country instrumentation.

It was in this dense atmosphere that Presley appeared 10 at Phillips' studio to cut a birthday record for his mother, two songs of his own choosing.[5] Some eight months later, in the summer of 1954, Phillips thought Elvis might be right for a ballad he had acquired. Although the recording session was unsuccessful, Phillips later thought that mixing minimal instrumentation behind Presley on vocals might be the right combination for merging the country and the rhythm and blues sounds for the pop market. After some six months rehearsal with Elvis and two local musicians familiar with the studio and the local club scene—Scotty Moore on guitar and Bill Black on bass—Phillips thought he had found his man.

Presley was the singer he had talked about so often. 11 Mississippi born, poor, religiously soaked, strictly raised, Beale Street smart, musically and theatrically adept though a complete amateur, young, and strikingly handsome in the face, Elvis was indeed the answer.

---

[4]*Billboard,* 17 July 1954.

[5]One was "My Happiness," a 1933 tune that had reached the pop and the country charts in 1948 in versions by Ella Fitzgerald, the Pied Pipers, Slim Whitman, and Jan and Sondra Steele. The other was an equally mawkish ballad "That's When Your Heartaches Begin," a 1940 tune released in 1952 but never making the national charts.

The selection of the tunes for the first record, dic- 12
tated certainly by Phillips, was as obvious as it was
effective: one-half black, one-half country, both pop.[6]
Memphis-based blues singer Arthur "Big Boy" Crudup's
"That's All Right Mama" was the "A" side. The tune
had been recorded by its writer for Victor's Bluebird
label in 1946 and had achieved only local jukebox play.
The "B" side was Bill Monroe's 1947 "Blue Moon of
Kentucky."

The two sides are both remarkable. The clean and 13
austere instrumentation of Scotty Moore's electric guitar
and Bill Black's string bass was unquestionably a country sound. Elvis' vocal style—tentative, self-consciously
experimenting, but exuberant—was, however, the main
part of the appeal. The manner on "That's All Right"
was softer and more balladlike compared to the more
exaggerated blues roughness of the "Blue Moon of
Kentucky" side. The deliberate stylistic reversal—the
black, up-tempo song done in an almost dreamy country
feeling and the slow country anthem unceremoniously
given a brusque treatment—is somehow acceptable
because of the youthful, honest, but playful voice. It was
in that reversal that Phillips saw the road to pop, and
he said so at that first session. All the garbled versions
of the tape contain Phillips' line, "That's different. That's
a pop song now." It should be clear that these first two
sides as well as the rest of the records Elvis made for
Sun were in the current reservoir of R&B and country
and western. They were *not* part of the folk stream. It
would be some years before Bill Monroe and Arthur
Crudup would be lionized by the museum wing of the
folk stream and the major record companies would
reissue their old records, RCA labeling Crudup the
"Father of Rock and Roll."[7]

---

[6]Robert Palmer, *A Tale of Two Cities: Memphis Rock and New Orleans Roll*
(Brooklyn: Brooklyn College of the City University of New York, 1979), p. 25.
[7]*Rolling Stone*, 9 December 1971, p. 10.

Presley's first record is clearly another candidate for 14
the first rocknroll record. Arguably, it was the first *re-gional hit* to launch a national star on the basis of his
performance. The "That's All Right" side brought an
R&B sound in a country voicing to pop, enlarging
rocknroll's young reservoir with a white as well as a
black component. The "Blue Moon of Kentucky" side
was a shrewd choice to record at that time. Nashville
was still assembling, not at all the "capital" of country
music it would become, and Bill Monroe's place as an
established easterner and hillbilly stalwart was an im-portant component for the Phillips strategy. Elvis, as a
deep southerner, did the song with such surprising bold-ness that his reach into white mountain music carried.
Presley's country music credentials, which he passed on
to his descendants a full decade later, were validated in
that record.

The question was where to expose these two sides. 15
Sam Phillips went to disk jockey Dewey Phillips (no
relation) who aired them to an immediate deluge. The
telephone board lit up; the radio audience wanted to
hear the record again and again, and they wanted to
know where they could buy it. They also wanted to
know something about the singer. Dewey Phillips, in the
radio interview that evening, quickly and diplomatically
identified Presley as white by answering a question about
what high school he had attended. "Humes High" was
more than a sufficient answer. L. C. Humes High School
was one of the all-white schools in the city. The tele-phone callers may have even recognized Elvis as the
acne-ridden, shy kid who wore the outrageous clothes
seen in Beale Street shop windows. He was certainly not
part of the school's leading crowd.

The first record sold well in the Memphis area. 16
Billboard put its "Review Spotlight" on Presley as "a
potent new chanter who can sock over a tune for either
the country or the r & b markets."[8] This success was

---

[8]*Billboard,* 7 August 1954, p. 39.

not enough. It was a blind alley, in fact, for Elvis to ignite the mixed white and black teenage radio audience with only the rhythm and blues side. He had to reach the country audience. This meant live appearances on the country circuit. Sam Phillips got Elvis onto Webb Pierce's tour, in the local clubs, and on the Opry itself within a few months. The reception was mixed. The name "Elvis Presley" was off-beat; so was the act. The conservative Opry audience was cool; Elvis was crushed. Phillips did not give up, nor did Elvis' first manager, Bob Neal, one of Memphis' senior country and western disk jockeys.

Neal proceeded to book him both locally and in the [17] "high minors" of the country circuit. The pop thrust was accentuated by naming Elvis' act (now formally including Scotty Moore and Bill Black) the Blue Moon Boys.[9] Following the traditional practice of placing an ad when a record is reviewed, the review and display ad appeared on the same page in *Billboard*. Note the now-common designation of the emerging style as "folk blues." This label served the obvious tactic of tying together Elvis' first record, "Blue Moon of Kentucky," to the authentic and unassailable country artist Bill Monroe. Elvis was on his way. The country music establishment designated Elvis as the "Most Promising Country Music Singer" of 1955. The trade press announced that the revival of country music was at hand, that a new day had arrived. Elvis' releases on Sun were highlighted in "Pick of the Week" reviews.

At the same time, an articulate minority of the country [18] music establishment was in opposition. It was clear to some that Sam Phillips was trying to use Elvis' country music style as a passport to the pop stream, while carrying a full case of rhythm and blues. They blew the whistle. The clearest statement appeared in, of all places, a front-page *Down Beat* article by a well-known country disk

---

[9]*Billboard*, 29 January 1955, p. 51.

jockey. Elvis, the major culprit, though unnamed, is not the only problem mentioned. Rhythm and blues was leaking into country, breaching the deepest line of cleavage in all the American popular musics. This voice did not come just from one petulant country disk jockey. The situation was recognized by the entire industry. Everyone saw the generational failure of country music to produce new talent, but the experts were divided on how their ranks were to be replenished.

Presley stayed with Sam Phillips for about a year. [19] When his contract expired, the mysterious Colonel Tom Parker took over. The sale of this poor Mississippi boy was about to commence. The Colonel saw in the nineteen-year-old not only what Sam Phillips and Bob Neal had seen, but he could also read the charts. By late spring of 1955, Elvis' latest Sun side, "Baby Let's Play House" (a cover of Arthur Gunter's R&B hit), was, for the first time, climbing the national country charts (but never making the pop charts). By fall, his "Mystery Train," a cover of Junior Parker's R&B hit of 1953 for Sun Records, and its flip side, "I Forgot to Remember to Forget," had topped the country charts.

Colonel Parker's vision was far grander than that of [20] either Phillips or Bob Neal; he had been closer to the pinnacle of the country music structure as Eddy Arnold's former manager and, by 1954, head of the Hank Snow Jamboree Attractions. The exact route that took Presley from Sun Records to Victor for $25,000 and the publishing rights from Hi Lo Music (Sun's publishing arm) to Hill and Range for $15,000 is well known, involving such familiar characters as Arnold Shaw and Bill Randle. Shaw, after hearing Elvis' records, met with Colonel Parker and then with Sam Phillips. On the basis of what the Colonel told him, that "Presley had not really made his mark on wax, that he was *dynamite* in personal appearances, affecting Southern girls, white and black—as Sinatra once had," he called Bill Randle. Randle, whose audience response was immediate and positive, arranged to have Elvis booked onto the Dorsey Brothers' "Stage Show."[10]

The personal appearances on television, particularly on the Ed Sullivan show, handed Elvis the nation. In spite of the blast of parental disapproval, more likely because of it, Elvis could do no wrong. He began the long march of some 150 records on the pop charts, and then it was off to the movies. Ever since a quarter of Tin Pan Alley had moved to California when the talkies appeared in 1928, there was an unflagging appetite for singers and bands in motion pictures. That appetite was fully fed by the ambitions of singers who wanted nothing more than the worldwide glamour accorded a movie star.

Comment

Ennis states that the "origin story," like all myths, simplifies the facts of history to resolve contradictions, solving them "in the air" rather than "on the ground," in a factual account. In his account of Elvis Presley's origin as a singer, Ennis states facts that correct a popular myth that ignores contradictory elements that merged in his career. He discusses those responsible for Presley's success, the moment in Southern history when he emerged as a singer, and the diverse musical world in which rock and roll was born.

Questions for Study and Discussion

1. What is the popular myth that Ennis is correcting in his account of Elvis Presley's origin as a singer?
2. What diverse musical styles joined to create the rock and roll that Presley popularized? In what cultures did these styles originate, and how diverse were these cultures?

---

[10]Arnold Shaw, *Honkers and Shouters* (New York; Collier Books, 1978), pp. 496-500; *Billboard*, 3 December 1955, p. 1.

3. What attributes made Presley the singer that Sam Phillips was looking for? What point is Ennis making in discussing Phillips?
4. What in Southern cultural history and in Memphis made Presley's success possible?
5. Did Presley gain national fame for the same reasons that he first gained success in the South?

Vocabulary Study

Give the meaning of the following in the paragraph cited:
1. *eschew, particularities* (paragraph 1)
2. *constellation, predisposed, confluence* (paragraph 2)
3. *nurture, egalitarian* (paragraph 3)
4. *entrepreneurial, augmented, pyramidal hierarchy* (paragraph 4)
5. *exploitation* (paragraph 8)
6. *incubations, whetted* (paragraph 9)
7. *adept* (paragraph 11)
8. *brusque* (paragraph 13)
9. *validated* (paragraph 14)
10. *articulate, cleavage, petulant* (paragraph 18)

Suggestion for Writing

Often an important scientific discovery or medical procedure is credited to a single person. Using the resources of your college library, investigate one of the following, or another of your choosing, to find out if it was the discovery of a single person, working alone. Write a report on your findings, citing the books, articles, and other sources you consult.
1. the discovery and medical use of insulin or penicillin
2. the development of a rabies or a polio vaccine
3. the discovery and medical use of X-rays
4. the description of the DNA molecule or the AIDS virus
5. the discovery of the planet Uranus or Pluto

Robert J. Samuelson

COMPUTER COMMUNITIES

In his column on economics for *Newsweek,* Robert J. Samuelson
writes frequently about federal economic policy and its effects on the
consumer and the marketer. His column on computer communities,
published on December 16, 1986, discusses changes in marketing and
consumption that have led to a "massive paradox."

This holiday season is also the high season for cata-   1
logs. I'm sitting with 30 of them, offering everything
from teddy bears to electronic scrabble games. They all
arrived at our house in recent months. My wife tells me
we get about 100 a year. This bothered me. Were we
such lavish consumers to attract every selling organization in America? I checked it out. We're about average.
There are roughly 10 billion catalogs mailed out annually, which is more than 50 for every American over 18,
and the number has more than doubled since 1978.

Historian Daniel Boorstin's apt phrase—consump-   2
tion communities—describes people connected by what
they buy, not where they live. The modern analogue is
computer communities. We are, in part, defined by the
computer lists we're on: the lists for catalogs, magazines,
credit cards, alumni associations, unions and trade
groups. They are windows to our pocketbooks, and
almost all can be rented. Bob Castle, a major list broker,
offers 40,000 lists. His biggest has 165 million Americans by age and address, but for a client selling an
executive jet, "I once rented a list of 40 oil sheiks living
in America."

Our language overflows with marketing jargon: 3
"niches," "segments" and "clusters." We're coded according to age, income, education, reading habits and
spending patterns, even if these things are inferred from
the census tract where we live. Lists are run against each
other to produce new lists with more information.

Suitably grouped, we're fair game for catalogs, chari-
table solicitations, political appeals and advertising fli-
ers. We're peddled mutual funds, insurance policies and
vacations. In 1985, third-class—alias "junk"—mail
totaled 52 billion pieces; it's growing four times faster
than other mail.

This direct-mail boom is said to cater to working   4
women. Shopping time is scarce. Nearly 60 percent of
people who order by mail or phone are women. This
pop theory, though true, is much overrated. Computers
have been the dominant agent of change by making it
cheaper to analyze and address Americans by groups.
Direct mail's rise, for example, does not parallel the
gradual increase of working women. The explosive
growth was triggered in 1979 by cuts in bulk-mail rates,
based on computerized presorting of letters to individual postal routes. Some third-class mail rates are now
lower than in 1978.

The computers are trying to straddle a huge schism   5
in national culture. Americans exalt individuality, but
our economic success rests on a mass market that stresses
commonality. By creating huge new groups—big enough
to produce economies of scale, but small enough to seem
personal—the computers seek to skirt this conflict.
Magazines and television audiences are dissected by the
same computerized scanning to determine which are
best for cameras and which for beer. All advertisers want
the right niche, which sounds like a cozy group. The
mass market is supposed to be dead, but, of course, any
niche worth selling has hundreds of thousands, usually
millions, of customers.

This hypocrisy—marketers trying to make us feel   6
select, when we're not—offends some. Columnist Richard Cohen of the *Washington Post* recently unleashed
this splendid tirade against the direct-mail avalanche:
"Every day, I come home to open a newly arrived stack
of lies. . . . The Book-of-the-Month Club tells me, in the
manner of the Marines, that it is seeking 'a few people

in Washington,' when, of course, it will take anyone it can get. . . . I get letters in which my name [is] misspelled each and every time: 'Yes, Rojhard Cohen, the whales are in danger.'"

Well, Rojhard, it's an old story. The early mail-order 7 houses—Montgomery Ward (1872) and Sears (1888)— succeeded in part by cultivating a personal bond with their customers. Confidence was essential, notes historian Boorstin, "to induce farmers to buy goods sight unseen from a distant warehouse." Many customers wrote personal letters that were answered. "I suppose you wondered why we haven't ordered anything from you since the fall," one letter to Ward's founder said. "Well, the cow kicked my arm and broke it and besides my wife was sick, and there was the doctor bill."

The pretense of exclusivity doesn't fool most of us. 8 We tolerate or enjoy the obvious deceptions of advertising, including direct mail. For all the excesses we secretly appreciate the attention. Even throwing the stuff away unopened provides a perverse satisfaction that someone wants our business. A friend of mine peruses catalogs while pedaling an exercise bike. She is surely treated to the constant surprises of the commercial imagination. A place in Maine will send you a telephone shaped like a piano (you dial on the keyboard) for $59, and then there's the $39 Snore Stopper from California:

"A snoring sleeper can cause a loving bedmate to en- 9 dure many a sleepless night. . . . The static electrical pulse which Snore Stopper emits, each time you snore, is very light—and it goes on for only 5/100 of a second. . . . [B]ut it will stop even the heaviest sleeper from snoring."

But the result of all this computerized marketing— 10 the obsession with niche building—is a massive paradox. The point of splintering consumers into finer subdivisions is to give vent to individual differences and choices. In fact, our high-tech marketing simply fosters new, more variegated styles of conformity. What the marketers call niches and segments, you and I call friends.

People don't compare themselves with strangers. They look at their peers: people like themselves. Most of us—along with our friends—are being bombarded by the same appeals for the same specialized products.

There's a shortening of the half-lives of fads and 11 fashions. Nothing remains novel very long, because the tools of mass marketing accelerate the introduction of new products aimed at particular groups: whether Yuppies, prosperous retirees or skiing buffs. Our marketers pander to the rhetoric of individuality, but in our new computer communities, differences are still hard to detect. The more refined customer markets become, the faster the spread of new products. The ultimate irony of computerized merchandising is that it's made being a snob a more exhausting and exacting exercise than ever.

Comment

In his discussion of Americans as consumers, Samuelson depends chiefly on classification and division to develop his thesis. He first shows how advertisers put consumers into a broad class, defined by Daniel Boorstin as "consumption communities." Samuelson then divides this class in various ways, and draws a number of conclusions about consumer attitudes and marketing technology. Comparison and causal analysis also play an important part in describing this technology. Samuelson uses his analysis to say something important about advertising and marketing today.

Questions for Study and Discussion

1. Into what groups do mail advertisers divide consumers?
2. Why do advertisers seek to create "huge new groups" of consumers? Why must these groups not be too big?
3. What point is Samuelson making in his comparison of consumption communities and computer communities (paragraph 2)? Where else does he use comparison, and what point does he make through this comparison?

4. What is the "massive paradox" that results from computerized marketing? What point is Samuelson making through discussion of this paradox? What is the "ultimate irony" of computerized marketing?
5. Samuelson is writing to increase our understanding of mail advertising. Does he have another purpose in writing—for example, to encourage readers of his *Newsweek* column to change their buying habits?

Vocabulary Study

Give the dictionary meaning of the following words. Then explain how Samuelson uses the word in the paragraph:
1. *analogue* (paragraph 2)
2. *inferred* (paragraph 3)
3. *schism, dissected, niche* (paragraph 5)
4. *exclusivity, perverse* (paragraph 8)
5. *paradox* (paragraph 10)
6. *irony* (paragraph 11)

Suggestions for Writing

1. Samuelson states: "The pretense of exclusivity doesn't fool most of us. We tolerate or enjoy the obvious deceptions of advertising, including direct mail. For all the excesses, we secretly appreciate the attention." Discuss the extent to which this statement describes your attitude toward mail advertising.
2. Discuss the extent to which the advertising of a particular product—for example, automobiles—illustrates one of the following statements in paragraph 11:
   a. "There's a shortening of the half-lives of fads and fashions."
   b. "Nothing remains novel very long, because the tools of mass marketing accelerate the introduction of new products aimed at particular groups. . . ."
   c. "Our marketers pander to the rhetoric of individuality, but in our new computer communities, differences are still hard to detect."

Paul Lancaster

EXHALE! . . . INHALE! . . . EXHALE! . . .

Paul Lancaster was a reporter and feature editor for the *Wall Street Journal* for sixteen years. He is the author of *Gentleman of the Press: The Life and Times of an Early Reporter* (1992), and has written a number of articles on popular history for *American Heritage,* in which the following on exercise appeared in October 1978. The American "cult of health," H. L. Mencken wrote in 1931, led in his time to "the striated muscle fetish." The American interest in exercise, Lancaster shows, has a long and fascinating history, marked by "periodic changes" in attitude and practice.

All you joggers out there dodging garbage trucks at dawn, listen to this: "I am fully convinced that exercise is bosh. . . . Find ways to exert yourself and you find ways to harm yourself. . . . Do not stand when you can sit; or sit when you can lie down; or just lie down when you can nap. Do not run if you can walk. . . . To have a strong heart it is essential to give up all unnecessary exercise."

In a day when sixty-year-olds train for marathons, middle-aged cyclists rack up the miles on their ten-speeds, and tennis players of all shapes and sizes crowd the courts, the advice sounds strange. But it was written little more than a generation ago by Dr. Peter Steincrohn, a reputable physician. His view was shared widely at the time. For anyone beyond the flush of youth, strenuous exercise was thought to carry the risk of heart strain. Now most physicians hold the precise opposite to be true: *failure* to engage regularly in vigorous exercise is believed to increase the risk of heart disease.

This about-face is only one of the periodic changes in direction that have occurred since Americans in large numbers began to concern themselves with exercise for the sake of health. That doesn't seem to have happened until sometime toward the end of the nineteenth century.

There had always been a few, of course, who kept playing games—cricket, rounders, and, later, baseball—after school days were over. The well-to-do took up golf and tennis in the last decades of the century. Young Theodore Roosevelt, an awkward but enthusiastic tennis player, battled through ninety-one games one day in 1882.

Cycling had its devotees beginning with the introduction of the high-wheeler in the 1870's, and there were also some early advocates of rigorous physical training routines. German immigrants of the mid-1800's transplanted the Turners, athletic societies devoted to gymnastics on rings, bars, and vaulting horses. In the 1870's some colleges started formal physical education classes where students tossed medicine balls and performed drills designed to improve posture. Even in the years just before his death at the age of eighty-three in 1878, William Cullen Bryant rose early to heft dumbbells for an hour and then strode the three miles from his house in lower Manhattan to the *New York Evening Post*. There, scorning the newfangled elevator, he ran up ten flights of stairs to his office, where he sometimes stopped at the door to seize the lintel and raise and lower himself by his arms several times.

But for most people of that era the physical demands of ordinary life were quite enough, and the notion that they should seek out extra work for their muscles would have seemed bizarre. That was particularly true for the great majority of Americans who still lived in rural areas—almost 75 percent in 1870—and for whom heavy farm labor from dawn to dusk was often the rule. But it also held true for many city dwellers. They drew water, chopped wood, walked to work and church. Understandably, technological advances that saved human effort—elevators, streetcars, telephones, running water—were seen as undiluted blessings.

Attitudes toward exercise were changing as 1890 approached, however. Urbanization was steadily reducing the proportion of Americans who had to spend their days wrestling plows and pitching hay. "Americans went indoors to serve machines, stand behind counters, or sit at desks," observes one historian. When a handful of self-proclaimed "experts" on physical fitness began spreading the message that the "nineteenth-century method of living" was making the nation soft, they found a receptive audience, and their numbers proliferated. "Professors" of physical culture opened gymnasiums where businessmen paid to swing Indian clubs and "in-hale! . . . ex-hale!" to the cadence of instructors. Doctors, who were often scornful of the physical culturists muscling into what they considered their purview, offered their own regimens. Books and magazine articles poured forth promoting one new system of exercise after another and exhorting readers to shape up in tones so stirring that it is almost impossible to dip into their musty pages today without instinctively squaring the shoulders and taking a deep breath.

If a man feels he is getting soft, the most obvious 7 solution is to acquire a handsome pair of biceps, and the early exercise manuals stressed straightforward muscle building. One was entitled *How to Get Strong.* Another demanded: "Why be weakly?" The goal was more modest than the exaggerated musculature of today's body-building cultists; one set of arm exercises was designed to produce arms "which look well either in rowing or exercising costume, that is, with nothing on them, or which set off a well-cut coat to great advantage." But the authors themselves were nevertheless pretty impressive specimens who were not at all reticent about their own physical accomplishments—one, for example, invited two-hundred-pounders to don heavy boots and take a running jump onto his abdomen and the clear implication was that readers could achieve similar physiques if only they would pay attention.

The recommended exercise was demanding, often 8 calling for the use of weights and other strengthening equipment. In the nineties many bedrooms were graced by A. G. Spalding & Bros. Victor No. 5 Machine, a contraption of pulleys and weights that attached to the wall. In the same decade, J. R. Judd, a professor of physical culture with a luxuriant handlebar mustache, published *Always Strong and Happy,* a course that required a whole array of equipment manufactured by Judd, including dumbbells weighing up to forty pounds, a racklike affair called the Extensor, and his Columbia Parlor General Exercising and Rowing Machine. After punishing himself with this paraphernalia, the victim was instructed to plunge into a cold bath, which was the standard conclusion for most of the exercise programs.

The best known of the early body builders was   9
Bernarr Macfadden. In 1898, when he was a sleek-muscled, narcissistic thirty-year-old, Macfadden published a five-cent pamphlet called *Physical Culture.* It evolved into a monthly magazine with a circulation of half a million and helped make Macfadden a cult figure among health faddists. Macfadden, who in time built a publishing enterprise that also included such magazines as *True Story* and *True Romance* and a sleazy newspaper known formally as the *New York Evening Graphic* but informally as the *Pornographic,* presented a body-building scheme, using a contrivance of pulleys and cords, in a book in 1900. Sprinkled among nude or near-nude photographs of Macfadden posing on a pedestal or on a leopard skin were stern admonitions: "Clear your system of accumulated corruption from inactivity, and live! . . . If you are weak, there is absolutely no excuse for your continuing so."

Macfadden's methods worked for him. He lived to   10
the age of eighty-seven, and he celebrated his seventy-fifth birthday by standing on his head during an interview and his eighty-third by making a parachute jump into the Hudson River. But in the eyes of many, muscle building had a couple of serious disadvantages. One was that it entailed considerable effort. The other was that no matter how hard they heaved and strained, when

most men stood before a mirror—Macfadden recommended exercising there—they were never going to see
a Greek god.

So another crop of experts came to the rescue with   11
the good news that large muscles were out of date. They
were contemptuous of the muscle builders. "The ordinary gymnasium 'professor' knows no more about the
principles of bodily development than he does about
ancient Coptic," scoffed a physician named Latson in
1910. Another doctor, writing in *Harper's*, warned that
muscle building was positively dangerous to the health.
Backing came from a 1910 editorial in the *New York
Times* deploring the emphasis on "brute strength" in
physical education. "The cultivation of huge muscles
belonged to the hunting, grazing, peasant, and warrior
stages of civilization," said the *Times*.

To replace arduous muscle building, the doctors and   12
others proposed less taxing calisthenics. There were
variations in the systems; one school held, for example,
that touching the toes without bending the knees was
beneficial, while a rival camp insisted that if God had
intended man to do that, He would not have provided
knee joints. But for the most part the movements were
similar—stretch, twist, turn, bend. They were the sort
of mild exercises a lot of people dutifully performed a
few decades ago upon arising, sometimes under the
guidance of an instructor on the radio or on a record—
and, indeed, that some people still do. Such calisthenics
can ease muscular kinks, but more fundamental benefits
seem to have been ruled out by competition among the
originators of the systems to see who could come up
with the easiest program. The ideal appeared to be
exercise that required no effort, and some of the systems
came close.

Dr. Latson, the critic of the physical culture profes-   13
sors, asserted that a great advantage of his own gentle
twists and turns was that "they require practically no
effort of body or mind." In 1907 Sanford Bennett, an

elderly eccentric from San Francisco, published *Exercising in Bed*. The book is exactly what the title indicates, a manual of exercises that can be done in bed, alone, without even throwing off the covers. "I believe that muscles develop more rapidly under these comfortable conditions than in the cold, bracing air usually advocated for physical exercise," explained Bennett.

The experts also vied to see who could devise the shortest exercise routines. Bernarr Macfadden had advocated working out as much as an hour a day, but in 1905 J. P. Müller, a Dane, began promoting *My System*—"15 Minutes' Work a Day for Health's Sake"— in America. Within a few years, however, competitors offered systems even less time-consuming, and so in 1924 Müller issued a revised version of his book called *The Daily Five Minutes*. Then somebody undercut this with a sure-fire four-minute program. 14

The most popular exercises in the 1920's were Walter Camp's Daily Dozen. Camp, a robust former Yale football star and the inventor of the All-American team, said he got the inspiration for his system by watching lions stretch at the Bronx Zoo. He gave the movements in his ten-minute routine alliterative names—hands, hips, head; grind, grate, grasp; crawl, curl, crouch; wave, weave, wing. "The essential thing is to go slowly," he advised. A casual test shows that the Daily Dozen will not raise a drop of sweat on a desk-bound forty-seven-year-old writer. The exercises approximate what a moderately serious jogger might do to loosen up before starting *real* exercise. 15

Considering the modest investment of effort, the benefits claimed for such exercises were truly remarkable. Constipation and dyspepsia, which seem to have afflicted people back then more than they do now, would vanish. So would sluggish livers, following a few repetitions of the "liver squeezer," a widely prescribed exercise that involved lying on the back and drawing the knees up to the chin. This was said to wring out the liver 16 like a sponge. Preoccupation with fat was frowned on. "A prejudice against fat amounting to an abhorrence ought to be condemned," wrote a Boston physician, Samuel Delano, in 1918. But if you did want to lose weight, it was no problem provided you conscientiously practiced the deep breathing that was part of most systems. "Deep, purposeful breathing in the open air prevents the accumulation of fat, as it acts like a pair of active bellows on a furnace fire," said William J. Cromie, an instructor of physical education at the University of Pennsylvania.

Now and then a voice from the past expresses ideas 17 about exercise not too far removed from present theories. As far back as 1890, a physical culturist named Edwin Checkley came out in favor of running, although he added sadly: "When I run for a few streets on a city thoroughfare, the populace look after me as if I were a 'freak,' or as if I were making off with something not belonging to me. . . ." Perhaps that explains why another pioneer jogger, Theodore Roosevelt, sometimes did his running at night while President, going out from the White House and trotting around the Washington Monument. Among medical men, Dudley A. Sargent, who directed physical education at Harvard from 1879 to 1919, sounded much like physicians today. Sustained, vigorous exertion that stimulates the heart and lungs strengthens the vital systems, he preached.

But where those of middle age or older were con- 18 cerned, Sargent and the other exercise specialists who agreed with him generally cautioned against really strenuous workouts of the sort their theories seemed to require, such as long runs. Some of the authorities said that "gentle" running was safe, but they really meant "gentle." C. Ward Crampton of New York, one of the first physicians to sound the alarm over the mounting number of heart attacks among Americans, insisted that the focus of exercise should be to strengthen the heart and that running was well suited for this purpose. But, he said in 1924, sixty-four steps "is sufficient for anyone." That's a couple of laps around the living room.

At the time, even that would have been considered overdoing it in some circles. It was commonly believed 19 that everyone was endowed with a fixed, limited supply of "vitality" and that strenuous exercise could lead to premature exhaustion of the supply, followed by invalidism or early death. A 1931 article on exercise in *Hygeia,* a health magazine published for laymen by the American Medical Association, commented: "It seems that the more prodigiously we give of our vitality the sooner we exhaust it."

To buttress their case, exponents of this theory seized 20 on every instance of an athlete dying young. Such deaths were not rare in those days; athletes, like nonathletes, could be struck down in their prime by infectious diseases since conquered by antibiotics. But the foes of strenuous exercise claimed in such cases that the athletes had squandered their vitality, weakening their hearts and their defenses against disease. Arthur A. McGovern, the proprietor of a gym in New York, kept a scrapbook of obituaries of athletes who had died by the age of forty, presumably to show clients who might be tempted to push themselves too hard.

McGovern and most of his fellow experts just about 21 ruled out vigorous exercise of any type for anyone over forty. It went without saying that running was foolhardy, and the list of potentially perilous activities usually included bicycling, rowing, squash, handball, and tennis—even doubles. Warning of the dire fate in store for "those disciples of strenuosity," Dr. Delano of Boston offered fairly typical advice. "The heart and breathing are not to be unduly juggled," he asserted. Beware of the bicycle, which has produced "many a damaged heart and circulation." Tennis is risky because "in the volleying much *qui vive* and much holding of breath is necessary. It does the heart up easily—especially in the case of the nervous temperament." The only sport Delano wholeheartedly approved was golf. As for calisthenics, the doctor propounded his own thirty-four-movement system in *How Shall I Take Exercise and Set-Up?* Judging from the illustrations, for which the rather modestly muscled doctor himself posed somewhat sheepishly ("Let not the eye fall at once on the quantity of muscle. . . . For muscle by itself we have, as the reader must know, but scant respect"), the exercises consisted mainly of assorted grimaces.

If exercise was fraught with peril for men, it was even more so for women. Fielding Yost, who dispensed advice on exercise besides coaching football at the University of Michigan, said women should quit tennis at thirty-five. The idea of exercises to strengthen female muscles was absurd on its face. As Dr. Delano put it: "Femininity was plainly created not to have much muscle." The permissible exercises for the ladies in their middy tops and bloomers were mild in the extreme, with a trim waist and a "graceful carriage" the primary goals. An article by a woman doctor in the *Ladies' Home Journal* in 1907 reflected the tone that prevailed for decades. It recommended the exercise of touching the toes ("Austrian officers, who are noted for their tapering waists, make a special point of its use"). It also said that "healthy girls"—but apparently not adult women—could hazard stationary running in the bathroom, provided they started with no more than twenty-five steps and lay down for at least five minutes immediately after. [22]

Clearly, even healthy girls couldn't tolerate much strain. Arthur McGovern, the gym proprietor, frowned on all strenuous competitive games for girls "as the element of excitement very easily leads to exertion injurious to the feminine physique." In a 1915 issue of the *Delineator*, Dr. B. Wallace Hamilton told the harrowing tale of fifteen-year-old Emily. She went off to boarding school, where she became nervous and jumpy from playing too much basketball. Hamilton prescribed a [23] transfer to a school where the staff appreciated the frailty of young women, and a switch to golf and croquet.

If the theory that each person has a fixed stock of 24 vitality is accepted as valid, then the logical conclusion must be that the wisest course is no exercise at all, and that is precisely the direction in which things moved. Whereas the electric horses that became popular in the early twenties demanded at least modest effort from the user, the abdominal massage machines that came into wide use a few years later required no exertion whatever. These machines, which whipped a broad belt back and forth on the user's stomach, supposedly stimulated the internal organs and dissolved fat, but by 1930 the American Medical Association, not always the most enlightened voice on the subject of exercise, felt compelled to state that they not only did no good but had caused some grievous injuries.

In 1925 a grim article entitled "Too Much Exercise" 25 appeared in the *Saturday Evening Post.* Citing "overwhelming evidence that a great many Americans, of middle age or beyond, are exercising too much," it warned that any man over forty "who persists in putting unnecessary strains on his heart is fixing to make the acquaintance of the undertaker." The article ridiculed calisthenics and went on to question the safety of golf, which was just about the only sport left to doddering forty-year-olds by then. The stress and exertion of golf were vastly underrated, readers were told, and the nation's courses were more or less littered with the corpses of players who had collapsed from the strain.

The ultimate stand against exercise was taken by 26 Peter Steincrohn, the doctor who dismissed all such activity as "bosh." In 1942 Steincrohn, a prolific writer on health topics, published a book that bore the alluring title *You Don't Have to Exercise* and the subtitle *"Rest Begins at Forty."* It sounds like satire now, but it was dead serious. In fact, when the book came out, it was quoted approvingly by Dr. Morris Fishbein, editor of the *Journal of the American Medical Association.*

Steincrohn's thesis was that the heart needed rest, 27 not exercise, to stay healthy. Therefore, on reaching middle age it was best to avoid all exertion beyond that necessary for conducting the business of life. "Don't lift a finger unnecessarily after forty" was Steincrohn's motto. "Bending over to tie and untie your shoes; bringing the fork to your mouth; the rubdown after a shower; laughing; talking and reading—all these furnish your daily exercise requirements." Steincrohn, then in his forties, made clear that he had managed to shake the exercise habit completely, but for those who insisted on continuing to play a bit of golf, he advised dawdling on the course and taking a break for a smoke and a drink between nines. As for old codgers of fifty who persisted in playing tennis, he had nothing but reproach—"infantile exhibitionism."

Steincrohn reiterated his antiexercise arguments, only 28 slightly hedged, in a 1968 book, but by then even he conceded that the tide of medical opinion had turned against him. A major force behind that change was Paul Dudley White, the cardiologist. In the 1930's White had become convinced that exercise to the point of pleasant fatigue—long bicycle rides were his favorite form— benefited the heart. When he came into the public eye after being summoned to treat President Dwight Eisenhower following his heart attack in 1955, White made use of his new prominence to promote the cause of exercise through speeches, articles, and interviews. Dr. White, who died in 1973 at the age of eighty-seven, was a dogged exerciser himself, pedaling his bicycle thirty miles a day even in his later years.

In the sixties and seventies White was joined in his 29 crusade by many other physicians and medical researchers. Their central message was that the most valuable exercise for general health was activity that forced the respiratory and circulatory systems to work hard for prolonged periods. Far from draining the organism of vitality, such exercise was said to increase the efficiency of the heart and to expand its capability. The exercise needed to achieve this effect involves considerable effort; there is no such thing as effortless exercise. A typical program might call, for example, for jogging as long as an hour several times a week, or perhaps for sustained stints of cycling or swimming. Most Americans still don't exercise much, of course, and many are still overweight, but, as the jogging craze in particular illustrates, millions have heeded the message. And their ranks include many well along in years. "Age is not a major obstacle to fitness," insists Dr. Kenneth H. Cooper. As the developer of the widely followed "aerobics" system, Cooper is more responsible than anyone else for starting Americans jogging.

It is conceivable that the new experts are wrong. But 30 the assumption has to be that the march of medical science is generally onward and upward and that the exercise advocates know what they're talking about. Moreover, they are beginning to gather some statistical evidence that backs them up. A report issued in 1977 on a study of seventeen thousand men who enrolled at Harvard between 1916 and 1950 concluded that those who habitually exercised intensively suffered markedly fewer heart attacks than those who didn't. Similar reports are not yet available on women, and indeed one recent medical study of top women athletes such as Olympics trainees revealed the curious fact that a prolonged program of heavy exercise temporarily makes some women stop menstruating. There seems to be every reason to think, however, that the beneficial results of regular, energetic exercise are not confined to males.

Then, too, there is the subjective evidence of those 31 who have found that they don't have to put aside games at forty and who derive deep satisfaction from the discovery that stamina can even grow with age. We are learning that we are not as delicate as was once thought and that we do not need to coddle ourselves, slow our step, and consign the tennis racket to the back of the closet shelf just because we are no longer young. In short, we are developing a whole new attitude toward growing old. And we can only feel sorry for all those who in the past were made to feel old before their time by the misguided fitness "experts" and the sedentary doctors.

Comment

In selecting evidence, the historian seeks evidence that represents typical attitudes and practices, and in presenting this evidence, must convince the reader that the evidence presented is representative. Paul Lancaster seeks to convince us through a series of examples and judicious quotations—focusing on prominent people who shaped public attitudes, describing popular exercise equipment, and quoting statements that highlight contrasting views of exercise. He also interprets his evidence and places it in its historical context. Woven into a single narrative, his evidence reveals a pattern or cycle of attitudes, "periodic changes in direction." Because these changes extend into our own time, Lancaster can appeal to our own experience and observation and use his exposition to give us a reminder. For even though his essay is expository in tracing the recent history of exercise, it also has an argumentative edge.

Questions for Study and Discussion

1. What point is Lancaster making in quoting Dr. Peter Steincrohn's statements about exercise?
2. What "periodic changes in direction" does Lancaster trace? Does he make an explicit or implicit point about these changes?
3. What does Bernarr Macfadden's personal history and career as a journalist tell us about the history of exercise in America?
4. How did the attitude toward female exercise differ from that of male exercise? Does the evidence presented suggest that attitudes toward female exercise changed less?
5. How does Lancaster reveal his own attitude toward exercise in the course of the essay? What direct or implied comment on or recommendation about exercise does he make?

Vocabulary Study

1. Lancaster reminds us that words often had a special meaning in the past. Use the *Oxford English Dictionary* and other dictionaries to discover the original meaning of *calisthenics* and find out whether the word is used in the same sense today.
2. Explain the following words and phrases:
   a. *flush of youth* (paragraph 2)
   b. *lintel* (paragraph 4)
   c. *purview* (paragraph 6)
   d. *physique* (paragraph 7)
   e. *paraphernalia* (paragraph 8)
   f. *alliterative* (paragraph 15)
   g. *buttress* (paragraph 20)
   h. *qui vive, sheepishly, grimace* (paragraph 21)
   i. *bloomers, tapering* (paragraph 22)
   j. *prolific* (paragraph 26)
   k. *exhibitionism* (paragraph 27)
   l. *aerobics* (paragraph 29)
   m. *coddle, sedentary* (paragraph 31)

Suggestions for Writing

1. Use current articles and advertisements in a variety of sources—newspapers, health and sports magazines, consumer newsletters and magazines, medical journals—to compare attitudes toward male and female exercise today. Distinguish between attitudes based on medical research and those based on social attitudes and popular conceptions of health. Develop a thesis based on your evidence. Document your sources, following instructions in your college handbook.
2. Use the same sources to determine current attitudes toward exercise by people over seventy. Distinguish between the same attitudes cited above. Limit your conclusions, and document your sources.

PART FOUR

STRATEGIES FOR ARGUING AND PERSUADING

*S*omewhere in the middle of every game, the same thing happens. A man is knocked down and writhes in pain. The team plays on.

Ellen Goodman

Argument, or proof, is different from exposition, but the two often occur together. Most arguments require explanation and illustration, and many explanations seek to prove an idea.

Arguments seek to establish the truth or falseness, or the degree of probability, of a statement. Arguments often have different purposes and use different kinds of evidence. A trial lawyer may argue the innocence of a client on the basis of eyewitness testimony and supporting circumstantial evidence. A scientist may argue on the basis of repeated experiments that heredity plays a role in some kinds of cancer. A newspaper editorialist may argue for equal educational opportunity for the handicapped through an appeal to constitutional precedents.

Inductive arguments seek to establish highly probable conclusions on the basis of personal experience, observation, experiment, and other factual evidence. The lawyer and the scientist are reasoning inductively in seeking to establish the probable innocence of the client and the probable role of heredity in cancer on the basis of factual or empirical evidence. *Deductive* arguments show that beliefs and long established truths imply or entail other truths. The editorialist is developing a deductive argument in showing that constitutional precedents imply equal opportunity for the handicapped.

An essay that contains argument usually does more than reason in these ways. In developing the argument, the writer usually is trying to change our thinking on an issue or encourage us to take action. The purpose of the argument in these instances is persuasive. The writer employs strategies intended to capture our attention and assent to the argument. But not all persuasive writing uses formal argument. Political cartoons as well as many satirical essays and poems are persuasive without using formal argument. In this part of the book, we will discuss argument and persuasion separately, though some of the essays in the four sections illustrate both.

✧

Inductive Argument

When we draw probable conclusions from personal experience, observation, experiments, facts and statistics, and other empirical evidence, we are reasoning inductively. We would be doing so if we predicted that it will rain on the upcoming Fourth of July because it has rained on previous Fourths in the past ten years. A scientist would do so in predicting that vaccines will be effective in fighting new viral diseases because of the success of vaccines in combatting polio, smallpox, and measles. In the essay that follows, Edward H. Peeples, Jr., uses various kinds of evidence—personal experience, social work, medical observation, testimony, statistical studies—to reach a conclusion concerning hunger and malnutrition in America.

Inductive arguments make predictions about the future on the basis of past and present experience or experimentation. Because it is based on experience, and experience changes, the prediction or conclusion of an inductive argument can be only probable, and it cannot go beyond the particular evidence presented. The probability increases that it will rain this Fourth of July if it did in fact rain on every Fourth of July in the last forty years. But the fact that it has rained does not guarantee that it will do so again; nor can we use the history of the Fourth to predict what will happen on other holidays. The success in treating viral disease suggests that vaccines may be effective in fighting new viral diseases; however, it does not prove that vaccination is the only effective method, or that it will be effective with newly discovered bacterial and other nonviral diseases.

The writer of an inductive argument must decide how much evidence is needed to draw a well-founded conclusion—to make the *inductive leap*. There is, of course, no end to the amount of evidence that can be presented for a conclusion such as Peeples reaches in the essay that follows.

280

> There are those who argue that we do not have enough hard data on the human consumption of pet foods. Must we wait for incontrovertible data before we seriously seek to solve the problems of hunger and malnutrition in America? I submit that we have data enough.

As Peeples suggests in this statement, the researcher must make the decision at some point in conducting an investigation that enough evidence has been found to warrant a conclusion. The conclusion, however, must be properly limited or qualified: the writer or researcher must tell us how broad a conclusion can be drawn from the evidence available. The phrase *inductive leap* sometimes means that the writer has drawn a conclusion too soon, on the basis of incomplete evidence.

Probably few writers are satisfied that they have found all the evidence needed to make the argument convincing to everyone. Like Peeples, they find it necessary to draw a conclusion from a limited amount of evidence because a current situation is growing critical and must be exposed at once:

> Isn't it sufficient to know that one American child or a single elderly person in this bountiful land is reduced to eating the forage of animals or exposed to unknown toxic levels of mercury, lead or salmonella to know that something very extraordinary must be done?

Peeples admits that his personal experience imposes a limit on his conclusions; he is careful to state this limitation. If writers have wide and expert experience in their subject, as Peeples has, their experience alone may be sufficient to give weight to the conclusion. But the greater the variety of evidence provided for the conclusion, the greater the weight it may possess.

Causal analysis—reasoning about causes and effects—is another kind of inductive argument: identifying causes that produce an event is the same as drawing a conclusion from particulars of experience. In his explanation of "computer communities," Robert J. Samuelson (p. 258) reasons about causes in arguing that computerized marketing has led to "niche building," or persuading consumers that they are special or "select," and with unexpected results:

> The point of splintering consumers into finer subdivisions is to give vent to individual differences and choices. In fact, our high-tech

> marketing simply fosters new, more variegated styles of conformity. What the marketers call niches and segments, you and I call friends. People don't compare themselves with strangers. They look at their peers: people like themselves. Most of us—along with our friends—are being bombarded by the same appeals for the same specialized products.   —"Computer Communities"

Though advertisers appeal to the "rhetoric of individuality" in aiming at a particular group or segment of consumers, individual differences turn out to matter little. Samuelson is appealing to our experience with mass marketing to argue this point. In the course of his essay, he gives examples of mass marketing that illustrate these effects. His causal analysis is inductive in drawing upon these particulars of experience.

The word *cause* has different meanings (see p. 86). Sometimes the word refers to the immediate event that produces an effect— failure of an engine part that leads to a car crash, a drought that leads to widespread starvation. Sometimes the word refers to one or more events that led to the engine failure or to the drought. The immediate cause of the event may be of less concern to us than the remote cause: we want to know why the engine failed or what changing weather patterns or atmospheric pollution, or both, led to the drought.

We sometimes use the word *condition* to refer to cause. We may speak of a condition necessary for an event to occur: wheat cannot grow without water. Water is a necessary condition, but water is not a sufficient condition; water alone is not enough to produce a strong crop. Other conditions must be present—fertile soil, proper cultivation, sunlight, to name a few. We would know the sufficient condition if we knew all the conditions that must be present to ensure a strong crop. It is difficult, however, to claim to know all conditions; knowledge of why things happen is seldom complete. The word *condition* is thus used to avoid this implication. Statements about causes and effects need to be qualified carefully.

An *analogy* is a point-by-point comparison of two unlike things, used for illustration (see p. 81) or to prove a thesis. An argument from analogy is inductive because, like causal analysis, it makes an appeal to experience. For example, you might argue that a candidate for the presidency should be elected on the basis of resemblances to an admired former president. Your analogy covers a range of similarities in character traits, policies, and governmental acts. In an effective argument from analogy, the points of similarity must be pertinent to the issue—here, the qualifications for the presidency. It would be immaterial to the argument if the candidate were shorter in height than the former president. Important differences would weaken the analogy: it would be a material difference if the candidate had no previous governmental experience. If the similarities noted are genuine and if no significant differences weaken the analogy, it can be argued that the candidate probably would make a good president.

Notice the qualification *probably.* The analogy does not allow us to say with certainty that the candidate will make a good president. Inductive arguments are probable only. As in causal analysis we can never be certain that we have discovered all the facts—that an exception may not exist to the conclusion drawn from the evidence. In inductive arguments the major problem is not to claim more in the conclusion than the evidence warrants. The conclusion must be limited properly.

Edward H. Peeples, Jr.

. . . MEANWHILE, HUMANS EAT PET FOOD

Edward H. Peeples, Jr., is associate professor of preventive medicine at Virginia Commonwealth University. Born in 1935 in Richmond, Virginia, Peeples attended Richmond Professional Institute, the University of Pennsylvania, and the University of Kentucky, where he received his Ph.D. in 1972. In the 1960s, he gained knowledge of urban poverty as a social worker in Richmond and South Philadelphia. He has been a leader of the Richmond Human Rights Coalition and Council on Human Relations and has long been concerned with the nutritional problems and medical care of poor people. His article appeared in *The New York Times* on December 16, 1975.

The first time I witnessed people eating pet foods 1
was among neighbors and acquaintances during my youth in the South. At that time it was not uncommon or startling to me to see dog-food patties sizzling in a pan on the top of a stove or kerosene space heater in

a dilapidated house with no running water, no refrigerator, no heat, no toilet and the unrelenting stench of decaying insects. I simply thought of it as the unfortunate but unavoidable consequence of being poor in the South.

The second time occurred in Cleveland in the summer of 1953. Like many other Southerners, I came to seek my fortune in one of those pot-at-the-end-of-the-rainbow factories along Euclid Avenue. Turned away from one prospective job after another ("We don't hire hillbillies," employers said), I saw my nest egg of $30 dwindle to nothing. As my funds diminished and my hunger grew, I turned to pilfering food and small amounts of cash. With the money, I surreptitiously purchased, fried and ate canned dog and cat food as my principal ration for several weeks.

I was, of course, humiliated to be eating something that, in my experience, only "trash" consumed. A merciless pride in self-sufficiency kept me from seeking out public welfare or asking my friends or family for help. In fact, I carefully guarded the secret from everyone, because I feared being judged a failure. Except for the humiliation I experienced, eating canned pet food did not at the time seem to be particularly unpleasant. The dog food tasted pretty much like mealy hamburger, while the cat food was similar to canned fish that I was able to improve with mayonnaise, mustard or catsup.

The next time I ate dog food was in 1956 while struggling through a summer session in college without income for food. Again, I was ashamed to admit it, fearing that people would feel sorry for me or that others who had even less than I would feel compelled to sacrifice for my comfort. I never again had to eat pet food. Later, while working as a hospital corpsman at the Great Lakes Illinois Naval Training Center in the late 1950's I had the opportunity to ask new recruits about their home life and nutrition practices. While I was not yet a disciplined scientist, I was able to estimate that about 5 to 8 percent of the thousands of young men who came to Great Lakes annually consumed pet foods and other materials not commonly thought to be safe or desirable for humans. Among these substances were baking soda, baking powder, laundry starch, tobacco, snuff, clay, dirt, sand and various wild plants.

My later experience as a public assistance caseworker in Richmond, a street-based community worker in South Philadelphia, and my subsequent travels and studies as a medical sociologist throughout the South, turned up instances of people eating pet food because they saw it as cheaper than other protein products. Through the years, similar cases found in the Ozarks, on Indian reservations and in various cities across the nation have also been brought to my attention.

While there do exist scattered scientific reports and commentary on the hazards and problems associated with eating such things as laundry starch and clay, there is little solid epidemiological evidence that shows a specific percentage of American households consume pet food. My experience and research, however, suggest that human consumption of pet food is widespread in the United States. My estimate, one I believe to be conservative, is that pet foods constitute a significant part of the diet of at least 225,000 American households, affecting some one million persons. Who knows how many more millions supplement their diet with pet-food products? One thing that we can assume is that current economic conditions are increasing the practice and that it most seriously affects the unemployed, poor people, and our older citizens.

There are those who argue that we do not have enough hard data on the human consumption of pet foods. Must we wait for incontrovertible data before we seriously seek to solve the problems of hunger and malnutrition in America? I submit that we have data enough. Isn't it sufficient to know that one American child or a single elderly person in this bountiful land is reduced to eating the forage of animals or exposed to unknown toxic levels of mercury, lead or salmonella to know that something very extraordinary must be done?

Questions for Study and Discussion

1. Why do people eat pet food, according to Peeples?
2. What is his purpose in writing, and where does he state it? What makes the essay inductive?
3. To what audience is he writing, and how do you know? Were he writing to public health officials only, would he approach the subject in a different way, or present different evidence?
4. How does Peeples qualify his conclusion that people who eat pet food are affected by it seriously—that is, how does he indicate the degree of probability that this is so?
5. Has Peeples persuaded you that the situation he describes is serious and that something must be done about it? If not, what other evidence would persuade you?

Vocabulary Study

1. Complete the following to show the meaning of the italicized words:
    a. His *disciplined* way of living was shown by
    b. A *conservative* action is one that
    c. An *incontrovertible* proof can never
    d. The *bountiful* harvest
2. Identify the denotative and connotative meanings of the following:
    a. *sizzling, dilapidated, stench* (paragraph 1)
    b. *pilfering, surreptitious* (paragraph 2)
    c. *"trash"* (paragraph 3)
    d. *cheaper* (paragraph 5)
    e. *extraordinary, forage* (paragraph 7)

Suggestions for Writing

1. Write an essay that builds to a thesis through a series of observations and experiences. Qualify your thesis by stating the limitations of your experience and knowledge of the subject.
2. Discuss an experience that resulted when you found yourself short of money. Discuss what you did and what you learned about yourself and perhaps about other people.
3. Discuss how your ideas about people changed through experiences in a world different from that you grew up in. Use this experience to persuade a particular audience to change their thinking about these people.

Ellen Goodman

PLAYING WITH PAIN

Ellen Goodman wrote for *Newsweek* and the *Detroit Free Press* before joining the staff of the *Boston Globe* in 1967 as feature writer and columnist. Her columns on a wide range of social and political issues are collected in *At Large* (1981), *Keeping in Touch* (1985), *Making Sense* (1989) and *Value Judgments* (1993), in which the essay reprinted here appears. In 1980 Goodman received the Pulitzer Prize for Commentary.

It was an average week. A separated shoulder or two, a few broken bones in one hand, ligament damage to a couple of knees. The football coverage sounded like Grand Rounds on the orthopedic ward. Your average scoreboard of injuries.

Then Jeff Fuller barreled his 49ers' helmet into an opponent on the 29-yard line. It was what the commentators call "a possible career-ending injury." It was also a possible walk-ending injury, a possible move-his-body-ending injury, but nobody put it that way at first. Was his neck broken? The game went on. Round up the usual casualties.

I am no football fan. I do not share the allure of this 3
alleged sport. Thousands of pounds of human flesh and
armor pound more thousands across the turf, Astro and
real, Saturdays, Sundays, Monday nights. But watching
Fuller being carefully carted off the field, I know why
I am hooked on the dynamics of the thing.

Somewhere in the middle of every game, the same 4
thing happens. A man is knocked down and writhes in
pain. The team plays on. A man is carted off on a
stretcher and replaced. The game goes on. As I watch
it now, I have come to wonder: Is this what men mean
when they talk about teammates and team players?

All my life, I have heard about the disadvantage 5
women have in business because most don't play team
sports. It is said that we don't know what it is like to
be turf buddies together, to get muddied together, to win
together. Togetherness.

The ultimate model is, I am told, this all-American, 6
only-American sport called football. It is true that on
this turf men work together for victory. But on this same
turf, they are trained to block a teammate's injury out
of their minds. Also trained to be carried out of the way.

This is the image of a team we take from football: 7
a group of people strong and close enough to go for it
together, but not intimate enough to stop and take care
of each other.

Not long ago, I talked with Harvard's Carol Gilligan, 8
who has studied moral development in children. She has
observed the different ways grade school boys and girls
generally deal with sports. When a boy is injured, he is
taken off the field while the others continue. When a
girl is injured, the game stops while they gather around
the one who was hurt.

When does that break occur? Most children, even 9
the littlest boys and girls, express compassion when
another of their kind is hurt. Is it taught out of boys
on the playing fields? Is it how they are prepared for
war or business or just manhood?

Recently, an open and friendly eighteen-year-old high 10
school football star, Brett Law, unselfconsciously told a
People magazine reporter, "Mostly I like knocking people
over." When do people learn that to be a "pro" in many
worlds you have to equip yourself with blinders against
the weak and the injured? Do they have to learn first
to ignore their own feelings?

I don't think every game should halt while a splinter 11
is removed or that every business deal should be sidetracked by injured feelings. Indeed, there are times when
people, especially women, get paralyzed by the opposite
problem: their fear of causing pain or even making
others angry.

But it occurs to me that this image of teamwork may 12
be all too successful a training for business in an era of
takeovers and lean, mean strategies. Today, "competitiveness" is the key word. Those who would be winners
often learn not to care when colleagues are cut from the
"team." The bottom line may indeed reward those who
aren't distracted by bodies on the field.

What would happen in America if just once the pros 13
stopped playing ball until they found out if a teammate
had indeed broken his neck? The producers, the coaches,
the advertisers would scream.

But they just might send abroad a startling new 14
image of a team player: not an interchangeable digit on
a shirt, not a group of men united by an external goal.
Somewhere down in the Pop Warner Leagues and in the
living room there would be a small flash of understanding: "Pros" also take care of each other.

In time, with this radical sort of teamwork, they 15
might even make the field a less dangerous place. And
in time, on more than one turf, in more than one office,
we might learn to play the serious games with much less
pain.

Comment

Long observation led Goodman to ask a question about football: "I have come to wonder: Is this what men mean when they talk about teammates and team players?" Other observations led Goodman to other questions and conclusions. The argument she makes is inductive in basing these questions and conclusions on experience and observation and in stating the conclusions as probabilities. How seriously we take Goodman's argument depends on how strongly the evidence presented accords with our experience and observations or persuades us to accept her conclusions.

Questions for Study and Discussion

1. What observations led Goodman to ask what conception of teammates and team playing men have in talking about football?
2. What other observations led Goodman to compare football to the conduct of business in the 1980s? With what general consideration does Goodman lead into this comparison?
3. Does Goodman give or imply an explanation for the way football is played and the way business is conducted?
4. How convincing do you find the evidence she presents for her statements about football and the attitudes of boys and girls toward sports injuries?

Vocabulary Study

State how the following words differ in meaning, and explain why Goodman uses the first word in each pair:
1. *writhes, suffers* (paragraph 4)
2. *intimate, friendly* (paragraph 7)
3. *compassion, pity* (paragraph 9)
4. *distracted, diverted* (paragraph 12)
5. *radical, extreme* (paragraph 15)

Suggestions for Writing

1. Discuss the extent to which your own experience and obser-
    vation support Goodman's image of football or the way boys
    and girls deal with sports injuries. Use your discussion to
    evaluate Goodman's general argument.
2. Discuss "the image of a team" you have of another sport, and
    compare this image with that of football or another sport.

Jane Tompkins

THE LANGUAGE OF WESTERNS

Jane Tompkins is professor of English at Duke University. Her books
on modern criticism and popular culture include *Sensational Designs:
The Cultural Work of American Fiction* (1985) and *West of Everything:
The Inner Life of Westerns* (1992), in which this section on the
language of Western movies appears. Tompkins states: "These are the
classic oppositions from which all Westerns derive their meaning: parlor
versus mesa, East versus West, woman versus man, illusion versus truth,
words versus things. It is the last of these oppositions I want to focus
on now because it stands for all the rest." Selection title by editor.

So it is with language. Westerns distrust language.   1
Time and again they set up situations whose message
is that words are weak and misleading, only actions
count; words are immaterial, only objects are real. But
the next thing you know, someone is using language
brilliantly, delivering an epigram so pithy and dense it
might as well be a solid thing. In fact, Westerns go in
for their own special brand of the bon mot, seasoned
with skepticism and fried to a turn. The product—
chewy and tough—is recognizable anywhere:

> Cow's nothin' but a heap o' trouble tied up in a leather bag.
> > *The Cowboys*, 1972

> A human rides a horse until he's dead and then goes on foot. An
> Indian rides him another 20 miles and then eats him.
> > *The Searchers*, 1956

A Texan is nothin' but a human man way out on a limb.

The Searchers

Kansas is all right for men and dogs but it's pretty hard on women and horses.

The Santa Fe Trail, 1940

God gets off at Leavenworth, and Cyrus Holliday drives you from there to the devil.

The Santa Fe Trail

There ain't no Sundays west of Omaha.

The Cowboys

This is hard country, double hard.

Will Penny, 1968

When you boil it all down, what does a man really need? Just a smoke and a cup of coffee.

Johnny Guitar, 1954

In the end you end up dyin' all alone on a dirty street. And for what? For nothin'.

High Noon, 1952

You can't serve papers on a rat, baby sister. You gotta kill 'em or let 'em be.

True Grit, 1969

He wasn't a good man, he wasn't a bad man, but Lord, he was a *man*.

The Ballad of Cable Hogue, 1969

Some things a man has to do, so he does 'em.

Winchester '73, 1950

Only a man who carries a gun ever needs one.

Angel and the Bad Man, 1947

Mr. Grimes: "God, dear God."
Yaqui Joe: "He won't help you."

100 Rifles, 1969

You haven't gotten tough, you've just gotten miserable.

Cowboy, 1958

The sayings all have one thing in common: they bring you down. Like the wisdom L'Amour offers his female protagonist out on the mesa top, these gritty pieces of advice challenge romantic notions. Don't call on God; he's not there. Think you're tough? You're just miserable. What do you die for? Nothin'. The sayings puncture big ideas and self-congratulation; delivered with perfect timing, they land like stones from a slingshot and make a satisfying thunk.

For the Western is at heart antilanguage. Doing, not 3 talking, is what it values. And this preference is connected to its politics, as a line from L'Amour suggests: "A man can . . . write fine words, or he can do something to hold himself in the hearts of the people" (*Treasure Mountain,* 1972). "Fine words" are contrasted not accidentally with "the hearts of the people." For the men who are the Western's heroes don't have the large vocabularies an expensive education can buy. They don't have time to read that many books. Westerns distrust language in part because language tends to be wielded most skillfully by people who possess a certain kind of power: class privilege, political clout, financial strength. Consequently, the entire enterprise is based on a paradox. In order to exist, the Western has to use words or visual images, but these images are precisely what it fears. As a medium, the Western has to pretend that it doesn't exist at all, its words and pictures, just a window on the truth, not really there.

So the Western's preferred parlance ideally consists 4 of abrupt commands: "Turn the wagon. Tie 'em up short. Get up on the seat" (*Red River*); "Take my horse. Good swimmer. Get it done, boy" (*Rio Grande,* 1950). Or epigrammatic sayings of a strikingly aggressive sort: "There's only one thing you gotta know. Get it out fast and put it away slow" (*Man Without a Star*); "When you pull a gun, kill a man" (*My Darling Clementine*). For the really strong man, language is a snare; it blunts his purpose and diminishes his strength. When Joey asks Shane if he knows how to use a rifle, Shane answers, and we can barely hear him, "Little bit." The understatement and the clipping off of the indefinite article are typical of the

minimalist language Western heroes speak, a desperate
shorthand, comic, really, in its attempt to communicate
without using words.

Westerns are full of contrasts between people who   5
spout words and people who act. At the beginning of
Sam Peckinpah's *The Wild Bunch* a temperance leader
harangues his pious audience; in the next scene a violent bank robbery makes a shambles of their proces-
sion through town. The pattern of talk canceled by
action always delivers the same message: language is
false or at best ineffectual; only actions are real. When
heroes talk, it is action: their laconic put-downs cut
people off at the knees. Westerns treat salesmen and
politicians, people whose business is language, with
contempt. Braggarts are dead men as soon as they
appear. When "Stonewall" Tory, in *Shane,* brags that
he can face the Riker gang any day, you know he's
going to get shot; it's Shane, the man who clips out
words between clenched teeth, who will take out the
hired gunman.

The Western's attack on language is wholesale and   6
unrelenting, as if language were somehow tainted in its
very being. When John Wayne, in John Ford's *The
Searchers,* rudely tells an older woman who is taking
more than a single sentence to say something, "I'd be
obliged, ma'am if you would get to the point," he
expresses the genre's impatience with words as a way
of dealing with the world. For while the woman is
speaking, Indians are carrying a prisoner off. Such a
small incident, once you unpack it, encapsulates the
Western's attitude toward a whole range of issues:

1. Chasing Indians—that is, engaging in aggressive physical
    action—is doing something, while talking about the situation
    is not.
2. The reflection and negotiation that language requires are
    gratuitous, even pernicious.
3. The hero doesn't need to think or talk; he just *knows.* Being
    the hero, he is in a state of grace with respect to the truth.

In a world of bodies true action must have a physical 7
form. And so the capacity for true knowledge must be
based in physical experience. John Wayne playing Ethan
Edwards in *The Searchers* has that experience and knows
what is right because, having arrived home after fighting
in the Civil War, he better than anyone else realizes that
life is "blood and death and a cold wind blowing and
a gun in the hand." In such a world, language constitutes an inferior kind of reality, and the farther one
stays away from it the better.

Language is gratuitous at best; at worst it is decep- 8
tive. It takes the place of things, screens them from view,
creates a shadow world where anything can be made to
look like anything else. The reason no one in the Glenn
Ford movie *Cowboy* can remember the proper words
for burying a man is that there aren't any. It is precisely
words that cannot express the truth about things. The
articulation of a creed in the Western is a sign not of
conviction but of insincerity. The distaste with which
John Wayne says, "The Lord giveth, the Lord taketh
away," as he buries a man in *Red River,* not only chal-
lenges the authority of the Christian God but also
expresses disgust at all the trappings of belief: liturgies,
litanies, forms, representations, all of which are betray-
als of reality itself.

The features I am describing here, using the abstract 9
language the Western shuns, are dramatically present in
a movie called *Dakota Incident* (1956), whose plot turns
in part on the bootlessness of words and, secondarily,
on the perniciousness of money (another system of representation the Western scorns). Near the beginning, a
windbag senator, about to depart on the stage from a
miserable town called Christian Flats, pontificates to a
crowd that has gathered to watch a fight, "There's no
problem that can't be solved at a conference table,"
adding, "Believe me, gentlemen, I know whereof I speak."
The next minute, two gunfights break out on Main

Street; in one of them the hero shoots and kills his own brother.

The theme of loquacity confounded by violence, 10 declared at the outset, replays itself at the end when the main characters have been trapped by some Indians in a dry creek bed. The senator has been defending the Indians throughout, saying that they're misunderstood, have a relationship with the land, and take from the small end of the horn of plenty. Finally, when he and the others are about to die of thirst, he goes out to parley with the Indians. He makes a long and rather moving speech about peace and understanding, and they shoot him; he dies clawing at the arrow in his chest.

In case we hadn't already gotten the point about the 11 ineffectuality of language, we get it now. But no sooner is the point made than the movie does an about-face. The other characters start saying that the senator died for what he believed, that he was wrong about the Indians "but true to himself." They say that perhaps his words "fell on barren ground: the Indians and us." And the story ends on a note of peaceful cooperation between whites and Indians (after the attacking Indians have been wiped out), with talk about words of friendship falling on fertile ground.

Language is specifically linked in this movie to a 12 belief in peace and cooperation as a way of solving conflicts. And though it's made clear from the start that only wimps and fools believe negotiation is the way to deal with enemies (the movie was made in 1956 during the Cold War), that position is abandoned as soon as "our side" wins. *Dakota Incident* is not the only Western to express this ambivalent attitude toward language and the peace and harmony associated with it. Such ambivalence is typical, but it is always resolved in the end. Language gets its day in court, and then it is condemned.

When John Wayne's young protégé in *The Searchers*, 13 for example, returns to his sweetheart after seven years, he's surprised to learn that she hasn't been aware of his affection. "But I always loved you," he protests. "I thought you knew that without me havin' to say it." For a moment here, John Ford seems to be making fun of the idea that you can communicate without language, gently ridiculing the young man's assumption that somehow his feelings would be known although he had never articulated them. But his silence is vindicated ultimately when the girl he loves, who was about to marry another man, decides to stick with him. The cowboy hero's taciturnity, like his awkward manners around women and inability to dance, is only superficially a flaw; actually, it's proof of his manhood and trueheartedness. In Westerns silence, sexual potency, and integrity go together.

Again, in *My Darling Clementine* Ford seems to make 14 an exception to the interdiction against language. When Victor Mature, playing Doc Holliday, delivers the "To be or not to be" speech from *Hamlet,* taking over from the drunken actor who has forgotten his lines, we are treated to a moment of verbal enchantment. The beauty and power of the poetry are recognized even by the hero, Wyatt Earp (played by Henry Fonda), who appreciates Shakespeare and delivers a long soliloquy himself over the grave of his brother. But when the old actor who has been performing locally leaves town, he tricks the desk clerk into accepting his signature on a bill in place of money. The actor, like the language he is identified with, is a lovable old fraud, wonderfully colorful and entertaining, but not, finally, to be trusted.

The position represented by language, always asso- 15 ciated with women, religion, and culture, is allowed to appear in Westerns and is accorded a certain plausibility and value. It functions as a critique of force and, even more important, as a symbol of the peace, harmony, and civilization that force is invoked in order to preserve. But in the end, that position is deliberately proven wrong—massively, totally, and unequivocally—with pounding hooves, thundering guns, blood and death. Because the genre is in revolt against a Victorian culture where the ability to manipulate language confers power, the Western equates power with "not-language." And not-language it equates with being male.

Comment

Tompkins argues her thesis through examples of Western movies from the 1940s to the early 1970s. She opens with a statement of her thesis and a series of sayings that illustrate it, then analyzes the attitude toward language in a number of typical statements and situations. She concludes by discussing three Westerns that seem to present exceptions to the attitude discussed. The greater the number of examples, the greater the claim the writer can make for the thesis. Tompkins presents a large number, and she strengthens her argument by choosing them from a variety of Westerns rather than a single type. The argument is inductive in this assembling of examples to support a thesis or generalization.

Questions for Study and Discussion

1. What is an epigram or bon mot, and how are the sayings quoted in paragraph 1 typical of the special kind of epigram or bon mot in Westerns? In what sense do the sayings "bring you down"? In what sense do they "challenge romantic notions"?
2. How do the Westerns discussed in paragraphs 5-8 illustrate the thesis, stated in paragraph 1?
3. Why must "the capacity for true knowledge . . . be based in physical experience" (paragraph 7)? How does Tompkins illustrate this point?
4. Tompkins states that "language is gratuitous at best; at worst it is deceptive" (paragraph 8). What does she mean, and how does she illustrate this statement?

5. How does *Dakota Incident* express an "ambivalent attitude toward language" (paragraph 12)? Is this attitude an exception to the general attitude toward language in Westerns?
6. Are the Westerns discussed in paragraphs 13 and 14 exceptions to the attitudes discussed by Tompkins? If not, what point is she making about these Westerns?

Vocabulary Study

Define the following words:
1. *parlance, minimalist* (paragraph 4)
2. *harangues, shambles, ineffectual, laconic* (paragraph 5)
3. *liturgies, litanies* (paragraph 8)
4. *perniciousness, pontificates* (paragraph 9)
5. *loquacity, confounded* (paragraph 10)
6. *soliloquy* (paragraph 14)
7. *plausibility, critique* (paragraph 15)

Suggestions for Writing

1. Tompkins argues that in the Western, "not-language" is synonymous with being male. Discuss the extent to which you find the same "not-language" in television Westerns or other action programs. Analyze a series of statements and situations to support your points.
2. Tompkins states that "Westerns treat salesmen and politicians, people whose business is language, with contempt." Discuss the depiction of salesmen or politicians in current movies or current television in light of this statement. Make your examples concise and informative.

Richard Moran

MORE CRIME AND LESS PUNISHMENT

Richard Moran, professor of sociology at Mount Holyoke College, has written on criminal law and crime in America in *Knowing Right from Wrong: The Insanity Defense of Daniel McNaughton* (1981) and in articles in *Newsweek* and other periodicals. His essay on problems created by the high crime rate in America is inductive in drawing inferences from particulars of experiences and statistical evidence. Moran also depends upon illustrative analogy (p. 81) to clarify his argument. His article appeared in *Newsweek* on May 7, 1984.

If you are looking for an explanation of why we don't get tough with criminals, you need only look at the numbers. Each year almost a third of the households in America are victimized by violence or theft. This amounts to more than 41 million crimes, many more than we have the capacity to punish. There are also too many criminals. The best estimates suggest that 36 million to 40 million people or 16 to 18 percent of the U.S. population have arrest records for nontraffic offenses. We already have 2.4 million people under some form of correctional supervision, 412,000 of them locked away in a prison cell. We don't have room for any more!

The painful fact is that the more crime there is the less we are able to punish it. This is why the certainty and severity of punishment must go down when the crime rate goes up. Countries like Saudi Arabia can afford to mete out harsh punishments precisely because they have so little crime. But can we afford to cut off the hands of those who committed more than 35 million property crimes each year? Can we send them to prison? Can we execute more than 22,000 murderers?

We need to think about the relationship between punishment and crime in a new way. A decade of sophisticated research has failed to provide clear and convincing evidence that the threat of punishment influences the rate of most major crimes committed. We assume that punishment deters crime, but it just might be the other way around. It just might be that crime deters punishment: that there is so much crime that it simply cannot be punished.

This is the situation we find ourselves in today. Just 4 as the decline in the number of high-school graduates has made it easier to gain admission to the college of one's choice, the gradual increase in the criminal population has made it more difficult to get into prison. While elite colleges and universities have held the line on standards of admissions, some of the most "exclusive" prisons now require about five prior felony convictions before an inmate is accepted into their correctional program. Our current crop of prisoners is an elite group, on the whole much more serious offenders than those who inhabited Alcatraz during its heyday.

Given the reality of the numbers it makes little sense 5 to blame the police, judges or correctional personnel for being soft on criminals. There is not much else they can do. The police can't find most criminals and those they find are difficult and costly to convict. Those convicted can't all be sent to prison. The social fact is that we cannot afford to do nothing about crime. The practical reality is that there is very little the police, courts or prisons can do about the crime problem. The criminal-justice system must then become as powerless as a parent who has charge of hundreds of teenage children and who is nonetheless expected to answer the TV message: "It's 10 o'clock! Do you know where your children are?"

A few statistics from the Justice Department's recent 6 "Report to the Nation on Crime and Justice" illustrate my point. Of every 100 felonies committed in America, only 33 are actually reported to the police. Of the 33 reported, about 6 are cleared by arrest. Of the six arrested, only three are prosecuted and convicted. The others are rejected or dismissed due to evidence or witness problems or diverted into a treatment program. Of the three convicted, only one is sent to prison. The other two are placed on probation or some form of supervision. Of the select few sent to prison, more than half receive a maximum sentence of five years. The average inmate, however, graduates into a community-based program in about two years. Most prisoners gain early release not because parole boards are soft on crime, but because it is much cheaper to supervise a criminal in the community. And, of course, prison officials must make room for the new entering class of recruits sent almost daily from the courts.

We could, of course, get tough with the people we 7
already have in prison and keep them locked up for longer periods of time. Yet when measured against the probable reduction in crime, prolonged incarceration is not worth the financial burden it imposes on state and local governments who pay the bulk of criminal-justice costs. Besides, those states that have tried to gain voter approval for bonds to build new prisons often discover that the public is unwilling to pay for prison construction.

And if it were willing to pay, prolonged incarceration 8
may not be effective in reducing crime. In 1981, 124,000 convicts were released from prison. If we had kept them in jail for an additional year, how much crime would have been prevented? While it is not possible to know the true amount of crime committed by people released from prison in any given year, we do know the extent to which those under parole are reconfined for major crime convictions. This number is a surprisingly low 6 percent (after three years it rises to only 11 percent). Even if released prisoners commit an average of two crimes each, this would amount to only 15,000 crimes prevented: a drop in the bucket when measured against the 41 million crimes committed annually.

More time spent in prison is also more expensive. 9
The best estimates are that it costs an average of $13,000 to keep a person in prison for one year. If we had a place

to keep the 124,000 released prisoners, it would have cost us $1.6 billion to prevent 15,000 crimes. This works out to more than $100,000 per crime prevented. But there is more. With the average cost of prison construction running around $50,000 per bed, it would cost more than $6 billion to build the necessary cells. The first-year operating cost would be $150,000 per crime prevented, worth it if the victim were you or me, but much too expensive to be feasible as a national policy.

Faced with the reality of the numbers, I will not be 10 so foolish as to suggest a solution to the crime problem. My contribution to the public debate begins and ends with this simple observation: getting tough with criminals is not the answer.

Comment

Statistical arguments that are worth considering include the following tests. The group sampled must be sufficiently broad and varied; that is, enough people must be interviewed to support a significant conclusion. A conclusion bearing on the whole population will be weak if the sample is based on two or three people or drawn from a single segment. The sample must not be based on unusual circumstances, and all pertinent facts and circumstances must be taken into account in interpreting the evidence. Furthermore, the conclusion must be warranted by the evidence; that is, the evidence must be pertinent to the conclusion, and the conclusion must not go beyond the limits of the evidence. Moran does not base his argument on the incidence of crime in a few densely populated areas with high unemployment—special circumstances that would call his conclusion into question; his statistical evidence covers the whole United States. Moran further draws a limited conclusion from his evidence: we must learn to think about crime in a new way. Finally, he qualifies his argument by noting the limitation of his evidence: he tells us that his estimate of crime in America is approximate, not exact, and he is not using this evidence to speculate about crime worldwide.

Questions for Study and Discussion

1. Why does Moran not propose a solution to the problems he discusses? Why does he consider his analysis useful even though he does not propose a solution?
2. Why can Moran not provide exact statistical information on the rate of crime in America? Why can he provide exact information on the reimprisonment of paroled criminals?
3. Does Moran say or imply that he would favor harsh punishments, including capital punishment, if it were practical to administer them? Or is he only pointing out a fact?
4. What kind of evidence does Moran present for his conclusion that public thinking about punishment is inconsistent? Why does Moran emphasize this inconsistency?
5. What use does Moran make of illustrative analogy?

Vocabulary Study

State the differences in meaning of the words in each group. Then explain why Moran uses the first of the words in the paragraph cited:

1. *severity* (paragraph 2), *intensity, harshness*
2. *sophisticated* (paragraph 3), *intense, serious*
3. *deters* (paragraph 3), *forbids, stops*
4. *felonies* (paragraph 6), *crimes, misdemeanors*
5. *incarceration* (paragraph 7), *punishment, penalty*

Suggestions for Writing

1. Analyze advertisements for similar products—for example, cosmetics and toothpaste—to discover what evidence each of the advertisers presents for statements about the product. Use your analysis to draw a conclusion about the particular advertising of these products. Limit your conclusion carefully.
2. Your college library contains reference books and government documents that report crime statistics for particular cities and regions of the United States. Locate statistical reports on crime in two large American cities—Miami and Los Angeles,

for example—and compare the information given about the crimes named. Use your comparison to draw a conclusion about the nature of crime in these cities.

Elizabeth Marshall Thomas

THE SOCIAL LIFE OF DOGS

As a young woman Elizabeth Marshall Thomas accompanied her father to the Kalahari Desert, in southwest Africa, where they taught dry-country farming to the !Kung Bushmen. Thomas describes the life and culture of the Bushmen in *The Harmless People* (1959), and she has written about other contemporary tribal people in *Warrior Herdsmen* (1981) and people of the later Stone Age in her novels *Reindeer Moon* (1987) and *The Animal Wife* (1990). *The Hidden Life of Dogs* (1993) describes eleven dogs of different breeds, five males, six females, living with Thomas and her husband. "I wanted to see what they would do when free to plan their own time and make their own decisions." Thomas states that "in the past even scientists have been led to believe that only human beings have thoughts or emotions. Of course, nothing could be further from the truth." Selection title by editor.

WHAT DO DOGS want most? They want to belong, and they want each other. Groups that form naturally, the children of a mated pair, are probably the most stable, but groups such as ours, which include a dog or two from the outside, can also be stable. Every dog might wish to be Dog One, but like us, most dogs want membership in the group even more than they want supremacy over others, so that as soon as each dog is content with his place, the social system must seem reassuringly solid to them, firm and dependable, like a good, strong ladder. Loss of a member then becomes deeply significant, which is why our dogs called to the night sky for Zooey.

Interestingly enough, the howl was one of very few pieces of obvious evidence for their powerful feelings of unity. Also in Virginia, another piece of evidence presented itself very dramatically, but the importance was inferential. The dogs made a den.

To understand why this is important, and what it   3
might mean, we should think of our own species and how we would react if what happened to these dogs should happen to us. What would we do, for instance, if eight or nine of us were dropped off somewhere in the woods, assuming that we were to stay for a while, that we weren't obliged to find our way elsewhere, and that our situation didn't deeply distress us?

To answer the question, we'd have to know what we   4
meant to one another. If we considered one another adversaries or suspicious-looking strangers, we would probably scatter to the four winds. If we were a team or a family, however, whether we expected to stay for a while or merely to figure out how to cope with our situation, our first act would probably be to make a camp. We would feel the need for a focus for our group and our activities. Whether we would make some kind of shelter, or clear some grass, or build a fire, or merely spread a blanket for a picnic, we would invariably alter the environment a little in a way that suited us. We would strongly, acutely feel the need to do that *first*, before we went searching for food or played a game or did whatever else seemed suitable to the occasion. Why? Because only with an established camp would we know where to place ourselves, where to come back to, where we could expect to find the others and they to find us.

To feel the need to prepare a campsite in such a   5
situation seems so obvious to most human beings as to be almost unworthy of mention, and no wonder. The need is very old, far older than our species. Surely the idea of using a central focal area, if only as a place where the young await the foraging adult or adults, is as old as the nesting dinosaurs and perhaps much older, so that today the variety of creatures using certain spots to keep their groups together is wide indeed—from nests to camps to dens, from crocodiles to birds to dogs to

people. That my dogs made a den in Virginia should not have come as a surprise.

But it did. One day we discovered what was surely ₆ the height of our dogs' achievements toward creating their own social cohesion: in spite of the numerous, comfortable, and substantial shelters we had provided for them—nice, dry shelters, some with small doors for shelter in winter, others wide open for breezy shade in summer, each shelter complete with hay and cedar shavings—the dogs had made themselves a den fully as ambitious and as brilliantly executed as any wolf den on Baffin. In fact, the den in Virginia was almost exactly like a wolf den, a tunnel penetrating horizontally for fifteen feet into the side of a hill. The dogs had chosen a well-drained place in compact, claylike earth, and had shaped the tunnel's ceiling like a shallow dome so that it wouldn't collapse on them. On one side of the tunnel near its far end they had excavated a chamber approximately three feet wide, two feet high, and three feet deep—big enough for a dog or two to sleep in.

What was most amazing about the den, though, or ₇ at least what seemed most amazing to me, was the secrecy that surrounded it. I visited the pen every day at least twice, usually much oftener, and I made a practice of walking all around it, checking for problems and possible attempts at escape. I also spent time with the dogs each day, either observing them or simply sitting in their presence, enjoying their company. Yet neither I nor any other person had the faintest notion that the dogs were working on their enormous excavation, even though the tunnel's entrance was only twenty yards from our front door. To be sure, now and then a dog or two would vanish mysteriously, but the pen was so large that they could have been elsewhere in it, and I never searched it so thoroughly that I could have said positively that the dogs in question weren't there. That the vanished dogs were deep in the earth simply never occurred to me, even though I might have been standing directly above them. Not even piles of excavated dirt betrayed their project; incredibly, they scattered more than six cubic yards of it, enough to fill a large dump truck, so carefully and so efficiently that no telltale mounds remained.

Was the secrecy intentional? I'm convinced that it 8 was. The tunnel's entrance, for instance, was hidden underneath a woodpile, which in turn was sheltered by the eaves of our garage, which formed part of the fence of the pen. The eaves would keep rain from running into the entrance, so other considerations besides secrecy may have figured in the plan, but unless the dogs wanted secrecy it is hard to explain why they never worked on the tunnel or even went in or out of it when a person was present.

One day, though, Maria slipped up. She had already 9 started into the entrance when I came into the pen, and when I happened to glance at the woodpile I was astonished to see her rump and tail disappearing between two of the logs. Now why would a dog squeeze down inside a woodpile? She had moved fairly smoothly, without the excitement she would have shown if she had been chasing, say, a small animal taking refuge there. Furthermore, the pile represented only the few trees we had cleared to build the garage. It was only about three logs deep, and the logs were fairly small in diameter, so that the whole pile didn't stand quite as high as a dog's shoulder. Yet Maria had vanished inside it as if by illusion. What was happening here?

I went over to look, and found a space about ten 10 inches wide between two of the logs. I moved them, revealing a similar space between the logs below. I moved them too, and underneath I found a great, gaping, elliptic hole shaped like the underside of a bridge and its reflection, twenty-two inches across the minor axis— about the diameter of a dog. Well! I got down on my hands and knees and tried to look inside, but about three feet in, the shaft curved slightly upward, so I couldn't see very far. And it was dark. I still hadn't fully understood the implications of what I was looking at when suddenly Maria popped up face to face with me. She looked startled. I was startled too. Somewhere inside was a space big enough for her to turn around in.

We then investigated the tunnel, probed it with a 11 long bamboo pole, learned its size, and marveled. We also saw reasons other than social reasons for digging a den. Deep in the earth, for instance, is the perfect climate. Always a constant temperature, about fifty-five degrees Fahrenheit year round, a den seems cool in summer but warm in winter and is always a refuge from the wind, mosquitoes, and the sun. So it was easy to see why the dogs liked it. What wasn't so obvious was the secrecy. Dogs are like wolves and wolves keep their dens secret, so the secrecy wasn't unprecedented, but why have it at all? Of course, the enormous amount of energy spent on the digging gives a den genuine economic value, so perhaps the owners fear that it will be taken from them. After all, the easy way to get a den is to let others dig it and then drive them off. Or perhaps the dogs felt a wolfish atavism to protect and hide their young of the future, even though all the important females had been spayed by that time.

Whatever the reason, once the dogs knew I knew 12 about the den, they dropped their security measures and came and went freely. Sometimes three or four dogs would go inside together and stay a long time, surely lined up one behind the other like peas in a pod. Only one, the last to enter, was sure to be staying voluntarily. The dogs deeper inside sometimes seemed to be staying simply because they couldn't get past the outer dog to freedom. No dog seemed particularly sensitive to the problem, either. Often after a long sojourn inside the tunnel, one dog would emerge calm and refreshed, but then two other, very agitated dogs might pop out right behind him and shake or run off somewhere, their fur full of dirt. They couldn't have been truly suffocating, since air could reach them through the corners of the ellipse, but after an hour or so with three dogs breathing, the tunnel probably seemed pretty close.

The den was the dogs' crowning achievement, and 13 the focus of their lives. Eventually, trails radiated from it to all corners of the pen. As if the dogs were wolves, Maria and one of the males—her second son, Windigo— made most use of the den. They, but not the others, frequently improved it by digging it deeper. We would know that one of them was working inside it when little showers of dirt came flying out of its mouth. In keeping with the idea that subordinate animals are but satellites of the alpha pair, the other females rarely used the den at all, and little Viva, the dingo and lowest-ranking female, never used it. Instead, with the highest-ranking male, Suessi, these females stayed very near and scraped alternate beds for themselves around it, in the dirt on the hill.

And as if they had removed themselves at last from 14 their ties with our species, the dogs seemed to have erased human beings from their consciousness. They were always nice to us, and had never been submissive to us, but we began to feel a difference even from that. When we returned from an absence, for instance, they greeted us very mildly, if at all, and they took no notice whatever of strangers. A burglar robbed the house, but the dogs saw no problem in his presence, although a similar burglary years before in Cambridge had left Koki in a state of nervous collapse, so that while the young man burgled, she cringed in terror behind a toilet, having chosen the smallest space in the smallest, darkest room as a place to hide. But in the woods in Virginia, on the hillside by the den, her dog's life had absorbed her utterly, so that the doings of people had faded from her mind. For Koki, who had grown up as a slave, that was quite a step.

Comment

"I began observing dogs by accident," Thomas tells us. In the course of complaints about her Siberian husky that habitually jumped a fence, she noticed that some were coming from sometimes six miles away—the dog ranging at the beginning over 130 square miles. Her later observation of den-building also occurred by chance. But the episode shows that, though chance observation often plays a role in inductive reasoning, it is not synonymous with it or scientific discovery. The popular view that scientists enter laboratories with blank minds and make chance discoveries by randomly mixing chemicals or looking through microscopes simplifies a complex process. Like Thomas, who was prepared by previous observations to notice the den-building, chance discovery is conditioned by previous experience and knowledge. Indeed, the scientist usually comes into the lab to test a theory or *hypothesis* arrived at through earlier experimentation and observation. Thomas is careful not to claim scientific precision. "I don't pretend that my experiment was scientific, or anything more than a casual (if lengthy) observation." An experiment such as hers can be the basis of scientific investigation if it can be tested by further observation and if, in the words of Karl R. Popper, "it has become possible to decide empirically between it and some rival theory" (*The Logic of Scientific Discovery,* Hutchinson, 1959, p. 278).

Questions for Study and Discussion

1. Thomas begins by stating that dogs have "powerful feelings of unity"—an observation drawn from previous observation of her dogs. What other experience and knowledge prepared her to notice these feelings—or, as she states in paragraph 5, "That my dogs made a den in Virginia should not have come as a surprise"?

2. How did the dogs try to keep their den-building a secret? How did Thomas discover that the dogs had built the den? What previous knowledge prepared her to make the discovery?

3. What possible explanations does Thomas give for the secrecy? Does Thomas make a claim for any of these?

4. What observations does Thomas make about life inside the den and the entry of the dogs into it and their exit from it? What inferences does she draw? What earlier observations of canine behavior prepare her to make these inferences?
5. How does the episode support her belief that dogs possess consciousness and have thoughts and emotions? What other evidence does she present in paragraph 14?

Vocabulary Study

1. Thomas states that "in Virginia, another piece of evidence presented itself very dramatically, but the importance was inferential" (paragraph 2)? Why was it "inferential" and not direct?
2. What is a "foraging adult" animal (paragraph 5)?
3. How does the building of the den and the behavior of the dogs illustrate their "social cohesion"?
4. What does Thomas mean by "wolfish atavism" (paragraph 11)?

Suggestions for Writing

1. Describe your own experience with a family pet or perhaps a group of animals you have cared for, and explain how this experience shaped one or more ideas about animal behavior.
2. Thomas states that, to understand how animals behave, "we'd have to know what we meant to one another" as human beings. Show how your relationship with friends and family influenced how you behaved in an episode comparable to being dropped off in the woods with eight or nine other people. Focus on those aspects of the episode that explain the relationship.

Wendell Berry

GETTING ALONG WITH NATURE

Wendell Berry taught English at the University of Kentucky from 1964 to 1977. He has written about his native Kentucky in numerous poems, novels, and essays. *Collected Poems* was published in 1985; his novels include *Nathan Coulter* (1960) and *The Memory of Old Jack* (1974); his essays appear in *The Long-Legged House* (1969) and other collections. Berry has long been associated with the environmental movement and its effort to preserve wilderness areas throughout the United States. His many essays on nature reveal what the critic Edward Abbey describes as "a certain nobility of spirit and sentiment" in Berry's writings—a "sanctity" springing "from his deliberate choice of an old and fundamental way of life, his apparently firm-rooted attachment to his original and right place on earth."

The defenders of nature and wilderness—like their 1 enemies the defenders of the industrial economy—sometimes sound as if the natural and the human were two separate estates, radically different and radically divided. The defenders of nature and wilderness sometimes seem to feel that they must oppose any human encroachment whatsoever, just as the industrialists often apparently feel that they must make the human encroachment absolute or, as they say, "complete the conquest of nature." But there is danger in this opposition, and it can be best dealt with by realizing that these pure and separate categories are pure ideas and do not otherwise exist.

Pure nature, anyhow, is not good for humans to live 2 in, and humans do not want to live in it—or not for very long. Any exposure to the elements that lasts more than a few hours will remind us of the desirability of the basic human amenities: clothing, shelter, cooked food, the company of kinfolk and friends—perhaps even of hot baths and music and books.

It is equally true that a condition that is *purely* 3 human is not good for people to live in, and people do not want to live for very long in it. Obviously, the more artificial a human environment becomes, the more the word "natural" becomes a term of value. It can be argued indeed, that the conservation movement, as we know it today is largely a product of the industrial revolution. The people who want clean air, clear streams, and wild forests, prairies and deserts are the people who no longer have them.

People cannot live apart from nature; that is the first principle of the conservationists. And yet people cannot live in nature without changing it. But this is true of *all* creatures; they depend upon nature, and they change it. What we call nature is, in a sense, the sum of the changes made by all the various creatures and natural forces in their intricate actions and influences upon each other and upon their places. Because of the woodpeckers nature is different from what it would be without them. It is different also because of the borers and ants that live in tree trunks, and because of the bacteria that live in the soil under the trees. The making of these differences is the making of the world.

Some of the changes made by wild creatures we would call beneficent: beavers are famous for making ponds that turn into fertile meadows; trees and prairie grasses build soil. But sometimes, too, we would call natural changes destructive. According to early witnesses, for instance, large areas around Kentucky salt licks were severely trampled and eroded by the great herds of hoofed animals that gathered there. The buffalo "streets" through hilly country were so hollowed out by hoof-wear and erosion that they remain visible almost two centuries after the disappearance of the buffalo. And so it can hardly be expected that humans would not change nature. Humans, like all other creatures, must make a difference; otherwise, they cannot live. But unlike other creatures, humans must make a choice as to the kind and scale of the difference they make. If they choose to make too small a difference, they diminish their humanity. If they choose to make too great a difference, they diminish nature, and narrow their subsequent choices; ultimately, they diminish or destroy themselves. Nature, then, is not only our source but also our limit and measure. Or, as the poet Edmund Spenser put it almost four hundred years ago, Nature, who is the "greatest goddesse," acts as a sort of earthly lieutenant of God, and Spenser represents her as both a mother and judge. Her jurisdiction is over the relations between the creatures; she deals "Right to all . . . indifferently," for she is "the equall mother" of all "And knittest each to each, as brother unto brother." Thus, in Spenser, the natural principles of fecundity and order are pointedly linked with the principle of justice, which we may be a little surprised to see that he attributes also to nature. And yet in his insistence on an "indifferent" natural justice, resting on the "brotherhood" of *all* creatures, not just of humans, Spenser would now be said to be on sound ecological footing.

In nature we know that wild creatures sometimes 6 exhaust their vital sources and suffer the natural remedy: drastic population reductions. If lynxes eat too many snowshoe rabbits—which they are said to do repeatedly—then the lynxes starve down to the carrying capacity of their habitat. It is the carrying capacity of the lynx's habitat, not the carrying capacity of the lynx's stomach, that determines the prosperity of lynxes. Similarly, if humans use up too much soil—which they have often done and are doing—they will starve down to the carrying capacity of *their* habitat. This is nature's "indifferent" justice. As Spenser saw in the sixteenth century, and as we must learn to see now, there is no appeal from this justice. In the hereafter, the Lord may forgive our wrongs against nature, but on earth, so far as we know, He does not overturn her decisions.

One of the differences between humans and lynxes is 7 that humans can see that the principle of balance operates between lynxes and snowshoe rabbits, as between humans and topsoil; another difference, we hope, is that humans have the sense to act on their understanding. We can see, too, that a stable balance is preferable to a balance that tilts back and forth like a seesaw, dumping a surplus of creatures alternately from either end. To say this is to renew the question of whether or not the human relationship with nature is necessarily an adversary relationship, and it is to suggest that the answer is not simple.

But in dealing with this question and in trying to do justice to the presumed complexity of the answer, we are up against an American convention of simple opposition to nature that is deeply established both in our minds and in our ways. We have opposed the primeval forests of the East and the primeval prairies and deserts of the West, we have opposed man-eating beasts and crop-eating insects, sheep-eating coyotes and chicken-eating hawks. In our lawns and gardens and fields, we oppose what we call weeds. And yet more and more of us are beginning to see that this opposition is ultimately destructive even of ourselves, that it does not explain many things that need explaining—in short, that it is untrue. 8

If our proper relation to nature is not opposition, then what is it? This question becomes complicated and difficult for us because none of us, as I have said, wants to live in a "pure" primeval forest or in a "pure" primeval prairie; we do not want to be eaten by grizzly bears; if we are gardeners, we have a legitimate quarrel with weeds; if, in Kentucky, we are trying to improve our pastures, we are likely to be enemies of the nodding thistle. But, do what we will, we remain under the spell of the primeval forests and prairies that we have cut down and broken; we turn repeatedly and with love to the thought of them and to their surviving remnants. We find ourselves attracted to the grizzly bears, too, and know that they and other great, dangerous animals remain alive in our imaginations as they have been all through human time. Though we cut down the nodding 9 thistles, we acknowledge their beauty and are glad to think that there must be some place where they belong. (They may, in fact, not always be out of place in pastures; if, as seems evident, overgrazing makes an ideal seedbed for these plants, then we must understand them as a part of nature's strategy to protect the ground against abuse by animals.) Even the ugliest garden weeds earn affection from us when we consider how faithfully they perform an indispensable duty in covering the bare ground and in building humus. The weeds, too, are involved in the business of fertility.

We know, then, that the conflict between the human 10 and the natural estates really exists and that it is to some extent necessary. But we are learning, or relearning, something else, too, that frightens us: namely, that this conflict often occurs at the expense of *both* estates. It is not only possible but altogether probable that by diminishing nature we diminish ourselves, and vice versa.

The conflict comes to light most suggestively, per- 11 haps, when advocates for the two sides throw themselves into absolute conflict where no absolute difference can exist. An example of this is the battle between defenders of coyotes and defenders of sheep, in which the coyote-defenders may find it easy to forget that the sheep ranchers are human beings with some authentic complaints against coyotes, and the sheep-defenders find it easy to sound as if they advocate the total eradication of both coyotes and conservationists. Such conflicts—like the old one between hawk-defenders and chicken-defenders—tend to occur between people who use nature indirectly and people who use it directly. It is a dangerous mistake, I think, for either side to pursue such a quarrel on the assumption that victory would be a desirable result.

The fact is that people need both coyotes and sheep, 12 need a world in which both kinds of life are possible. Outside the heat of conflict, conservationists probably know that a sheep is one of the best devices for making coarse foliage humanly edible and that wool is ecologically better than the synthetic fibers, just as most shepherds will be aware that wild nature is of value to them and not lacking in interest and pleasure.

The usefulness of coyotes is, of course, much harder   13
to define than the usefulness of sheep. Coyote fur is not a likely substitute for wool, and, except as a last resort, most people don't want to eat coyotes. The difficulty lies in the difference between what is ours and what is nature's: What is ours is ours because it is directly useful. Coyotes are useful *indirectly,* as part of the health of nature, from which we and our sheep alike must live and take our health. The fact, moreover, may be that sheep and coyotes need each other, at least in the sense that neither would prosper in a place totally unfit for the other.

This sort of conflict, then, does not suggest the   14
possibility of victory so much as it suggests the possibility of a compromise—some kind of peace, even an alliance, between the domestic and the wild. We know that such an alliance is necessary. Most conservationists now take for granted that humans thrive best in ecological health and that the test or sign of this health is the survival of a diversity of wild creatures. We know, too, that we cannot imagine ourselves apart from those necessary survivals of our own wildness that we call our instincts. And we know that we cannot have a healthy agriculture apart from the teeming wilderness in the topsoil, in which worms, bacteria, and other wild creatures are carrying on the fundamental work of decomposition, humus making, water storage, and drainage. "In wildness is the preservation of the world," as Thoreau said, may be a spiritual truth, but it is also a practical fact.

On the other hand, we must not fail to consider the   15
opposite proposition—that, so long at least as humans are in the world, in human culture is the preservation of wildness—which is equally, and more demandingly,

true. If wildness is to survive, then *we* must preserve it. We must preserve it by public act, by law, by institutionalizing wildernesses in some places. But such preservation is probably not enough. I have heard Wes Jackson of the Land Institute say, rightly I think, that if we cannot preserve our farmland, we cannot preserve the wilderness. That said, it becomes obvious that if we cannot preserve our cities, we cannot preserve the wilderness. This can be demonstrated practically by saying that the same attitudes that destroy wildness in the topsoil will finally destroy it everywhere; or by saying that if *everyone* has to go to a designated public wilderness for the necessary contact with wildness, then our parks will be no more natural than our cities.

But I am trying to say something more fundamental 16 than that. What I am aiming at—because a lot of evidence seems to point this way—is the probability that nature and human culture, wildness and domesticity, are not opposed but are interdependent. Authentic experience of either will reveal the need of one for the other. In fact, examples from both past and present prove that a human economy and wildness can exist together not only in compatibility but to their mutual benefit.

One of the best examples I have come upon recently 17 is the story of two Sonora Desert oases in Gary Nabhan's book, *The Desert Smells Like Rain*. The first of these oases, A'al Waipia, in Arizona, is dying because the park service, intending to preserve the natural integrity of the place as a bird sanctuary for tourists, removed the Papago Indians who had lived and farmed there. The place was naturally purer after the Indians were gone, but the oasis also began to shrink as the irrigation ditches silted up. As Mr. Nabhan puts it, "an odd thing is happening to their 'natural' bird sanctuary. They are losing the heterogeneity of the habitat, and with it, the birds. The old trees are dying. . . . These riparian trees are essential for the breeding habitat of certain birds. Summer annual seed plants are conspicuously absent. . . . Without the

soil disturbance associated with plowing and flood irrigation, these natural foods for birds and rodents no
longer germinate."

The other oasis, Ki:towak, in old Mexico, still thrives   18
because a Papago village is still there, still farming. The
village's oldest man, Luis Nolia, is the caretaker of the
oasis, cleaning the springs and ditches, farming, planting
trees: "Luis . . . blesses the oasis," Mr. Nabhan says,
"for his work keeps it healthy." An ornithologist who
accompanied Mr. Nabhan found twice as many species
of birds at the farmed oasis as he found at the bird
sanctuary, a fact that Mr. Nabhan's Papago friend,
Remedio, explained in this way: "That's because those
birds, they come where the people are. When the people
live and work in a place, and plant their seeds and water
their trees, the birds go live with them. They like those
places, there's plenty to eat and that's when we are
friends to them."

Another example, from my own experience, is sugges-   19
tive in a somewhat different way. At the end of July
1981, while I was using a team of horses to mow a small
triangular hillside pasture that is bordered on two sides
by trees, I was suddenly aware of wings close below me.
It was a young red-tailed hawk, who flew up into a
walnut tree. I mowed on to the turn and stopped the
team. The hawk then glided to the ground not twenty
feet away. I got off the mower, stood and watched, even
spoke, and the hawk showed no fear. I could see every
feather distinctly, claw and beak and eye, the creamy
down of the breast. Only when I took a step toward him,
separating myself from the team and mower, did he fly.
While I mowed three or four rounds, he stayed near,
perched in trees or standing erect and watchful on the
ground. Once, when I stopped to watch him, he was
clearly watching me, stooping to see under the leaves
that screened me from him. Again, when I could not find
him, I stooped, saying to myself, "This is what he did to
look at me," and as I did so I saw him looking at me.

Why had he come? To catch mice? Had he seen me   20
scare one out of the grass? Or was it curiosity?

A human, of course, cannot speak with authority of   21
the motives of hawks. I am aware of the possibility of
explaining the episode merely by the hawk's youth and
inexperience. And yet it does not happen often or depen-
dably that one is approached so closely by a hawk of
any age. I feel safe in making a couple of assumptions.
The first is that the hawk came because of the conjunction of the small pasture and its wooded borders, of
open hunting ground and the security of trees. This is
the phenomenon of edge or margin that we know to be
one of the powerful attractions of a diversified landscape, both to wildlife and to humans. The human eye
itself seems drawn to such margins, hungering for the
difference made in the countryside by a hedgy fencerow,
a stream, or a grove of trees. And we know that these
margins are biologically rich, the meeting of two kinds
of habitat. But another difference also is important here:
the difference between a large pasture and a small one,
or, to use Wes Jackson's terms, the difference between
a field and a patch. The pasture I was mowing was a
patch—small, intimate, nowhere distant from its edges.

My second assumption is that the hawk was   22
emboldened to come so near because, though he obviously recognized me as a man, I was there with the team
of horses, with whom he familiarly and confidently
shared the world.

I am saying, in other words, that this little visit   23
between the hawk and me happened because the kind
and scale of my farm, my way of farming, and my
technology *allowed* it to happen. If I had been driving
a tractor in a hundred-acre cornfield, it would not have
happened.

In some circles I would certainly be asked if one can   24
or should be serious about such an encounter, if it has
any value. And though I cannot produce any hard
evidence, I would unhesitatingly answer yes. Such

encounters involve another margin—the one between domesticity and wildness—that attracts us irresistibly; they are among the best rewards of outdoor work and among the reasons for loving to farm. When the scale of farming grows so great and obtrusive as to forbid them, the *life* of farming is impoverished.

But perhaps we do find hard evidence of a sort when   25 we consider that *all* of us—the hawk, the horses, and I—were there for our benefit and, to some extent, for our *mutual* benefit: The horses live from the pasture and maintain it with their work, grazing, and manure; the team and I together furnish hunting ground to the hawk; the hawk serves us by controlling the fieldmouse population.

These meetings of the human and the natural estates,   26 the domestic and the wild, occur invisibly, of course, in any well-farmed field. The wilderness of a healthy soil, too complex for human comprehension, can yet be husbanded, can benefit from human care, and can deliver incalculable benefits in return. Mutuality of interest and reward is a possibility that can reach to any city backyard, garden, and park, but in any place under human dominance—which is, now, virtually everyplace—it is a possibility that is *both* natural and cultural. If humans want wildness to be possible, then they have to make it possible. If balance is the ruling principle and a stable balance the goal, then, for humans, attaining this goal requires a consciously chosen and deliberately made partnership with nature.

In other words, we can be true to nature only by   27 being true to human nature—to our animal nature as well as to cultural patterns and restraints that keep us from acting like animals. When humans act like animals, they become the most dangerous of animals to themselves and other humans, and this is because of another critical difference between humans and animals: Whereas animals are usually restrained by the limits of physical appetites, humans have mental appetites that can be far more gross and capacious than physical ones. Only humans squander and hoard, murder and pillage because of notions.

The work by which good human and natural possibilities are preserved is complex and difficult, and it probably cannot be accomplished by raw intelligence and information. It requires knowledge, skills, and restraints, some of which must come from our past. In the hurry of technological progress, we have replaced some tools and methods that worked with some that do not work. But we also need culture-borne instructions about who or what humans are and how and on what assumptions they should act. The Chain of Being, for instance— which gave humans a place between animals and angels in the order of Creation—is an old idea that has not been replaced by any adequate new one. It was simply rejected, and the lack of it leaves us without a definition. 28

Lacking that ancient definition, or any such definition, we do not know at what point to restrain or deny ourselves. We do not know how ambitious to be, what or how much we may safely desire, when or where to stop. I knew a barber once who refused to give a discount to a bald client, explaining that his artistry consisted, not in the cutting off, but in the knowing when to stop. He spoke, I think, as a true artist and a true human. The lack of such knowledge is extremely dangerous in and to an individual. But ignorance of when to stop is a modern epidemic; it is the basis of "industrial progress" and "economic growth." The most obvious practical result of this ignorance is a critical disproportion of scale between the scale of human enterprises and their sources in nature. 29

The scale of the energy industry, for example, is too big, as is the scale of the transportation industry. The scale of agriculture, from a technological or economic point of view, is too big, but from a demographic point of view, the scale is too small. When there are enough people on the land to use it but not enough to husband 30

it, then the wildness of the soil that we call fertility
begins to diminish, and the soil itself begins to flee from
us in water and wind.

If the human economy is to be fitted into the natural   31
economy in such a way that both may thrive, the human
economy must be built to proper scale. It is possible to
talk at great length about the difference between proper
and improper scale. It may be enough to say here that
difference is *suggested* by the difference between amplified and unamplified music in the countryside, or the
difference between the sound of a motorboat and the
sound of oarlocks. A proper human sound, we may say,
is one that allows other sounds to be heard. A properly
scaled human economy or technology allows a diversity
of other creatures to thrive.

"The proper scale," a friend wrote to me, "confers   32
freedom and simplicity . . . and doubtless leads to long
life and health." I think that it also confers joy. The
renewal of our partnership with nature, the rejoining of
our works to their proper places in the natural order,
reshaped to their proper scale, implies the reenjoyment
both of nature and of human domesticity. Though our
task will be difficult, we will greatly mistake its nature
if we see it as grim, or if we suppose that it must always
be necessary to suffer at work in order to enjoy ourselves
in places specializing in "recreation."

Once we grant the possibility of a proper human   33
scale, we see that we have made a radical change of
assumptions and values. We realize that we are less interested in technological "breakthroughs" than in technological elegance. Of a new tool or method we will no
longer ask: Is it fast? Is it powerful? Is it a labor saver?
How many workers will it replace? We will ask instead:
Can we (and our children) afford it? Is it fitting to our
real needs? Is it becoming to us? Is it unhealthy or ugly?
And though we may keep a certain interest in innovation
and in what we may become, we will renew our interest
in what we have been, realizing that conservationists

must necessarily conserve *both* inheritances, the natural and the cultural.

To argue the necessity of wildness to, and in, the human economy is by no means to argue against the necessity of wilderness. The survival of wilderness—of places that we do not change, where we allow the existence even of creatures we perceive as dangerous—is necessary. Our sanity probably requires it. Whether we go to those places or not, we need to know that they exist. And I would argue that we do not need just the great public wildernesses, but millions of small private or semiprivate ones. Every farm should have one; wildernesses can occupy corners of factory grounds and city lots—places where nature is given a free hand, where no human work is done, where people go only as guests. These places function, I think, whether we intend them to or not, as sacred groves—places we respect and leave alone, not because we understand well what goes on there, but because we do not. 34

We go to wilderness places to be restored, to be instructed in the natural economies of fertility and healing, to admire what we cannot make. Sometimes, as we find to our surprise, we go to be chastened or corrected. And we go in order to return with renewed knowledge by which to judge the health of our human economy and our dwelling places. As we return from our visits to the wilderness, it is sometimes possible to imagine a series of fitting and decent transitions from wild nature to the human community and its supports: from forest to woodlot to the "two-story agriculture" of tree crops and pasture to orchard to meadow to grainfield to garden to household to neighborhood to village to city—so that even when we reached the city we would not be entirely beyond the influence of the nature of that place. 35

What I have been implying is that I think there is a bad reason to go to the wilderness. We must not go there to escape the ugliness and the dangers of the present human economy. We must not let ourselves feel that to 36 go there is to escape. In the first place, such an escape is now illusory. In the second place, if, even as conservationists, we see the human and the natural economies as necessarily opposite or opposed, we subscribe to the very opposition that threatens to destroy them both. The wild and the domestic now often seem isolated values, estranged from one another. And yet these are not exclusive polarities like good and evil. There can be continuity between them, and there must be.

What we find, if we weight the balance too much 37
in favor of the domestic, is that we involve ourselves in dangers both personal and public. Not the least of these dangers is dependence on distant sources of money and materials. Farmers are in deep trouble now because they have become too dependent on corporations and banks. They have been using methods and species that enforce this dependence. But such a dependence is not safe, either for farmers or for agriculture. It is not safe for urban consumers. Ultimately, as we are beginning to see, it is not safe for banks and corporations—which, though they have evidently not thought so, are dependent upon farmers. Our farms are endangered because—like the interstate highways or modern hospitals or modern universities—they cannot be inexpensively used. To be usable at all they require great expense.

When the human estate becomes so precarious, our 38
only recourse is to move it back toward the estate of nature. We undoubtedly need better plant and animal species than nature provided us. But we are beginning to see that they can be too much better—too dependent on us and on "the economy," too expensive. In farm animals, for instance, we want good commercial quality, but we can see that the ability to produce meat or milk can actually be a threat to the farmer and to the animal if not accompanied by qualities we would call natural: thriftiness, hardiness, physical vigor, resistance to disease and parasites, ability to breed and give birth without assistance, strong mothering instincts. These natural

qualities decrease care, work, and worry; they also decrease the costs of production. They save feed and time; they make diseases and cures exceptional rather than routine.

We need crop and forage species of high productive ability also, but we do not need species that will not produce at all without expensive fertilizers and chemicals. Contrary to the premise of agribusiness advertisements and of most expert advice, farmers do not thrive by production or by "skimming" a large "cash flow." They cannot solve their problems merely by increasing production or income. They thrive, like all other creatures, according to the difference between their income and their expenses.

One of the strangest characteristics of the industrial economy is the ability to increase production again and again without ever noticing—or without acknowledging—the *costs* of production. That one Holstein cow should produce 50,000 pounds of milk in a year may appear to be marvelous—a miracle of modern science. But what if her productivity is dependent upon the consumption of a huge amount of grain (about a bushel a day), and therefore upon the availability of cheap petroleum? What if she is too valuable (and too delicate) to be allowed outdoors in the rain? What if the proliferation of her kind will again drastically reduce the number of dairy farms and farmers? Or, to use a more obvious example, can we afford a bushel of grain at a cost of five to twenty bushels of topsoil lost to erosion?

"It is good to have Nature working for you," said Henry Besuden, the dean of American Southdown breeders. "She works for a minimum wage." That is true. She works at times for almost nothing, requiring only that we respect her work and give her a chance, as when she maintains—indeed, improves—the fertility and productivity of a pasture by the natural succession of clover and grass or when she improves a clay soil for us by means of the roots of a grass sod. She works for us by

preserving health or wholeness, which for all our ingenuity we cannot make. If we fail to respect her health,
she deals out her justice by withdrawing her protection
against disease—which we *can* make, and do.

To make this continuity between the natural and the   42
human, we have only two sources of instruction: nature
herself and our cultural tradition. If we listen only to
the apologists for the industrial economy, who respect
neither nature nor culture, we get the idea that it is
somehow our goodness that makes us so destructive:
The air is unfit to breathe, the water is unfit to drink,
the soil is washing away, the cities are violent and the
countryside neglected, all because we are intelligent,
enterprising, industrious, and generous, concerned only
to feed the hungry and to "make a better future for our
children." Respect for nature causes us to doubt this,
and our cultural tradition confirms and illuminates our
doubt: No good thing is destroyed by goodness; good
things are destroyed by wickedness. We may identify
that insight as Biblical, but it is taken for granted by
both the Greek and the Biblical lineages of our culture,
from Homer and Moses to William Blake. Since the start
of the industrial revolution, there have been voices urging
that this inheritance may be safely replaced by intelligence,
information, energy, and money. No idea, I believe,
could be more dangerous.

Comment

Berry uses particulars of experience to state probable truths. Berry
begins his discussion by citing a mistaken view of nature shared by
conservationists and industrialists; he wants to correct this view and
find a basis for reconciliation between opposing views. Because so
much misunderstanding on the issue of conservation exists, he needs
to correct mistaken assumptions before arguing the basis for reconciliation. In the concluding paragraphs, Berry suggests measures that
conservationists and their opponents can take to satisfy what he has
shown to be mutual needs.

Questions for Study and Discussion

1. What evidence does Berry present in paragraphs 1-9 for the statement that "our proper relation to nature is not opposition"? If this relation is not an opposition, in what sense is there a "conflict" between sheep and coyotes and other animals, and between human beings and nature in general?

2. What is the difference between the direct and indirect use of nature (paragraph 11), and how does Berry illustrate these different uses? How does this distinction advance his discussion?

3. In what way does human culture preserve nature (paragraph 15)? In what way do the "same attitudes that destroy wildness in the topsoil . . . finally destroy it everywhere"?

4. Berry builds up to his thesis, a statement of the basis for reconciliation between conservationists and industrialists, in paragraph 16. What is the basis of reconciliation? How do the examples given in paragraphs 17-25 illustrate and support Berry's thesis?

5. What point is Berry making about human nature and animal nature in paragraph 27? How does this point advance his argument?

6. How can conservationists and industrialists fit the "human economy" into the "natural economy" and in this way meet the needs of nature and human beings? How does Berry develop this point in paragraphs 34 and 35?

7. What dangers does Berry explore in paragraphs 36-40? How does this discussion further develop his thesis?

8. How does Berry remind the reader of the conflicting claims of conservationists and industrialists in paragraphs 41 and 42, and also restate his thesis?

Vocabulary Study

1. How do the details of paragraph 21 explain what Berry means by "the phenomenon of edge or margin"?

2. What does he mean in paragraph 24 by the margin between "domesticity and wildness"?

3. Explain the following words and phrases:
   a. *encroachment* (paragraph 1)
   b. *human amenities* (paragraph 2)
   c. *ecological* (paragraph 5)
   d. *habitat* (paragraph 6)
   e. *primeval, humus* (paragraph 9)
   f. *domesticity* (paragraph 16)
   g. *silted* (paragraph 17)
   h. *conjunction* (paragraph 21)
   l. *notions* (paragraph 27)
   j. *illusory, polarities* (paragraph 36)
   k. *precarious* (paragraph 38)

Suggestions for Writing

1. Write a summary or précis of Berry's essay, paraphrasing (in your own words) his chief ideas. A précis usually omits examples and supporting details, but you may wish to include any that you consider essential to the argument.
2. Look up the phrase "Chain of Being" (or "Great Chain of Being") in an encyclopedia or other reference book, noting its origin and implications. Then write a short essay on how Berry's essay illustrates the idea.
3. Discuss a statement in Berry's essay with which you strongly agree or disagree and explain why you do. Base your essay on personal experiences and observation, perhaps your own encounter with "pure nature" or with a wild animal.

Deductive Argument

Deductive arguments show that statements the author believes to be true imply other truths. In the essay that follows, "Confessions of a Miseducated Man," Norman Cousins presents his basic argument as follows:

> In order to be at home anywhere in the world I had to forget the things I had been taught to remember. It turned out that my ability to get along with other peoples depended not so much upon my comprehension of the uniqueness of their way of life as upon my comprehension of the things we had in common.

Cousins restates this argument in subsequent paragraphs:

> Only a few years ago an education in differences fulfilled a specific if limited need. That was at a time when we thought of other places and peoples largely out of curiosity or in terms of exotic vacations. It was the mark of a rounded man to be well traveled and to know about the fabulous variations of human culture and behavior. But it wasn't the type of knowledge you had to live by and build on.
>
> Then overnight came the great compression. Far-flung areas which had been secure in their remoteness suddenly became jammed together in a single arena. And all at once a new type of education became necessary, an education in liberation from tribalism. . . .

Cousins summarizes his argument in the following statement:

> The old emphasis upon superficial differences had to give way to education for mutuality and for citizenship in the human community.

We may restate Cousins's argument informally:

> Since getting along with other people depends on understanding what we have in common, an education that teaches only the differences between people doesn't prepare us to live in a world that has become a single arena.

This argument may be restated in positive terms and arranged as a formal argument or *syllogism:*

> *[Major premise]* An education that prepares us to live in a world that has become a single arena is an adequate one.
>
> *[Minor premise]* An education that teaches what we have in common with other people prepares us to live in a world that has become a single arena.
>
> *[Conclusion]* Such an education is an adequate one.

Such an argument is called deductive because it makes an inference from statements assumed to be true—beliefs held as "self-evident" or axiomatic or truths established by experience, observation, or experimentation. A deductive argument says that *if* the premises of the formal argument are true, the conclusion or inference properly drawn from these statements must also be true. We know that Cousins holds the first two statements to be true because he says so in introducing his basic argument:

> As I write this, I have the feeling that my words fail to give vitality to the idea they seek to express. Indeed, the idea itself is a truism which all peoples readily acknowledge even if they do not act on it.

In arguing, we often omit one of the premises or the conclusion. We do so because we consider the omitted premise or conclusion obvious. Shortened arguments of this sort are called *enthymemes.* Here are some examples:

> Since an education that teaches what we have in common prepares us to live in a world that has become a single arena, such an education is adequate. [Major premise omitted: *An adequate education prepares us to live in a world that has become a single arena.*]
>
> Since an adequate education prepares us to live in a world that has become a single arena, an education that teaches what we have in common with other people is an adequate one. [Minor premise omitted: *An education that teaches what we have in*

common with others prepares us to live in a world that has become a single arena.]

An adequate education prepares us to live in a world that has become a single arena, and an education that teaches what we have in common with other people prepares us to live in such a world. [Conclusion implied: *Such an education is adequate.*]

These examples are typical of arguments we hear every day—arguments that require us to supply one of the premises or even the conclusion. In other words, we need to consider implied as well as explicit statements in testing the validity of an argument and weighing its soundness.

A deductive argument is considered *sound* if its premises are true and the process of reasoning is proper or *valid*. If the process of reasoning is faulty or invalid or the premises are untrue—if the premises are "glittering generalities" or are statements that cannot be defended or do not cover all instances—the argument is considered unsound. Cousins's argument would be judged unsound *if* an opponent could disprove his assertion that teaching what people have in common is necessary to live in a changing world.

Here is a valid argument:

Successful farmers are hard-working people.
My parents are successful farmers.
My parents are hard-working people.

What is true of all successful farmers must be true of anyone who belongs to the same class. But note this much different argument:

Successful farmers are hard-working people.
My parents are hard-working people.
My parents are successful farmers.

This argument is invalid because neither premise claims that all hard-working people are successful farmers. Some may be farmers, and some may not be. Deductive arguments take many forms and the tests of validity are therefore complex—the subject of formal logic. Common sense often can detect an error in invalid arguments, but many deceptive arguments require a knowledge of these formal tests. Here are two simple ones:

First, no conclusion can be drawn from two negative premises. If one of the premises is negative, so must be the conclusion. The following informal argument is invalid because it draws a conclusion when none is possible:

> Since no sick people are happy people, and none of us are sick people, we must be happy people.

Second, the terms of the argument must not shift in meaning:

> Since sick people are not happy people, and bigots are sick people, bigots are not happy people.

The phrase *sick people* ordinarily refers to the physically ill. If the word *sick* in the minor premise refers to mental aberration, then the term has shifted in meaning in this argument. Bigots may very well be unhappy people, but not for the reason stated.

Writers know that people will disagree with their premises—with the beliefs, assumptions, truisms on which they base the argument. For this reason a writer may explain or illustrate one or both of the premises—for example, by showing *how* what we have in common with other people helps us to live with them to mutual advantage. Cousins does so in describing the education he favors. The argument is nevertheless deductive in showing what truths the premises entail if the argument is sound.

Norman Cousins

CONFESSIONS OF A MISEDUCATED MAN

Norman Cousins edited the *Saturday Review* from 1940 to 1971, and again from 1971 to 1973. During these years he wrote editorially on a wide range of topics relating to national and international issues. *Present Tense* (1967) contains editorials Cousins wrote between 1940 and 1966; the editorial reprinted here appeared on May 10, 1952. Cousins's other books include *In God We Trust: The Religious Beliefs of the Founding Fathers* (1958), *Doctor Schweitzer of Lambaréné* (1960), *The Celebration of Life* (1975), *The Human Option* (1981), *The Healing Heart* (1983), and *The Pathology of Power* (1987). *Anatomy of an Illness* (1979) describes how he overcame a serious illness. Among his numerous awards are the Benjamin Franklin citation for magazine journalism in 1956, the Eleanor Roosevelt Peace award in 1963, and the United National Peace medal in 1971. Cousins died in 1991.

These notes are in the nature of a confession. It is 1
the confession of a miseducated man.

I have become most aware of my lack of a proper 2
education whenever I have had the chance to put it to
the test. The test is a simple one: am I prepared to live
in and comprehend a world in which there are 3 billion
people? Not the world as it was in 1850 or 1900, for
which my education might have been adequate, but the
world today. And the best place to apply that test is
outside the country—especially Asia or Africa.

Not that my education was a complete failure. It 3
prepared me superbly for a bird's-eye view of the world.
It taught me how to recognize easily and instantly the
things that differentiate one place or one people from
another. Geography had instructed me in differences of
terrain, resources, and productivity. Comparative culture had instructed me in the differences of background
and group interests. Anthropology had instructed me in
the differences of facial bone structure, skin pigmenta-
tion, and general physical aspect. In short, my education
protected me against surprise. I was not surprised at the
fact that some people lived in mud huts and others in
bamboo cottages on stilts; or that some used peat for
fuel and others dung; or that some enjoyed music with
a five-note scale and others with twelve; or that some
people were vegetarian by religion and others by preference.

In those respects my education had been more than 4
adequate. But what my education failed to do was to
teach me that the principal significance of such differences was that they were largely without significance.
The differences were all but obliterated by the similarities. My education had by-passed the similarities. It had
failed to grasp and define the fact that beyond the
differences are realities scarcely comprehended because
of their shattering simplicity. And the simplest reality of
all was that the human community was one—greater
than any of its parts, greater than the separateness

imposed by the nations, greater than the divergent faiths and allegiances or the depth and color of varying cultures. This larger unity was the most important central fact of our time—something on which people could build at a time when hope seemed misty, almost unreal.

As I write this, I have the feeling that my words fail 5 to give vitality to the idea they seek to express. Indeed, the idea itself is a truism which all peoples readily acknowledge even if they do not act on it. Let me put it differently, then. In order to be at home anywhere in the world I had to forget the things I had been taught to remember. It turned out that my ability to get along with other peoples depended not so much upon my comprehension of the uniqueness of their way of life as upon my comprehension of the things we had in common. It was important to respect these differences, certainly, but to stop there was like clearing the ground without any idea of what was to be built on it. When you got through comparing notes, you discovered that you were both talking about the same neighborhood, i.e., this planet, and the conditions that made it congenial or hostile to human habitation.

Only a few years ago an education in differences 6 fulfilled a specific if limited need. That was at a time when we thought of other places and peoples largely out of curiosity or in terms of exotic vacations. It was the mark of a rounded man to be well traveled and to know about the fabulous variations of human culture and behavior. But it wasn't the type of knowledge you had to live by and build on.

Then overnight came the great compression. Far- 7 flung areas which had been secure in their remoteness suddenly became jammed together in a single arena. And all at once a new type of education became necessary, an education in liberation from tribalism. For tribalism had persisted from earliest times, though it had taken refined forms. The new education had to teach man the most difficult lesson of all: to look at someone anywhere in the world and be able to recognize the image of himself. It had to be an education in self-recognition. The old emphasis upon superficial differences had to give way to education for mutuality and for citizenship in the human community.

In such an education we begin with the fact that the universe itself does not hold life cheaply. Life is a rare occurrence among the millions of galaxies and solar systems that occupy space. And in this particular solar system life occurs on only one planet. And on that one planet life takes millions of forms. Of all these countless forms of life, only one, the human species, possesses certain faculties in combination that give it supreme advantages over all the others. Among those faculties or gifts is a creative intelligence that enables man to reflect and anticipate, to encompass past experience, and also to visualize future needs. There are endless other wondrous faculties the mechanisms of which are not yet within the understanding of their beneficiaries—the faculties of hope, conscience, appreciation of beauty, kinship, love, faith.

Viewed in planetary perspective, what counts is not that the thoughts of men lead them in different directions but that all men possess the capacity to think; not that they pursue different faiths but that they are capable of spiritual belief; not that they write and read different books but that they are capable of creating print and communicating in it across time and space; not that they enjoy different art and music but that something in them enables them to respond deeply to forms and colors and ordered vibrations of sounds.

These basic lessons, then, would seek to provide a proper respect for man in the universe. Next in order would be instruction in the unity of man's needs. However friendly the universe may be to man, it has left the conditions of human existence precariously balanced. All men need oxygen, water, land, warmth, food. Remove any one of these and the unity of human needs is attacked and man with it. The next lesson would concern the human situation itself—how to use self-understanding in the cause of human welfare; how to control the engines created by man that threaten to alter the precarious balance on which life depends; how to create a peaceful society of the whole.

With such an education, it is possible that some nation or people may come forward not only with vital understanding but with the vital inspiration that men need no less than food. Leadership on this higher level does not require mountains of gold or thundering propaganda. It is concerned with human destiny; human destiny is the issue; people will respond.

Questions for Study and Discussion

1. Is Cousins saying that an adequate education presents only what people have in common? Or does an adequate education also include the differences between people?
2. Cousins states that "what counts" is the capacity for "spiritual belief" and not the pursuit of different beliefs or faiths. Is he saying that differences in belief or faith are superficial and of no consequence or value?
3. What special view of people does a "planetary perspective" provide of human life? What conclusions does Cousins draw from this view?
4. Why does an adequate education "begin with the fact that the universe itself does not hold life cheaply"? Why should education not begin with the qualities people have in common?
5. Do you agree with Cousins that a person who is aware only of differences between people and cultures is miseducated? What is the basis of your agreement or disagreement with Cousins?

Vocabulary Study

1. Give synonyms for the following words:
    a. *comprehend* (paragraph 2)
    b. *terrain, productivity* (paragraph 3)
    c. *obliterated, allegiances* (paragraph 4)

d. *mutuality* (paragraph 7)
e. *mechanisms* (paragraph 8)
f. *perspective* (paragraph 9)
g. *precarious* (paragraph 10)
h. *propaganda* (paragraph 11)
2. What does the word *tribalism* mean in paragraph 7, and how do you know?
3. Cousins concludes with the statement that "human destiny is the issue." What does he mean by *destiny?*

Suggestions for Writing

1. Discuss one or more ways in which you find your education lacking. Explain why it is lacking—what you should have been taught and what the cost of your miseducation has been.
2. State the qualities that you believe mark the educated person. Then explain why you hold these beliefs. Illustrate these qualities from personal experience or observation.
3. State why you agree or disagree with one of Cousins's statements. Then defend your reasons for agreeing or disagreeing by drawing on personal experience and observation.

Timothy S. Healy, S. J.

IN DEFENSE OF DISORDER

Timothy S. Healy, for many years president of Georgetown University in Washington, D.C., served later as director of the New York Public Library. A specialist in the poetry of John Donne, the Rev. Healy previously taught English at Fordham University and also served as vice chancellor for academic affairs at the City University of New York and on federal government commissions on education. Healy died in 1991. His essay on interruption of unpopular university speakers explores this specific issue. His essay appeared in *Newsweek* on May 23, 1983.

Over the past weeks, the nation's colleges have taken 1
a beating because of loudmouths who shouted down

invited speakers. Eldridge Cleaver at Wisconsin, Ambassador Jeane Kirkpatrick at Berkeley and Sheik Ahmad Zaki Yamani at Kansas were the speakers, and the noise raised in their defense is only slightly less deafening than the shouts that drowned their speeches. No one in the academy approved or condoned the shouting: the clearest defense of the university as an open forum has come from university people themselves through the national associations that represent presidents, faculty members and students.

Whether or not they are aware of it, our critics   2
misread our vulnerability to disruption. They seem to think that universities are orderly places, and if they aren't, presidents and trustees ought to make them so, even by force. Force is, however, our last and least resource, and order in the universities has seldom been more than skin-deep. We order our planning, our upkeep, our payroll and the lawns. But where our most serious work is done, messiness, not to say a kind of anarchy, is part of our nature.

Look first at our teaching. Our job is to put students   3
in touch with beauty or thought and then watch what happens. A young mind seeing for the first time into Virgil, Plato or Burke undergoes an intellectual chain reaction that is uncontrollable. Great works and young minds are "fire and powder which as they kiss consume."

There is an anarchy in the being of our students. The   4
chaos of living in a 20-year-old body translates into the 20-year-old's steady probing at authority. Most students at one time or another tangle with it, not because they want it removed, but because they want to see whether it will stand still long enough for them to measure themselves against it.

At times, the faculty, like parents, cry out in Shake-   5
spearean eloquence:

Let me not live . . . to be the snuff
Of younger spirits, whose apprehensive senses

All but new things disdain; whose judgments are
Mere fathers of their garments; whose constancies
Expire before their fashions.

But faculty, too, are caught up in our disorderly process.
A good class crackles with intensity. The professor knows
the long reach of his ideas and the challenge they put
not only to his students but to himself. He is also aware
of how hard he must crowd and pull to make student
growth go as far as it can. The wrestle of mind on mind
fills both, and neither faculty member nor student has
much time for the dull business of keeping the world,
even the world of the university, in good trim. To learn
and to teach are beautiful things, but at their intense
best, like laughter or pain, they distort.

The faculty knows also the messiness of research. 6
Every scholar who finds himself treading ground no one
has trod before feels as though he has been spun off his
native planet into a solitary and chaotic orbit of specula-
tion, hypothesis and doubt. Anarchy and loneliness go
together. Scholarship in which facts stay in line or ideas
in order is either vulgarization or echo.

Our critics take as given the basic tidiness of gov- 7
ernment, industry and the press, but authority within a
university is tentative and dispersed. No one is completely in charge, and no one should be. Academic
decisions are made by faculties. Students want a large
say in the conduct of their lives on campus. Presidents
and deans distribute the seven goods of the university
(people, space, money, books, equipment, location and
reputation) but are bigger fools than they look if they
confuse the ground they walk with the windy heights
where the young learn and grow.

That growth touches all of us. The faculty offer their 8
experience and knowledge and the students their imagination and energy. The shock between them remakes all
our worlds, including our democracy. Alfred North
Whitehead's vision of the university as the smithy where
a people's ideas and forms are rethought and recast in

"the imaginative acquisition of knowledge" is still true. That vision doesn't work where premises or conclusions go untried or where a false neatness is forcibly laid on.

Because we are open in our process and open in our 9 places, we are deliberately vulnerable to ill-aimed force, which can at times attack our own freedom. The very being of a university makes it easy to disrupt, and our centuries have taught us that we are weakly defended by policemen. A university's great gift is the grant of room for young and old to speculate, to dream, to rear great buildings of ideas. A second gift is an absolution from consequence should those ideas crash down about our ears. Unless the young learn firsthand how supple and strengthening our freedoms are, they will never learn to defend them. Imposed order is a poor teacher for any free people.

Our strong defense, on halcyon as on stormy days, 10 is a discipline as old as man's mind. The worst of our errors are academic and intellectual and we can, given time, correct them. Correction comes not by crowd control, but by reason, by the slow, wearing rub of mind on mind. We live in a glass house that beckons the booby's stone, and none of the numerical barbed wire at the gates of admission can keep out boobies. All of us deal with disrupters, but we try to civilize them, or at least hold them at bay in the strong toils of talk, thought, persuasion. All of us know the acrid shame of failure whenever we must resort to force. We also know that authority alone can never lead a student out of "the prison of his days."

If America's colleges are to be roundly condemned 11 because they feel the best way to handle disruption is to educate disrupters, then something of value to all of us will be lost. Our faculties have at least one large body of allies: the parents of their students. Parents know how hard it is for the young to grow without error, indeed how impossible. They understand why colleges react so

often with ambiguous patience. We who teach distrust
force because we take parentage of the mind seriously,
because like parents we still at heart love our own.

Comment

Healy's argument is a deductive one. In paragraph 5 he states his
conception of the ideal class and the ideal professor: "A good class
crackles with intensity. The professor knows the long reach of his
ideas and the challenge they put not only to his students but to himself." From this belief and others concerning the purpose and nature
of education and the nature of twenty-year-old college students, he
makes inferences or deductions and uses these to explain the behavior of students who disrupt speakers at college campuses. Healy supports his argument with observations drawn from his experience as
a university president; he states that college administrations, trustees, and faculty cannot make universities tidy and well-behaved.

Questions for Study and Discussion

1.   What does Healy tell us in paragraphs 3 through 5 about the
     purpose and nature of education and the nature of college
     students? How does he develop his ideas about education in
     paragraphs 8 and 9?
2.   What conclusions does he draw about campus life and, in
     particular, disruption of speakers from these ideas?
3.   Why do college administrators, trustees, and faculty not have
     the power to control college life? Is Healy saying that anarchy
     is desirable or necessary? Is he saying that administrators and
     faculty should not discourage disruption of speakers?
4.   What appeal to experience does he make to conclude the essay?

Vocabulary Study

1.   What meanings of *order* does Healy explore in paragraphs 2
     and 9? What is the meaning of *discipline* in paragraph 10?

What kind of order does he believe is possible and desirable on a college campus?

2. In what sense of the word is there *anarchy* in twenty-year-old college students?

3. What images and ideas do the words *wrestle* (paragraph 5), *smithy* (paragraph 8), and *rub* (paragraph 10) convey? How are these metaphors related in idea?

4. What meanings do the words *parent* and *parentage* have in paragraph 11?

Suggestion for Writing

Write an essay stating your views on one of the following issues. In the course of your essay, state and answer objections to your position:

1. Disrupting speakers on college campuses
2. Appointing students to serve as college trustees
3. Requiring college students to study a foreign language
4. Refusing to publish offensive advertisements in the college newspaper

Margaret Mead and Rhoda Metraux

CRIME: BROKEN CONNECTIONS

Margaret Mead (1901-1978), one of America's most distinguished anthropologists, was a curator of ethnology at the Museum of Natural History in New York City from 1926 to 1969. She also taught at Columbia and other universities, and participated in the work of numerous United States and United Nations agencies. She traveled widely and wrote about many cultures, including her own, in such widely read books as *Growing Up in New Guinea* (1930), *And Keep Your Powder Dry* (1942), and *Male and Female* (1949).

Rhoda Metraux has done field work in anthropology in many countries. She has been on the staff of various government agencies and a research associate at the Museum of Natural History. She and Margaret Mead worked together for many years, collaborating in the writing of *The Study of Culture at a Distance* (1953) and *Themes in French Culture* (1954). Their essay appeared in *Redbook* in May, 1978.

"That's terrible! That's a crime! Someone should do   1
something about it!" How often have you heard that
said—or said it yourself?

Heard apart from the act that triggered the reaction,   2
these are just trite words. But like so many other well-
worn phrases, they may carry a very heavy load of
emotion—indignation, fear, anger. And better than many
more learned definitions, they sum up people's response
to crime the world over, in nations with modern, sophisticated penal codes and in tiny societies of a few hundred
persons who still live by their own unwritten, customary
law. A crime is something that people regard as very
wrong—something terrible—that someone should do
something about.

In our kind of society it is the police who should do   3
something, and when we have reported what may be a
crime to a law-enforcement officer we can, and usually
do, put it out of our minds. Unless, of course, we happen
to be the victim who has been robbed or assaulted or
otherwise harmed. But sometimes what seems to a layperson to be a crime is not so in the law; then the police
can take no action. At other times we would not consider reporting acts that every one of us knows very well
are illegal, and the police too may close their eyes.
During prohibition almost every adult in town knew
exactly where to buy a drink and how to contact a
bootlegger. Today even young teen-agers in a city can
easily find out where hard drugs are bought and sold
more or less openly and with impunity.

What differs extremely around the world is the cul-   4
tural conception of what constitutes a crime, who should
do something about it and what should be done. There
are societies in which vulnerable persons, such as pregnant women, mourners, little children or men starting
out on some large enterprise, must wear deterrent amu-
lets or be magically charmed or ritually treated to protect them from danger—to ward off the evil eye, the angry ghost, the malicious curse, the enemy spear. Elsewhere,

victims or their kin turn to the nearest sorcerer in search of vengeance. Or a malefactor may be banished from his community so that he has no one to back him up, no one to protect him in a time of need. Or the murderer may be obliged to take the place of his victim—become a husband to his victim's wife, a father to his victim's children, knowing that one day, when least expected, he too will be killed.

There seems to be no end to human ingenuity when it comes to defining what is a crime, and especially what should be done about it. In advanced civilizations the idea of some kind of penal code, clear and impersonal, is very ancient. But we only recently have begun to realize the extraordinarily arbitrary nature of both our private beliefs about crime and criminals and of our laws and to discover the depth of our emotional commitment to particular forms of punishment, legal and extralegal.

There are no societies that are totally free of crime. In every society, as far as we know, there are likely to be a very few individuals who cannot be socialized, that is, who cannot learn to control their violent, destructive impulses and who therefore are dangerous and endangered. In a very small society or in a stable, homogeneous small community where everyone knows a great deal about everyone else, the danger may be minimized by watchful awareness—not always successfully, to be sure, but most of the time.

The hazards are greater in a very populous and complex urban society. For the most part such asocial individuals are unidentifiable—unknown strangers until by some violent act they come into public view. In our society the life history of a person even with a long record of maladaptive or criminal acts may be known only superficially or in fragments, and often reform schools and penitentiaries are only too eager to rid themselves, on any pretext, of such endlessly troublesome prisoners. But the number of fundamentally violent or asocial individuals in our very large population is not great. Recently John Boone, the former Commissioner of Corrections in Massachusetts, estimated that in the whole United States there are no more than 5,000 to 6,000 such persons.

For the rest, we make our own criminals, and their 8 crimes are congruent with the national culture we all share. It has been said that a people get the kind of political leadership they deserve. I think they also get the kinds of crime and criminals they themselves bring into being. As in every culture, it is a circular system. For instance, in a society in which people believe in sorcery, there undoubtedly will be sorcerers, and they in turn will foster effectively the practice of sorcery.

In our country white-collar crimes by educated, well- 9 to-do and socially respected businessmen and professionals, juvenile delinquency at every social level, burglaries and armed robberies, muggings of defenseless old women and men, the prostitution of runaway teen-aged girls and boys, the drug dealing, the wife beating and child abuse, the hijackings, the senseless killing of unknown persons, the arson and vandalism that today stretch from factories and shops and public buildings to inner-city slums and suburban communities and even to the remotest rural places—all these and many other forms of crime are not simply accidental. They are the products of the way we organize the country, the way we both proclaim and reject social responsibility, the way we dichotomize our thinking about and treatment of human beings, protecting some privileged individuals from the consequences of their acts and punishing others whom from their earliest years we first neglect and then treat as expendable. Their behavior, like anyone else's, is an expression of our national culture for which all of us ultimately must take responsibility.

I believe we have concentrated too much on crimi- 10 nals, on the flaws in their character and the weaknesses in their background, instead of asking what needs they serve and what general attitudes in our society—or in the whole of modern society—are reflected in their actions. I do not argue for the point of view that has confounded so many of our attempts at reform, namely, that because a society is ultimately responsible for the behavior of its members, the individual criminal has been made a misfit who must not be held responsible for his acts.

Instead, I am asking what we are doing that is 11 encouraging a rising tide of violence and crime and that has permitted men at the very top of national law-enforcement agencies—an attorney general of the United States and the long-time head of the FBI—to believe that it is right to deal harshly with criminals and at the same time that it is all right for them, and other men like them, to commit highly illegal acts.

I am asking also what has led us to avoid responsible 12 action to bring about change. For there is a great deal of evidence that this is what we are doing. Consider, for example, the vast contemporary proliferation of insurance as a principal method of coping not only, very legitimately, with natural disasters, with illness, accident and death and with the needs of young families, but also with almost every form of delinquency and crime—including the damage our own children may inflict on the property of others.

Today insurance has become a highly organized, 13 profitable way of accepting the existence of carelessness, irresponsibility, delinquency and almost every form of crime, from the destruction or loss of property to the loss of life. Insurance protects each of us individually—or at least those of us who can afford to buy this protection—from loss. In addition there are hidden costs, for businesses simply pass on to their customers the rising cost of insurance against shoplifting, hijacking, vandalism and other kinds of crime to which they are subject. But this still appears to be cheaper and easier for us than it would be to make the moral effort to alter attitudes and the conditions of living in which crime flourishes.

Would making such a moral effort be too high a price to pay? 14

I do not think so. But I believe the problem lies else- 15
where.

What we are suffering from—and I do mean suffer- 16
ing—is a whole series of broken connections between different aspects of our behavior, our thinking and feeling. Changes, including vast changes in scale as our society has grown and become technologically sophisticated, have obscured the connections between our beliefs and our actions, have fragmented our awareness of one another. Consequently our response has been to turn away from the hard problems we have solved badly or left unsolved.

We value human rights, for example, but we do not 17
see the connection between our rejection of the elderly and the handicapped and whatever of value they have to offer us, on the one hand, and on the other the mugging of the old by street children and the scandalous exploitation of the elderly in lonely rooms or frightening welfare "hotels" or nursing homes. We believe that the nation's children are the keepers of the future, but we do not see the connection between juvenile crime and living conditions of families in inner cities or the poverty-stricken countryside, between such crime and our deteriorating schools in which children are demeaned and punished because we have failed them as teachers and interpreters of our culture. We do not see the connection between the very high rates of joblessness among young people who have few skills and no resources and who have lost their readiness to learn and the extremely high rate of crime, especially violent crime, among these adolescents and young adults.

The right to a second—or a third or fourth—new 18
chance is central in our culture. But we have lost the connection between our perceptions of whole groups in

our population—particularly those whom we have already put down, ripped off and denigrated as human beings by the conditions of life to which they are condemned because they are poor, members of minority groups or illegal immigrants, young, unskilled and feared—and our handling of criminals. We have lost the connection between the conditions in the places of detention for young offenders (among whom are the runaways, so often children already offended against) and in the reformatories and penitentiaries, where once optimistic reformers hoped that prisoners would be treated as penitents, and the increasing number of persons, today women as well as men, who have become hopelessly addicted to a life of crime.

But there is still another, a further and final step. We have lost the connection between our ambiguous apparent admiration for and rejection of criminals whom we believe to be irreparably violent and our increasingly loud insistence that the only legitimate response to violence is violence. [19]

In our private lives we insist that citizens must retain the right to be armed and to have at hand the lethal weapons that threaten the lives not only of intruders but also of members of their families and, indeed, anyone against whom an individual may turn in a temporary excess of rage or fear. In parts of the country where hunting still is a sanctioned traditional sport, the young may be instructed in the care of guns and taught to respect them as dangerous. But not so in cities. [20]

And almost everywhere, law-enforcement officers have spent millions of dollars on sophisticated weapons. But what has happened is that individual policemen have become correspondingly warier of being attacked and more trigger-ready to shoot to kill before they know whether the suspected wrongdoer is also armed and about to attack. [21]

When the Supreme Court effectively abolished the death sentence for crime, it seemed possible that we [22] might now reconsider the whole connection between violent crime and violent retribution. Instead, the legislatures of many states are attempting to draft new state laws that will permit us, after all, to go on legally killing members of our own society, members of our own human species, whom we have utterly rejected.

Can we do this now without also strengthening the belief that lethal violence can be legitimate? I do not believe so. Far from providing a deterrent, the reinstated death penalty—for different crimes in different states—will increase the belief in violence not only among ordinary criminals but also among those disturbed and distorted persons who seek some highly publicized goal by means of arson, kidnapping or hijacking and killing well-known individuals or groups of helpless, uninvolved persons, children and adults.   23

Is there no alternative?   24

I believe there is, providing we will accept the responsibility for our decisions and our subsequent actions.   25

Comment

Mead and Metraux write as anthropologists about crime in various societies, and they also write as citizens of a large American city about crime in America. Their argument is deductive in their statement of long-tested truths, derived from personal observation and experience, and their inferences or conclusions drawn from these truths. The inferences drawn are sometimes immediate and obvious. If, for example, an urban society is "very populous and complex," then it follows that "asocial individuals" are harder to identify, in contrast to small societies where no one is a stranger. From other truths, discussed at length, they draw more far-reaching inferences about crime—its causes and remedies.

Questions for Study and Discussion

1. Why are the conceptions of crime and efforts to prevent it in various societies important to Mead and Metraux in considering crime in America?

2. Mead and Metraux state that "we make our own criminals, and their crimes are congruent with the national culture we all share" (paragraph 8). How do they restate and develop this statement in paragraph 9?

3. What evidence do they present for the claim that Americans "avoid responsible action to bring about change" (paragraph 12)?

4. Why do they reject the argument that "because a society is ultimately responsible for the behavior of its members, the individual criminal has been made a misfit who must not be held responsible for his acts" (paragraph 10)? Do they reject the initial premise?

5. To what disconnection do Mead and Metraux attribute the reluctance of Americans to reduce crime? What consequence do they deduce from this attitude?

6. Are Mead and Metraux opposed to the private ownership of guns and other weapons because they are dangerous to the owners? Would they be opposed if everyone was trained to respect and care for firearms? How do you know?

7. What truths or assumptions underlie the argument against the death penalty in paragraphs 22 and 23? Do Mead and Metraux state these truths, or are they implied in their discussion?

Vocabulary Study

How does the context or surrounding words help to explain the following words and phrases:

1. *trite words, sophisticated penal codes* (paragraph 2)
2. *layperson, impunity* (paragraph 3)
3. *cultural conception, malefactor* (paragraph 4)
4. *homogeneous* (paragraph 6)
5. *maladaptive* (paragraph 7)
6. *congruent, circular system* (paragraph 8)

7. *proliferation* (paragraph 12)
8. *fragmented* (paragraph 16)
9. *denigrated, penitents* (paragraph 18)
10. *ambiguous, irreparably* (paragraph 19)
11. *sanctioned* (paragraph 20)

Suggestions for Writing

1. Argue for or against private ownership of firearms or the death penalty, explaining why you agree or disagree with Mead and Metraux on the issue. State the assumptions or truths that support your argument, explaining why you hold them and how you reason from these to your position on the issue.
2. Argue whether or not parents should be held responsible for the damage their children inflict. State the assumptions or truths on which you base your argument.
3. Discuss what the term *human rights* means to you. State the beliefs or assumptions that underlie your view.

Alan M. Dershowitz

JUST "A LITTLE CENSORSHIP"

Alan M. Dershowitz, professor of law at Harvard University, is the author of numerous books on civil liberties and American law, including *The Best Defense* (1982), *Reversal of Fortune: Inside the Von Bulow Case* (1986), and *Taking Liberties* (1988). Dershowitz gives details of his life and career in his autobiography *Chutzpah!* (1991). His essay on censorship appears in his collection of essays *Contrary to Popular Opinion* (1992).

Almost everyone supports freedom of speech—in theory. But most would insist on some "limited" exceptions to complete freedom of expression. "Just this itsy-bitsy exception wouldn't cause any harm" is the argument I hear all the time. The problem is that everyone has a *different* itsy-bitsy exception, and in a nation of equal protection, it is difficult to pick and choose among the preferred exceptions. If we were to accept them all, there would be little left of the First Amendment.

I recall an incident at Harvard several years ago that illustrates this principle of "ism equity." A feminist instructor circulated a memorandum objecting to the fact that the Harvard library contained *"Playboy* magazine." She was "offended" by that particular item and could not understand why Harvard's money should be used to subscribe to an item that offended her. I wrote a tongue-in-cheek response in which I applauded her proposal and suggested taking it to its logical extreme: Every member of the Harvard community should have the power to demand that the library not carry one genre of material that he or she found offensive. I submitted my own particular favorite: books and articles that call for censorship. I argued that if every member of the Harvard community got to veto one offensive genre of writing, we could close down the costly library system, move the few remaining volumes to a few file cabinets, and convert Widener Library into squash courts—unless, of course, someone was offended by squash.

In a nation—or university—committed to equality, there can never be just "a little" censorship. The choice is between what I call "the taxi-cab theory of free speech" and a "system of censorship." Just as a taxi cab must accept all law-abiding passengers who can pay the fare without discriminating on the basis of where they are going or why they are going there, so, too, a government or university may not pick and choose between what books or magazines may be offensive. Once it gets into the business of picking and choosing among writings, then it must create a fair and equitable *system* of censorship based on articulated principles. If it decides that items offensive to some women can be banned, then it will have difficulty rejecting the claims of offensiveness made by blacks, Jews, gays, fundamentalist Christians, atheists, vegetarians, antifur proponents, and other politically correct and incorrect groups. I used to be able to argue that under such a system the only book left would be *Little Red Riding Hood*. But recently that children's classic was banned on the grounds that it promoted the killing of animals by glorifying the hunter as well as the drinking of wine by elderly grandmothers.

Comment

A writer may state the premises of an argument as *given* truths, requiring no defense, though these *givens* may be explained and illustrated in the course of the essay. If a premise or assumption is controversial, the writer may defend it, perhaps by citing long-tested observations that support it. Dershowitz defends a central assumption or belief about freedom of expression that forms his attitude. The defense takes the form of the traditional *reductio ad absurdum*— reducing or disproving an argument by showing that it leads to an absurdity. His brief and incisive argument is deductive in showing that censorship entails certain contradictions and absurdities.

Questions for Study and Discussion

1. What effect would a slight limit or exception to freedom of expression have on the First Amendment?
2. How did Dershowitz demonstrate the absurdity of censorship in the controversy over the presence of *Playboy* in the Harvard library?
3. What is "the taxi-cab theory of free speech," and how does he use this theory in defending unlimited freedom of expression?
4. What other contradictions or absurdities of censorship does Dershowitz discuss? Why do you think he concludes his defense with these absurdities?

Vocabulary Study

Use the formal definitions and synonym listings in your college dictionary to determine the difference between the following words: *freedom, liberty, license, privilege.* Then write sentences that illustrate these meanings.

Suggestions for Writing

1. Argue against a proposed or existing law or policy as Dershowitz does, by showing that it leads to contradictions or absurdities.
2. Develop your argument further by showing the benefits of not enacting the law or policy or of abolishing it.

George F. Will

BEARBAITING AND BOXING

George F. Will taught politics at Michigan State University and other universities, and later observed the workings of government as a congressional aide. Since 1972, he has given his full time to journalism, first as editor of the *National Review,* and later as a columnist for the *Washington Post* and *Newsweek,* and as commentator for the American Broadcasting Company. In 1977, Will received the Pulitzer Prize for Commentary. His columns have been collected in a number of books, including *The Pursuit of Virtue, and Other Tory Notions* (1982), *The Morning After* (1986), *Suddenly: The American Idea Abroad and at Home* (1990), and *Political Essays* (1990). His book *Statecraft as Soulcraft: What Government Does* (1983) is a theoretical study of government.

For 150 years people have been savoring Macaulay's   1
judgment that the Puritans hated bearbaiting not because it gave pain to the bear but because it gave pleasure to the spectators. However, there are moments, and this is one, for blurting out the truth: The Puritans were

right. The pain to the bear was not a matter of moral indifference, but the pleasure of the spectators was sufficient reason for abolishing that entertainment.

Now another boxer has been beaten to death. The brain injury he suffered was worse than the injury the loser in a boxing match is supposed to suffer. It is hard to calibrate such things—how hard an opponent's brain should be banged against the inside of his cranium—in the heat of battle.

From time immemorial, in immemorial ways, men have been fighting for the entertainment of other men. Perhaps in a serene, temperate society boxing would be banned along with other blood sports—if, in such a society, the question would even arise. But a step toward the extinction of boxing is understanding why that is desirable. One reason is the physical injury done to young men. But a sufficient reason is the quality of the pleasure boxing often gives to spectators.

There is no denying that boxing, like other, better sports, can exemplify excellence. Boxing demands bravery and, when done well, is beautiful in the way that any exercise of finely honed physical talents is. Furthermore, many sports are dangerous. But boxing is the sport that has as its object the infliction of pain and injury. Its crowning achievement is the infliction of serious trauma on the brain. The euphemism for boxing is "the art of self-defense." No. A rose is a rose is a rose, and a user fee is a revenue enhancer is a tax increase, and boxing is aggression.

It is probable that there will be a rising rate of spinal cord injuries and deaths in football. The force of defensive players (a function of weight and speed) is increasing even faster than the force of ball carriers and receivers. As a coach once said, football is not a contact sport—dancing is a contact sport—football is a collision sport. The human body, especially the knee and spine, is not suited to that. But football can be made safer by equipment improvements and rules changes such as those proscribing certain kinds of blocks. Boxing is fundamentally impervious to reform.

It will be said that if two consenting adults want to 6
batter each other for the amusement of paying adults, the essential niceties have been satisfied, "consent" being almost the only nicety of a liberal society. But from Plato on, political philosophers have taken entertainments seriously, and have believed the law should, too. They have because a society is judged by the kind of citizens it produces, and some entertainments are coarsening. Good government and the good life depend on good values and passions, and some entertainments are inimical to these.

Such an argument cuts no ice in a society where the 7
decayed public philosophy teaches that the pursuit of happiness is a right sovereign over all other considerations; that "happiness" and "pleasure" are synonyms, and that there is no hierarchy of values against which to measure particular appetites. Besides, some persons will say, with reason, that a society in which the entertainment menu includes topless lady mud wrestlers is a society past worrying about.

Some sports besides boxing attract persons who want 8
their unworthy passions stirred, including a lust for blood. I remember Memorial Day in the Middle West in the 1950s, when all roads led to the Indianapolis Speedway, where too many fans went to drink Falstaff beer and hope for a crash. But boxing is in a class by itself.

Richard Hoffer of the *Los Angeles Times* remembers 9
the death of Johnny Owen, a young 118-pound bantamweight who died before he had fulfilled his modest ambition of buying a hardware store back home in Wales. Hoffer remembers that "Owen was put in a coma by a single punch, carried out of the Olympic (arena) under a hail of beer cups, some of which were filled with urine."

The law can not prudently move far in advance of 10
mass taste, so boxing can not be outlawed. But in a world in which many barbarities are unavoidable, perhaps it is

not too much to hope that some of the optional sorts will be outgrown.

Comment

The statement on bearbaiting by the nineteenth-century English historian Thomas B. Macaulay on Oliver Cromwell and the English Puritans, who ruled from 1649 to 1660, is often quoted in the course of ridiculing puritanical views. Will defends the Puritan ethical view as "sufficient reason" for discouraging boxing. He shows that boxing resembles football and automobile racing in different ways, but he focuses on boxing because he considers the sport to be "in a class by itself." His argument is based on what he considers obvious truths about the ideal society. Recognizing that probably few boxing fans would agree with him, he supports his argument with factual evidence. His argument is a deductive one, however, in making inferences directly from these truths.

Questions for Study and Discussion

1. What is Will's definition of the ideal society, and where does he present it?
2. What inference does Will draw from this definition about the entertainments of a society?
3. Why does American society fall short of that ideal? What factual evidence does Will present to support this judgment?
4. How does boxing resemble football and automobile racing? Why does Will believe boxing is "in a class by itself"?
5. In paragraph 10, Will states an obvious truth and draws an inference from it. What is that truth and what is the inference?

Vocabulary Study

1. Find information on bearbaiting in a sports dictionary or other reference book. To what extent did bearbaiting in the seventeenth century and other times resemble the sports criticized by Will?

2. Give synonyms for the following:

    a. *calibrate* (paragraph 2)
    b. *temperate* (paragraph 3)
    c. *honed, trauma, euphemism* (paragraph 4)
    d. *proscribing, impervious* (paragraph 5)
    e. *niceties, inimical* (paragraph 6)
    f. *sovereign, hierarchy* (paragraph 7)
    g. *prudently* (paragraph 10)

Suggestions for Writing

1. State whether or not you agree with Will on the issue of boxing. Explain your reasons for your agreement or disagreement.
2. Use the resources of your library to write a research paper on one of the following topics. Limit the topic to a particular period—perhaps a decade in which a large number of fatalities or accidents occurred—or to an aspect on which you find sufficient information to support a significant thesis. Your research paper might be an informative one that provides facts needed to understand an existing situation. Or your paper might be persuasive: you might use your findings to argue for or against a proposal or an existing policy:

    a. Professional boxing fatalities and the public response
    b. Injuries in stock car and other automobile races and the public response
    c. Injuries in college and professional football
    d. Gunshot deaths in the United States and Great Britain
    e. Drug-related crime in two American cities
    f. Infant mortality in the United States
    g. Chemical warfare since 1913
    h. Causes of homelessness in America in the 1980s
    i. The increasing cost of hospitalization in the 1990s
    j. Standards of welfare eligibility in two American cities

Strategies of Persuasion

Writers direct their arguments to a particular audience, and to make their arguments persuasive, they organize them in light of that audience's knowledge and beliefs. We saw that inductive arguments generalize from particulars of experience and similar kinds of evidence, and that deductive arguments reason from premises to conclusions they entail. The persuasiveness of the inductive argument depends on the strength of the facts presented, but the order in which these facts and generalizations are presented is not fixed: the writer may decide to lead from the facts to the generalizations they support, as Edward H. Peeples, Jr., does (p. 283), or begin with the generalizations and proceed to the facts. The decision depends on what order the writer decides will be most persuasive to a particular audience. The same is true of the deductive essay. Here the conclusion of the argument may be stated first as a way of focusing attention on the point of most concern. Or the writer may start with the least controversial statement (or premise) and end with the most controversial. The order of ideas does not affect the strength or soundness of the argument itself.

Roger Rosenblatt's essay on the Air Florida crash in Washington, D.C., on January 14, 1982, builds from an account or narrative of the crash to a description of acts of heroism that challenge the widespread belief that "people are powerless in the world." The description of one of the heroic acts leads to a question about the nameless man who performed it: "Yet there was something else about our man that kept our thoughts on him, and which keeps our thoughts on him still." What is true of the nameless man in the water is true also of the others who risked their lives. And, Rosenblatt continues, leading to his thesis, their acts remind us of our real feelings about ourselves, no matter what we say about what people can do in the world.

361

Rosenblatt thus appeals to experience to support a truth about people. He might have begun the essay with a statement of this truth, but in order to challenge the skeptical reader he shows that the acts of the three men were indeed heroic before he explores the meaning of their acts. Using a simple, direct style, he presents the facts without overdramatizing them. His simple, eloquent language brings the essay to a fitting emotional climax:

> So the man in the water had his own natural powers. He could not make ice storms, or freeze the water until it froze the blood. But he could hand life over to a stranger, and that is a power of nature too.

The essay is persuasive not only in its precise statement of the facts that build to a controversial thesis, but in the simplicity and eloquence of the language.

A writer has available numerous persuasive means. In dramatizing the episode, Rosenblatt allows the reader to imagine the situation of the man in the water. This appeal to imagination is one important persuasive device. Another is humor, if appropriate to the subject. To change our thinking on an issue or encourage us to take action, the writer may appeal to shame and guilt or to our common humanity. The satirist employs ridicule to correct bad manners or unethical or vicious behavior. The simple, precise statement of the facts of a case, exact in its details, is sometimes more persuasive than a highly emotional appeal, as the letter on strip mining that concludes this section shows.

Roger Rosenblatt

THE MAN IN THE WATER

Roger Rosenblatt attended New York University and Harvard University, where he later taught English. From 1973 to 1975 he was director of education for the National Endowment for the Humanities. He has also been literary editor of *The New Republic* and an essayist for *Time* and *Life* magazines and the *MacNeil-Lehrer NewsHour* on the Public Broadcasting Service. Rosenblatt is the author of *Black Fiction* (1974); *Children of War* (1983); and *The Man in the Water* (1994), a collection of essays. In 1982 he received the George Polk Award for magazine reporting. His essay on an airplane crash in Washington, D. C., originally appeared in *Time* on January 25, 1982.

As disasters go, this one was terrible, but not unique, certainly not among the worst on the roster of U.S. air crashes. There was the unusual element of the bridge, of course, and the fact that the plane clipped it at a moment of high traffic, one routine thus intersecting another and disrupting both. Then, too, there was the location of the event. Washington, the city of form and regulations, turned chaotic, deregulated, by a blast of real winter and a single slap of metal on metal. The jets from Washington National Airport that normally swoop around the presidential monuments like famished gulls are, for the moment, emblemized by the one that fell; so there is that detail. And there was the aesthetic clash as well—blue-and-green Air Florida, the name a flying garden, sunk down among gray chunks in a black river. All that was worth noticing, to be sure. Still, there was nothing very special in any of it, except death, which, while always special, does not necessarily bring millions to tears or to attention. Why, then, the shock here?

Perhaps because the nation saw in this disaster something more than a mechanical failure. Perhaps because people saw in it no failure at all, but rather something successful about their makeup. Here, after all were two forms of nature in collision: the elements and human character. Last Wednesday, the elements, indifferent as ever, brought down Flight 90. And on that same afternoon, human nature—groping and flailing in mysteries of its own—rose to the occasion.

Of the four acknowledged heroes of the event, three are able to account for their behavior. Donald Usher and Eugene Windsor, a park police helicopter team, risked their lives every time they dipped the skids into the water to pick up survivors. On television, side by side in bright blue jumpsuits, they described their courage as all in the line of duty. Lenny Skutnik, a 28-year-old employee of the Congressional Budget Office, said: "It's something I never thought I would do"—referring to his jumping into the water to drag an injured woman to shore. Skutnik added that "somebody had to go in the water," delivering every hero's line that is no less admirable for its repetitions. In fact, nobody had to go into the water. That somebody actually did so is part of the reason this particular tragedy sticks in the mind.

But the person most responsible for the emotional impact of the disaster is the one known at first simply as the man in the water." (Balding, probably in his 50s, an extravagant mustache.) He was seen clinging with five other survivors to the tail section of the airplane. This man was described by Usher and Windsor as appearing alert and in control. Every time they lowered a lifeline and flotation ring to him, he passed it on to another of the passengers. "In a mass casualty, you'll find people like him," said Windsor. "But I've never seen one with that commitment." When the helicopter came back for him, the man had gone under. His selflessness was one reason the story held national attention; his anonymity another. The fact that he went unidentified invested him with a universal character. For a while he was Everyman, and thus proof (as if one needed it) that no man is ordinary.

Still, he could never have imagined such a capacity in himself. Only minutes before his character was tested, he was sitting in the ordinary plane among the ordinary passengers, dutifully listening to the stewardess telling him to fasten his seat belt and saying something about the "no smoking sign." So our man relaxed with the others, some of whom would owe their lives to him. Perhaps he started to read, or to doze, or to regret some harsh remark made in the office that morning. Then suddenly he knew that the trip would not be ordinary. Like every other person on that flight, he was desperate to live, which makes his final act so stunning.

For at some moment in the water he must have realized that he would not live if he continued to hand over the rope and ring to others. He *had* to know it, no matter how gradual the effect of the cold. In his judgment he had no choice. When the helicopter took off with what was to be the last survivor, he watched everything in the world move away from him, and he deliberately let it happen.

Yet there was something else about our man that [7] kept our thoughts on him, and which keeps our thoughts on him still. He was *there,* in the essential, classic circumstance. Man in nature. The man in the water. For its part, nature cared nothing about the five passengers. Our man, on the other hand, cared totally. So the timeless battle commenced in the Potomac. For as long as that man could last, they went at each other, nature and man; the one making no distinctions of good and evil, acting on no principles, offering no lifelines; the other acting wholly on distinctions, principles and, one supposes, on faith.

Since it was he who lost the fight, we ought to come [8] again to the conclusion that people are powerless in the world. In reality, we believe the reverse, and it takes the act of the man in the water to remind us of our true feelings in this matter. It is not to say that everyone would have acted as he did, or as Usher, Windsor and Skutnik. Yet whatever moved these men to challenge death on behalf of their fellows is not peculiar to them. Everyone feels the possibility in himself. That is the abiding wonder of the story. That is why we would not let go of it. If the man in the water gave a lifeline to the people gasping for survival, he was likewise giving a lifeline to those who observed him.

The odd thing is that we do not even really believe [9] that the man in the water lost his fight. "Everything in Nature contains all the powers of Nature," said Emerson. Exactly. So the man in the water had his own natural powers. He could not make ice storms, or freeze the water until it froze the blood. But he could hand life over to a stranger, and that is a power of nature too. The man in the water pitted himself against an implacable, impersonal enemy; he fought it with charity; and he held it to a standoff. He was the best we can do.

Questions for Study and Discussion

1. Rosenblatt does not give us all the facts of the crash. What facts does he present, and what aspects does he emphasize?
2. Is Rosenblatt writing only to those readers familiar with the circumstances of the crash, or is he also providing information for those unfamiliar with what happened?
3. Rosenblatt builds from the details of the crash to reflections about it. In what order are these details presented? Is Rosenblatt describing the events in the order they occurred?
4. How does he explain the heroism of the man in the water, the helicopter police, and Larry Skutnik?
5. Rosenblatt builds to his thesis, instead of stating it toward the beginning of the essay. What is his thesis, and what is gained by building to it? Do you agree with it?

Vocabulary Study

1. How does the context of the final sentence in paragraph 4 help us to understand the reference to Everyman?
2. In what sense is Rosenblatt using the word *classic* in paragraph 7?
3. Does the word *power* have more than one meaning in paragraph 9?

Suggestions for Writing

1. Explain the following sentence in light of the whole essay: "If the man in the water gave a lifeline to the people gasping for survival, he was likewise giving a lifeline to those who observed him."
2. Explain the statement of Emerson, "Everything in Nature contains all the powers of Nature," in light of the final paragraph. Then illustrate it from your own experience.
3. First state the conception of heroism Rosenblatt presents in the essay. Then discuss the extent to which this conception fits an act of heroism you have observed, or accords with your idea of what makes a person heroic.

4.   Discuss a recent event that taught you an important truth about people or life. Describe the event for readers unfamiliar with it, and build to your thesis as Rosenblatt does.

Henry Louis Gates, Jr.

TRADING ON THE MARGIN

Henry Louis Gates, Jr., is W.E.B. DuBois Professor of Humanities and chairman of the Department of Afro-American Studies at Harvard University. A graduate of Yale and Cambridge universities, Gates has taught at Yale, Cornell, and Duke. His many books on Afro-Americans and American education include *Race Writing and Difference* (1986), *Figures in Black* (1987), *The Souls of Black Folk* (1989), *Bearing Witness* (1991), and *Loose Canons: Notes on the Culture Wars* (1992), in which this opening section of an essay on multiculturalism appears.

I recently asked the dean of a prestigious liberal arts college if he thought that his school would ever have, as Berkeley has, a majority nonwhite enrollment. "Never," he replied candidly. "That would completely alter our identity as a center of the liberal arts."

The assumption that there is a deep connection between the shape of a college curriculum and the ethnic composition of its students reflects a disquieting trend in American education. Political representation has been confused with the "representation" of various ethnic identities in the curriculum, while debates about the nature of the humanities and core curricula have become marionette theaters for larger political concerns.

The cultural right, threatened both by these demographic shifts and by the demand for curricular change, has retreated to a stance of intellectual protectionism, arguing for a great and inviolable "Western tradition" which contains the seeds, fruit, and flowers of the very best that has been thought or uttered in human history, while the cultural left demands changes to accord with

population shifts in gender and ethnicity (along the way
often providing searching indictments of the sexism and
racism that have plagued Western culture, and to which
the cultural right sometimes turns a blind eye). Both, it
seems to me, are wrongheaded.

As a humanist, I am just as concerned that so many   4
of my colleagues, on the one hand, feel that the prime
motivation for a diverse curriculum is these population
shifts, as I am that those opposing diversity see it as
foreclosing the possibility of a shared "American" identity. Both sides quickly resort to a grandly communitarian
rhetoric. Both think they're struggling for the very soul
of America. But if academic politics quickly becomes a
bellum omnium contra omnes, perhaps it's time to wish
a *pax* on both their houses.

What is multiculturalism, and why are they saying   5
such terrible things about it? We've been told it threatens
to fragment American culture into a warren of ethnic
enclaves, each separate and inviolate. We've been told
that it menaces the Western tradition of literature and
the arts. We've been told it aims to politicize the school
curriculum, replacing honest historical scholarship with
a "feel good" syllabus designed solely to bolster the self-
esteem of minorities. The alarm has been sounded, and
many scholars and educators—liberals as well as conservatives—have responded to it. After all, if multiculturalism is just a pretty name for ethnic chauvinism, who
needs it?

There is, of course, a liberal rejoinder to these con-   6
cerns, which says that this isn't what multiculturalism
is—or at least not what it ought to be. The liberal
pluralist insists that the debate has been miscast from
the beginning and that it is worth setting the main issues
straight.

There's no denying that the multicultural initiative   7
arose, in part, because of the fragmentation of American
society by ethnicity, class, and gender. To make it the
culprit for this fragmentation is to mistake effect for

cause. Mayor Dinkins's metaphor about New York as a "gorgeous mosaic" is catchy but unhelpful, if it means that each culture is fixed in place and separated by grout. Perhaps we should try to think of American culture as a conversation among different voices—even if it's a conversation that some of us weren't able to join until recently. Perhaps we should think about education, as the conservative philosopher Michael Oakeshott proposed, as "an invitation into the art of this conversation in which we learn to recognize the voices," each conditioned, as he says, by a different perception of the world. Common sense says that you don't bracket 90 percent of the world's cultural heritage if you really want to learn about the world.

To insist that we "master our own culture" before 8 learning others only defers the vexed question: What gets to count as "our" culture? What makes knowledge worth knowing? Unfortunately, as history has taught us, an Anglo-American regional culture has too often masked itself as universal, passing itself off as our "common culture," and depicting different cultural traditions as "tribal" or "parochial." So it's only when we're free to explore the complexities of our hyphenated American culture that we can discover what a genuinely common American culture might actually look like. Common sense (Gramscian* or otherwise) reminds us that we're *all* ethnics, and the challenge of transcending ethnic chauvinism is one we all face.

Granted, multiculturalism is no magic panacea for 9 our social ills. We're worried when Johnny can't read. We're worried when Johnny can't add. But shouldn't we be worried, too, when Johnny tramples gravestones in a Jewish cemetery or scrawls racial epithets on a dormitory wall? It's a fact about this country that we've entrusted our schools with the fashioning and refashioning

---

Gramscian: Referring to a theory of social change associated with the Italian philosopher Antonio Gramsci (1891-1937). [Ed.]

of a democratic polity; that's why the schooling of
America has always been a matter of political judgment.
But in America, a nation that has theorized itself as
plural from its inception, our schools have a very special
task.

The *society* we have made simply won't survive with-   10
out the values of tolerance. And cultural tolerance comes
to nothing without cultural understanding. In short, the
challenge facing America in the next century will be the
shaping, at long last, of a truly common public culture,
one responsive to the long-silenced cultures of color. If
we relinquish the ideal of America as a plural nation,
we've abandoned the very experiment that America
represents.

Comment

In his opening paragraphs Gates introduces the topic of his essay,
multiculturalism, through the views of major opponents in the
debate—the cultural "left" and the cultural "right." He then states
his central topic—"What is multiculturalism, and why are they
saying such terrible things about it?"—and briefly reviews the
argument against it (paragraph 5). In many argumentative essays,
the thesis statement, supporting arguments, and refutation or answer to opponents follow the introduction and background of the
case (p. 434). Gates states what multiculturalism is and answers
objections to this definition (paragraphs 6-7), then states his thesis—"we're *all* ethnics" (paragraph 8)—and discusses it (paragraphs
9-10). The writer may decide to build up to a controversial thesis,
as Gates does, and may also, like Gates, combine his supporting
arguments with his refutation or answer to objections. These decisions depend on what the audience knows about the subject and
how it may best may be informed and persuaded.

Questions for Study and Discussion

1. What opposing views in the debate about curriculum does Gates identify in paragraphs 1-4? How do these views reflect his own concerns about American education?
2. According to Gates, what social and political conditions led to the demand for multiculturalism in the schools?
3. How does Gates answer the objection that we should "master our own culture" before learning about other cultures? In his view, what limited views of culture do the two sides in the debate about multiculturalism share?
4. What broader definition of American culture does he suggest would encompass these views? What would the ideal multicultural curriculum include?
5. What does Gates gain in building to his thesis instead of stating it early in the essay?

Vocabulary Study

Explain how Gates uses the first word in the paragraph cited and how the word differs in meaning from those following:

1. *ethnic* (paragraph 2), *racial, cultural*
2. *gender* (paragraph 3), *masculinity, femininity*
3. *humanist* (paragraph 4), *humanitarian, philanthropist*
4. *chauvinism* (paragraph 5), *patriotism, jingoism*
5. *parochial* (paragraph 8), *local, provincial*

Suggestions for Writing

1. Discuss the extent to which Norman Cousins (p. 334) would agree with Gates on the aims of education and ways of achieving them.
2. Discuss what you gained most from your high school education and what you found missing. Then recommend changes that would improve the curriculum.

E. B. White

THE DECLINE OF SPORT
(A Preposterous Parable)

E. B. White (1899-1985), the distinguished essayist, humorist, and
editor, was born in Mount Vernon, New York. He was long
associated with *The New Yorker* as a writer and editor and also
wrote for *Harper's Magazine* and other publications. His books
include *Charlotte's Web* (1952) and *Stuart Little* (1945), both for
children, and *One Man's Meat* (1943), *The Second Tree from the
Corner* (1954), and *The Points of My Compass* (1962), collections of
essays. A paragraph-length essay of White's appeared on page 40.

In the third decade of the supersonic age, sport   1
gripped the nation in an ever-tightening grip. The horse
tracks, the ballparks, the fight rings, the gridirons, all
drew crowds in steadily increasing numbers. Every time
a game was played, an attendance record was broken.
Usually some other sort of record was broken, too—
such as the record for the number of consecutive doubles
hit by left-handed batters in a Series game, or some such
thing as that. Records fell like ripe apples on a windy
day. Customs and manners changed, and the five-day
business week was reduced to four days, then to three,
to give everyone a better chance to memorize the scores.
Not only did sport proliferate but the demands it   2
made on the spectator became greater. Nobody was
content to take in one event at a time, and thanks to
the magic of radio and television nobody had to. A Yale
alumnus, class of 1962, returning to the Bowl with
197,000 others to see the Yale-Cornell football game
would take along his pocket radio and pick up the
Yankee Stadium, so that while his eye might be following a fumble on the Cornell twenty-two-yard line, his
ear would be following a man going down to second
in the top of the fifth, seventy miles away. High in the
blue sky above the Bowl, skywriters would be at work

writing the scores of other major and minor sporting contests, weaving an interminable record of victory and defeat, and using the new high-visibility pink news-smoke perfected by Pepsi-Cola engineers. And in the frames of the giant video sets, just behind the goalposts, this same alumnus could watch Dejected win the Futurity before a record-breaking crowd of 349,872 at Belmont, each of whom was tuned to the Yale Bowl and following the World Series game in the video and searching the sky for further news of events either under way or just completed. The effect of this vast cyclorama of sport was to divide the spectator's attention, over-subtilize his appreciation, and deaden his passion. As the fourth supersonic decade was ushered in, the picture changed and sport began to wane.

A good many factors contributed to the decline of sport. Substitutions in football had increased to such an extent that there were very few fans in the United States capable of holding the players in mind during play. Each play that was called saw two entirely new elevens lined up, and the players whose names and faces you had familiarized yourself with in the first period were seldom seen or heard of again. The spectacle became as diffuse as the main concourse in Grand Central at the commuting hour.

Express motor highways leading to the parks and stadia had become so wide, so unobstructed, so devoid of all life except automobiles and trees that sport fans had got into the habit of travelling enormous distances to attend events. The normal driving speed had been stepped up to ninety-five miles an hour, and the distance between cars had been decreased to fifteen feet. This put an extraordinary strain on the sport lover's nervous system, and he arrived home from a Saturday game, after a road trip of three hundred and fifty miles, glassy-eyed, dazed, and spent. He hadn't really had any relaxation and he had failed to see Czlika (who had gone in for Trusky) take the pass from Bkeeo (who had gone in for Bjallo) in the third period, because at that moment a youngster named Lavagetto had been put in to pinch-hit for Art Gurlack in the bottom of the ninth with the tying run on second, and the skywriter who was attempting to write "Princeton O—Lafayette 43" had banked the wrong way, muffed the "3," and distracted everyone's attention from the fact that Lavagetto had been whiffed.

Cheering, of course, lost its stimulating effect on 5 players, because cheers were no longer associated necessarily with the immediate scene but might as easily apply to something that was happening somewhere else. This was enough to infuriate even the steadiest performer. A football star, hearing the stands break into a roar before the ball was snapped, would realize that their minds were not on him, and would become dispirited and grumpy. Two or three of the big coaches worried so about this that they considered equipping all players with tiny ear sets, so that they, too, could keep abreast of other sporting events while playing, but the idea was abandoned as impractical, and the coaches put it aside in tickler files, to bring up again later.

I think the event that marked the turning point in 6 sport and started it downhill was the Midwest's classic Dust Bowl game of 1975, when Eastern Reserve's great right end, Ed Pistachio, was shot by a spectator. This man, the one who did the shooting, was seated well down in the stands near the forty-yard line on a bleak October afternoon and was so saturated with sport and with the disappointments of sport that he had clearly become deranged. With a minute and fifteen seconds to play and the score tied, the Eastern Reserve quarterback had whipped a long pass over Army's heads into Pistachio's waiting arms. There was no other player anywhere near him, and all Pistachio had to do was catch the ball and run it across the line. He dropped it. At exactly this moment, the spectator—a man named Homer T. Parkinson, of 35 Edgemere Drive, Toledo, O.—suffered at least three other major disappointments in the realm of sport. His horse, Hiccough, on which he had a five-hundred-dollar bet, fell while getting away from the starting gate at Pimlico and broke its leg (clearly visible in the video); his favorite shortstop, Lucky Frimstitch, struck out and let three men die on base in the final game of the Series (to which Parkinson was tuned); and the Governor Dummer soccer team, on which Parkinson's youngest son played goalie, lost to Kent, 4-3, as recorded in the sky overhead. Before anyone could stop him, he drew a gun and drilled Pistachio, before 954,000 persons, the largest crowd that had ever attended a football game and the *second*-largest crowd that had ever assembled for any sporting event in any month except July.

This tragedy, by itself, wouldn't have caused sport to decline, I suppose, but it set in motion a chain of other tragedies, the cumulative effect of which was terrific. Almost as soon as the shot was fired, the news flash was picked up by one of the skywriters directly above the field. He glanced down to see whether he could spot the trouble below, and in doing so failed to see another skywriter approaching. The two planes collided and fell, wings locked, leaving a confusing trail of smoke, which some observers tried to interpret as a late sports score. The planes struck in the middle of the nearby eastbound coast-to-coast Sunlight Parkway, and a motorist driving a convertible coupe stopped so short, to avoid hitting them, that he was bumped from behind. The pileup of cars that ensued involved 1,482 vehicles, a record for eastbound parkways. A total of more than three thousand persons lost their lives in the highway accident, including the two pilots, and when panic broke out in the stadium, it cost another 872 in dead and injured. News of the disaster spread quickly to other sport arenas, and started other panics among the crowds trying to get to the exits, where they could buy a paper and study a list of the dead. All in all the afternoon of sport cost 20,003 lives, a record. And nobody had much to show for it, except one small Midwestern boy who hung around the smoking wrecks of the planes, captured

some aero news-smoke in a milk bottle, and took it
home as a souvenir.

From that day on, sport waned. Through long,   8
noncompetitive Saturday afternoons, the stadia slum-
bered. Even the parkways fell into disuse as motorists
rediscovered the charms of old, twisty roads that led
through main streets and past barnyards, with their mild
congestions and pleasant smells.

Comment

Satire is an important kind of persuasive writing. An essay may be
entirely satirical, as in E. B. White's on the American obsession with
sports, or it may be satirical in part. The chief means of persuasion
is ridicule: the satirist makes fun of attitudes or behavior or holds
them up to shame. The targets of social satire are foolish attitudes
or behavior—social snobbery, pretentious talk, slobbish eating, and
the like. Though amusing and sometimes even disgusting, these have
no very serious consequences for the individual or for society. The
targets of ethical satire are vicious attitudes and behavior—for
example, racial or religious prejudice, dishonesty, hypocrisy—that
do have serious consequences. Social satire is usually humorous;
ethical satire may be humorous, as in many political cartoons like
Doonesbury, but it is more often bitter or angry. Many satires like
Twain's *Huckleberry Finn* contain both types.

Some satirists are direct in their criticism—their statements are
angry and biting. Others like E. B. White, James Thurber, and Art
Buchwald depend on humorous understatement or exaggeration.
These are forms of irony. An ironic statement generally implies more
through inflection of voice or phrasing than the words actually say;
sarcasm is a bitter kind of irony. You are being ironic when you
smile or wink while saying something supposedly serious.

Questions for Study and Discussion

1.   What attitudes or habits is White satirizing in the America of
     late 1947, when this essay first appeared? Are the targets of

the satire limited to attitudes and habits relating to sport, or does White have also in mind general attitudes and habits?

2. Is the satire social or ethical? Is White satirizing merely foolish or, instead, vicious attitudes or behavior?

3. To what extent does White depend on exaggeration or over-statement? Does he also use understatement?

4. Names like "Dejected" can be satirical as well as humorous. Do you find other humorous names in the essay, and are they used satirically?

5. White refers to the "high-visibility pink news-smoke perfected by Pepsi-Cola engineers." Why does he refer to "Pepsi-Cola" rather than to "U.S. Steel" or "Dow Chemical"?

6. Do you think the essay describes attitudes toward sport and the behavior of sports fans in the eighties? Do you find the satire persuasive?

Vocabulary Study

1. What is a "parable"? What does the subtitle "A Preposterous Parable" show about White's intention?

2. Write a paraphrase of paragraph 2 or paragraph 6—a sentence-for-sentence rendering in your own words. Be sure to find substitutes for *proliferate*, *interminable*, and *over-subtilize* (paragraph 2), or *deranged*, *whipped*, and *drilled* (paragraph 6). Try to retain the tone of White's original paragraph.

Suggestions for Writing

1. Identify the targets of White's satire and explain how you discover them in the course of reading.

2. Discuss the extent to which White's predictions in 1947 have come true. Cite contemporary events and attitudes that support the predictions or that show White to be mistaken.

3. Write a satirical essay of your own on a contemporary social or political issue. You may not discover the best strategy or tone until you have written several paragraphs. Revise your draft to make the strategy and tone consistent throughout.

James Thurber

THE PRINCESS AND THE TIN BOX

James Thurber (1894-1961) worked as a journalist on the *Columbus Dispatch* and *Chicago Tribune* before beginning his long association with *The New Yorker* in 1925, the year it began publication. Most of his stories, sketches, and cartoons appeared in that magazine. Thurber was a humorist and a satirist of many aspects of American life. His many books include *My Life and Hard Times* (1933), *Fables for Our Time* (1943), *The Thurber Carnival* (1945), and *Thurber Country* (1953).

Once upon a time, in a far country, there lived a king whose daughter was the prettiest princess in the world. Her eyes were like the cornflower, her hair was sweeter than the hyacinth, and her throat made the swan look dusty. 1

From the time she was a year old, the princess had been showered with presents. Her nursery looked like Cartier's window. Her toys were all made of gold or platinum or diamonds or emeralds. She was not permitted to have wooden blocks or china dolls or rubber dogs or linen books, because such materials were considered cheap for the daughter of a king. 2

When she was seven, she was allowed to attend the wedding of her brother and throw real pearls at the bride instead of rice. Only the nightingale, with his lyre of gold, was permitted to sing for the princess. The common blackbird, with his boxwood flute, was kept out of the palace grounds. She walked in silver-and-samite slippers to a sapphire-and-topaz bathroom and slept in an ivory bed inlaid with rubies. 3

On the day the princess was eighteen, the king sent a royal ambassador to the courts of five neighboring kingdoms to announce that he would give his daughter's hand in marriage to the prince who brought her the gift she liked the most. 4

The first prince to arrive at the palace rode a swift white stallion and laid at the feet of the princess an enormous apple made of solid gold which he had taken from a dragon who had guarded it for a thousand years. It was placed on a long ebony table set up to hold the gifts of the princess's suitors. The second prince, who came on a gray charger, brought her a nightingale made of a thousand diamonds, and it was placed beside the golden apple. The third prince, riding on a black horse, carried a great jewel box made of platinum and sapphires, and it was placed next to the diamond nightingale. The fourth prince, astride a fiery yellow horse, gave the princess a gigantic heart made of rubies and pierced by an emerald arrow. It was placed next to the platinum-and-sapphire jewel box.

Now the fifth prince was the strongest and handsomest of all the five suitors, but he was the son of a poor king whose realm had been overrun by mice and locusts and wizards and mining engineers so that there was nothing much of value left in it. He came plodding up to the palace of the princess on a plow horse and he brought her a small tin box filled with mica and feldspar and hornblende which he had picked up on the way.

The other princes roared with disdainful laughter when they saw the tawdry gift the fifth prince had brought to the princess. But she examined it with great interest and squealed with delight, for all her life she had been glutted with precious stones and priceless metals, but she had never seen tin before or mica or feldspar or hornblende. The tin box was placed next to the ruby heart pierced with an emerald arrow.

"Now," the king said to his daughter, "you must select the gift you like best and marry the prince that brought it."

The princess smiled and walked up to the table and picked up the present she liked the most. It was the platinum-and-sapphire jewel box, the gift of the third prince.

"The way I figure it," she said, "is this. It is a very large and expensive box, and when I am married, I will meet many admirers who will give me precious gems with which to fill it to the top. Therefore, it is the most valuable of all the gifts my suitors have brought me and I like it the best."   10

The princess married the third prince that very day in the midst of great merriment and high revelry. More than a hundred thousand pearls were thrown at her and she loved it.   11

Moral: All those who thought the princess was going to select the tin box with worthless stones instead of one of the other gifts will kindly stay after class and write one hundred times on the blackboard "I would rather have a hunk of aluminum silicate than a diamond necklace."   12

Comment

As in "The Princess and the Tin Box," Thurber's humor often arises in his fables and stories from incongruities between what we expect to see in people or expect to happen to them and what does happen. Another incongruity is found in Thurber's language. Disparities of this sort are a major source of irony—the sardonic discovery that life is different from what we expect it to be, that appearances deceive. Many authors do not comment on what they show; they allow truths and ironies to emerge from the details of the story—from the setting, happenings, statements of characters. Thurber does comment in the moral he attaches to his story. But this moral by no means expresses all the truths contained in what the princess does and says.

Questions for Study and Discussion

1.   How do the details of the first six paragraphs lead you to believe that the princess will choose the fifth prince? Is the order of these details important?

2. At what point do you discover the real character of the princess? What does her manner of speaking or choice of words contribute to this discovery?
3. Thurber, in his moral, talks to us in a language different from that of the story. What exactly is this difference, and what humor arises from it?
4. What idea or attitude is Thurber satirizing? Is he also satirizing the princess or the reader of the essay or possibly both? Do you find other truths in the story?
5. Do you find Thurber's moral pertinent to the world today?

Vocabulary Study

Look up the following words: *parable, fairy tale, fable, allegory.* How closely does "The Princess and the Tin Box" fit the definitions you found?

Suggestions for Writing

1. Write a fairy tale or fable or parable of your own that develops an idea or truth about people.
2. Write a nonsatirical essay that examines the idea or values Thurber writes about from your point of view and experience. If you take a different view of these values, compare your view with Thurber's.

Harold J. Morowitz

THE SIX MILLION DOLLAR MAN

Harold J. Morowitz, professor of molecular biophysics and biochemistry at Yale University, is the author of *Life on the Planet* (1974) and other books on biophysics. His essays are collected in *The Wine of Life* (1979), in which the essay reprinted here appears. Morowitz is writing humorously but also with a persuasive aim, and in doing so conveys considerable information about the human body.

Another annual cycle inevitably passed and the pain 1 was eased by a humorous birthday card from my daughter and son-in-law. The front bore the caption "According to BIO-CHEMISTS the materials that make up the HUMAN BODY are only worth 97¢" (Hallmark 25B 121-8, 1975). Before I could get to the birthday greeting I began to think that if the materials are only worth ninety-seven cents, my colleagues and I are really being taken by the biochemical supply companies. Lest the granting agencies were to find out first, I decided to make a thorough study of the entire matter.

I started by sitting down with my catalogue from the 2 (name deleted) Biochemical Co. and began to list the ingredients. Hemoglobin was $2.95 a gram, purified trypsin was $36 a gram, and crystalline insulin was $47.50 a gram. I began to look at slightly less common constituents such as acetate kinase at $8,860 a gram, alkaline phosphatase at $225 a gram, and NADP at $245 a gram. Hyaluronic acid was $175 a gram, while bilirubin was a bargain at $12 a gram. Human DNA was $768 a gram, while collagen was as little as $15 a gram. Human albumin was down at $3 a gram, whereas bradykinin was $12,000 for a gram. The real shocker came when I got to follicle-stimulating hormone at $4,800,000 a gram—clearly outside the reach of anything that Tiffany's could offer. I'm going to suggest it as a gift for people who have everything. For the really wealthy, there is prolactin at $17,500,000 a gram, street price.

Not content with a brief glance at the catalogue, I averaged all the constituents over the best estimate of the percent composition of the human body and arrived at $245.54 as the average value of a gram dry weight of human being. With that fact burning in my head I rushed over to the gymnasium and jumped on the scale. There it was, 168 pounds, or, after a quick go-round with my pocket calculator, 76,364 grams. Remembering that I was 68% water, I calculated my dry weight to be 24,436 grams. The next computation was done with a great sense of excitement. I had to multiply $245.54 per gram dry weight by 24,436 grams. The number literally jumped out at me—$6,000,015.44. I was a Six Million Dollar Man—no doubt about it—and really an enormous upgrade to my ego after the ninety-seven cent evaluation!

Assuming that the profits of the biochemical companies are considerably less than the 618,558,239% indicated above, we must still strike a balance between the ninety-seven cent figure and the six million dollar figure. The answer is at the same time very simple and very profound: information is much more expensive than matter. In the six million dollar figure I was paying for my atoms in the highest informational state in which they are commercially available, while in the ninety-seven cent figure I was paying for the informationally poorest form of coal, air, water, lime, bulk iron, etc.

This argument can be developed in terms of proteins as an example. The macromolecules of amino acid subunits cost somewhere between $3 and $20,000 a gram in purified form, yet the simpler, information-poorer amino acids sell for about twenty-five cents a gram. The proteins are linear arrays of the amino acids that must be assembled and folded. Thus we see the reason for the expense. The components such as coal, air, water, limestone and iron nails are, of course, simple and correspondingly cheap. The small molecular weight monomers are much more complex and correspondingly more expensive, and so on for larger molecules.

This means that my six million dollar estimate is much too low. The biochemical companies can sell me their wares for a mere six million because they isolate them from natural products. Doubtless, if they had to synthesize them from ninety-seven cents worth of material they would have to charge me six hundred million or perhaps six billion dollars. We have, to date, synthesized only insulin and ribonuclease. Larger proteins would be even more difficult. 6

A moment's reflection shows that even if I bought all the macro molecular components, I would not have purchased a human being. A freezer full of unstable molecules at −70° C does not qualify to vote or for certain other inalienable rights. At six billion it would certainly qualify for concern over my −70° deep freezer, which is always breaking down. 7

The next step is to assemble the molecules into organelles. Here the success of modern science is limited as we are in a totally new area of research. A functionally active subunit of ribosomes has been assembled from the protein and RNA constituents. Doubtlessly other cellular structures will similarly yield to intensive efforts. The ribosome is perhaps the simplest organelle, so that considerably more experimental sophistication will be required to get at the larger cell components. One imagines that if I wanted to price the human body in terms of synthesized cellular substructures, I would have to think in terms of six hundred billion or perhaps six trillion dollars. Lest my university begin to salivate about all the overhead they would get on these purchases, let me point out that this is only a thought exercise, and I have no plans to submit a grant request in this area. 8

Continuing the argument to its penultimate conclusion, we must face the fact that my dry-ice chest full of organelles (I have given up the freezer, at six trillion it 9 simply can't be trusted) cannot make love, complain, and do all those other things that constitute our humanity. Dr. Frankenstein was a fraud. The task is far more difficult than he ever realized. Next, the organelles must be assembled into cells. Here we are out on a limb estimating the cost, but I cannot imagine that it can be done for less than six thousand trillion dollars. Do you hear me, Mr. Treasury Secretary, Mr. Federal Reserve Chairman? Are these thoughts taking a radical turn?

A final step is necessary in our biochemical view of 10
man. An incubator of 76,364 grams of cell culture at 37°C still does not measure up, even in the crassest material terms, to what we consider a human being. How would we assemble the cells into tissues, tissues into organs, and organs into a person? The very task staggers the imagination. Our ability to ask the question in dollars and cents has immediately disappeared. We suddenly and sharply face the realization that each human being is priceless. We are led cent by dollar from a lowly pile of common materials to a grand philosophical conclusion—the infinite preciousness of each person. The scientific reasons are clear. We are, at the molecular level, the most information-dense structures around, surpassing by many orders of magnitude the best that computer engineers can design or even contemplate by miniaturization. The result must, however, go beyond science and color our view of the world. It might even lead us to Alfred North Whitehead's conclusion that "the human body is an instrument for the production of art in the life of the human soul."

Comment

Morowitz uses exposition—his catalog of body chemicals and explanation of how molecules are formed—to argue a thesis. The exposition is used in a special way, for the argument has a satirical edge: Morowitz is showing the absurdity of a purely biochemical view of the human being by taking the view as far as he can, to its ultimate conclusion. He is amused at the birthday card and its implications, but he has a serious point to make about them. The persuasiveness of the argument derives in large part from the exactness of the details, both in the catalog and in the explanation of molecular assembly that form the argument.

Questions for Study and Discussion

1. Where does Morowitz first state his thesis? Where does he restate it? What does he gain by stating and restating the thesis where he does?
2. In discussing the biochemical view of the human being, what other way of viewing people does Morowitz have in mind? Does he refer to this view directly?
3. Morowitz develops his thesis by inviting us to look at ourselves from an unusual viewpoint. From what other viewpoint might he have developed his thesis?
4. What does Morowitz assume about the knowledge and interests of his readers? How does this assumption or estimate influence the way he chooses to make the argument persuasive?

Vocabulary Study

1. What does Morowitz mean by *information* in the statement that "information is much more expensive than matter" (paragraph 4)? How do the details of paragraphs 3 and 4 help to explain the meaning of the word? In what sense are humans "information-dense structures" (paragraph 10)?
2. What is the difference between "macromolecular components" (paragraph 7) and molecules?
3. What is the "penultimate conclusion" of an argument (paragraph 9), in contrast to its ultimate conclusion?
4. What is the meaning of *radical* in the concluding sentence of paragraph 9?

Suggestions for Writing

1. Discuss a way that Morowitz might have chosen to make his thesis persuasive for a different audience.
2. Discuss the implications of a greeting card caption that catches your attention, and use your discussion to develop a thesis.

Suzanne Falter-Barns

IN CHELSEA, BACK TO SLEEP

Suzanne Falter-Barns is a novelist and essayist. Her novel, *Doin' the Box Step,* was published in 1992. Her essays have appeared in *The New York Times, Adweek,* and other periodicals. Her essay on a murder on the street outside her apartment in the Chelsea district of Manhattan appeared in the *Times* on November 25, 1989.

On a cool night recently, a woman was murdered in front of my apartment in Chelsea. She was sleeping in her car when someone—evidently trying to steal her car radio—was surprised by her, and slashed her throat with a knife.

The woman killed was only a few years older than I, and her photograph in the papers was familiar. Many neighbors had seen her coming and going from the Buddhist temple next door, and so she was one of us— another daily face you'd pass, unknown but still part of the surroundings. That she slept in her car was not even surprising, just another thing people do in New York. We regarded it with the silence with which one sees everything in this city—the silence of blasé acceptance.

Here is the core of the tragedy. An upstairs neighbor, wakened by her car horn, watched from his window as the stabbed woman staggered from her car, made her way up the steps of the temple and rattled the doorknob in vain. In the darkness, he could not see her profuse bleeding, but he could hear her speaking strangely, asking for what sounded like her mother. She was drunk, he assumed, or high, and he watched her make her way back to the car and drive away quickly. She died a few moments later.

Even at 4 o'clock in the morning, on a deserted block 4 in Chelsea, what our neighbor saw did not seem unusual. He had the New York reaction of the 1980's, and assumed she was just another one of the city's huge corps of the deranged, the homeless, the addicted, the drunk. He didn't even consider going downstairs to help her; after all, how many dozens didn't he help just that day? To do so would have taken hours and dollars that cannot be spared, so my neighbor did what any of us would have done. He went back to sleep.

I cannot say I blame him. I was sitting in my living 5 room while the murder took place right in front of my windows. In my sleeplessness, I was drinking hot milk and flipping through a travel magazine, steadfastly ignoring the weird murmurings of the girl outside. In fact, I didn't even think of getting up to see what might be wrong. Years of living in New York City had trained me: The distress you hear is nothing serious. It's only a drunk or a bum.

A few hours later, when the detectives questioned 6 me, I was ashamed to admit what I had heard. Perhaps it wasn't her, but it probably was. If only I hadn't been so smug, if only I'd gone to the window, perhaps I could have done something. The doctor next door says no one could have saved her, but I tell myself I could have held her, or reassured her, or even tried to get a description of the assailant. At least she wouldn't have died so pitifully, ignored by her neighbors because they thought she was a drunk, when in fact, she was looking for help.

That this should be a normal reaction says some- 7 thing about our life here. What begins as compassion, when you first arrive, gets ground to dust by the daily barrage of people dressed in garbage bags, passed out in doorways, making loud, plaintive pitches on the subway or displaying their mutilated limbs in an attempt to get some change. The sheer numbers of these people exhaust the soul. To live here at all, you have to be callous.

The morning after the murder, I washed away the 8 victim's bloodstains that covered the sidewalk; as I did, a stream of people in business clothes walked by, neatly picking their way past the stains, papers and briefcases tucked under their arms. No one seemed to notice or care what I was doing. No one asked what had happened. They averted their eyes—avoiding the pain— keeping their mind on more important things. That someone died here was just another incident to file away, another fact of this strange place.

Comment

Suzanne Falter-Barns gives us "the core of the tragedy" in her neighbor's response and her own to the murder of a woman outside her New York City apartment building. In discussing the tragedy, she reflects on the attitude of New Yorkers toward the impoverished and the homeless of the city. Though she does not make a direct appeal for action, her reflective essay has an "argumentative edge"— the vivid details forcing us to imagine the situation of the murdered woman, that of Falter-Barns and her neighbor, and of those passing the murder scene.

Questions for Study and Discussion

1. Why does Falter-Barns not give us a physical description of the woman? What is the purpose of the details that she does give us?
2. Is she critical of the people who pass her on the sidewalk? Is she asking for a change in attitude and response? How do you know?

3. How much does Falter-Barns tell us about herself and her neighbor? How much does she need to tell us to achieve her purpose in describing the episode?
4. How many references to images of silence do you find in the essay? What do these references and images contribute to its effect?

Vocabulary Study

Explain why the first word fits the sentence in the paragraph cited better than the second:

1. *blasé* (paragraph 2), *indifferent*
2. *profuse* (paragraph 3), *lavish*
3. *murmurings* (paragraph 5), *whisperings*
4. *compassion* (paragraph 7), *sympathy*
5. *barrage* (paragraph 7), *parade*

Suggestions for Writing

1. Identify the causes that Falter-Barns states or implies for her own attitude and response and those of others to homelessness and urban poverty. Describe your own attitude and response to people and situations like those described in paragraph 7.
2. Describe your own response to an accident or a crime or some other event in which you did not intervene. Explain why you didn't and what you think now about your response.

Harvey and Nancy Kincaid

A LETTER ON STRIP MINING

Harvey and Nancy Kincaid lived with their seven children in Fayetteville, West Virginia, near Buffalo Creek at the time they wrote the following letter. On February 26, 1972, a dam consisting of slag from the mines and owned by a local coal company burst. The ensuing flood killed 125 people and injured many thousands; most of the victims were coal miners and members of their families. In 1971 Mrs. Kincaid had spoken about strip mining to the Congress Against Strip Mining, in Washington, D.C. Her letter was read before the West Virginia State Legislature and it helped to pass the Anti-Strip-Mining Bill. Mrs. Kincaid told an interviewer, "It used to be that the kids could keep fish, catfish, and minnows in the creeks. Now you can see the rocks in the creek where the acid has run off the mountains, off the limestone rocks. The rocks in the creek are reddish-looking, like they're rusted. There's nothing living in the creek now."

Gentlemen:

I don't believe there could be anyone that would like 1 to see the strip mines stopped any more than my husband and myself. It just seems impossible that something like this could happen to us twice in the past three and one half years of time. We have been married for thirteen years and worked real hard at having a nice home that was ours and paid for, with a nice size lot of one acre. Over the thirteen years, we remodeled this house a little at a time and paid for it as we worked and did the work mostly ourselves. The house was located about a quarter of a mile off the road up Glenco Hollow at Kincaid, Fayette County, West Virginia, where it used to be a nice, clean neighborhood.

Then the strippers came four years ago with their big 2 machinery and TNT. I know that these men need jobs and need to make a living like everyone else, but I believe there could be a better way of getting the coal out of these mountains. Have you ever been on a mountaintop and looked down and seen about five different strips on one mountain in one hollow?

My husband owns a Scout Jeep and he can get to ₃
the top of the strip mines with the Scout. I would like
to invite you to come and visit us sometime and go for
a ride with us. It would make you sick to see the way
the mountains are destroyed.

First they send in the loggers to strip all the good ₄
timber out and then they come with their bulldozers. If
their engineers make a mistake in locating the coal they
just keep cutting away until they locate the seam of coal.
When the rains come and there isn't anything to stop
the drainage, the mountains slide, and the spoil banks
fall down to the next spoil bank and so on until the
whole mountain slides. There is a small creek in the
hollow and when the spring rains come, its banks won't
hold the water.

So where does it go?—into people's yards, into their ₅
wells, under and into their houses. You have rocks, coal,
and a little bit of everything in your yards. When the
strippers came they started behind our house in the fall
sometime before November. There was a hollow behind
our house and we asked them not to bank the spoil the
way they did, because we knew what would happen
when the spring rains came. My father-in-law lived beside
us and the property all ran together in a nice green
lawn—four acres.

But the rains came in the spring and the spoil bank ₆
broke and the water and debris came into our property
every time it rained. It would only take a few minutes
of rain and this is what we had for three years.

Then the damage comes to your house because of ₇
so much dampness. The doors won't close, the foundation sinks and cracks the walls in the house, your tile
comes up off your floors, your walls mold, even your
clothes in your closets. Then your children stay sick with
bronchial trouble, then our daughter takes pneumonia—X-rays are taken, primary T.B. shows up on the X-
ray. This is in July of two years ago. About for a year
this child laid sick at home. In the meantime we have

already filed suit with a lawyer in Oak Hill when the water started coming in on us, but nothing happens. For three years we fight them for our property—$10,000. The lawyer settles out of court for $4,500. By the time his fee comes out and everything else we have to pay, we have under $3,000 to start over with.

So what do we have to do? Doctor's orders, move 8 out for child's sake and health. We sell for a little of nothing—not for cash, but for rent payments, take the $3,000 and buy a lot on the main highway four miles up the road toward Oak Hill.

The $3,000 goes for the lot, digging of a well and 9 a down payment on a new house. Here we are in debt for thirty years on a new home built and complete by the first of September. We moved the first part of September and was in this house *one month* and what happens? The same strip company comes up the road and puts a blast off and damages the new house— $1,400 worth. When they put one blast off that will crack the walls in your house, the foundation cracked the carport floor straight across in two places, pull a cement stoop away from the house and pull the grout out of the ceramic tile in the bathroom. This is what they can get by with.

How do they live in their $100,000 homes and have 10 a clear mind, I'll never know. To think of the poor people who have worked hard all their lives and can't start over like we did. They have to stay in these hollows and be scared to death every time it rains. I know by experience the many nights I have stayed up and listened to the water pouring off the mountains and the rocks tumbling off the hills.

I remember one time when the strippers put a blast 11 off up the hollow a couple years ago and broke into one of the old mines that had been sealed off for 30 years. They put their blast off and left for the evening. Around seven o'clock that evening it started. We happened to look up the hollow, and thick mud—as thick as pudding—

was coming down the main road in the hollow and made itself to the creek and stopped the creek up until the creek couldn't even flow.

The water was turned up into the fields where my husband keeps horses and cattle. I called the boss and told him what was happening and the danger we were in and what did he say? "There isn't anything I can do tonight. I'll be down tomorrow." I called the agriculture and they told us, whatever we did, not to go to bed that night because of the water backed up in those mines for miles.   12

This is just some of the things that happen around a strip mine neighborhood. But they can get by with it, unless they are stopped. Even if they are stopped it will take years for the trees and grass—what little bit they put on them—to grow enough to keep the water back and stop the slides.   13

Mr. and Mrs. Harvey Kincaid

Comment

The Swiss writer Henri Frédéric Amiel wrote in his journal: "Truth is the secret of eloquence and of virtue, the basis of moral authority." The Kincaids' great letter is an example of eloquence achieved through simple words that state facts plainly and exactly. Instead of reviewing the rights and wrongs of strip mining, Mr. and Mrs. Kincaid describe what happened to them and the land—in enough detail for the reader to imagine the life of people in the hollow. At the end of the letter they state the issue simply and without elaboration: "But they can get by with it, unless they are stopped."

Questions for Study and Discussion

1. The Kincaids state how their life was changed by strip mining. How do they show that their experiences were typical of people in the area?

2. Is the damage caused by strip mining the result of neglect or carelessness, or is it inherent in the process itself—given the details of the letter? Are the Kincaids mainly concerned with this question?

3. What is the central issue for them? Are they arguing against strip mining on moral grounds? Or are they concerned only with the practical consequences? What assumptions about the rights of individuals underlie their argument?

4. Are the Kincaids addressing a general or specific audience? How do you know?

5. What is the tone of the letter, and what in the letter creates it? What do the various questions asked in the letter contribute?

Vocabulary Study

Explain how the letter helps you understand the following words and phrases: *hollow, strips, spoil banks, grout, pudding.*

Suggestions for Writing

1. Write a letter protesting an activity that has changed your life in some way. Let the details of the change carry the weight of your protest.

2. Use the *New York Times Index, Social Sciences Index,* and other periodical indexes to find articles that state contrasting opinions on strip mining or a recent environmental or political issue. Analyze the assumptions and reasoning of each writer, noting similarities and differences. Then state which of the writers makes the stronger case, and why you think the writer does.

Chief Joseph

SURRENDER STATEMENT AND
STATEMENT TO THE U.S. CONGRESS

In 1877, following the theft of Nez Percé Indian horses by white settlers in the Wallowa Valley in southwest Washington, several young warriors killed eighteen settlers. When government troops were sent to deal with the Nez Percé, Chief Joseph sought to lead his band of 400 to 500 to Canada. In the course of four months, the outnumbered band defeated four army columns in more than twelve battles, inflicting heavy casualties, and despite their own casualties continued their march through more than a thousand miles of mountain terrain. On October 5, 1877, Chief Joseph was forced to surrender thirty miles from the Canadian border. Two years later he addressed the U.S. Congress but failed to gain redress. He was for a time imprisoned in Kansas, where five of his children died of disease. In 1904 he died on a reservation in Washington State. The entire surrender statement and the opening and concluding portions of his 1879 address to Congress are reprinted here from the report of Brigadier General O. O. Howard in the *Annual Report of the Secretary of War* (Washington, 1877) and *The North American Review,* 128 (April 1879). In the portion omitted here, Chief Joseph describes the events leading up to his surrender.

Surrender Statement, October 5, 1877

Tell General Howard I know his heart. What he told 1
me before I have in my heart. I am tired of fighting. Our chiefs are killed. Looking Glass is dead. Too-hul-hulsote is dead. The old men are all dead. It is the young men who say yes or no. He who led on the young men is dead. It is cold and we have no blankets. The little children are freezing to death. My people, some of them, have run away to the hills, and have no blankets, no food; no one knows where they are—perhaps freezing to death. I want to have time to look for my children and see how many of them I can find. Maybe I shall find them among the dead. Hear me, my chiefs. I am tired; my heart is sick and sad. From where the sun now stands I will fight no more forever.

Statement to U.S. Congress, January 14, 1879

My friends, I have been asked to show you my heart. ₂
I am glad to have a chance to do so. I want the white
people to understand my people. Some of you think an
Indian is like a wild animal. This is a great mistake. I
will tell you all about our people, and then you can
judge whether an Indian is a man or not. I believe much
trouble and blood would be saved if we opened our
hearts more. I will tell you in my way how the Indian
sees things. The white man has more words to tell you
how they look to him, but it does not require many
words to speak the truth. What I have to say will come
from my heart, and I will speak with a straight tongue.
Ah-cum-kin-i-ma-me-hut (the Great Spirit) is looking at
me, and will hear me.

My name is In-mut-too-yah-lat-lat (Thunder travel- ₃
ing over the Mountains). I am chief of the Wal-lam-wat-
kin band of Chute-pa-lu, or Nez Percés (nose-pierced
Indians). I was born in eastern Oregon, thirty-eight
winters ago. My father was chief before me. When a
young man, he was called Joseph by Mr. Spaulding, a
missionary. He died a few years ago. There was no stain
on his hands of the blood of a white man. He left a good
name on the earth. He advised me well for my people.

Our fathers gave us many laws, which they had ₄
learned from their fathers. These laws were good. They
told us to treat all men as they treated us; that we should
never be the first to break a bargain; that it was a
disgrace to tell a lie; that we should speak only the truth;
that it was a shame for one man to take from another
his wife, or his property without paying for it. We were
taught to believe that the Great Spirit sees and hears
everything, and that he never forgets; that hereafter he
will give every man a spirit-home according to his deserts:
if he has been a good man, he will have a good home;
if he has been a bad man, he will have a bad home. This
I believe, and all my people believe the same.

We did not know there were other people besides the ⁵
Indian until about one hundred winters ago, when some
men with white faces came to our country. They brought
many things with them to trade for furs and skins. They
brought tobacco, which was new to us. They brought
guns with flint stones on them, which frightened our
women and children. Our people could not talk with
these white-faced men, but they used signs which all
people understand. These men were Frenchmen, and
they called our people "Nez Percés," because they wore
rings in their noses for ornaments. Although very few
of our people wear them now, we are still called by the
same name. These French trappers said a great many
things to our fathers which have been planted in our
hearts. Some were good for us, but some were bad. Our
people were divided in opinion about these men. Some
thought they taught more bad than good. An Indian
respects a brave man, but he despises a coward. He loves
a straight tongue, but he hates a forked tongue. The
French trappers told us some truths and some lies.

The first white men of your people who came to our ⁶
country were named Lewis and Clark. They also brought
many things that our people had never seen. They talked
straight, and our people gave them a great feast, as a
proof that their hearts were friendly. These men were
very kind. They made presents to our chiefs and our
people made presents to them. We had a great many
horses, of which we gave them what they needed, and
they gave us guns and tobacco in return. All the Nez
Percés made friends with Lewis and Clark, and agreed
to let them pass through their country, and never to
make war on white men. This promise the Nez Percés
have never broken. No white man can accuse them of
bad faith, and speak with a straight tongue. It has
always been the pride of the Nez Percés that they were
the friends of the white men. When my father was a
young man there came to our country a white man who
talked spirit law. He won the affections of our people

because he spoke good things to them. At first he did not say anything about white men wanting to settle on our lands. Nothing was said about that until about twenty winters ago, when a number of white people came into our country and built houses and made farms. At first our people made no complaint. They thought there was room enough for all to live in peace, and they were learning many things from the white men that seemed to be good. But we soon found that the white men were growing rich very fast, and were greedy to possess everything the Indian had. My father was the first to see through the schemes of the white men, and he warned his tribe to be careful about trading with them. He had suspicion of men who seemed so anxious to make money. I was a boy then, but I remember well my father's caution. He had sharper eyes than the rest of our people.

Next there came a white officer, who invited all the   7
Nez Percés to a treaty council. After the council was opened he made known his heart. He said there were a great many white people in the country, and many more would come; that he wanted the land marked out so that the Indians and white men could be separated. If they were to live in peace it was necessary, he said, that the Indians should have a country set apart for them, and in that country they must stay. My father, who represented his band, refused to have anything to do with the council, because he wished to be a free man. He claimed that no man owned any part of the earth, and a man could not sell what he did not own.

Mr. Spaulding took hold of my father's arm and said,   8
"Come and sign the treaty." My father pushed him away, and said: "Why do you ask me to sign away my country? It is your business to talk to us about spirit matters, and not to talk to us about parting with our land." Governor Stevens urged my father to sign his treaty, but he refused. "I will not sign your paper," he said; you go where you please, so do I; you are not a

child, I am no child; I can think for myself. No man can think for me. I have no other home than this. I will not give it up to any man. My people would have no home. Take away your paper. I will not touch it with my hand."

My father left the council. Some of the chiefs of the other bands of the Nez Percés signed the treaty, and then Governor Stevens gave them presents of blankets. My father cautioned his people to take no presents, for "after a while," he said, "they will claim that you have accepted pay for your country." Since that time four bands of the Nez Percés have received annuities from the United States. My father was invited to many councils, and they tried hard to make him sign the treaty, but he was firm as the rock, and would not sign away his home. His refusal caused a difference among the Nez Percés.

Eight years later (1863) was the next treaty council. A chief called Lawyer, because he was a great talker, took the lead in this council, and sold nearly all the Nez Percés country. My father was not there. He said to me: "When you go into council with the white man, always remember your country. Do not give it away. The white man will cheat you out of your home. I have taken no pay from the United States. I have never sold our land." In this treaty Lawyer acted without authority from our band. He had no right to sell the Wallowa *(winding water)* country. That had always belonged to my father's own people, and the other bands had never disputed our right to it. No other Indians ever claimed Wallowa.

In order to have all people understand how much land we owned, my father planted poles around it and said: "Inside is the home of my people—the white man may take the land outside. Inside this boundary all our people were born. It circles around the graves of our fathers, and we will never give up these graves to any man."

The United States claimed they had bought all the Nez Percés country outside of Lapwai Reservation, from

Lawyer and other chiefs, but we continued to live on this land in peace until eight years ago, when white men began to come inside the bounds my father had set. We warned them against this great wrong, but they would not leave our land, and some bad blood was raised. The white men represented that we were going upon the war-path. They reported many things that were false.

The United States Government again asked for a 13 treaty council. My father had become blind and feeble. He could no longer speak for his people. It was then that I took my father's place as chief. In this council I made my first speech to white men. I said to the agent who held the council: "I did not want to come to this council, but I came hoping that we could save blood. The white man has no right to come here and take our country. We have never accepted any presents from the Government. Neither Lawyer nor any other chief had authority to sell this land. It has always belonged to my people. It came unclouded to them from our fathers, and we will defend this land as long as a drop of Indian blood warms the hearts of our men."

The agent said he had orders, from the Great White 14 Chief at Washington, for us to go upon the Lapwai Reservation, and that if we obeyed he would help us in many ways. "You *must* move to the agency," he said. I answered him: "I will not. I do not need your help; we have plenty, and we are contented and happy if the white man will let us alone. The reservation is too small for so many people with all their stock. You can keep your presents; we can go to your towns and pay for all we need; we have plenty of horses and cattle to sell, and we won't have any help from you; we are free now; we can go where we please. Our fathers were born here. Here they lived, here they died, here are their graves. We will never leave them." The agent went away, and we had peace for a little while.

Soon after this my father sent for me. I saw he was 15 dying. I took his hand in mine. He said: "My son, my body is returning to my mother earth, and my spirit is going very soon to see the Great Spirit Chief. When I am gone, think of your country. You are the chief of these people. They look to you to guide them. Always remember that your father never sold his country. You must stop your ears whenever you are asked to sign a treaty selling your home. A few years more, and white men will be all around you. They have their eyes on this land. My son, never forget my dying words. This country holds your father's body. Never sell the bones of your father and your mother." I pressed my father's hand and told him I would protect his grave with my life. My father smiled and passed away to the spirit-land.

I buried him in that beautiful valley of winding 16 waters. I love that land more than all the rest of the world. A man who would not love his father's grave is worse than a wild animal.

For a short time we lived quietly. But this could not 17 last. White men had found gold in the mountains around the land of winding water. They stole a great many horses from us, and we could not get them back because we were Indians. The white men told lies for each other. They drove off a great many of our cattle. Some white men branded our young cattle so they could claim them. We had no friend who would plead our cause before the law councils. It seemed to me that some of the white men in Wallowa were doing these things on purpose to get up a war. They knew that we were not strong enough to fight them. I labored hard to avoid trouble and bloodshed. We gave up some of our country to the white men, thinking that then we could have peace. We were mistaken. The white man would not let us alone. We could have avenged our wrongs many times, but we did not. Whenever the Government has asked us to help them against other Indians, we have never refused. When the white men were few and we were strong we could have killed them all off, but the Nez Percés wished to live at peace.

If we have not done so, we have not been to blame.   18
I believe that the old treaty has never been correctly
reported. If we ever owned the land we own it still, for
we never sold it. In the treaty councils the commission-
ers have claimed that our country had been sold to the
Government. Suppose a white man should come to me
and say, "Joseph, I like your horses, and I want to buy
them." I say to him, "No, my horses suit me, I will not
sell them." Then he goes to my neighbor, and says to
him: "Joseph has some good horses. I want to buy them,
but he refuses to sell." My neighbor answers, "Pay me
the money, and I will sell you Joseph's horses." The
white man returns to me, and says, "Joseph, I have
bought your horses, and you must let me have them."
If we sold our lands to the Government, this is the way
they were bought.

On account of the treaty made by the other bands   19
of the Nez Percés, the white men claimed my lands. We
were troubled greatly by white men crowding over the
line. Some of these were good men, and we lived on
peaceful terms with them, but they were not all good.

Nearly every year the agent came over from Lapwai   20
and ordered us on to the reservation. We always replied
that we were satisfied to live in Wallowa. We were
careful to refuse the presents or annuities which he
offered.

Through all the years since the white men came to   21
Wallowa we have been threatened and taunted by them
and the treaty Nez Percés. They have given us no rest.
We have had a few good friends among white men, and
they have always advised my people to bear these taunts
without fighting. Our young men were quick-tempered,
and I have had great trouble in keeping them from doing
rash things. I have carried a heavy load on my back ever
since I was a boy. I learned then that we were but few,
while the white men were many, and that we could not
hold our own with them. We were like deer. They were
like grizzly bears. We had a small country. Their country

was large. We were contented to let things remain as the Great Spirit Chief made them. They were not; and would change the rivers and mountains if they did not suit them.

. . . .

. . . I have heard talk and talk, but nothing is done. [22] Good words do not last long unless they amount to something. Words do not pay for my dead people. They do not pay for my country, now overrun by white men. They do not protect my father's grave. They do not pay for all my horses and cattle. Good words will not give me back my children. Good words will not make good the promise of your War Chief General Miles. Good words will not give my people good health and stop them from dying. Good words will not get my people a home where they can live in peace and take care of themselves. I am tired of talk that comes to nothing. It makes my heart sick when I remember all the good words and all the broken promises. There has been too much talking by men who had no right to talk. Too many misrepresentations have been made, too many misunderstandings have come up between the white men about the Indians. If the white man wants to live in peace with the Indian he can live in peace. There need be no trouble. Treat all men alike. Give them all the same law. Give them all an even chance to live and grow. All men were made by the same Great Spirit Chief. They are all brothers. The earth is the mother of all people, and all people should have equal rights upon it. You might as well expect the rivers to run backward as that any man who was born a free man should be contented when penned up and denied liberty to go where he pleases. If you tie a horse to a stake, do you expect he will grow fat? If you pen an Indian up on a small spot of earth, and compel him to stay there, he will not be contented, nor will he grow and prosper. I have asked some of the great white chiefs where they get their authority to say to the Indian that he shall stay in one place, while he sees white men going where they please. They can not tell me.

I only ask of the Government to be treated as all 23 other men are treated. If I can not go to my own home, let me have a home in some country where my people will not die so fast. I would like to go to Bitter Root Valley. There my people would be healthy; where they are now they are dying. Three have died since I left my camp to come to Washington.

When I think of our condition my heart is heavy. I 24 see men of my race treated as outlaws and driven from country to country, or shot down like animals.

I know that my race must change. We can not hold 25 our own with the white men as we are. We only ask an even chance to live as other men live. We ask to be recognized as men. We ask that the same law shall work alike on all men. If the Indian breaks the law, punish him by the law. If the white man breaks the law, punish him also.

Let me be a free man—free to travel, free to stop, 26 free to work, free to trade where I choose, free to choose my own teachers, free to follow the religion of my fathers, free to think and talk and act for myself—and I will obey every law, or submit to the penalty.

Whenever the white man treats the Indian as they treat 27 each other, then we will have no more wars. We shall all be alike—brothers of one father and one mother, with one sky above us and one country around us, and one government for all. Then the Great Spirit Chief who rules above will smile upon this land, and send rain to wash out the bloody spots made by brothers' hands from the face of the earth. For this time the Indian race are waiting and praying. I hope that no more groans of wounded men and women will ever go to the ear of the Great Spirit Chief above, and that all people may be one people.

In-mut-too-yah-lat-lat has spoken for his people. 28

YOUNG JOSEPH.
WASHINGTON CITY, D.C.

Comment

Chief Joseph's brief surrender statement is an outstanding example of native American eloquence. The statement exists in different versions that vary slightly. Brigadier General O. O. Howard, whose version is reprinted here, states that the reply was "taken verbatim on the spot" by his aide-de-camp, Lieutenant C. E. S. Wood. "In accordance with this pledge, Joseph himself, accompanied by four or five of his warriors, came inside our lines, and Joseph set the example by offering me his rifle. . . ." Chief Joseph's address to Congress two years later, contains the same persuasive qualities that distinguish the surrender statement.

Questions for Study and Discussion

1. What qualities of the surrender statement do you find most striking? Would the statement have been more eloquent if Chief Joseph had reviewed in more detail the circumstances that led to the surrender?
2. How does Chief Joseph seek to persuade the U.S. Congress that the Nez Percé Indians suffered wrongs? What wrongs does he cite?
3. What qualities does the address to Congress share with the surrender statement? What suggests that they are statements by the same person?
4. What do the surrender statement and the address tell you about Chief Joseph as a person and a leader?

Suggestion for Writing

The image of the native American has changed in recent years, largely through the Indian Rights movement and increased attention to the writings of native Americans about their own history and culture, and also popular films like *Dances with Wolves* and *Thunderheart.* Peter Nabokov's *Native American Testimony: A Chronicle of Indian-White Relations from Prophecy to the Present, 1492-1992* (Viking, 1992) contains a wide selection of these writings by native Americans as early as Tecumseh in the early 1800s.

Important firsthand accounts of historical events and autobiographical writings include the following:

Althea Bass, *The Arapaho Way: A Memoir of an Indian Boyhood* (Potter, 1966)

Black Hawk: An Autobiography, ed. Donald Jackson (University of Illinois Press, 1964)

Mary C. Dog and Richard Erdoes, *Lakota Woman* (Grove, 1990)

Hopi Voices: Recollections, Traditions and Narratives of the Hopi Indians, ed. Harold Courlander (University of New Mexico Press, 1982)

I Am an Indian, ed. Kent Gooderham (Dent, 1969)

I Am the Fire of Time: The Voices of Native American Women, ed. Jane B. Katz (Dutton, 1977)

Luther Standing Bear, *My People* (Houghton Mifflin, 1928)

The Zunis: Self-Portrayals (University of New Mexico Press, 1972)

Discuss how two or more of these or other primary sources increase your understanding of native American life and change your perception of the native American, perhaps altering a stereotype like those discussed in Kenneth Lincoln's *Indi'n Humor* (Oxford University Press, 1993).

✦

Controversy

Much of our persuasive writing is directed to specific issues of the day and usually to specific audiences—perhaps a person or group with whom we disagree. The controversy or question at issue usually defines the specific matters to be addressed. In the debate over the federal deficit in 1993, the administration and Congress agreed that reduction of the enormous deficit is essential. But how to reduce it required discussion of a number of controversial issues, including the cost of federal health programs and an increase in taxes for people of high income. Vigorous national debate and numerous proposals from those in government as well as the general public assured that these issues would be discussed.

But what should be the chief focus or point at issue in the debate was a major topic of discussion. For some the point to be debated was the cost of health care; for others, a decrease in government spending. Much of the debate centered on the point at issue—on what was to be argued and negotiated. The debate on the deficit resembles that of our own arguments with friends on particular issues. We may agree that measures must be taken to reduce crime or protect the environment, but we may not agree on what measures deserve discussion.

Participants in debates usually find it necessary to define the central point at issue, and in addition the terms to be used in the argument (defining human life is a central issue in the debate over abortion). In the course of debate, assumptions need to be identified and defended. The appeal to experience and other kinds of evidence may also be controversial. Experimental and statistical evidence considered reliable by one participant may be considered unreliable by another. Indeed, debate often centers on the relevance of a particular kind of evidence.

In writing a persuasive essay, you will want to anticipate the views of opponents on the matters just discussed. You will need to defend the point at issue as you see it, as well as the kind of evidence you intend to present (you may need to argue that statistical evidence of public attitudes has bearing on the issue—or has no bearing). If you know that agreement exists on the point of issue or relevant evidence, you may decide to devote most of your essay to the issue itself. In writing a persuasive essay, as in writing other kinds of papers, making an estimate of your audience is essential.

Animals in Research

Stephen Kaufman

MOST ANIMAL EXPERIMENTATION DOES NOT BENEFIT HUMAN HEALTH

Dr. Stephen Kaufman, an ophthalmologist at St. Luke's Hospital, Cleveland, Ohio, received his M.D. degree from Case Western Reserve University. In the course of his career he has been senior resident in ophthalmology at New York University and vice-chairman of the Medical Research Modernization Committee in New York City, a group of health professionals seeking to improve biomedical research. In his essay Dr. Kaufman reviews animal experimentation in various kinds of research.

Increasing numbers of scientists and clinicians have   1
criticized animal research on scientific grounds. Animal studies have always been unreliable and of tenuous value, but proponents have argued that there were no alternatives. Today, there are many alternatives that are less expensive and more valid. However, we continue to waste billions of tax dollars on irrelevant, often misleading animal research. This situation, which is tragic for both people and animals, occurs in large part because the thousands of scientists who make a living doing animal research defend the status quo vigorously and

effectively. They claim that animal research has been valuable to human health and that it will continue to benefit human patients.

Scientists frequently make statements such as, "Animal experimentation is an essential component of biomedical and behavioral research, a critical part of efforts to prevent, cure, and treat a vast range of ailments."[1] However, Reines showed that most of the key discoveries in several areas, such as heart disease and cancer, were made by clinical research, observations of patients, and human autopsies.[2] Animal research served primarily to "prove" in animals what had already been demonstrated in people. 2

Historical Impact of Animal Research

The scientific tradition that medical hypotheses must be "proven" in the lab has had unfortunate consequences. Frequently, effective therapies have been delayed because of the difficulty of finding an animal model that "works." For example, research with the animal model of polio resulted in a misunderstanding of the mechanism of infection. This delayed the development of the tissue culture, which was critical to the discovery of a vaccine.[3] 3

Misleading animal tests can be devastating for human health. For example, prior to 1963, every prospective and retrospective study of human patients, dozens in all, demonstrated that cigarette smoking causes cancer. Unfortunately, health warnings were delayed for years, and thousands of people subsequently died of cancer, because laboratory results were conflicting. In 4

---

[1]Committee on the Use of Laboratory Animals in Biomedical and Behavioral Research: *Use of Laboratory Animals in Biomedical and Behavioral Research.* Washington, D.C.: National Academy Press, 1988.

[2]Reines, B.R. *Masked Men of Medicine.* New York: Paragon House, 1989 (in press).

[3]Paul, J.R. *A History of Poliomyelitis.* New Haven: Yale University Press, 1971.

fact, a leading scientist wrote in the 1950s, "The failure of many investigators . . . to induce experimental cancers, except in a handful of cases, during fifty years of trying, cast serious doubt on the validity of the cigarette-lung cancer theory."[4]

How could widespread beliefs about the value of animal models be inaccurate? Academic researchers, many of whom do animal research, teach medical students and graduate students, write the textbooks students study, and edit the journals that all professionals read. Thus, they have the ability to disseminate widely among professionals a self-serving interpretation of medical history. For example, it is widely believed that the surgical therapy that cured the "blue babies," who suffered from a congenital heart defect known as tetralogy of Fallot, was derived from laboratory research. In fact, Dr. Taussig suggested a helpful surgical procedure based on human autopsy studies. In order to "prove" that the surgery would help, scientists tried to create an animal "model." Since it was impossible to produce tetralogy of Fallot in dogs, researchers cut out lung tissue of lab dogs instead. Thus, the lab animal "model" and the babies with tetralogy of Fallot had fundamentally different disease processes. Indeed, the only similarity was that they were both blue. Then, a surgical procedure, which was different from the one that was later used in patients, was tried on the dogs. While most dogs did poorly, some seemed to do a little better. Despite the irrelevance and poor outcome of the laboratory research, scientists claimed that this was an animal research success story. For example, Glaser wrote, "The experiments were so successful and confirmed Dr. Taussig's theory so completely that Blalock felt he could venture to operate on one of the poor children. . . ."[5]

_____

[4]Northrup, E. Men, mice, and smoking. *Science looks at smoking.* New York: Coward-McCann, 1957, p. 133.
[5]Glaser, H. *The Miracle of Heart Surgery.* London: Lutterworth Press, 1961, p. 59.

While scientists have attempted to re-write medical 6 history, many clinicians have recognized the primary role of clinical research. For example, renowned physician Paul Beeson, reviewing the history of hepatitis, concluded:

> Progress in the understanding and management of human disease must begin, and end, with studies of man. . . . Hepatitis, although an almost 'pure' example of progress by the study of man, is by no means unusual; in fact, it is more nearly the rule. To cite other examples: appendicitis, rheumatic fever, typhoid fever, ulcerative colitis and hyperparathyroidism.[6]

It is surprising that animal research has contributed 7 little to human health, given the billions of dollars invested in animal experimentation annually. An underlying problem with animal research is that it is difficult, if not impossible, to gain insight into a human disease by studying a superficially similar but fundamentally different nonhuman disease in a nonhuman animal. Even though dogs with surgically removed lungs and babies with tetralogy of Fallot were both blue, the dog "model" was not valid. Animal models of human disease have never been reliable, but researchers have argued that they were needed to study ongoing disease processes. While autopsies have always been a vital clinical research tool, they are rarely useful for the study of human disease before its lethal stage. However, many modern research techniques, such as CAT scans, PET scans, needle biopsies, and tissue cultures, permit safe, ethical investigation of human diseases with human patients and human tissues.

Contemporary Animal Models: Cancer

In 1971, the National Cancer Act initiated a "War 8 on Cancer," which many sponsors predicted would cure

---

[6]Beeson, P.B. The growth of knowledge about a disease hepatitis. *American Journal of Medicine.* Vol 67; 1979; pp. 366-370.

cancer by 1976. However, despite spending over one billion dollars a year on cancer research, the program has been, according to Harvard's Dr. John Bailar III, a "qualified failure." Bailar reported in 1986 that, "Age-adjusted mortality rates (from cancer) have shown a slow and steady increase over several decades, and there is no evidence of a recent downward trend."[7] However, in order to encourage continued support for cancer research, scientists have misled the public. According to the U.S. General Accounting Office, the National Cancer Institute's statistics, ". . . artificially inflate in the amount of 'true' progress."[8] The GAO found that simple five year survival statistics used by the NCI did not consider important statistical biases. Furthermore, claims of cancer "cures" based on five year survival ignore the fact that certain cancers, such as breast cancer and melanoma, often kill the patient more than five years after detection.

Why has progress against cancer failed to be commensurate with the research effort? One possibility is that, in our enthusiasm to cure cancer, we have uncritically funded many less-promising projects. In addition, Dr. Irwin Bross noted that, since cancer reflects failure of the body's own defense system, substantial differences between man and animals have hindered efforts to cure cancer with animal models.[9] Dr. Bailar, commenting on the discouraging results of our research efforts on cancer treatment, stated that ". . . the more promising areas are in cancer prevention. . . ."[7]

Recently, researchers have advocated use of animal models of AIDS. However, no immunologically normal animal besides man develops the AIDS syndrome. Only

9

10

---

[7]Bailar, J.C., and Smith, E.M. Progress against Cancer? *New England Journal of Medicine.* Vol 314; 1986: pp. 1226-1232.

[8]U.S. General Accounting Office. *Cancer Patient Survival: What Progress Has Been Made?* Washington, D.C.: General Accounting Office, 1987.

[9]Bross, I. *Crimes of Official Science.* Buffalo: Biomedical Metatechnology Press, 1987.

chimpanzees can be infected with the virus, but they develop a mild flu-like illness only. Furthermore, since AIDS is an infectious disease, the chimpanzees must be kept in isolation. This is very stressful for chimpanzees, who are social animals. Since stress affects the immune system and since AIDS attacks the immune system, this animal "model" of AIDS is of dubious value.

Because chimpanzees are a threatened species, many 11 researchers are studying simian (monkey) AIDS. However, Power et al. wrote, ". . . a molecular clone of the prototype SAIDS virus. . . has no notable similarity in either genetic organization or sequence to the human AIDS retroviruses."[10] Not surprisingly, the critical insights into the understanding, prevention, and treatment of human AIDS has come from research using human subjects and tissues. Although future advances against this disease are most likely to come from clinical investigation, a large fraction of the research on AIDS is being devoted to animal research.

Psychiatry

Animal models of psychiatric diseases have come 12 under particularly vigorous attack. For example, there have been hundreds of "learned helplessness" studies, in which animals are repeatedly shocked or otherwise traumatized until they stop trying to escape. This "learned helplessness," researchers maintain, is similar to human depression, in which patients feel helpless and hopeless. However, these animals do not have other symptoms of human depression, such as sleeplessness, loss of appetite, guilt, or suicidal behavior and ideas. Psychiatrist Dallas Pratt wrote, "Surely these experimenters are contributing little or nothing to an understanding of the complexities of human anxiety or depressive states. If

---

[10]Power, J.D., Marx, P.A., Bryant, M.L., Gardner, M.B., Barr, P.J., Luciw, P.A., Nucleotide sequence or SRV-1, a type D simian acquired immune deficiency syndrome retrovirus. *Science.* Vol 231; 1987: pp. 438-446.

anything, these tortured and terrified dogs appear to be suffering from a traumatic reaction, similar to the soldier's 'shell-shock'. . . ."[11] Indeed, we do not know if animals exhibiting "learned helplessness" are experiencing depression, anxiety, shock, or a type of mental state unfamiliar to our species. As in all animal models of psychiatric diseases, it is not possible to determine the mental state of the animal, because it cannot communicate its feelings. The only way to understand human depression is to interview and study depressed people.

Similarly, Midgely criticized Harlow's monkey maternal deprivation experiments, in which infants were separated from their mothers and consequently exhibited "depression" and other psychopathology:

> The existences of the species barrier confronts experimenters like Harlow with only two clear alternatives: (1) Human beings and rhesus monkeys are indeed very closely comparable emotionally. In this case his results, though slight, may have some validity for human beings, and he is guilty of cruelty so enormous that hardly any theoretical advance could justify it. (2) Human beings and rhesus monkeys are not closely comparable emotionally. In this case he may be guilty of callousness. . . but is convicted of enormous and wasteful intellectual confusion, and his results are void.[12]

Harlow himself wrote, ". . . most experiments are not worth doing and the data obtained are not worth publishing."[13] Indeed, former behavioral psychologist Roger Ulrich recalled, "When I finished my dissertation on pain-producing aggression, my Mennonite mother asked me what it was about. When I told her she replied, 'Well, we knew that. Dad always warned us to stay away from

[11]Pratt, D. *Alternatives to Pain in Experimentation on Animals*. New York: Argus Archives, 1980, p. 68.

[12]Midgely, M. Why knowledge matters. In Sperlinger, D. (ed). *Animals in Research*. New York: John Wiley & Sons, 1981.

[13]Rollin, B.E. *Animal Rights and Human Morality*. Buffalo: Prometheus Books, 1981.

animals in pain because they are more likely to attack.'"[13] Giannelli concluded:

> I believe the most valuable things we have learned through animal experimentation are insights into the human mentality. These insights have arisen from direct analysis of researchers at work, not from tenuous extrapolations to ourselves based on animal behavior in highly artificial laboratory environments. We have learned that otherwise compassionate people can become remarkably desensitized and detached from the suffering they inflict upon animals. We have learned that highly intelligent people can be engaged in the most trivial or eccentric research yet convince themselves that their work is important.[14]

Regarding the development of drugs for psychiatric diseases, Reines observed, ". . . the antidepressants and antipsychotics were discovered by clinical serendipity. This was common knowledge among psychopharmacologists until N.E. Miller and other animal research enthusiasts started rewriting medical history."[15]

Toxicity Tests

Several prevalent animal toxicity tests have been widely criticized by toxicologists and humanitarians. For example, the LD50 test, which determines how much of a drug, chemical, or cosmetic is needed to kill 50% of test animals, uses about 60-100 animals, most of whom suffer greatly. However, it has several scientific flaws.[16] First, extrapolation of results from rodents to man is highly unreliable. Second, since the results can depend on such variables as strains within species, age,

---

[14]Giannelli, M.A.: Three blind mice, see how they run: a critique of behavioral research with animals. In Fox, M.W., and Mickley, L.D., (eds). *Advances in Animal Welfare Science 1985/86*. Washington, D.C.: Humane Society of the United States, 1985.

[15]Reines, B.R. Animal rights and research. *American Journal of Psychiatry.* Vol 145; 1987: pp. 539-540.

[16]Zbinden, G., and Flury-Roversi, M.: Significance of the LD50 test for the toxicological evaluation of chemical substances. *Archives of Toxicology.* Vol 47; 1981: pp. 77-99.

sex, and weight, different laboratories often obtain widely disparate results for the same substances. Third, LD50 data cannot be applied to most human poisoning victims, because the quantity and even the type of substance(s) ingested are often unknown. Finally, in an emergency, one needs to know how much of a substance is dangerous and which organs are at risk, but the LD50 indicates only the meaningless statistic of how much is lethal to 50% of individuals. While the LD50 is nearly worthless, alternative protocols could yield more relevant information while using 80-90% fewer animals.[17]

Similarly, the Draize eye irritation test, in which 15 unanesthetized rabbits have substances instilled in their eyes, is scientifically unsound. Fundamental anatomical differences between rabbits and people in the eyelids, tearing mechanisms, and corneas make the Draize results of dubious validity. In fact, when Draize data for 14 household and cosmetic products were compared to accident[al] human eye exposures, they differed by a factor 18 to 250. On the other hand, modern *in vitro* assays have compared well with existing databases.[18] A battery of *in vitro* tests would be less expensive, and probably more accurate, than the Draize test.

Animal tests for cancer causing substances are noto- 16 riously unreliable. Of the 19 known human oral carcinogens, only seven caused cancer in the NCI protocol. This standard screening test is so insensitive that a substance that did not appear to be carcinogenic in experimental animals could still cause cancer in up to one million Americans.[19] On the other hand, an international study

---

[17]Schutz, E., and Fuchs, H.: A new approach to minimizing the number of animals used in acute toxicity testing and optimizing the information of test results. *Archives of Toxicology.* Vol 51; 1982: pp. 197-200.

[18]Goldberg, A.N. (ed). *In Vitro Toxicology: Approaches to Validation.* New York: Mary Ann Liebert, 1987.

[19]Rowan, A.N. *Of Mice, Models, & Men: A Critical Evaluation of Animal Research.* Albany: SUNY Press, 1984.

demonstrated that new *in vitro* tests were more sensitive and more accurate than the animal tests.[20]

Why Animal Research Persists

If animal experimentation is indeed of little value, why does it persist? There are several possible explanations. First, animal research is easy. It is simple to take a well-defined animal model, change a variable, and produce a paper for publication. This is a strong incentive to do animal research in the "publish or perish" world of academia. Second, animal research is fast. Human diseases tend to span over many years, but laboratory animals, with shorter lifespans, tend to have more rapidly progressive disease processes. This again facilitates quick publication of papers. Third, many scientists are trained in and comfortable with animal research techniques. They are reluctant to adopt alternative methodologies, such as tissue cultures, which would require extensive re-training. A final attraction is that scientists can control research variables much more tightly in animal experiments than is possible with human clinical research. It is possible to take genetically similar animals, give identical disease conditions, and then try two different research strategies to see which works better. The problem, however, is known as "garbage in, garbage out." If the animal model is irrelevant to human disease, it is most unlikely to provide information of clinical value. The ability to control variables, which permits consistent, reproducible results, has led to a widespread belief among scientists that animal research is more "scientific" than clinical research. While controlling variables is desirable, it does not justify the use of poorly conceived animal models.

---

[20]De Serres, F.J. Panel discussion. In *Trends in Bioassay Methodology: in vivo, in vitro and mathematical approaches*. Washington, D.C.: U.S. Department of Health and Human Services, 1981.

Redirect Animal Research Funds

In conclusion, it appears that, for political reasons, 18 the value of animal research has been grossly overstated. Not all animal research is irrelevant, but its value is severely limited by anatomical, physiological, and pathological differences between people and nonhuman animals. Most of the billions of dollars invested annually in animal research could be used much more effectively in clinical research or public health programs.

Comment

Kaufman begins by defining the point at issue for him in the debate on animal experimentation. This opening definition, often the central issue itself in debate, allows him to focus on research for which exaggerated claims have been made, not on research that is relevant and may benefit human health—a topic for additional discussion and debate. Kaufman reviews certain kinds of research like toxicity tests that have been under most attack. The documentation provided in the notes allows his opponent to test the accuracy of his claims and allows the general reader to study the kinds of research discussed and compare positions and claims.

Questions for Study and Discussion

1. What is the point at issue for Kaufman in the debate over animal research?
2. What traditional method of scientific research does Kaufman criticize in paragraphs 3-5? Does he say that the traditional method is faulty or invalid, or that it has been misused? What do his examples in paragraphs 3-6 show?
3. How is "clinical research" different from animal research? What examples does he give of clinical research?
4. How does the discussion of cancer and AIDS research in paragraphs 9-10 support Kaufman's claim that animal research in invalid?

5. Is Kaufman making the same points about the use of animals in research into psychiatric diseases and in toxicity tests? Is the discussion of these kinds of research essential to the case he is making?
6. Is Kaufman arguing that if "animal studies have always been unreliable and of tenuous value," they are of no value and ought to be halted?
7. What alternatives to animal research does Kaufman cite?

Vocabulary Study

Explain the following words and phrases:

1. *tenuous value, proponents, status quo* (paragraph 1)
2. *human autopsies* (paragraph 2)
3. *medical hypotheses* (paragraph 3)
4. *disseminate, congenital* (paragraph 5)
5. *needle biopsies* (paragraph 7)
6. *statistical biases* (paragraph 8)
7. *syndrome, immune system* (paragraph 10)
8. *genetic organization, retroviruses* (paragraph 11)
9. *traumatized* (paragraph 12)
10. *psychopathology, extrapolations, antipsychotics, clinical serendipity* (paragraph 13)
11. *toxicologists, humanitarians, protocols* (paragraph 14)
12. *in vitro assays* (paragraph 16)

Suggestion for Writing

Using *Index Medicus* and other guides to medical research, find articles in scientific and medical journals that discuss one of the kinds of animal research discussed in the essay. Take notes on the method of research described and the scientific or medical justification given in the article for the particular method. In a report on your findings, discuss the kind of claims or case the authors make—or would be likely to make—for animal experimentation. Where possible, compare the case made with Kaufman's comments on animal research.

Meg Greenfield

IN DEFENSE OF ANIMALS

Meg Greenfield graduated from Smith College in 1952, and afterward studied as a Fulbright scholar at Cambridge University in England, again at Smith College, and at Georgetown University. Her career as a journalist began with *The Reporter* magazine; her association with the *Washington Post* began in 1968, and since 1979 she has been editor of the editorial page. Greenfield also writes a regular column in *Newsweek,* in which the following essay on the use of animals in experiments appeared on April 17, 1989.

I might as well come right out with it: contrary to some of my most cherished prejudices, the animal-rights people have begun to get to me. I think that in some part of what they say they are right.

I never thought it would come to this. As distinct from the old-style animal rescue, protection and shelter organizations, the more aggressive newcomers, with their "liberation" of laboratory animals and periodic championship of the claims of animal well-being over human well-being when a choice must be made, have earned a reputation in the world I live in as fanatics and just plain kooks. And even with my own recently (relatively) raised consciousness, there remains a good deal in both their critique and their prescription for the virtuous life that I reject, being not just a practicing carnivore, a wearer of shoe leather and so forth, but also a supporter of certain indisputably agonizing procedures visited upon innocent animals in the furtherance of human welfare, especially experiments undertaken to improve human health.

So, viewed from the pure position, I am probably only marginally better than the worst of my kind, if that: I don't buy the complete "speciesist" analysis or even the fundamental language of animal "rights" and continue to find a large part of what is done in the name of that cause harmful and extreme. But I also think, patronizing as it must sound, that the zealots are required early on in any movement if it is to succeed in altering the sensibility of the leaden masses, such as me. Eventually they get your attention. And eventually you at least feel obliged to weigh their arguments and think about whether there may not be something there.

It is true that this end has often been achieved—as 4 in my case—by means of vivid, cringe-inducing photographs, not by an appeal to reason or values so much as by an assault on squeamishness. From the famous 1970s photo of the newly skinned baby seal to the videos of animals being raised in the most dark, miserable, stunting environment as they are readied for their life's sole fulfillment as frozen patties and cutlets, these sights have had their effect. But we live in a world where the animal protein we eat comes discreetly prebutchered and prepacked so the original beast and his slaughtering are remote from our consideration, just as our furs come on coat hangers in salons, not on their original proprietors; and I see nothing wrong with our having to contemplate the often unsettling reality of how we came by the animal products we make use of. Then we can choose what we want to do.

The objection to our being confronted with these 5 dramatic, disturbing pictures is first that they tend to provoke a misplaced, uncritical and highly emotional concern for animal life at the direct expense of a more suitable concern for human suffering. What goes into the animals' account, the reasoning goes, necessarily comes out of ours. But I think it is possible to remain stalwart in your view that the human claim comes first and in your acceptance of the use of animals for human betterment and *still* to believe that there are some human interests that should not take precedence. For we have become far too self-indulgent, hardened, careless and cruel in the pain we routinely inflict upon these creatures for the most frivolous, unworthy purposes. And I also think that the more justifiable purposes, such as medical research, are shamelessly used as cover for other activities that are wanton.

For instance, not all of the painful and crippling 6 experimentation that is undertaken in the lab is being conducted for the sake of medical knowledge or other purposes related to basic human well-being and health. Much of it is being conducted for the sake of super-refinements in the cosmetic and other frill industries, the noble goal being to contrive yet another fragrance or hair tint or commercially competitive variation on all the daft, fizzy, multicolored "personal care" products for the medicine cabinet and dressing table, a firmer-holding hair spray, that sort of thing. In other words, the conscripted, immobilized rabbits and other terrified creatures, who have been locked in boxes from the neck down, only their heads on view, are being sprayed in the eyes with different burning, stinging substances for the sake of adding to our already obscene store of luxuries and utterly superfluous vanity items.

Oddly, we tend to be very sentimental about animals 7 in their idealized, fictional form, and largely indifferent to them in realms where our lives actually touch. From time immemorial, humans have romantically attributed to animals their own sensibilities—from Balaam's Biblical ass who providently could speak and who got his owner out of harm's way right down to Lassie and the other Hollywood pups who would invariably tip off the good guys that the bad guys were up to something. So we simulate phony cross-species kinship, pretty well drown in the cuteness of it all—Mickey and Minnie and Porky—and ignore, if we don't actually countenance, the brutish things done in the name of Almighty Hair Spray.

This strikes me as decadent. My problem is that it 8 also causes me to reach a position that is, on its face philosophically vulnerable, if not absurd—the muddled, middling, inconsistent place where finally you are saying it's all right to kill them for some purposes, but not to hurt them gratuitously in doing it or to make them suffer horribly for one's own trivial whims.

I would feel more humiliated to have fetched up on 9 this exposed rock, if I didn't suspect I had so much company. When you see pictures of people laboriously trying to clean the Exxon gunk off of sea otters even knowing that they will only be able to help out a very few, you see this same outlook in action. And I think it *can* be defended. For to me the biggest cop-out is the one that says that if you don't buy the whole absolutist, extreme position it is pointless and even hypocritical to concern yourself with lesser mercies and ameliorations. The pressure of the animal-protection groups has already had some impact in improving the way various creatures are treated by researchers, trainers and food producers. There is much more in this vein to be done. We are talking about rejecting wanton, pointless cruelty here. The position may be philosophically absurd, but the outcome is the right one.

Comment

Meg Greenfield devotes several paragraphs to defining the point at issue in the debate over animal rights. In doing so, she explains how she reached her position and states her view of the animal rights movement and its rhetoric or means of persuasion. Greenfield might have devoted the rest of the essay to the experiments that concern her; she instead focuses on the animal rights movement because the movement and its rhetoric present her (and possibly her readers) with a dilemma. Greenfield builds up to this dilemma in the concluding paragraphs, stating it and then discussing how to resolve it. Among the ways of resolving a dilemma, the most common are "seizing the horns" (the sharply opposed, exclusive alternatives) and "going between the horns." In "seizing the horns," the debater shows that one of the alternatives is false as stated; in "going between the horns," the debater shows that a better alternative exists to those presented. Greenfield uses one of these techniques to resolve her dilemma. (A less common but effective technique is to present a counter-dilemma.)

Questions for Study and Discussion

1. What prompted Greenfield to consider the argument in favor of animal rights? What attitudes and practices originally led her to be indifferent or skeptical? Is the point at issue for her in the debate the same as for Kaufman?

2. What in the argument and rhetoric of the animal rights movement does Greenfield reject? What has she come to accept, and why?

3. In paragraph 8 Greenfield states the dilemma that she faced in thinking about animal rights. What is that dilemma, and how do paragraphs 2-7 explain how she came to face it? How does Greenfield resolve the dilemma?

4. What audience is Greenfield addressing in the essay? Is she talking directly to the animal rights movement, to its opponents, or to both? Or is she addressing readers who have been indifferent to the issue, or skeptical of arguments for and against animal rights?

Vocabulary Study

Explain the following words and phrases:

1. *critique, prescription, carnivore* (paragraph 2)
2. *zealots* (paragraph 3)
3. *squeamishness, proprietors* (paragraph 4)
4. *stalwart, wanton* (paragraph 5)
5. *simulate, cross-species kinship* (paragraph 7)
6. *muddled, middling, gratuitously* (paragraph 8)
7. *cop-out, absolutist, ameliorations* (paragraph 9)

Suggestion for Writing

Using the *Essay Index, Readers' Guide to Periodical Literature, Social Sciences Index,* and other indexes and reference guides, locate an article that argues for or against animal research. Write an essay comparing the article with Greenfield's essay, giving attention to the following:

1. Statement and defense of the point at issue
2. Nature of the arguments opposing animal research
3. Persuasive devices used by each writer
4. Introduction of opposing arguments and response to them

Ron Karpati

A SCIENTIST: "I AM THE ENEMY"

Ron Karpati, fellow in pediatric oncology and bone marrow transplantation at the University of California, San Francisco, writes about animal research from the point of view of a pediatrician concerned with immunological research. His essay appeared in *Newsweek* on December 18, 1989.

I am the enemy! One of those vilified, inhumane   1
physician-scientists involved in animal research. How strange, for I have never thought of myself as an evil person. I became a pediatrician because of my love for children and my desire to keep them healthy. During medical school and residency, however, I saw many children die of leukemia, prematurity and traumatic injury—circumstances against which medicine has made tremendous progress, but still has far to go. More important, I also saw children, alive and healthy, thanks to advances in medical science such as infant respirators, potent antibiotics, new surgical techniques and the entire field of organ transplantation. My desire to tip the scales in favor of the healthy, happy children drew me to medical research.

My accusers claim that I inflict torture on animals ₂ for the sole purpose of career advancement. My experiments supposedly have no relevance to medicine and are easily replaced by computer simulation. Meanwhile, an apathetic public barely watches, convinced that the issue has no significance, and publicity-conscious politicians increasingly give way to the demands of the activists.

We in medical research have also been unconsciona- ₃ bly apathetic. We have allowed the most extreme animal-rights protesters to seize the initiative and frame the issue as one of "animal fraud." We have been complacent in our belief that a knowledgeable public would sense the importance of animal research to the public health. Perhaps we have been mistaken in not responding to the emotional tone of the argument created by those sad posters of animals by waving equally sad posters of children dying of leukemia or cystic fibrosis.

Much is made of the pain inflicted on these animals ₄ in the name of medical science. The animal-rights activists contend that this is evidence of our malevolent and sadistic nature. A more reasonable argument, however, can be advanced in our defense. Life is often cruel, both to animals and human beings. Teenagers get thrown from the back of a pickup truck and suffer severe head injuries. Toddlers, barely able to walk, find themselves at the bottom of a swimming pool while a parent checks the mail. Physicians hoping to alleviate the pain and suffering these tragedies cause have but three choices: create an animal model of the injury or disease and use that model to understand the process and test new therapies; experiment on human beings—some experiments will succeed, most will fail—or finally, leave medical knowledge static, hoping that accidental discoveries will lead us to the advances.

Some animal-rights activists would suggest a fourth ₅ choice, claiming that computer models can simulate animal experiments, thus making the actual experiments unnecessary. Computers can simulate, reasonably well, the effects of well-understood principles on complex systems, as in the application of the laws of physics to airplane and automobile design. However, when the principles themselves are in question, as is the case with the complex biological systems under study, computer modeling alone is of little value.

One of the terrifying effects of the effort to restrict the use of animals in medical research is that the impact will not be felt for years and decades: drugs that might have been discovered will not be; surgical techniques that might have been developed will not be; and fundamental biological processes that might have been understood will remain mysteries. There is the danger that politically expedient solutions will be found to placate a vocal minority, while the consequences of those decisions will not be apparent until long after the decisions are made and the decision makers forgotten.

Fortunately, most of us enjoy good health, and the trauma of watching one's child die has become a rare experience. Yet our good fortune should not make us unappreciative of the health we enjoy or the advances that make it possible. Vaccines, antibiotics, insulin and drugs to treat heart disease, hypertension and stroke are all based on animal research. Most complex surgical procedures, such as coronary-artery bypass and organ transplantation, are initially developed in animals. Presently undergoing animal studies are techniques to insert genes in humans in order to replace the defective ones found to be the cause of so much disease. These studies will effectively end if animal research is severely restricted.

In America today, death has become an event isolated from our daily existence—out of the sight and thoughts of most of us. As a doctor who has watched many children die, and their parents grieve, I am particularly angered by people capable of so much compassion for a dog or a cat, but with seemingly so little for a dying human being. These people seem so insulated from the reality of human life and death and what it means.

Make no mistake, however: I am not advocating the 9 needlessly cruel treatment of animals. To the extent that the animal-rights movement has made us more aware of the needs of these animals, and made us search harder for suitable alternatives, they have made a significant contribution. But if the more radical members of this movement are successful in limiting further research, their efforts will bring about a tragedy that will cost many lives. The real question is whether an apathetic majority can be aroused to protect its future against a vocal, but misdirected, minority.

Comment

Like Meg Greenfield, Ron Karpati devotes a major part of his essay to defining the point at issue in the debate over animal research. And like Greenfield, he is also concerned with finding points of agreement with his opponents, for he knows that working out a solution depends on finding a common ground. To persuade his audience, Karpati draws on his own experience as a physician and researcher. This rational appeal is one of the three that the Greek philosopher Aristotle identified in persuasive discourse. The other two are the appeal to emotion and the ethical appeal that invites the reader to recognize that the speaker or writer is a person of good character and is arguing for good motives. The appeals that Karpati makes to the reader seek to make his essay persuasive.

Questions for Study and Discussion

1. How does Karpati define the point at issue in the debate over animal rights? Where does he restate it in the course of the essay? Is the point at issue the same as for Greenfield and for Kaufman?

2. What arguments in opposition to animal research does Karpati reject? How does he answer these opponents? How varied is the evidence he presents in support of animal research?
3. In what order does he introduce opposing arguments and his responses to them?
4. Where does Karpati state his main point or thesis? How does he give it emphasis?
5. What appeals does he make in seeking to persuade his readers?

Vocabulary Study

Explain the following words and phrases:

1. *vilified, leukemia, prematurity, traumatic injury* (paragraph 1)
2. *apathetic, computer simulation* (paragraph 2)
3. *cystic fibrosis* (paragraph 3)
4. *malevolent, sadistic, alleviate* (paragraph 4)
5. *placate* (paragraph 6)
6. *coronary-artery bypass* (paragraph 7)
7. *radical* (paragraph 9)

Suggestions for Writing

1. Extend your investigation of the debate over animal research (p. 409) by finding and analyzing additional articles pro and con. On the basis of this limited investigation, discuss points of agreement on which the issue might be conciliated or resolved. Take note also of differences that make conciliation and resolution difficult.
2. State your own views on animal research, explaining why you hold them, and responding to the arguments of Greenfield or Karpati or both.

Drugs in College:
To Test or Not to Test

James C. Puffer

N.C.A.A. PLAN IS DETERRENT

A member of the Division of Family Medicine at U.C.L.A. Medical Center, Dr. James C. Puffer was head physician of the U.S. Summer Olympic Team and chairperson of the National Collegiate Athletic Association (N.C.A.A.) Competitive Safeguards Committee in 1988, the year he wrote this article. His argument in favor of collegiate drug testing is based on his experience with safety and health in intercollegiate athletic programs.

The untimely deaths of Len Bias and Don Rogers 1 two years ago focused our attention on the tragic role that substance abuse plays in the lives of performing athletes. The tremendous pressures placed upon them to perform to expectations that are often unrealistic have created circumstances in which athletes frequently turn to drug use either to escape from these pressures or to enhance performance. In fact, the widespread use of performance-enhancing drugs has perhaps become the single most important threat to the integrity of amateur and professional sport.

The use of drugs to enhance performance is not a 2 recent phenomenon. The writings of Homer documented ingestion of mushrooms by Greek athletes in the third century B.C. during the ancient Olympic Games. In the 19th century there were reports of widespread use of caffeine, alcohol, nitroglycerin, ethyl ether and opium by European athletes.

However, it was not until the death of Kurt Enemar 3 Jensen, a Danish cyclist, at the 1960 Summer Olympic Games in Rome that considerable attention was focused on this mounting problem. Jensen and two of his teammates had taken amphetamines in an attempt to improve their performance in the 100-kilometer team cycling trials and this helped contribute to Jensen's death. These events motivated the International Olympic Committee to begin to question the integrity of games in which athletes were using artificial substances in an effort to enhance performance.

The rest is well known. The International Olympic   4
Committee instituted drug testing in the 1968 Olympics in both Grenoble and Mexico City and has tested for drugs since that time. For a time, drug testing remained a phenomenon that was predominantly limited to international events such as the Olympic Games and world championships. However, in the past several years drug testing has become widespread and is used by both the National Collegiate Athletic Association and numerous member institutions in an attempt to stem the increasing use of drugs by athletes.

The N.C.A.A. has just reported that 1.3 percent of   5
the 1,589 athletes who were tested at championship events last fall tested positive for banned substances. This was a slight increase over the 1 percent of the 3,360 who tested positive in the 1986-87 academic year. Given the seemingly small number of positive tests, why would any organization or institution wish to invest the tremendous amount of financial and human resources necessary to conduct an exemplary drug testing program? In order to understand the reasoning, it is essential to understand the notion that drug testing is an adjunctive tool that is used to deter drug use. The low number of positive samples speaks to the positive effect that testing has had.

Is drug testing indeed a deterrent to drug use? It would   6
appear that it is. Reports from certified laboratories at which drug testing is performed indicate that when testing is voluntary and nonpunitive, as many as 50 percent of the samples may be positive. The institution of man-

datory drug testing at N.C.A.A. championship events two years ago has had a profound effect on significantly reducing the use of injectable anabolic steroids by college athletes. This is based on the fact that a recent N.C.A.A. survey indicated that approximately 8 percent of college athletes admitted to using steroids. The performance of athletes in certain weight events in last year's N.C.A.A. track and field championships were far below those from the previous year, further testimony that drug testing can have a dramatic effect on the final results.

Many argue that while testing is an effective deterrent in the use of certain types of drugs, it nevertheless violates the personal rights of individual athletes as well as presumes guilt. It is important to note that six court cases have been brought against either the N.C.A.A. or its member institutions in the past year and a half in an attempt to resolve this issue. The cases have yet to resolve the issue satisfactorily.   7

While the preliminary results from one hearing would indicate that, in fact, drug testing may violate some of the personal rights of athletes in the state of California, others have determined that drug testing may not be an unreasonable condition of participation in intercollegiate athletics. If one appreciates the notion that drug testing is, in fact, a deterrent to drug use, and its sole purpose is to prevent athletes from using banned substances altogether, one can certainly dismiss the notion of presumptive guilt; it is the explicit intent of drug testing programs to find no positive samples if indeed the program is successful.   8

Finally, some comment must be made about the attitudes of the athletes who undergo drug testing. Numerous surveys on college campuses that conduct their own testing programs have shown that the overwhelming majority of athletes favor drug testing. They think that it guarantees the opportunity to participate in a drug-free environment and provides a valuable crutch that allows them to say no to drugs. This fact   9 has been repeatedly demonstrated by the decreasing use of drugs by college athletes as documented by drug testing at these institutions since the inception of their programs.

Even though testing is far from totally eradicating drug use by college athletes, when used in conjunction with a sound drug education program, it serves as the best method for deterring drug use. Until better means become available, drug testing remains our best option in guaranteeing the safety and well-being of athletes who participate in sport.

10

Comment

Essays that debate an issue often use an organization that originated in the legal orations of the ancient Greeks. This kind of persuasive essay usually contains the following:

1. an *introduction* that states the topic of the paper and seeks to generate interest in the proposal at issue;
2. the *background* or essential facts of the case, called the *narrative;*
3. a statement of the *thesis,* often following the narrative;
4. arguments in support of the thesis, called the *confirmation;*
5. *refutation* of opposing arguments; and
6. a *conclusion* that may restate the thesis, summarize the supporting arguments and evidence, and ask the audience to accept the argument.

Some writers combine supporting arguments with the refutation, making a case for the proposal in the course of answering objections to it.

James C. Puffer's argument in support of drug testing does the latter. Puffer introduces his main topic—the threat of performance-enhancing drugs—by reminding us of recent drug-related deaths of prominent collegiate athletes and the death of a bicyclist at the Olympic Games in Rome in 1960. This background leads into a statement of the central thesis (paragraph 5). Following a brief defense of his thesis (paragraph 6), Puffer turns to his main argument in support of drug testing—deterrence (paragraph 7). In the remaining paragraphs, Puffer makes his case for drug testing in the course of answering objections to the procedure. He concludes with a restatement of his thesis. This type of organization presents the argument in an economical and effective way.

Questions for Study and Discussion

1. How does Puffer establish the importance of the subject in his opening paragraphs?
2. What is his thesis, and how does he defend it following its introduction in paragraph 5? What does he gain by defending drug testing in the course of answering objections to it?
3. What are the objections to drug testing, and how does Puffer answer them? What kind of evidence does he present in this refutation?
4. Why does Puffer conclude with the opinions of college athletes? Is he concluding with the strongest evidence in favor of drug testing? If a majority of college athletes opposed drug resting, would Puffer consider his argument to be weakened or refuted?
5. To what audience is Puffer addressing his argument? Is he writing to a special audience—specifically, those opposed to drug testing? Or is he writing to a general audience—to people who hold various opinions on drug testing or none? How do you know?

Vocabulary Study

Explain the following words and phrases:

1. *performance-enhancing* (paragraph 1)
2. *ingestion, amphetamines* (paragraph 3)
3. *adjunctive tool* (paragraph 5)
4. *anabolic steroids* (paragraph 6)
5. *presumptive guilt* (paragraph 8)

Suggestions for Writing

1. Write a persuasive essay on a current issue, using the form of argument outlined above. Address those people who hold opinions opposite to yours. You may wish to combine the arguments supporting your thesis with your refutation of opposing arguments, or you may wish to separate them. Make your thesis prominent by stating it in key places in the essay, as Puffer does.

2. Rewrite your persuasive essay, addressing it to a general audience—to people who hold various opinions on the issue. Present your supporting arguments and your refutation of opponents in an order best able to convince your audience.

Allen L. Sack

RANDOM TESTS ABUSE DIGNITY

Allen L. Sack, chairman of the Honors program at the University of New Haven, writes in opposition to the N.C.A.A. policy, defended by James C. Puffer in his essay on drug testing. Puffer's and Sack's essays appeared together in *The New York Times* on May 29, 1988.

Nothing better illustrates the low regard that the National Collegiate Athletic Association has often had for the rights of student athletes than its random drug-testing policy. There are a number of alternatives for addressing the problem of substance abuse. Unfortunately, the N.C.A.A. chooses an approach that protects the public relations image of its member institutions but shows little or no concern for the dignity and privacy of the vast majority of hard-working young athletes who are drug-free.

Random drug-testing treats all athletes like suspected criminals when there is no probable cause for doing so, and it expects them to surrender rights docilely that are the cornerstone of American democracy. Most disturbing is the fact that this policy was approved without even the slightest consultation with the athletes themselves.

The actual procedure for gathering urine samples from randomly selected athletes is precisely spelled out in N.C.A.A. documents. Immediately following participation in a championship event, student-athletes are selected for drug-testing, and are instructed to report to a urine collection station within one hour. At the collection station, what the N.C.A.A. calls a "urine validator" monitors the furnishing of the specimen.

Judge Conrad L. Rushing of the Superior Court of California describes the process graphically. "Under the N.C.A.A. program last year, Jennifer Hill was accompanied to a doorless bathroom stall by the monitor, who stood a few feet away and watched while Hill removed her shorts and undergarments . . . and urinated into a beaker."

Why should an athlete who has exhibited no behavior that would give rise to suspicion of illegal activity have to submit to this sort of humiliation, inconvenience, and violation of privacy? Why should athletes who only an hour before may have participated in the greatest athletic event of their careers have to agree to be herded like cattle into a urine-collection station and to be treated like common criminals?

One way to justify the extreme diminution of Fourth Amendment rights implicit in a search without probable cause is to argue that random drug testing of college athletes is crucial to public safety. Few people oppose the kinds of general searches that are carried out at airports while passengers are preparing to board planes. The fact that it is impossible to tell from the outside whether a person is carrying a weapon and the fact that weapons carried illegally onto a plane could take the lives of hundreds of passengers seem like fairly strong justifications for performing searches without reasonable suspicion of a particular individual. In a similar vein, there may be compelling reasons for performing random drug tests on airline pilots and nuclear power operators.

The case for testing college athletes without probable 7 cause seems far less compelling. It is difficult to argue that athletes hold positions of responsibility analogous to those of pilots or air-traffic controllers. There is little doubt that athletes serve as role models for millions of young people. But no one can seriously believe that isolated instances of drug use by college athletes have been a major cause of the rampant substance abuse that plagues this nation. Tragic incidents such as the death of Len Bias of Maryland of a drug overdose can have a devastating effect on a university's public image, but a concern with preventing bad publicity does not justify an assault on the Bill of Rights. Subjecting all athletes to random testing when other less intrusive methods for fighting substance abuse exist seems like the kind of policy the framers of the United States Constitution would have opposed.

It is not my intention here to cover the many com- 8 plex constitutional issues surrounding random drug testing. My argument is simple. The vast, vast majority of college athletes are good, decent, dedicated and drug-free. If the N.C.A.A. had respected these athletes as students and as sensitive human beings, random drug testing would have been instituted only as a last resort, and even then, only after encouraging athletes to consider the constitutional issues involved.

Efforts to fight substance abuse in college sports 9 must be concerned with more than keeping athletes drug-free in the short-term. The goal should be to help athletes understand the role that drugs play in our society and to prepare them to fight drug abuse throughout their lives. The N.C.A.A. should take the hundreds of thousands of dollars that are going into random drug testing and undertake a massive program in drug education. Drug education should be an integral part of every athletic department curriculum, and should consist of far more than a couple of talks by prominent athletes.

Drug education should extend to coaches and others 10 who work closely with athletes. Coaches should be taught the symptoms of substance abuse so that they can refer athletes for counseling and treatment. They should also be able (in conjunction with a team physician and the athletic director) to insist that an athlete submit to a drug test if there is some observance of suspicious activity. Athletes who abuse drugs should be subject to strict disciplinary action. Repeat offenders should lose athletic eligibility.

Drug education and drug testing based on probable 11 cause will probably not be as effective in deterring short-term substance abuse as having random drug-testing programs at every university in the country. It should be noted however that a democratic society has to be concerned with more than deterrence. There is no doubt in my mind that certain types of crime could be substantially reduced if the police could ignore large segments of the Constitution. The case of Nazi Germany offers considerable proof that searching people's property and their persons without probable cause can be an effective deterrent. But the price that is exacted is a wholesale assault on human dignity and personal freedom. Such measures have little place in a democracy, and they clearly cannot be justified in college sport.

Comment

Sack summarizes his argument against random drug testing and presents the background of the issue (paragraphs 1-5); then states arguments in support of the N.C.A.A. policy and refutes them (paragraphs 6-7). In his concluding paragraphs, he restates his thesis, makes recommendations, and presents a final argument in opposition to the policy. Sack points out that, in a brief argument on the issue, he cannot explore all of the complex issues related to drug testing. But he can establish the point at issue in drug testing and argue that point as fully as space permits.

Questions for Study and Discussion

1. Sack states his general topic in his opening sentence—the "low regard" for students revealed in the N.C.A.A. policy; then summarizes the faults of the policy. What are these faults, and in what order does Sack present them in paragraphs 1 and 2?

2. Sack argues that the N.C.A.A. humiliates the student athlete and gives an example of such humiliation in paragraph 4. If an alternate procedure that did not humiliate the student could be established, would Sack be less opposed to random drug testing?

3. What analogy in support of the N.C.A.A. policy does Sack criticize?

4. What additional evidence does Sack present for his thesis in his concluding paragraph? Why does he save this evidence for the end of the essay?

5. Is Sack addressing a special audience or a general one (see p. 435)? How do you know?

6. Do you agree in whole or in part with Sack on random drug testing? Or do you disagree completely? Have you other reasons for supporting or opposing the N.C.A.A. policy?

Suggestions for Writing

1. In an essay on the issue of drug testing, state your own opinion, citing observations you have made, personal beliefs, your reasons for agreeing or disagreeing with Puffer and Sack. You might introduce the ideas of Puffer and Sack in your opening paragraphs, as part of your background or narrative. Or you might save mention of Puffer and Sack until after you have stated your own position.

2. Compare the kind of arguments present in the essays of Puffer and Sack on drug testing, noting any similarities or differences in the evidence they present. Does either writer argue

from fundamental beliefs or assumptions from which they draw direct conclusions and perhaps illustrate these? Does either argue from well-founded opinion or judgments based on particulars of experience, analogy, causes and effects— inductive evidence that leads to a probable conclusion?

PART FIVE

EFFECTIVE
SENTENCES
AND
DICTION

*P*aul Schimmel has access to a
computer inside his brain, which
goes to work as soon as he enters a
subway car, sizing up the audience.

Mark Singer

The sentences we speak and write derive from sentences we hear and read from day to day. The same is true of the words we use. We adopt new words and new turns of phrase and ways of giving ideas emphasis usually without realizing we have done so. And usually the change is slight, for habits of speech and writing are established early and are not easy to change. Adopting new words is, however, easier for us than adopting new sentence patterns.

How conscious we are of language depends on the formality of the speaking or writing situation. Each of us has an informal and a formal way of speaking—each appropriate to different occasions, each expressive and useful. We make adjustments in our spoken language usually without realizing we are doing so. Writing calls for more deliberate choice, particularly in tightening sentences that derive from our informal speech.

The following is a transcription of spoken English:

> In the minor leagues we spent a lot of hours riding in buses, and they were so hot and you didn't have too many stops to eat. You ate poorly because you had bad meal money. We got $1.50 a day. But you were young. When I was with a class B league, I got a long distance call. My wife went to the hospital in labor. It was the first baby. I had to get home. The ticket was forty-some dollars. We didn't have it between us—the manager, everybody. I got there a day late.   —Studs Terkel, *Working*

These informal sentences are expressive despite the loose organization and the looseness of the first sentence and the fragmented sound of the short sentences that follow. Informal writing usually follows the same loose patterns of speech and uses familiar phrases, colloquial words, and contracted words:

> The excitement of the rodeo comes not so much from the competition between the cowboys themselves as from the competition between man and animal. The fans, of course, are partisans; they root for their own species. The crowd always cheers when a cowboy wins even if they've never heard of the chap. But the animals must be good, or the contest will be no fun. The horses, bulls, steers, and calves are thus all bred and raised especially for their spunk.   —Ray Raphael, *Edges*

At its best, as in this statement on rodeos, informal writing stays close to colloquial patterns. It becomes inexpressive and monotonous, however, when most of the sentences are short or loosely strung together.

To convey meaning when we speak, we depend on voice pitch and inflection. The baseball player above probably stressed particular words in the series of short sentences that conclude his statement. Not all resources in speech are available to the writer. Written sentences therefore must be tighter than the fragmented or run-on sentences we sometimes speak. In our formal writing as in our formal speech, we give even more attention to precision and emphasis. When formal writing deals with ideas, it uses a large number of abstract words and words that are also chosen for their exactness:

> Lincoln was a pre-eminent example of that self-help which Americans have always so admired. He was not, of course, the first eminent American politician who could claim humble origins, nor the first to exploit them. But few have been able to point to such a sudden ascent from relative obscurity to high eminence; none has maintained so completely while scaling the heights the aspect of extreme simplicity; and none has combined with the attainment of success and power such an intense awareness of humanity and moral responsibility.   —Richard Hofstadter, *The American Political Tradition*

The coordination of clauses in the first sentence of this formal passage is tighter than that in the statement on rodeos. The diction is also frequently abstract *(the aspect of extreme simplicity, the attainment of success and power, awareness of humanity and moral responsibility)* and the choice of words is exact *(ascent* rather than the informal *rise, high eminence* rather than *fame).* Formal writing, it should also be noted, sometimes depends on the passive voice more than informal writing does:

> Technological solutions to many formerly unremitting medical problems are at hand. Today, when penicillin, protein, and vaccines can be manufactured for pennies, no child should die from diseases, especially deficiency-related diseases, that can be relatively easily prevented or cured. To the extent that the quality of life is marred for so many of the world's people, the remedies are to be sought in expanded knowledge of human interactions. Profound socioeconomic adjustments could solve or ameliorate the overwhelming majority of distribution problems that cause

the benefits of modern medical advances to be withheld from appalling numbers of the world's medically burdened populations. An appreciation of the impressive personal efforts by the outstanding leaders we subsume as traditional healers, coupled with knowledge of the tremendous obstacles to survival that have been overcome through the biological mechanisms of evolutionary selection, should contribute to an attitude of optimism, indeed confidence, that the remaining tasks, the social readjustments that lie ahead, should not be insurmountable.   —Corinne Shear Wood, *Human Sickness and Health*

An abstract subject such as success in politics invites a formal style, a concrete subject like the rodeo an informal style; but both subjects might be written about in informal and formal language. Much depends on what style the writer believes is suited to a particular audience or its expectations.

Much writing today avoids the extremes of highly formal or highly informal English. *General English* is the term given to a spoken and written standard that shares characteristics of both. General English is much tighter than informal spoken English, but it is looser than the formal sentences just quoted—conveying the rhythm of ordinary speech, more often the rhythm of the active voice than the passive. It uses a plain vocabulary where possible, depending on abstract and technical words when simpler words will not express the intended ideas.

The Joan Didion essay on bureaucrats that follows illustrates general English, and so do most of the essays in this book. Compare the baseball player's statement (p. 445) with the following from Didion's essay:

Mere driving on the freeway is in no way the same as participating in it. Anyone can "drive" on the freeway, and many people with no vocation for it do, hesitating here and resisting there, losing the rhythm of the lane change, thinking about where they came from and where they are going. Actual participants think only about where they are. Actual participation requires a total surrender, a concentration so intense as to seem a kind of narcosis, a rapture-of-the-freeway. *The mind goes clean. The rhythm takes over.* A distortion of time occurs, the same distortion that characterizes the instant before an accident. [emphasis added]

Didion varies these sentences to considerable effect. The italicized short sentences make the impact they do because Didion uses them sparingly. Short sentences need not be as dramatic as these; the effect depends on the ideas they express.

At the same time, sentences that depart markedly from patterns of speech may sound stilted. In speaking, we usually begin with the main idea and add to it supporting details and other modifiers, or link the main idea to another as Didion does in the passage above:

> Anyone can "drive" on the freeway, and many with no vocation for it do, hesitating here and resisting there, losing the rhythm of the lane change, thinking about where they came from and where they are going.

Because so many spoken sentences open with the main clause, variation from this pattern catches the reader's attention:

> The closed door upstairs at 120 South Spring Street in downtown Los Angeles is marked OPERATIONS CENTER. In the window-less room beyond the closed door a reverential hush prevails. From six A.M. until seven P.M. in this windowless room men sit at consoles watching a huge board flash colored lights.

The second and third sentences—called *periodic* because the subject and verb of the main clause come at the end—catch our attention because of the dramatic build-up from the opening modifiers. Sentences such as these make their impact because Didion varies them to catch the pauses, interruptions, and nuances of talk.

Informal, formal, and general English use concrete and abstract words, specific and general ones. The passages quoted from Didion contain all of these. And writing at these three levels also contains metaphors and other figures of speech. In expressive writing like Annie Dillard's on the coming of spring (p. 513), metaphor dramatically expresses the special feeling and perceptions of the writer:

> This is the hoop of flame that shoots the rapids in the creek or spins across the dizzy meadows; this is the arsonist of the sunny woods. . . .

In informative writing, as in Robert J. Samuelson's description of computer communities, figurative language is not so obvious:

> The computers are trying to straddle a huge schism in national culture.

Every style has its hazards. Formal sentences that depart too far from colloquial English become hard to understand. Technical words or jargon are often essential in writing about technical subjects; usually only the special audience knows the meaning of these terms. The formal writer wants to be precise, but precision can become a fault as in the following sentence:

> But already at a point in economic evolution far antedating the emergence of the lady, specialized consumption of goods as an evidence of pecuniary strength had begun to work out in a more or less elaborate system.   —Thorstein Veblen, *Theory of the Leisure Class*

This overprecise sentence uses abstract, theoretical terms to state simple ideas. "Pecuniary strength" means nothing more than having money; "specialized consumption of goods" means buying things because they look expensive. In colloquial English, people are "putting on the dog."

At the three levels, overused phrases can make writing sound stale. A phrase like "putting on the dog"—a popular colloquialism—loses its color in writing through overfamiliarity. We refer to phrases of this kind as *clichés*. A piece of writing may also seem too colorful—overcrowded with metaphor and other figures. But deciding what is overfamiliar or overcolorful is not easy. There are no rules for deciding what sentence style or kind of diction is appropriate to particular subjects or audiences. A sense of appropriateness comes only with wide reading and the awareness that writers achieve different effects with different means and in unpredictable ways.

Joan Didion

BUREAUCRATS

Joan Didion has had a varied career since her graduation from the University of California at Berkeley in 1956. She has been an editor of *Vogue* and a columnist for *The Saturday Evening Post*. She reported on the Salvadoran civil war in *Salvador* (1983), and described southern Florida in the 1980s in *Miami* (1988). She has also written screenplays, numerous essays, and novels about contemporary American life including *Play It as It Lays* (1971), *The Book of Common Prayer* (1977), and *Democracy* (1984). "Bureaucrats" shows her concern with urban problems today and, in particular, her ironic view of the workings of government. It is reprinted from *The White Album* (1979), a collection of Didion's essays.

The closed door upstairs at 120 South Spring Street 1 in downtown Los Angeles is marked OPERATIONS CENTER. In the windowless room beyond the closed door a reverential hush prevails. From six A.M. until seven P.M. in this windowless room men sit at consoles watching a huge board flash colored lights. "There's the heart attack," someone will murmur, or "we're getting the gawk effect." 120 South Spring is the Los Angeles office of Caltrans, or the California Department of Transportation, and the Operations Center is where Caltrans engineers monitor what they call "the 42-Mile Loop." The 42-Mile Loop is simply the rough triangle formed by the intersections of the Santa Monica, the San Diego and the Harbor freeways, and 42 miles represents less than ten percent of freeway mileage in Los Angeles County alone, but these particular 42 miles are regarded around 120 South Spring with a special veneration. The Loop is a "demonstration system," a phrase much favored by everyone at Caltrans, and is part of a "pilot project," another two words carrying totemic weight on South Spring.

The Loop has electronic sensors embedded every 2 half-mile out there in the pavement itself, each sensor counting the crossing cars every twenty seconds. The Loop has its own mind, a Xerox Sigma V computer which prints out, all day and night, twenty-second readings on what is and is not moving in each of the Loop's eight lanes. It is the Xerox Sigma V that makes the big board flash red when traffic out there drops below fifteen miles an hour. It is the Xerox Sigma V that tells the Operations crew when they have an "incident" out there. An "incident" is the heart attack on the San Diego, the jackknifed truck on the Harbor, the Camaro just now tearing out the Cyclone fence on the Santa Monica. "Out there" is where incidents happen. The windowless room at 120 South Spring is where incidents get "verified." "Incident verification" is turning on the closed-circuit TV on the console and watching the traffic slow down to see (this is "the gawk effect") where the Camaro tore out the fence.

As a matter of fact there is a certain closed-circuit 3 aspect to the entire mood of the Operations Center. "Verifying" the incident does not after all "prevent" the incident, which lends the enterprise a kind of tranced distance, and on the day recently when I visited 120 South Spring it took considerable effort to remember what I had come to talk about, which was that particular part of the Loop called the Santa Monica Freeway. The Santa Monica Freeway is 16.2 miles long, runs from the Pacific Ocean to downtown Los Angeles through what is referred to at Caltrans as "the East-West Corridor," carries more traffic every day than any other freeway in California, has what connoisseurs of freeways concede to be the most beautiful access ramps in the world, and appeared to have been transformed by Caltrans, during the several weeks before I went downtown to talk about it, into a 16.2-mile parking lot.

The problem seemed to be another Caltrans "demon- 4 stration," or "pilot," a foray into bureaucratic terrorism they were calling "The Diamond Lane" in their promotional literature and "The Project" among themselves.

That the promotional literature consisted largely of schedules for buses (or "Diamond Lane Expresses") and invitations to join a car pool via computer ("Commuter Computer") made clear not only the putative point of The Project, which was to encourage travel by car pool and bus, but also the actual point, which was to eradicate a central Southern California illusion, that of individual mobility, without anyone really noticing. This had not exactly worked out. "FREEWAY FIASCO," the *Los Angeles Times* was headlining page-one stories. "THE DIAMOND LANE: ANOTHER BUST BY CALTRANS." "CALTRANS PILOT EFFORT ANOTHER IN LONG LIST OF FAILURES." "OFFICIAL DIAMOND LANE STANCE: LET THEM HOWL."

All "The Diamond Lane" theoretically involved was reserving the fast inside lanes on the Santa Monica for vehicles carrying three or more people, but in practice this meant that 25 percent of the freeway was reserved for 3 percent of the cars, and there were other odd wrinkles here and there suggesting that Caltrans had dedicated itself to making all movement around Los Angeles as arduous as possible. There was for example the matter of surface streets. A "surface street" is anything around Los Angeles that is not a freeway ("going surface" from one part of town to another is generally regarded as idiosyncratic), and surface streets do not fall directly within the Caltrans domain, but now the engineer in charge of surface streets was accusing Caltrans of threatening and intimidating him. It appeared that Caltrans wanted him to create a "a confused and congested situation" on his surface streets, so as to force drivers back to the freeway, where they would meet a still more confused and congested situation and decide to stay home, or take a bus. "We are beginning a process of deliberately making it harder for drivers to use freeways," a Caltrans director had in fact said at a transit conference some months before. "We are prepared to endure considerable public outcry in order to pry John

Q. Public out of his car. . . . I would emphasize that this is a political decision, and one that can be reversed if the public gets sufficiently enraged to throw us rascals out."

Of course this political decision was in the name of the greater good, was in the interests of "environmental improvement" and "conservation of resources," but even there the figures had about them a certain Caltrans opacity. The Santa Monica normally carried 240,000 cars and trucks every day. These 240,000 cars and trucks normally carried 260,000 people. What Caltrans described as its ultimate goal on the Santa Monica was to carry the same 260,000 people, "but in 7,800 fewer, or 232,200 vehicles." The figure "232,200" had a visionary precision to it that did not automatically create confidence, especially since the only effect so far had been to disrupt traffic throughout the Los Angeles basin, triple the number of daily accidents on the Santa Monica, prompt the initiation of two lawsuits against Caltrans, and cause large numbers of Los Angeles County residents to behave, most uncharacteristically, as an ignited and conscious proletariat. Citizen guerrillas splashed paint and scattered nails in the Diamond Lanes, Diamond Lane maintenance crews expressed fear of hurled objects. Down at 120 South Spring the architects of the Diamond Lane had taken to regarding "the media" as the architects of their embarrassment, and Caltrans statements in the press had been cryptic and contradictory, reminiscent only of old communiqués out of Vietnam.

To understand what was going on it is perhaps necessary to have participated in the freeway experience, which is the only secular communion Los Angeles has. Mere driving on the freeway is in no way the same as participating in it. Anyone can "drive" on the freeway, and many people with no vocation for it do, hesitating here and resisting there, losing the rhythm of the lane change, thinking about where they came from and where they are going. Actual participants think only about

where they are. Actual participation requires a total
surrender, a concentration so intense as to seem a kind
of narcosis, a rapture-of-the-freeway. The mind goes
clean. The rhythm takes over. A distortion of time occurs,
the same distortion that characterizes the instant before
an accident. It takes only a few seconds to get off the
Santa Monica Freeway at National-Overland, which is
a difficult exit requiring the driver to cross two new
lanes of traffic streamed in from the San Diego Freeway,
but those few seconds always seem to me the longest
part of the trip. The moment is dangerous. The exhilaration is in doing it. "As you acquire the special skills
involved," Reyner Banham observed in an extraordinary chapter about the freeways in his 1971 *Los Angeles: The Architecture of Four Ecologies,* "the freeways
become a special way of being alive . . . the extreme
concentration required in Los Angeles seems to bring on
a state of heightened awareness that some locals find
mystical."

Indeed some locals do, and some nonlocals too.   8
Reducing the number of lone souls careering around the
East-West Corridor in a state of mechanized rapture
may or may not have seemed socially desirable, but
what it was definitely not going to seem was easy.
"We're only seeing an initial period of unfamiliarity,"
I was assured the day I visited Caltrans. I was talking
to a woman named Eleanor Wood and she was thoroughly and professionally grounded in the diction of
"planning" and it did not seem likely that I could interest her in considering the freeway as regional mystery.
"Any time you try to rearrange people's daily habits,
they're apt to react impetuously. All this project requires
is a certain rearrangement of people's daily planning.
That's really all we want."

It occurred to me that a certain rearrangement of   9
people's daily planning might seem, in less rarefied air
than is breathed at 120 South Spring, rather a great deal
to want, but so impenetrable was the sense of higher

social purpose there in the Operations Center that I did not express this reservation. Instead I changed the subject, mentioned an earlier "pilot project" on the Santa Monica: the big electronic message boards that Caltrans had installed a year or two before. The idea was that traffic information transmitted from the Santa Monica to the Xerox Sigma V could be translated, here in the Operations Center, into suggestions to the driver, and flashed right back out to the Santa Monica. This operation, in that it involved telling drivers electronically what they already knew empirically, had the rather spectral circularity that seemed to mark a great many Caltrans schemes, and I was interested in how Caltrans thought it worked.

"Actually the message boards were part of a larger pilot project," Mrs. Wood said. "An ongoing project in incident management. With the message boards we hoped to learn if motorists would modify their behavior according to what we told them on the boards." [10]

I asked if the motorists had. [11]

"Actually no," Mrs. Wood said finally. "They didn't react to the signs exactly as we'd hypothesized they would, no. *But*. If we'd *known* what the motorist would do. . . then we wouldn't have needed a pilot project in the first place, would we." [12]

The circle seemed intact. Mrs. Wood and I smiled, and shook hands. I watched the big board until all lights turned green on the Santa Monica and then I left and drove home on it, all 16.2 miles of it. All the way I remembered that I was watched by the Xerox Sigma V. All the way the message boards gave me the number to call for CAR POOL INFO. As I left the freeway it occurred to me that they might have their own rapture down at 120 South Spring, and it could be called Perpetuating the Department. Today the California Highway Patrol reported that, during the first six weeks of the Diamond Lane, accidents on the Santa Monica, which normally range between 49 and 72 during a six-week [13] period, totaled 204. Yesterday plans were announced to extend the Diamond Lane to other freeways at a cost of $42,500,000.

Questions for Study and Discussion

1. What variations of sentence length do you find in paragraphs 1-6?
2. How many sentences in paragraphs 1-6 are built by addition of detail? How many are built by qualification and modification?
3. The greater the number of simple and compound sentences, the greater the informality of the essay. How informal is this essay?
4. Does Didion state her attitude toward Caltrans directly, or instead imply it through her details?
5. In what ways is the Los Angeles freeway symbolic of Los Angeles life? Does Didion see the freeway as symbolic or representative of California or perhaps American life, generally?

Vocabulary Study

1. What is Didion saying about the word *verified* and the other forms of it she cites in paragraphs 2 and 3?
2. What points is she making about other special terms she discusses—for example, *surface street*?
3. Why does she use the word *proletariat* rather than *population* or *citizenry* in paragraph 6?
4. Why does she use the phrase *secular communion* instead of *being together*—"the only way of being together that Los Angeles has"—in paragraph 7?
5. Explain the italicized words:

   This operation, in that it involved telling drivers electronically what they already knew *empirically,* had the rather *spectral circularity* that seemed to mark a great many Caltrans schemes, and I was interested in how Caltrans thought it worked.

Suggestions for Writing

1. Use the traffic of your hometown or city to comment on its quality of life or atmosphere. Make your details as specific as you can.
2. Discuss an "improvement" that in your opinion has worsened the situation it was intended to make better. Describe the situation in detail.

Emphasis

Giving ideas exact emphasis requires attention to sentence coordination and subordination. When you *coordinate* you use the words *and, but, for, or, nor,* and *yet* to connect words, phrases, and clauses of the same weight and importance. The three opening clauses in the following sentence are independent and coordinate:

> The cold night had come, *and* Ukwane in the frosty grass was shivering, *yet* he sat for an hour keeping his patience, putting his hands into the cold blood of the springbok to trace veins to their source, prefacing all his answers with positive, qualifying remarks.   —Elizabeth Marshall Thomas, *The Harmless People*

To stress a close relation between ideas, the writer may coordinate clauses with semicolons, with or without supporting or conjunctive adverbs like *however* and *furthermore* or adverbial phrases:

> Long-range planning and organization on a national scale are obviously essential. There is nothing unfamiliar about this; indeed, we've been engaged in a coordinated national effort for over two decades, through the established processes of the National Institutes of Health.
>
> In basic research, everything is just the opposite. What you need at the outset is a high degree of uncertainty; otherwise it isn't likely to be an important problem. You start with an incomplete roster of facts, characterized by their ambiguity; often the problem consists of discovering the connections between unrelated pieces of information.   —Lewis Thomas, "A Long Line of Cells"

When you *subordinate* you attach to independent clauses phrases and clauses that cannot stand alone. In Elizabeth Marshall Thomas's sentence above, the heavily stressed subordinate phrases that conclude the sentence contain specific details that explain the independent clauses:

> . . . yet he sat for an hour keeping his patience, putting his hands into the cold blood of the springbok to trace veins to their source, prefacing all his answers with positive, qualifying remarks.

English sentences often reserve the end of the sentence for the most important idea or for new ideas and details. This end-focus is evident in the stress given final words in speaking:

> My wife's parents live in NEW YORK.

Even if another word in the sentence is stressed, the final word still receives a degree of stress:

> My WIFE'S parents live in NEW YORK (my wife's parents, not my own parents).

End-focus has important consequences for building sentences and varying them. It means that the speaker or writer can "load" the end of the sentence, adding ideas and details that cannot easily go at the beginning. You speak or write the following sentence without thinking about its structure:

> (1) I know they won't come if they decide to go to Newark.

You would not say or write:

> (2) That they won't come if they decide to go to Newark I know.

But you can open the sentence with a shorter complement:

> (3) That they're coming I have no doubt.

Notice that the complement *[that] they won't come* in (1) is followed by a modifying subordinate clause *(if they decide to go to Newark)* and therefore cannot appear at the beginning of the sentence. The unmodified complement in (3)—*That they're coming*—can appear at the beginning. By contrast, phrasal modifiers can be added to the end of the sentence without difficulty:

> A school of minnows swam by, each minnow with its small individual shadow, doubling the attendance, so clear and sharp, in the sunlight.   —E. B. White, "Once More to the Lake"

> Most commonly we come to books with blurred and divided minds, asking of fiction that it shall be true, of poetry that it shall be false, of biography that it shall be flattering, of history that it shall enforce our own prejudices.   —Virginia Woolf, "How Should One Read a Book?"

Compound sentences, which coordinate independent clauses to emphasize their connection, can run on indefinitely:

> The height of the ginning season in that part of the country is early October, and in that time the loaded wagons are on the road before the least crack of daylight, the waiting is endless hours, and the gin is still pulsing and beating after dark.   —James Agee, "Cotton"

This sentence might continue further. The familiar definition of a sentence as a complete thought is of no use in deciding when to end sentences of this kind. For the completeness of the thought lies in the mind of the speaker or writer, who seeks to emphasize each component idea and who alone knows when everything necessary has been said. At the same time, the emphasis or force diminishes for the reader if the sentence seems to run on or drift monotonously.

Richard P. Feynman

THE AMATEUR SCIENTIST

Richard P. Feynman was professor of theoretical physics at the California Institute of Technology, where he taught from 1950 until his death in 1988. Feynman was born in Far Rockaway, New York, in 1918, and studied at the Massachusetts Institute of Technology and Princeton University. From 1943 to 1946 he worked as a nuclear physicist at Los Alamos, New Mexico. In 1965 Feynman received the Nobel Prize in physics for his contribution to quantum mechanics, which increased understanding of the fundamental forces of nature. *"Surely You're Joking, Mr. Feynman!"* is a collection of personal essays that form a memoir of his life. In the essay reprinted here from this collection, Feynman describes how he began to think and experiment like a scientist.

When I was a kid I had a "lab." It wasn't a labora- 1 tory in the sense that I would measure, or do important experiments. Instead, I would play: I'd make a motor, I'd make a gadget that would go off when something passed a photocell, I'd play around with selenium; I was piddling around all the time. I did calculate a little bit for the lamp bank, a series of switches and bulbs I used as resistors to control voltages. But all that was for application. I never did any laboratory kind of experiments.

I also had a microscope and *loved* to watch things 2 under the microscope. It took patience: I would get something under the microscope and I would watch it interminably. I saw many interesting things, like everybody sees—a diatom slowly making its way across the slide, and so on.

One day I was watching a paramecium and I saw 3 something that was not described in the books I got in school—in college, even. These books always simplify things so the world will be more like *they* want it to be: When they're talking about the behavior of animals, they always start out with, "The paramecium is extremely simple; it has a simple behavior. It turns as its slipper shape moves through the water until it hits something, at which time it recoils, turns through an angle, and then starts out again."

It isn't really right. First of all, as everybody knows, 4 the paramecia, from time to time, conjugate with each other—they meet and exchange nuclei. How do they decide when it's time to do that? (Never mind; that's not my observation.)

I watched these paramecia hit something, recoil, turn 5 through an angle, and go again. The idea that it's mechanical, like a computer program—it doesn't look that way. They go different distances, they recoil different distances, they turn through angles that are different in various cases; they don't always turn to the right; they're very irregular. It looks random, because you don't know what they're hitting; you don't know all the chemicals they're smelling, or what.

One of the things I wanted to watch was what 6 happens to the paramecium when the water that it's in dries up. It was claimed that the paramecium can dry up into a sort of hardened seed. I had a drop of water on the slide under my microscope, and in the drop of water was a paramecium and some "grass"—at the scale of the paramecium, it looked like a network of jack-straws. As the drop of water evaporated, over a time of fifteen or twenty minutes, the paramecium got into a tighter and tighter situation: there was more and more of this back-and-forth until it could hardly move. It was stuck between these "sticks," almost jammed.

Then I saw something I had never seen or heard of: the paramecium lost its shape. It could flex itself, like an amoeba. It began to push itself against one of the sticks, and began dividing into two prongs until the division was about halfway up the paramecium, at which time it decided *that* wasn't a very good idea, and backed away.

So my impression of these animals is that their behavior is much too simplified in the books. It is not so utterly mechanical or one-dimensional as they say. They should describe the behavior of these simple animals correctly. Until we see how many dimensions of behavior even a one-celled animal has, we won't be able to fully understand the behavior of more complicated animals.

I also enjoyed watching bugs. I had an insect book when I was about thirteen. It said that dragonflies are not harmful; they don't sting. In our neighborhood it was well known that "darning needles," as we called them, were very dangerous when they'd sting. So if we were outside somewhere playing baseball, or something, and one of these things would fly around, everybody would run for cover, waving their arms, yelling, "A darning needle! A darning needle!"

So one day I was on the beach, and I'd just read this book that said dragonflies don't sting. A darning needle came along, and everybody was screaming and running around, and I just sat there. "Don't worry!" I said. "Darning needles don't sting!"

The thing landed on my foot. Everybody was yelling 11
and it was a big mess, because this darning needle was
sitting on my foot. And there I was, this scientific wonder,
saying it wasn't going to sting me.

You're *sure* this is a story that's going to come out 12
that it stings me—but it didn't. The book was right. But
I did sweat a bit.

I also had a little hand microscope. It was a toy 13
microscope, and I pulled the magnification piece out of
it, and would hold it in my hand like a magnifying glass,
even though it was a microscope of forty or fifty power.
With care you could hold the focus. So I could go
around and look at things right out in the street.

When I was in graduate school at Princeton, I once 14
took it out of my pocket to look at some ants that were
crawling around on some ivy. I had to exclaim out loud,
I was so excited. What I saw was an ant and an aphid,
which ants take care of—they carry them from plant to
plant if the plant they're on is dying. In return the ants
get partially digested aphid juice, called "honeydew." I
knew that; my father had told me about it, but I had
never seen it.

So here was this aphid and sure enough, an ant came 15
along, and patted it with its feet—all around the aphid,
pat, pat, pat, pat, pat. This was terribly exciting! Then
the juice came out of the back of the aphid. And because
it was magnified, it looked like a big, beautiful, glisten-
ing ball, like a balloon, because of the surface tension.
Because the microscope wasn't very good, the drop was
colored a little bit from chromatic aberration in the
lens—it was a gorgeous thing!

The ant took this ball in its two front feet, lifted it off 16
the aphid, and *held* it. The world is so different at that
scale that you can pick up water and hold it! The ants
probably have a fatty or greasy material on their legs
that doesn't break the surface tension of the water when
they hold it up. Then the ant broke the surface of the
drop with its mouth, and the surface tension collapsed

the drop right into his gut. It was *very* interesting to see this whole thing happen!

In my room at Princeton I had a bay window with 17 a U-shaped windowsill. One day some ants came out on the windowsill and wandered around a little bit. I got curious as to how they found things. I wondered, how do they know where to go? Can they tell each other where food is, like bees can? Do they have any sense of geometry?

This is all amateurish; everybody knows the answer, 18 but *I* didn't know the answer, so the first thing I did was to stretch some string across the U of the bay window and hang a piece of folded cardboard with sugar on it from the string. The idea of this was to isolate the sugar from the ants, so they wouldn't find it accidentally. I wanted to have everything under control.

Next I made a lot of little strips of paper and put 19 a fold in them, so I could pick up ants and ferry them from one place to another. I put the folded strips of paper in two places: Some were by the sugar (hanging from the string), and the others were near the ants in a particular location. I sat there all afternoon, reading and watching, until an ant happened to walk onto one of my little paper ferries. Then I took him over to the sugar. After a few ants had been ferried over to the sugar, one of them accidentally walked onto one of the ferries nearby, and I carried him back.

I wanted to see how long it would take the other ants 20 to get the message to go to the "ferry terminal." It started slowly, but rapidly increased until I was going mad ferrying the ants back and forth.

But suddenly, when everything was going strong, I 21 began to deliver the ants from the sugar to a *different* spot. The question now was, does the ant learn to go back to where it just came from, or does it go where it went the time before?

After a while there were practically no ants going to 22 the first place (which would take them to the sugar), whereas there were many ants at the second place, mill-ing around, trying to find the sugar. So I figured out so far that they went where they just came from.

In another experiment, I laid out a lot of glass 23 microscope slides, and got the ants to walk on them, back and forth, to some sugar I put on the windowsill. Then, by replacing an old slide with a new one, or by rearranging the slides, I could demonstrate that the ants had no sense of geometry: they couldn't figure out where something was. If they went to the sugar one way, and there was a shorter way back, they would never figure out the short way.

It was also pretty clear from rearranging the glass 24 slides that the ants left some sort of trail. So then came a lot of easy experiments to find out how long it takes a trail to dry up, whether it can be easily wiped off, and so on. I also found out the trail wasn't directional. If I'd pick up an ant on a piece of paper, turn him around and around, and then put him back onto the trail, he wouldn't know that he was going the wrong way until he met another ant. (Later, in Brazil, I noticed some leaf-cutting ants and tried the same experiment on them. They *could* tell, within a few steps, whether they were going toward the food or away from it—presumably from the trail, which might be a series of smells in a pattern: A, B, space, A, B, space, and so on.)

I tried at one point to make the ants go around in 25 a circle, but I didn't have enough patience to set it up. I could see no reason, other than lack of patience, why it couldn't be done.

One thing that made experimenting difficult was that 26 breathing on the ants made them scurry. It must be an instinctive thing against some animal that eats them or disturbs them. I don't know if it was the warmth, the moisture, or the smell of my breath that bothered them, but I always had to hold my breath and kind of look to one side so as not to confuse the experiment while I was ferrying the ants.

One question that I wondered about was why the   27
ant trails look so straight and nice. The ants look as if
they know what they're doing, as if they have a good
sense of geometry. Yet the experiments that I did to try
to demonstrate their sense of geometry didn't work.

Many years later, when I was at Caltech and lived   28
in a little house on Alameda Street, some ants came out
around the bathtub. I thought, "This is a great opportunity." I put some sugar on the other end of the bathtub, and sat there the whole afternoon until an ant
finally found the sugar. It's only a question of patience.

The moment the ant found the sugar, I picked up a   29
colored pencil that I had ready (I had previously done
experiments indicating that the ants don't give a damn
about pencil marks—they walk right over them—so I
knew I wasn't disturbing anything), and behind where
the ant went I drew a line so I could tell where his trail
was. The ant wandered a little bit wrong to get back
to the hole, so the line was quite wiggly, unlike a typical
ant trail.

When the next ant to find the sugar began to go   30
back, I marked his trail with another color. (By the way,
he followed the first ant's return trail back, rather than
his own incoming trail. My theory is that when an ant
has found some food, he leaves a much stronger trail
than when he's just wandering around.)

This second ant was in a great hurry and followed,   31
pretty much, the original trail. But because he was going
so fast he would go straight out, as if he were coasting,
when the trail was wiggly. Often, as the ant was "coasting," he would find the trail again. Already it was
apparent that the second ant's return was slightly
straighter. With successive ants the same "improvement"
of the trail by hurriedly and carelessly "following" it
occurred.

I followed eight or ten ants with my pencil until their   32
trails became a neat line right along the bathtub. It's
something like sketching: You draw a lousy line at first;

then you go over it a few times and it makes a nice line after a while.

I remember that when I was a kid my father would 33 tell me how wonderful ants are, and how they cooperate. I would watch very carefully three or four ants carrying a little piece of chocolate back to their nest. At first glance it looks like efficient, marvelous, brilliant cooperation. But if you look at it carefully, you'll see that it's nothing of the kind: They're all behaving as if the chocolate is held up by something else. They pull at it one way or the other way. An ant may crawl over it while it's being pulled at by the others. It wobbles, it wiggles, the directions are all confused. The chocolate doesn't move in a nice way toward the nest.

The Brazilian leaf-cutting ants, which are otherwise 34 so marvelous, have a very interesting stupidity associated with them that I'm surprised hasn't evolved out. It takes considerable work for the ant to cut the circular arc in order to get a piece of leaf. When the cutting is done, there's a fifty-fifty chance that the ant will pull on the wrong side, letting the piece he just cut fall to the ground. Half the time, the ant will yank and pull and yank and pull on the wrong part of the leaf, until it gives up and starts to cut another piece. There is no attempt to pick up a piece that it, or any other ant, has already cut. So it's quite obvious, if you watch very carefully, that it's not a brilliant business of cutting leaves and carrying them away; they go to a leaf, cut an arc, and pick the wrong side half the time while the right piece falls down.

In Princeton the ants found my larder, where I had 35 jelly and bread and stuff, which was quite a distance from the window. A long line of ants marched along the floor across the living room. It was during the time I was doing these experiments on the ants, so I thought to myself, "What can I do to stop them from coming to my larder without killing any ants? No poison; you gotta be humane to the ants!"

What I did was this: In preparation, I put a bit of ³⁶
sugar about six or eight inches from their entry point
into the room, that they didn't know about. Then I made
those ferry things again, and whenever an ant returning
with food walked onto my little ferry, I'd carry him over
and put him on the sugar. Any ant coming toward the
larder that walked onto a ferry I also carried over to the
sugar. Eventually the ants found their way from the sugar
to their hole, so this new trail was being doubly rein-
forced, while the old trail was being used less and less.
I knew that after half an hour or so the old trail would
dry up, and in an hour they were out of my larder. I
didn't wash the floor; I didn't do anything but ferry ants.

Comment

Feynman's essay seems like an extended answer to a question he
might have been asked while conversing with a friend; his sentences are colloquial in structure—a series of details or short explanatory phrases and clauses often are added to a base sentence;
some clauses are compounded in a series, sometimes without verbal conjunctions:

> Instead, I would play: I'd make a motor, I'd make a gadget that
> would go off when something passed a photocell, I'd play around
> with selenium; I was piddling around all the time.

Feynman is making a point through the details of the experiments he
describes. Through these details the reader makes discoveries about
Feynman.

Questions for Study and Discussion

1. What features make the sentences in paragraphs 32 and 33
   colloquial—that is, suggestive of spoken English?
2. What implicit point is Feynman making about each of his
   various experiments? Is he making the same point in each
   instance?

3. Which of the author's personal qualities emerge in his narrative of these experiments? Are the experiments the central focus of the essay, or is Feynman the experimenter the focus? How do you know?
4. Does Feynman leave you with the sense that he has more to tell about his amateur experiments and has merely broken off the narrative? Or does he conclude the essay informally or formally?
5. If you were writing a formal essay on experiments you performed as an adolescent, how different would your essay be in structure from Feynman's? What features in general make an essay formal?

Sentence Study

1. All but the first sentence in paragraph 1 consist of main clauses. Construct additional complex sentences by subordinating some of these main clauses. What change in emphasis occurs in your revision? Does the revision change Feynman's meaning?
2. Feynman coordinates a series of main clauses in the following sentences. Recast each sentence, combining these clauses or subordinating one or more. What change in emphasis occurs in your revision?
    a. "It took patience: I would get something under the microscope and I would watch it interminably." (paragraph 2)
    b. "I had a drop of water on the slide under my microscope, and in the drop of water was a paramecium and some 'grass'—at the scale of the paramecium, it looked like a network of jackstraws." (paragraph 6)
    c. "Then the ant broke the surface of the drop with its mouth, and the surface tension collapsed the drop right into his gut." (paragraph 16)
3. Try to reduce the repetition of words in the following sentence:

    They go different distances, they recoil different distances, they turn through angles that are different in various cases; they don't always turn to the right; they're very irregular. (paragraph 5)

    What is gained or lost by your revision?

4. The concluding clause in the following sentence adds infor-
    mation about the larder. Speaking the sentence, we would
    probably raise our voice with *which* to show that it modifies
    larder. Revise the sentence so that *which* immediately follows
    larder:

    In Princeton the ants found my larder, where I had jelly and
    bread and stuff, which was quite a distance from the window.
    (paragraph 35)

    What problems did you meet in revising the sentence? Is your
    revision an improvement over Feynman's sentence?

Suggestions for Writing

1. Write about a series of related experiences that define your
    interests. Let the reader draw conclusions from your details.
    Don't draw these conclusions yourself.
2. Write a characterization of Feynman on the basis of what he
    tells you about his interests and how he presents them.

William Zinsser

JURY DUTY

William Zinsser was born in 1922 in New York City and has written
much about life there in numerous articles and books. He attended
Princeton University and later was a feature writer, film critic, and
drama editor for the *New York Herald Tribune* and a columnist for
Look and *Life.* Zinsser taught at Yale University from 1971 to 1979.
His books include *Pop Goes America* (1966), *The Lunacy Room*
(1970), and *On Writing Well,* 4th ed. (1990).

Jury duty again. I'm sitting in the "central jurors'   1
room" of a courthouse in lower Manhattan, as I do
every two years, waiting to be called for a jury, which
I almost never am. It's an experience that all of us have
known, in one form or another, as long as we can
remember: organized solitude.

The chair that I sit in is a little island of apartness. 2
I sit there alone, day after day, and I go out to lunch
alone, a stranger in my own city. Strictly, of course, I'm
not by myself. Several hundred other men and women
sit on every side, as closely as in a movie theater, also
waiting to be called for a jury, which they almost never
are. Sometimes we break briefly into each other's lives,
when we get up to stretch, offering fragments of talk to
fill the emptiness. But in the end each of us is alone,
withdrawn into our newspapers and our crossword
puzzles and our sacred urban privacy.

The room intimidates us. It is a dreary place, done 3
in thirties Bureaucratic, too dull to sustain more than
a few minutes of mental effort. On the subconscious
level, however, it exerts a strong and uncanny hold. It
is the universal waiting room. It is the induction center
and the clinic; it is the assembly hall and the office where
forms are filled out. Thoughts come unbidden there,
sneaking back from all the other moments—in the army,
at camp, on the first day of school—when we were part
of a crowd and therefore lonely.

The mere taking of roll call by a jury clerk will 4
summon back the countless times when we have waited
for our name to be yelled out—loud and just a little
wrong. Like every person whose job is to read names
aloud, the jury clerk can't read names aloud. Their
shapes mystify him. They are odd and implausible names,
as diverse as the countries that they came from, but
surely the clerk has met them all before. *Hasn't* he? Isn't
that what democracy—and the jury system—is all about?
Evidently not.

We are shy enough, as we wait for our name, with- 5
out the extra burden of wondering what form it will
take. By now we know most of the variants that have
been imposed on it by other clerks in other rooms like
this, and we are ready to answer to any of them, or to
some still different version. Actually we don't want to
hear our name called at all in this vast public chamber.
It is so private, so vulnerable. And yet we don't want

to *not* hear it, for only then are we reassured of our identity, really certain that we are known, wanted, and in the right place. Dawn over Camp Upton, 1943: Weinberg, Wyzanski, Yanopoulos, Zapata, Zeccola, Zinsser. . . .

I don't begin my jury day in such a retrospective 6 state. I start with high purpose and only gradually slide into mental disarray. I am punctual, even early, and so is everybody else. We are a conscientious lot—partly because we are so surrounded by the trappings of justice, but mainly because that is what we are there to be. I've never seen such conscientious-looking people. Observing them, I'm glad that American law rests on being judged by our peers. In fact, I'd almost rather be judged by my peers than judged by a judge.

Most of us start the day by reading. Jury duty is 7 America's gift to her citizens of a chance to catch up on "good" books, and I always bring *War and Peace*. I remember to bring it every morning and I keep it handy on my lap. The only thing I don't do is read it. There's something about the room . . . the air is heavy with imminent roll calls, too heavy for tackling a novel that will require strict attention. Besides, it's important to read the newspaper first: sharpen up the old noggin on issues of the day. I'm just settling into my paper when the clerk comes in, around ten-twenty-five, and calls the roll ("Zissner?" "Here!"). Suddenly it is 1944 and I am at an army base near Algiers, hammering tin to make a hot shower for Colonel McCloskey. That sort of thing can shoot the whole morning.

If it doesn't, the newspaper will. Only a waiting juror 8 knows how infinite the crannies of journalism can be. I read "Arrival of Buyers," though I don't know what they want to buy and have nothing to sell. I read "Soybean Futures," though I wouldn't know a soybean even in the present. I read classified ads for jobs that I didn't know were jobs, like "key-punch operators." What keys do they punch? I mentally buy 4bdrm 1½bth splt lvl homes w/fpl overlooking Long Island Sound and dream of taking 1/2 bath there. I read dog news and horoscopes ("bucking others could prove dangerous today") and medical columns on diseases I've never heard of, but whose symptoms I instantly feel.

It's an exhausting trip, and I emerge with eyes blurry and mind blank. I look around at my fellow jurors. Some of them are trying to work—to keep pace, pitifully, with the jobs that they left in order to come here and do nothing. They spread queer documents on their knees, full graphs and figures, and they scribble on yellow pads. But the papers don't seem quite real to them, or quite right, removed from the tidy world of filing cabinets and secretaries, and after a while the workers put the work away again.

Around twelve-forty-five the clerk comes in to make an announcement. We stir to attention: we are needed! "Go to lunch," he says. "Be back at two." We straggle out. By now the faces of all my fellow jurors are familiar (we've been here eight days), and I keep seeing them as we poke around the narrow streets of Chinatown looking for a restaurant that isn't the one where we ate yesterday. I smile tentatively, as New Yorkers do, and they smile tentatively back, and we go our separate ways. By one-fifty-five we are seated in the jurors' room again, drowsy with Chinese food and American boredom—too drowsy, certainly, to start *War and Peace*. Luckily, we all bought the afternoon paper while we were out. Talk about remote crannies of journalism!

Perhaps we are too hesitant to talk to each other, to invite ourselves into lives that would refresh us by being different from our own. We are scrupulous about privacy—it is one of the better gifts that the city can bestow, and we don't want to spoil it for somebody else. Yet within almost every New Yorker who thinks he wants to be left alone is a person desperate for human contact. Thus we may be as guilty as the jury system of not putting our time to good use.

What we want to do most, of course, is serve on a   12
jury. We believe in the system. Besides, was there ever
so outstanding a group of jurors as we, so intelligent and
fair-minded? The clerks have told us all the reasons why
jurors are called in such wasteful numbers: court schedules are unpredictable; trials end unexpectedly; cases are
settled at the very moment when a jury is called; prisoners plead guilty to a lesser charge rather than wait
years for a trial that might prove them innocent. All this
we know, and in theory it makes sense.

In practice, however, somebody's arithmetic is wrong,   13
and one of America's richest assets is being dribbled
away. There must be a better way to get through the
long and tragic list of cases awaiting a solution—and,
incidentally, to get through *War and Peace*.

Comment

Zinsser's opening paragraph illustrates important kinds of sentence
emphasis. A brief phrase, "Jury duty again," serves as the opening
topic sentence, contrasting with the two longer sentences that follow. The first of these adds qualifying clauses and a qualifying phrase
to the opening main clause:

> I'm sitting in the "central jurors' room" of a courthouse in lower
> Manhattan, as I do every two years, waiting to be called for a
> jury, which I almost never am.

The second sentence—the concluding sentence of the paragraph—
uses basically the same structure, but with an important difference:

> It's an experience that all of us have known, in one form or
> another, as long as we can remember: organized solitude.

A complement to the opening main clause of the sentence, the concluding phrase, *organized solitude,* gains emphasis at the end of the
sentence. In many of his sentences Zinsser takes advantage of terminal emphasis. But he uses this effect sparingly. His sentences have
the ring of spoken sentences, depending on coordination and occasionally italics to convey vocal inflection:

They are odd and implausible names, as diverse as the countries that they came from, but surely the clerk has met them all before. *Hasn't* he? Isn't that what democracy—and the jury system—is all about?

Questions for Study and Discussion

1. Which sentences in paragraph 5 are coordinate only? How many sentences consist of one introductory main clause, and one or more subordinate clauses? Do any of the sentences join subordinate to coordinate clauses?
2. Paragraph 6 contains a series of short emphatic opening sentences. Does Zinsser maintain this kind of emphasis in the rest of the paragraph?
3. How different is paragraph 7 from paragraph 6 in sentence construction? What use does Zinsser make of ellipsis? How much emphasis (through pitch and volume) should the parenthetical statements be given?
4. How much subordination do you find in paragraph 8? How many sentences are built through modification?
5. How does Zinsser establish a point of view and a dominant tone? Or do you find changes in tone throughout the essay?
6. Why would Zinsser "almost rather be judged by [his] peers than judged by a judge"?

Vocabulary Study

Write a sentence using each of the following pairs of words, and explain the difference between them. The first word in each pair is Zinsser's:

1. *fragments* (paragraph 2), *parts*
2. *intimidates* (paragraph 3), *threatens*
3. *bureaucratic* (paragraph 3), *governmental*
4. *uncanny* (paragraph 3), *strange*
5. *implausible* (paragraph 4), *unconvincing*
6. *vulnerable* (paragraph 5), *weak*
7. *scrupulous* (paragraph 11), *careful*
8. *bestow* (paragraph 11), *give*

Suggestions for Writing

1. Describe a waiting room and your feelings in it. Make your details specific, and use your description to make a comment about your general situation. Develop several of your sentences with modification, as Zinsser does. Where you can, combine coordinate clauses with subordinate phrases and clauses.

2. Analyze two of the final paragraphs of Zinsser's essay, showing how coordination and subordination are used to give emphasis to particular ideas.

Parallelism

Words, phrases, and clauses that are similar in structure and perform the same function in a sentence are said to be *parallel,* as indicated by the italicized words in the examples below:

> I have never seen a *maladroit, clumsy,* or *blundering* cat.
> —Lewis Thomas, "To Err Is Human" [parallel words]

> Everyone says, stay away from ants. They have no lessons for us; they are crazy little instruments, *inhuman, incapable of controlling themselves, lacking manners, lacking souls.* —Lewis Thomas, "The Tucson Zoo" [parallel words and phrases]

Sentences in a paragraph may be parallel in structure—in whole or in part:

> Science is undeniably hard. *Often, it can seem* quite boring. *It is unfortunately too often presented* as laws to be memorized instead of mysteries to be explored. *It is too often kept a secret* that science, like art, takes a well developed esthetic sense. —K. C. Cole, "Women and Physics"

Parallelism makes the reader aware of the similarity in ideas. If the ideas are not similar, the parallelism may seem awkward. Writers in the past sometimes made parts of sentences exactly parallel, using almost the same number of words in phrases and clauses. This kind of sentence sometimes occurs today in formal speeches, or addresses, like the following:

> Do not let us speak of darker days; let us rather speak of sterner days. These are not dark days: these are great days—the greatest days our country has ever lived. . . . —Winston S. Churchill, an address delivered on October 29, 1941

Modern writers favor a looser parallelism and may vary the length of parallel elements and vary the wording, to avoid a formal effect:

> He watched Martin slip the lens into his pocket, he sighed, he struggled for something else to say, and silently he lumbered into his bedroom.   —Sinclair Lewis, *Arrowsmith*

Rachel Carson

SUMMER'S END

Rachel Carson (1907-1964) is one of the great writers on nature. In her books *Under the Sea-Wind* (1941), *The Sea Around Us*, which received the National Book Award in 1951, and *The Edge of the Sea* (1955), she drew upon her experiences as an aquatic biologist at the Marine Biological Laboratory at Woods Hole, Massachusetts, and, from 1936 to 1952, with the United States Fish and Wildlife Service. She is perhaps best known for her book *Silent Spring* (1962), which warned of the dangers of pesticides to the environment. The National Council of Women in the United States gave Carson its first "Woman of Conscience" citation in 1963. The section reprinted here from *Under the Sea-Wind* describes an island on the southeastern coast of the United States. Carson tells us that Ship's Shoal is a "point of land . . . where the sea had broken through the barrier island to the sound years before." Mullet Pond is "half encircled by marsh, between the eastern end of the dunes and the inlet beach."

It was September before the sanderlings, now in   1
whitening plumage, ran again on the island beach or
hunted Hippa crabs in the ebbing tide at the point of
land called Ship's Shoal. Their flight from the northern
tundras had been broken by many feeding stops on the
wide mud flats of Hudson Bay and James Bay and on
the ocean beaches from New England southward. In
their fall migration the birds were unhurried, the racial
urge that drove them northward in the spring having
been satisfied. As the winds and the sun dictated, they
drifted southward, their flocks now growing as more
birds from the north joined them, now dwindling as
more and more of the migrants found their customary

winter home and dropped behind. Only the fringe of the great southward wave of shore birds would push on and on to the southernmost part of South America.

As the cries of the returning shore birds rose once ₂ more from the frothy edge of the surf and the whistle of the curlews sounded again in the salt marshes, there were other signs of the summer's end. By September the eels of the sound country had begun to drop down-stream to the sea. The eels came down from the hills and the upland grasslands. They came from cypress swamps where black-watered rivers had their begin-nings; they moved across the tidal plain that dropped in six giant steps to the sea. In the river estuaries and in the sounds they joined their mates-to-be. Soon, in silvery wedding dress, they would follow the ebbing tides to the sea, to find—and lose—themselves in the black abysses of mid-ocean.

By September, the young shad, come from the eggs ₃ shed in river and stream by the spawning runs of spring, were moving with the river water to the sea. At first they moved slowly in the vaster currents as the sluggish rivers broadened toward their estuaries. Soon, however, the speed of the little fish, no longer than a man's finger, would quicken, when the fall rains came and the wind changed, chilling the water and driving the fish to the warmer sea.

By September the last of the season's hatch of young ₄ shrimp were coming into the sounds through the inlets from the open sea. The coming of the young was sym-bolic of another journey which no man had seen and no man could describe—a journey taken weeks before by the elder generation of shrimp. All through the spring and summer more and more of the grown shrimp, come to maturity at the age of a year, had been slipping away from the coastal waters, journeying out across the con-tinental shelf, descending the blue slopes of undersea valleys. From this journey they never returned, but their young, after several weeks of ocean life, were brought by the sea into the protected inside waters. All through the summer and fall the baby shrimp were brought into the sounds and river mouth—seeking warm shallows where brackish water lay over muddy bottoms. Here they fed eagerly on the abundant food and found shelter from hungry fish in the carpeting eel grass. And as they grew rapidly, the young turned once more to the sea, seeking its bitter waters and its deeper rhythms. Even as the youngest shrimp from the last spawning of the season came through the inlets on each flood tide of September, the larger young were moving out through the sounds to the sea.

By September the panicles of the sea oats in the dunes 5 had turned a golden brown. As the marshes lay under the sun, they glowed with the soft greens and browns of the salt meadow grass, the warm purples of the rushes, and the scarlet of the marsh samphire. Already the gum trees were like red flares set in the swamps of the river banks. The tang of autumn was in the night air, and as it rolled over the warmer marshes it turned to mist, hiding the herons who stood among the grasses at dawn; hiding from the eyes of the hawks the meadow mice who ran along the paths they had made through the marshes by the patient felling of thousands of marsh-grass stems; hiding the schools of silversides in the sound from the terns who fluttered above the rolling white sea, and caught no fish until the sun had cleared away the mists.

The chill night air brought a restlessness to many fish 6 scattered widely throughout the sound. They were steely gray fish with large scales and a low, four-spined fin set on the back like a spread sail. The fish were mullet who had lived throughout the summer in the sound and estuary, roving solitary among the eel grass and widgeon grass, feeding on the litter of animal and vegetable fragments of the bottom mud. But every fall the mullet left the sounds and made a far sea journey, in the course of which they brought forth the next generation. And so the first chill of fall stirred in the fish the feeling of the sea's rhythm and awakened the instinct of migration.

The chilling waters and tidal cycles of the summer's 7
end brought to many of the young fish of the sound
country, also, a summons to return to the sea. Among
these were the young pompano and mullet, silversides
and killifish, who lived in the pond called Mullet Pond,
where the dunes of the barrier island fell away to the
flat sands of the Ship's Shoal. These young fish had been
spawned in the sea, but had found their way to the pond
through a temporary cut earlier that year.

On a day when the full harvest moon sailed like a 8
white balloon in the sky, the tides, which had grown in
strength as the moon swelled to roundness, began to
wash out a gully across the inlet beach. Only on the
highest tides did the torpid pond receive water from the
ocean. Now the beat of the waves and the strong back-
wash that sucked away the loose sand had found the
weak place in the beach, where a cut had been made
before, and in less time than it took a fishing launch to
cross from the mainland docks to the banks a narrow
gully or slough had been cut through to the pond. Not
more than a dozen feet across, it made a bottleneck into
which the surf rolled as the waves broke on the beach.
The water surged and seethed as in a mill race, hissing
and foaming. Wave after wave poured through the slough
and into the pond. They dug out an uneven, corrugated
bottom over which the water leaped and tobogganed.
They spread out into the marshes that backed the pond,
seeping silently and stealthily among the grass stems and
the reddening stalks of the marsh samphire. Into the
marshes they carried the frothy brown scud thrown off
by the waves. The sandy foam filled the spaces between
the grass stalks so closely that the marsh looked like a
beach thickly grown with short grass; in reality the grass
stood a foot in water and only the upper third of the
stalks showed above the froth.

Leaping and racing, foaming and swirling, the in- 9
coming flood brought release to the myriads of small
fishes that had been imprisoned in the pond. Now in
thousands they poured out of the pond and out of the

marshes. They raced in mad confusion to meet the clean, cold water. In their excitement they let the flood take them, toss them, turn them over and over. Reaching mid-channel of the slough they leaped high in the air again and again, sparkling bits of animate silver, like a swarm of glittering insects that rose and fell, rose again and fell. There the water seized them and held them back in their wild dash to the sea, so that many of them were caught on the slopes of the waves and held, tails uppermost, struggling helplessly against the might of the water. When finally the waves released them they raced down the slough to the ocean, where they knew once more the rolling breakers, the clean sandy bottoms, the cool green waters.

How did the pond and the marshes hold them all? 10 On they came, in school after school, flashing bright among the marsh grasses, leaping and bounding out of the pond. For more than an hour the exodus continued, with scarcely a break in the hurrying schools. Perhaps they had come in, many of them, on the last spring tide when the moon was a pencil stroke of silver in the sky. And now the moon had grown fat and round and another spring tide, a rollicking, roistering, rough-and-ready tide, called them back to the sea again.

On they went, passing through the surf line where 11 the white-capped waves were tumbling. On they went, most of them, past the smoother green swells to the second line of surf, where shoals tripped the waves coming in from the open sea and sent them sprawling in white confusion. But there were terns fishing above the surf, and thousands of the small migrants went no farther than the portals of the sea.

Comment

Carson uses parallelism to highlight similar as well as contrasting actions, as in the following sentence from paragraph 1:

As the winds and the sun dictated, they drifted southward, their flocks *now growing as more birds from the north joined them, now dwindling as more and more of the migrants found their customary winter home and dropped behind.* Only the fringe of the great southward wave of shore birds *would push on and on* to the southernmost part of South America. [italics added]

The parallel construction of the italicized participial phrases in the first sentence highlights the contrasting growth of the flocks of birds and their dwindling. The phrase *would push on and on* in the second sentence emphasizes the contrast with the birds that dropped from the migration. The parallelism of the following sentence from paragraph 5 allows Carson to combine a large number of contrasting actions and descriptive details without confusion or a loss of focus:

The tang of autumn was in the night air, and as it rolled over the warmer marshes it turned to mist, *hiding the herons who stood among the grasses at dawn; hiding from the eyes of the hawks the meadow mice who ran along the paths they had made through the marshes by the patient felling of thousands of marsh-grass stems; hiding the schools of silversides in the sound from the terns who fluttered above the rolling white sea, and caught no fish until the sun had cleared away the mists.* [italics added]

Occasionally Carson makes these elements similar in length as well as construction and wording:

The water surged and seethed as in a mill race, hissing and foaming. [paragraph 8]

This balancing of sentence elements helps to convey the rhythms of nature that Carson wishes the reader to experience.

Questions for Study and Discussion

1. What in the behavior of the sanderlings and the eel, shad, and other fish marks summer's end?
2. In what way is the coming of the young shrimp "symbolic of another journey"?
3. What changes in the weather and in the flora or vegetation of the island does Carson describe, and for what purpose?

4. What natural process is Carson describing in paragraphs 8, 9, and 10? Is she making a point about this process?

Sentence Study

Identify the parallel elements in the following sentences. What does the parallelism contribute to the clarity or effect of the sentence?

1. "As the marshes lay under the sun, they glowed with the soft greens and browns of the salt meadow grass, the warm purples of the rushes, and the scarlet of the marsh samphire." [paragraph 5]
2. "The fish were mullet who had lived throughout the summer in the sound and estuary, roving solitary among the eel grass and widgeon grass, feeding on the litter of animal and vegetable fragments of the bottom mud." [paragraph 6]
3. "These young fish had been spawned in the sea, but had found their way to the pond through a temporary cut earlier that year." [paragraph 7]
4. "On they went, most of them, past the smoother green swells to the second line of surf, where shoals tripped the waves coming in from the open sea and sent them sprawling in white confusion." [paragraph 11]

Suggestions for Writing

1. Describe a seasonal change in plant life and wildlife you have observed in your town or city or a place you have visited. Organize your description to make a point. Let your reader discover the point or idea through the details of your description.
2. Describe changes in everyday life that occur in your neighborhood during a change of weather or change of season. Let your details make a point—perhaps a point about the people of your neighborhood or town.

Sentence Variety

Sentences need to be varied to avoid a sense of monotony. Thus, a series of short simple sentences like the following will soon lose the reader's attention:

> You are watching coal miners at work. You realize momentarily what different universes people inhabit. It is a sort of world apart down there. One can quite easily go through life without ever hearing about that world. Probably a majority of people would even prefer not to hear about it.

Here is the actual version of the sentences above:

> Watching coal miners at work, you realize momentarily what different universes different people inhabit. *Down there* where coal is dug it is a sort of world apart *which* one can quite easily go through life without ever hearing about. Probably a majority of people would even prefer not to hear about it. —George Orwell, *The Road to Wigan Pier* [italics added]

Orwell varied his sentences probably as most writers do—without much conscious attention. The italicized connectives come naturally to us as we speak or write; indeed, it takes some effort to write in so disjointed a way. A series of disconnected sentences is not only monotonous but hard to understand because we must continually refocus our attention.

As a rule, the more varied the length and construction of our sentences, the less monotonous they are likely to be, and the more apparent the natural emphasis we wish to give our ideas. Notice the choices open to the writer in combining the following:

> You are watching coal miners at work. You realize momentarily what different universes people inhabit.

Orwell might have written the following:

> As you watch coal miners at work, you realize momentarily what different universes people inhabit.

> You realize momentarily what different universes people inhabit, as you watch coal miners at work.

> Watching coal miners at work makes one realize momentarily what different universes people inhabit.

These varied sentences achieve emphasis in different ways. In the first, the emphasis falls on the idea of different universes; in the second, on watching the miners at work. The third sentence gives the same emphasis to both ideas. Which sentence the writer chooses depends on what is emphasized in the whole paragraph or essay. As Orwell's sentences show, the choice can depend on making the connection of ideas clear.

Russell Baker

THE BEER CULTURE

Russell Baker was born in 1925 in Loudon County, in northern Virginia, and was raised in a Blue Ridge mountain community and later in Newark, New Jersey, and Baltimore, Maryland—very different worlds described in his autobiographical *Growing Up* (1982) and *The Good Times* (1989). Upon graduating from Johns Hopkins University in 1947, Baker began reporting for the *Baltimore Sun*. From 1954 to 1962 he reported on Washington and national politics for *The New York Times*. Since 1963 he has written a column for the *Times*. His many columns on national politics and American life—many of them humorous—have been collected in *So This Is Depravity* (1980) and other books. In 1979 Baker received the Pulitzer Prize for distinguished commentary, and the Pulitzer Prize for biography in 1983 for *Growing Up*.

The people of Beer World are named Buck, Mike, Al and Mac. There are no Algernons in Beer World, no Marmadukes, no Gaylords. Beer World has hair on its chest. [1]

Yes, there are a few women in Beer World. They are ²
named Gladys, though there is one named Elvira. You
have seen the woman who brings a tray of beer to Buck,
Mike, Al and Mac while they are sitting in the beer
parlor in their mackinaws being rugged and jolly? Of
course you have seen her. That woman is Gladys.

You may also have seen Buck recently having his ³
beer at a distinctly sissified ski lodge in company with
a lissome young woman. That woman is Elvira. Buck
sometimes takes Elvira to these sissy places in order to
experience the perfection of beer without sweating.

Buck often feels guilty after these perspiration-free ⁴
outings with Elvira, for in Beer World it is man's duty
to heave and grunt until his pores open and let the
honest body juices cascade freely. Only then does he
truly deserve beer. Beer is the reward for manly toil in
Beer World.

How often have you seen Buck, Mike, Al and Mac ⁵
exhausted at the end of an honest day's work on the
firing squad, sleeves rolled up, shirt collars opened,
perspiration dampening their cheeks as they labor to rid
the world of malcontents, looters and sissies—how often
have you seen them joyfully throw down their tools as
the sun sets, embrace each other merrily and tramp over
to Gladys's place for their beer?

Now comes beer time. The beer has been created for ⁶
Buck, Mike, Al and Mac in recognition of their labor,
in recognition of all they do. The beer is for them. Not
for Algernon. Not for Marmaduke and Gaylord. Someone will object that we never really see the boys putting
in a full day's work on the firing squad, that all we ever
see are the final few executions at sunset. But of course;
in Beer World, sunset is the only time of day. The sun
stands eternally in the setting position. Shortly after
Buck, Mike, Al and Mac throw down their rifles, or
their scythes or their big tractor-trailers, and receive
their beer from Gladys, they tramp out into the sunset
again and finish building a skyscraper so they can throw

down their rivet guns and march back to Gladys's place for another round of well-earned beer.

Why does Buck occasionally sneak away to sissified 7 places with Elvira to drink his beer in dry clothing? Surely Buck would rather be with Mike, Al and Mac arriving at Beer World's cottage by the lake in their plaid fishing shirts.

Of course, Buck would. It is much more fun racing 8 to the refrigerator with Mike, Al and Mac and discovering four bottles of chilled beer than it is sitting across a table from Elvira. Is Buck—let us phrase the question as delicately as possible—is Buck soft on women?

The question is often raised by Mike, Al and Mac 9 when they are all having dinner together in order to deserve a beer, or jogging twenty miles together just at sunset in order to earn the right really to enjoy a beer. Once they even asked Doc—Beer World's psychiatrist— to put Buck on the couch, give him a bottle of beer and find out if he was really one of the boys.

Doc had just finished whipping a massive superego 10 down to size and was headed to Gladys's place for his beer when he conducted the examination. He pronounced Buck a perfectly normal beer guy with a slight woman problem.

It seems Buck had a mother, which is very rare in 11 Beer World. In his youth, "Old Moms," as Buck called her, used to send him to the corner saloon to buy her what she called "a bucket of suds." "Old Moms" had since been deported under Beer World's rigid legal code, which denies citizenship to most women, especially if, like "Old Moms," they sit around the house in dresses made from flour sacks drinking beer out of tin buckets.

The law was necessary because people like "Old 12 Moms" created a bad image of Beer World, which wanted to be viewed as a sweaty but clean-cut place full of boys whose beer had fewer calories and whose mothers, if they must have mothers, wouldn't be caught dead wearing flour sacks. In short, Buck felt bad about the old lady's deportation; when he took Elvira out for beer, he was really taking out his mother who had learned to dress expensively and to drink her beer out of a glass.

Elvira actually despises beer and would much prefer a drink with Amaretto in it, but doesn't dare order it for fear Buck would accuse her of not being one of the boys and walk out of her life forever. The women of Beer World do not have much opportunity to get out for a good time. Elvira has often asked Gladys to go out and have some Amaretto with her, but Gladys is afraid that if the boys learned about it they would call her a sissy.

Comment

Baker satirizes not just the characters and situations in beer ads but also, in the phrase of Walker Gibson, their "tough talk." Gibson characterizes tough talk through its "short sentences, 'crude' repetitions of words, simple grammatical structures with little subordinating." Seeking a "tense intimacy with his assumed reader, another man who has been around," the tough talker favors "colloquial patterns from oral speech and . . . a high frequency of the definite article. He lets his reader make logical and other connections between elements" *(Tough, Sweet, and Stuffy)*. Tough talk is marked by the monotony of its sentences—the lack of variety that Baker is imitating.

Questions for Study and Discussion

1. The essay opens with three short simple sentences—all lacking modification. These illustrate one of the characteristics of Gibson's "tough talk." What other paragraphs also contain relatively simple or short sentences, compound or complex sentences?
2. How many "'crude' repetitions of words" do you find throughout the essay?
3. How often does Baker depend on "colloquial patterns from oral speech" and a "high frequency of the definite article"?

4. In imitating the tough talker through the style of the essay, Baker is characterizing the tough-talking advertiser. What does he gain satirically in imitating the speech of this person?
5. What does the essay reveal about Baker's personality, outlook, and sense of humor?
6. What satirical points is Baker making not only about beer ads but also about the "beer culture"? Is the essay closer to social satire than to ethical satire (p. 376)?
7. How effective do you find the satire?

Vocabulary Study

Baker depends on connotation—the associations and emotional auras of words—to convey the tone and attitudes about the beer culture. What do the following words mean? What connotations do they convey?

1. *lissome* (paragraph 3)
2. *cascade* (paragraph 4)
3. *malcontents, sissies* (paragraph 5)
4. *massive superego, slight woman problem* (paragraph 10)
5. *Amaretto* (paragraph 13)

Suggestions for Writing

1. Write an essay analyzing another series of ads that depict a different kind of world or culture—perhaps that of sports car owners. Develop a thesis suggested by the similarities in these ads.
2. Use the same ads to write a satirical essay. Again, use the similarities in these ads to make your point. But do not state this point directly; let your descriptive details and tone convey it, as in Baker's satirical picture of "Beer World."

Mark Singer

MR. PERSONALITY

A native of Tulsa, Oklahoma, Mark Singer is a graduate of Yale
University. A staff writer for *The New Yorker* magazine, he is the
author of *Funny Money* (1985) and *Mr. Personality* (1989), a
collection of profiles and talk pieces. Singer is a keen observer of
people and life in New York City, where he lives.

When Paul Schimmel does his regular work—he's 1
involved in the printing business—he's just plain Paul
Schimmel. When he plays his clarinet during rush hour
on the F train, he physically resembles just plain Paul
Schimmel, but his inner self has actually metamorphosed
into Mr. Personality. The money that Mr. Personality
collects from passengers in the subway Paul Schimmel
in turn uses to underwrite free concerts in hospitals and
nursing homes. Paul Schimmel arranges the concert dates,
and then he arranges for Mr. Personality to show up
with his clarinet. In the end, the Goodnicks of America—
Paul Schimmel happens to be the founder and at the
moment the only member of this organization—gets
credit for a good deed. Full circle comes the enterprise.

Seven days a week, Paul Schimmel ventures into the 2
subway with his clarinet. In the IND station at Sixth
Avenue and Forty-second Street one recent afternoon, he
paid his fare with a free pass. Various good deeds and
diplomatic gestures across the years have enabled Paul
Schimmel to forge friendships with employees of the
Transit Authority who evidently believe that he qualifies
for a senior citizen's discount. In fact, he is only sixty-
three. He was wearing black slacks, a blue blazer, a
light-blue shirt, a blue necktie, a black topcoat, a brown
leather cap with earflaps, and black shoes with a fresh
shine. "For the shoes, today I decided to splurge," he
said. He wears eyeglasses with thick lenses and thick
black frames, and he has gray hair, a round, jowly face,

and the torso of a born Santa Claus. On the downtown platform, he paused. After assembling his clarinet, he left its case open at his feet and spread a hand towel across it. Atop that he rested a straw basket, and then he displayed a plastic-sheathed copy of a letter from Mary Duffy, an employee of the geriatric-psychiatric-services division of Coney Island Hospital. The letter verified that Mr. Personality is a habitual doer of good deeds.

Warming up, Paul Schimmel said, "I can imitate Benny Goodman. Wanna hear?" He played "Let's Dance." "I can imitate all the bandleaders. Let's say Artie Shaw—all right?" He played "Begin the Beguine." 3

A shuttle train went by on the local tracks, followed a couple of minutes later by an F train. Paul Schimmel has access to a computer inside his brain, which goes to work as soon as he enters a subway car, sizing up the audience. A soft, sweet song usually breaks the ice. Aboard the F, he braced himself against a pole and played "The Shadow of Your Smile" and then "Sorrento," each song punctuated by loudspeaker announcements explaining that there was congestion at Thirty-fourth Street and the train would begin moving shortly. Paul Schimmel's idea of a perfect audience is a bunch of jolly young professionals "that appreciate artistic endeavor." When he finished "Sorrento," he said, "I belong to the Goodnicks of America. Our motto is 'Happiness through music.' Ladies and gentlemen, any contributions you make will go to support concerts in nursing homes and hospitals." By the time the train reached Thirty-fourth Street, there was fifty cents in the straw basket, and Paul Schimmel's transformation into Mr. Personality was complete. 4

Mr. Personality is partial to less-than-full trains—he needs room to maneuver—and to Broadway musicals. When he plays songs from *South Pacific*, he interlards them with impersonations of Ezio Pinza, Mary Martin, and Juanita Hall. He does the voice of Carol Channing 5 announcing that Mr. Personality will now play "Hello, Dolly!" Offering a synopsis of *West Side Story*, he says that Tony and Maria once planned an assignation aboard the F train.

He worked his way through Tommy Dorsey (a medley, 6 beginning with "I'm Getting Sentimental Over You"), Count Basie ("Stomping at the Woodside"), and Duke Ellington ("Folks, never mind what train you think you got on. This is now the A train"). He has been known to segue from "Take the 'A' Train" to "Chattanooga Choo Choo." His Tommy Dorsey medley is preceded by a set speech: "Ladies and gentlemen, in 1938 Tommy Dorsey came to the Paramount Theatre, a theatre that contained all the juvenile delinquents of that day, who are the grandmothers of today. They attended the shows illegally, because they were truants from New Utrecht High School or someplace. The truant officers would come in and say, 'All you kids, go back to school.' And they'd dance in the aisles and ignore the truant officer. If you don't believe me, ask your grandmother. Tell her Mr. Personality says, 'Ask your grandmother.'"

A sanitation worker in green work clothes and an 7 orange cap boarded at Fourteenth Street, accompanied by a brown-haired young woman wearing black leather and carrying a stereo boom box. The sanitation worker said, "Hey, Benny Goodman."

The young woman said, "I played clarinet for two 8 years. Then my lips got tired."

Mr. Personality's musicianship is such that he gets the 9 melodies mostly right. He doesn't necessarily land on every note as precisely as Rodgers and Hammerstein, Billy Strayhorn, or Leonard Bernstein might have preferred. Once in a while, a passenger suggests that maybe Mr. Personality should consider playing his clarinet on another train or in a large empty space. When this happens, Mr. Personality does what he can to restrain himself.

"Ladies and gentlemen," he said as the train rolled 10 out of the West Fourth Street station, "I'm now going to take you on an imaginary trip to Brazil. We're gonna leave on an imaginary airline. I'm the captain of the ship. We're about to land in Rio de Janeiro and we're looking over Copacabana Beach, and there are half-nude Cariocas dancing and swaying and you hear the music, and it's this." He played "Corcovado" and "The Girl from Ipanema," saying when he had finished, "Excuse me. Mariachi dancers and Margaritas are now being served in the bar car. It should only happen, right?"

Approaching East Broadway and Canal, he detoured to Paris by way of "La Vie en Rose." He told two young women to think of him as Charles Boyer or Maurice Chevalier, either one. Under the East River, he played "Gigi." On a good run—say, from midtown Manhattan to downtown Brooklyn—he brings in about ten dollars. At York Street, the first stop in Brooklyn, he usually gets out, because it is possible to cross the platform there and catch a Manhattan-bound train without climbing a stairway. Paul Schimmel knows all the Brooklyn subway stations, because he has lived in Brooklyn most of his life. He learned to play the clarinet as a teenager but gave it up at the age of nineteen, when he went into the printing business. Now, as Mr. Personality, he feels that he is carrying out a preordained plan. "There's no question that when I do this I'm fulfilling my destiny," he said. "So I'm a late bloomer is all." 11

In the summer of 1983, Mr. Personality and his clarinet logged a lot of hours at the Brighton Beach Baths. For two years, he worked at Bonaparte's Restaurant, on Avenue M, in Midwood. "That's where I practiced my craft," he said. "That's where I learned how to banter." 12

On the F train back to Manhattan, he spotted a Chassidic passenger, and the computer inside his brain told him to play "Bei Mir Bist Du Schön." That somehow led into "Oklahoma!" and on to "Camelot." When the train reached Thirty-fourth Street, he decided to take a rest. 13

"The body tells me when to cool it down," he said   14
while carrying his paraphernalia up a stairway and a
ramp. "But Mr. Personality is coming through today,
right? If I feel fatigued or a little stilted, it's no good. It
doesn't give Mr. Personality a chance to take over. Mr.
Personality has to generate his own fuel. I wouldn't know
what to say for a whole hour onstage. But *Mr. Personality* does. The key is improvisational ability. I don't
know what I'm going to do in the next thirty seconds,
you understand. Here you got a guy—*I* don't know Mr.
Personality any more than *you* do. He's a third dimension. Follow? It's improvisation and unpredictability that
give you the edge. That's the beautiful part of Mr. Personality. You wanna get an ice-cream cone?"

At a refreshment stand near the top of the ramp, he   15
said, "Gimme a custard. Vanilla."

Between bites, he discussed a concert he gave not   16
long ago at a Bronx nursing home, where his mother,
who is now ninety-five, resides. Evidently, fifty years ago
she discouraged him from pursuing a career in music.
The recent concert forced her to reconsider. "Now she
says to me, 'O.K., Paul, you wanna play the clarinet,
play the clarinet.'"

When the cone was gone, it was time to go back to   17
work. Instinct told Mr. Personality to switch from the
Sixth Avenue line to an uptown N train. "I'm a gambler
in life," he said. "I'm a great believer in the laws of
probability. Do you believe in ghosts? I sort of believe
in ghosts. If I go into a subway car and spill all my
stuff—unfortunately, it's happened—I have a feeling that
some ghost did that to me. It's a very artistic feeling.
I don't believe anything happens accidentally. Everything has a destiny, and you have variables. Now, we're
gonna take the N train next. O.K., maybe the F train
will blow up and I'll think, Gee, how lucky. But it was
meant to be that way. Anyway, I want to get on the N
train because it has a more artistic crowd. It stops at
Fifty-ninth Street, near Bloomingdale's."

A possibly artistic woman passenger on the N train 18
read an Edith Wharton novel and ignored Mr. Personality while he played "Sorrento," "Danny Boy," "Glocca
Morra," "Cabaret," and some klezmer tunes. A possibly artistic girl in chinos and a denim jacket snapped
her chewing gum and smiled at all his jokes. Mr. Personality played snatches of the theme from *The God-
father* and also "Over the Rainbow," "June Is Bustin'
Out All Over," "It Might As Well Be Spring," "In the
Mood," and "Marie." When he paused after "Marie,"
a middle-aged woman in a red wool coat looked up at
him and said, "Tommy Dorsey! I feel like I'm in my
living room."

Comment

Singer writes as if conversing with us about "Mr. Personality." He
coordinates ideas as we do in the loose manner of informal speech:

> Paul Schimmel arranges the concert dates, *and then* he arranges
> for Mr. Personality to show up with his clarinet *[coordinate
> clauses]*.

He interrupts to explain a statement, as we often do in pausing for
clarification:

> When Paul Schimmel does his regular work—*he's involved in the
> printing business*—he's just plain Paul Schimmel.

He adds a series of explanatory details to an opening main clause,
the core of the sentence:

> Paul Schimmel has access to a computer inside his brain, *which
> goes to work as soon as he enters a subway car [subordinate
> clause], sizing up the audience [subordinate phrase]*.

Singer stays close to colloquial patterns, but his sentences are also
tighter and more varied than spoken ones, opening sometimes with
an explanatory or transitional phrase instead of with the main clause,
as in the sentences above:

In the IND station at Sixth Avenue and Forty-second Street one recent afternoon, he paid his fare with a free pass.

In fact, he is only sixty-three.

On the downtown platform, he paused.

Sentence variation not only prevents monotony, but allows Singer to give emphasis to key ideas at the end of the sentence. Notice the change in meaning and emphasis in the following revision:

He paused on the downtown platform.

Questions for Study and Discussion

1. How does Singer vary the sentence openings in paragraph 4? How does he vary the length of the sentences in the whole paragraph?
2. In what ways does Singer vary his sentences in paragraphs 5 and 6?
3. How does Mr. Personality's manner of speaking help to characterize him? How do his statements contrast with Singer's own in the whole essay?
4. Does Singer approve or disapprove of Schimmel and his subway performances, or is he not making a judgment? Is he making a point or developing a thesis?

Vocabulary Study

Explain the difference between the following words. Then explain how Singer uses the first word in the paragraph cited:

1. *metamorphosed* (paragraph 1), *changed*
2. *punctuated* (paragraph 4), *interrupted*
3. *interlards* (paragraph 5), *interrupts*
4. *impersonations* (paragraph 5), *imitations*
5. *preordained* (paragraph 11), *scheduled*
6. *paraphernalia* (paragraph 14), *equipment*
7. *improvisational* (paragraph 14), *inventive*

Suggestions for Writing

1. Explain what Paul Schimmel means by the statement that "Mr. Personality has to generate his own fuel" (paragraph 14) and how the details of the essay illustrate it.
2. Describe an unusual person, giving details of his speech and his actions. Let the details reveal to your reader what is unusual about the person.

Concreteness

To make an idea *concrete* is to make it exist for the reader through the senses. The statement "That car's a beauty!" expresses a general attitude and feeling but nothing more. If we want readers to share our experience we must give particulars or details, as in this explanation of what California teenagers mean by the expression "low and slow, mean and clean":

> The car a lowrider drives—almost always a sedan produced by the General Motors Corporation—is also called a lowrider, or a ride. If it has been altered with conspicuous success—a multi-colored lacquer paint job, say, and metal-spoke wheels, and skimpy tires that seem to belong on a Datsun rather than a 1967 Chevrolet Impala, and a welded-chain steering wheel no bigger around than a 45-r.p.m. record—it is called a clean ride, or a bad ride. "Low and slow," lowriders sometimes say. "Mean and clean." —Calvin Trillin and Edward Koren, "Low and Slow, Mean and Clean"

Not all abstract ideas can be expressed entirely through physical details. We can, however, show their application to experience, suggest how we came to the idea, or give a partial illustration, as in the following statement on ancient Egyptian burial practices:

> In Egypt, as has been said, the reality of the unseen world slowly overshadowed that of the seen, but invisible though it was, it remained substantial. The dead bodies must be preserved from returning to dust; they must be placed in tombs that were underground fortresses safe from disturbance; they must be surrounded by all the furnishings they had made use of in life.
> —Edith Hamilton, *The Greek Way*

The idea has been made concrete. At the same time, we must be careful not to give more details than needed to make the idea clear.

Writing can be so colorful—so crowded with details and descriptive
words—that the reader is distracted from the main idea.

William G. Wing

CHRISTMAS COMES FIRST ON THE BANKS

William G. Wing was a veteran correspondent of the *New York
Herald Tribune*. A specialist on natural resources and conservation, he
has written for *Audubon Magazine*, *The New York Times*, and other
periodicals. This evocative essay, based on a trip on a Gloucester,
Massachusetts, trawler, shows how a popular subject can be written
about freshly from a new and unusual point of view.

The Christmas sun rises first, in America, on   1
trawlermen fishing the undersea meadows of Georges
Bank.

At the moment before sunrise a hundred miles east   2
of Cape Cod, the scene aboard a trawler is so unchang-
ing it can be imagined. The net has been hauled and
streamed again. The skipper is alone in the pilot house,
surrounded by the radio-telephone's racket and the green
and amber eyes of electronic instruments, instruments
that are supposed to tell him not only where he is but
where the fish are, too. But this is only hope, not science.
Despite the instruments, despite the boat's resemblance
to a plow horse, methodically criss-crossing the meadow,
her men are not engineers or farmers, but hunters who
seek their prey in the wilderness of the sea. The
trawlermen are, in fact, the last tribe of nomadic hunts-
men left in the East.

The skipper is alone, then, with a huntsman's anxi-   3
eties: the whereabouts of the prey, the uncertainties of
the weather, the chances of hitting a good market. On
deck before him the men are processing the catch just
brought aboard. They sit in a circle of brilliance, the
deck lights reflecting from their yellow and Daybrite-

orange oilskins and from the brown curve of the riding sail above. They sit on the edges of the pens, holding the big white and silver fish between their knees, ripping with knives and tearing with hands, heaving the disemboweled bodies into a central basket. Nothing is visible beyond the cone of light but the occasional flash of a whitecap or comber. There is much noise, though—wind and water and seabirds that have gathered in mobs for the feast of haulback.

There is an appropriateness to Christmas in this 4 scene, east of the sleeping mainland, so marked that it seems quaint. The names of the trawlers themselves—*Holy Family, Immaculate Conception, St. Mary, St. Joseph*—give the flavor. On the engine room bulkhead of a trawler *Holy Cross,* beyond the ugga-chugging Atlas diesel, is a painting of Christ at Gethsemane. There is an appropriateness, too, among the men. They share alike—equal shares of profit, equal shares of danger. To work together in such small quarters and stern conditions requires a graciousness of spirit that is the essence of Christmas.

The sun is up and the pens are empty. As the deck 5 is hosed down and the trash fish pitchforked overboard, the noise from the birds rises hysterically—barnyard sounds, shrieks, whistles, klaxon horns. Now the birds can be seen flying in a circle around the boat. Each can hold position for only a few moments beside the point where the remains of fish are washing over. Then it falls astern and has to come up to windward on the other side of the boat, cross ahead and fall backward to the critical point. The birds pumping up the windward side look like six-day bicycle riders, earnest and slightly ridiculous, but when they reach the critical point there is a miraculous moment of aerobatics as the birds brake, wheel and drop in the broken air.

Gulls snatch, gannets plunge, but the little kittiwakes 6 balance delicately, their tails spread like carved ivory fans. There is a column of descending, shrieking birds, a scintillating feathered mass. The birds revolving about the boat have made themselves not only guests at the feast but have formed the wreath as well.

Christmas Day has begun, but for the men it is time to sleep. They hose each other off and then disappear through the whaleback for a mug-up below. Boots and oilskins off, they will have a minute or two for a James Bond novel or a crossword puzzle in the bunks, braced against the elevator motions of the hull, not hearing the sounds of Niagara outside. Then the instant unconsciousness that seamen and children know. The skipper alone remains awake, watching Christmas come. 7

Christmas came first to men on lonely meadows. It will come first again to the men on the lonely meadows offshore, fishing the Bank in boats wreathed by seabirds. 8

Comment

Wing tells us that he will seek to make the moment before the sun rises concrete: he will find images that convey the mood and experience of the moment. He does so in the details of the boat, the trawlermen, their relations—"equal shares of profits, equal shares of danger." The seabirds have an unexpected appropriateness, for they wreathe the boats in their circlings. Through careful selection of details, Wing succeeds in his purpose; through his description, he is able to make a point without stating it directly.

Questions for Study and Discussion

1. What point is Wing making through his description? Is it important to him where the Christmas sun first rises in America?
2. Is the order of details governed by space (moving from one part of the scene to another) or by time, or possibly both?
3. What details make the idea of Christmas in the essay concrete?

4. Is Wing saying that the life aboard the trawler and the relations between the men are different during the Christmas season or on Christmas Day?
5. How does Wing make transitions throughout the essay?
6. What is the point of the concluding comparison?

Vocabulary Study

For each of the following words, list at least two synonyms that suggest a more specific meaning or use. For example, *forecast* is more specific than *foretell* when referring to a weather prediction.

1. *large*
2. *small*
3. *dirty*
4. *clean*
5. *law*
6. *run*

Suggestions for Writing

1. Describe a scene at a particular moment—for example, the moment of impact in an automobile accident. Select details that contribute to a central impression, but do not state the impression directly.
2. Describe a day of work, showing how the season of the year affects you and your fellow workers. Use your description to develop a thesis.
3. Describe an unusual day in your life—one that perhaps was spent in an unusual setting, away from home. Stress those feelings and details that made the day unusual and memorable.

Elizabeth Janeway

WATER

Elizabeth Janeway is the author of numerous short stories and novels, including *Daisy Kenyon* (1945) and *Accident* (1964), and she has written about the role of women in various societies and the changes in women's lives in recent years. Her books on women include *Man's World, Woman's Place: A Study in Social Mythology* (1971), *Between Myth and Morning: Women Awakening* (1974), and *Powers of the Weak* (1980). Her essay on water, first published in *House and Garden* magazine, makes a number of abstract ideas concrete.

Water is a universal symbol. Tamed and trickling out 1 of the tap, softened and fluoridated, warmed in the boiler by fires burning million-year-old oil, it is still not quite a commodity. Even for city dwellers some dim memory stirs from time to time of those ancient eons when water or the lack of it ruled everything—the sites of habitation, the paths through the wilderness, the limits of hunting grounds, famine and abundance, life and death. It can still shatter human hopes and plans. Thirty years ago, the top soil in the plain states rose into the sky and blew away. Men had ploughed grazing land, counting on rain to bind the soil where the tough grass roots had been cut, and the rain did not come. A migration as great as that of the Mongols poured out of the Dust Bowl toward California. Steinbeck, in *The Grapes of Wrath*, recorded what happened to one bit of flotsam on one stream of this Diaspora. Today, I read in the papers, the Russians are ploughing the virgin Siberian lands as, in the last century, we ploughed the Dakotas. But the stubborn old gods of rivers and rains have not yet submitted to Marxist-Leninist discipline. Disappointing harvests are reported.

Water. "It has caused more wars in the Middle East," 2 writes Freya Stark in one of her brilliant travel books, "than even religion." In the Middle East, that is quite a feat. But there are historians who trace the breakdown of the ancient civilizations along the Tigris, the Euphrates and the Indus to wars and raiding parties which breached dams and ruined irrigation and drainage systems. Whether the cities fell first and the aqueducts and irrigation ditches silted up through neglect, or whether they were deliberately destroyed to strangle the cities, they have never been rebuilt. Let us not imagine, in our smug pride of modernity, that engineers have yet become more powerful than statesmen, for even today, there is desert where once there was fertile land. Civilization takes water for granted, but that is civilization's mistake.

It's not a mistake, though, that will ever be made by those who live past the limits of "city water." Amidst all the denouncing of suburbia, let us give it credit for this: suburban dwellers must face some of the old facts of life, of living and of weather. In the country, water comes out of a well—save for that blessed, lucky trickle which flows to a favored few from a gravity-fed spring (and that is a trickle which, in August, may dwindle disastrously). Civilization, of course, has changed the Old Oaken Bucket into an electric motor pumping so many gallons a minute to a cistern from an artesian well, but it has not changed the nature of the emotions that go with procuring this water, only bunched them together into patches of intensity with stretches of complacence in between. But when the power goes out in a storm, so does the water supply.

Where we used to live, seventy miles from New York, the power had a habit of failing before the telephone lines went. Why this should be, I don't know. But the prudence of the telephone company in locating its poles and stringing its wires allowed messages to get through from neighbor to neighbor before the telephone lines went down and silence followed darkness. Thus, a spreading rash of calls would ripple out from the center of casualty: "We've lost our power. If you still have yours, fill the bathtubs quick." Then the householder (or his

wife, if he was a commuter who spent his days in an
ivory tower in the city) would go into action and fill tubs
and buckets and pots and pans against the drought to
come. After one ice storm, the water famine lasted for a
week in some parts of the township, and luckier folk
invited their neighbors in for baths.

From time to time, as families grew in size or new   5
houses went up with their demanding machines for
washing clothes and dishes, new wells had to be dug.
Then the drillers would come with their rig and thump
away at the ancient granite beneath our green countryside, and the owners would groan and shake a little, too,
at the dollars that each hour of thumping represented.
There was water, the drillers would report encourag-
ingly, but not yet quite enough, three gallons a minute,
five gallons a minute—would they never find the level
that would deliver the necessary eight gallons a minute?
On and on they went, like persevering, unsuccessful
disciples of Moses, smiting the rock. Once a friend of
ours, in despair after weeks of fruitless pounding, called
in a water dowser. Our friend is the founder of one of
the oldest and most respected public opinion polls. It
seemed quaintly appropriate to think of an old man with
a hazel twig in his hands questioning every foot of the
poll taker's land on its water content. At last he said,
"Dig here," and they dug, and found water. Of course,
it was simply luck—whatever that means.

Water. It is a universal symbol, I wrote, but a symbol   6
of what? Of birth and beginnings, as the scientists, the
first chapter of Genesis and Dr. Freud all tell us? Life
began in the sea, say the biochemists, when lightning
discharges awoke, in the thin soup of almost life, some
monstrous protein molecules which married each other:
this is our most modern mythology. An older story tells
us that the Spirit of God moved on the face of the waters
even before His command created Light: which might,
after all, be simply a more majestic way of describing
the same event. As for Freud, when he had rummaged

through enough people's heads and stitched thousands of fragments of dreams together, he came to the cautious conclusion that "to dream of being in water or passing through a stream often symbolized the act of birth." Which is a nice, pedantic, and quite useless conclusion, for it leaves us with another set of waters unexplained. What shall we make of "the bitter, salt, estranging sea," or the rivers of Styx and of Lethe, which are the rivers of death?

We must think again. Water can symbolize birth, as 7 it can symbolize death, but essentially its meaning is greater and simpler, and includes both. At the deepest level, water stands as the symbol of Change. Indeed, when St. John, in the Revelations, wished to describe the eternal landscape that would follow upon the Day of Judgment, he said, "There was no more sea." Changeless eternity could go no further.

Water is the present tense. It flows. It will not take 8 a shape of its own, but will fill indifferently any jug or pitcher or cup, and then flow out and on, indifferent still, forgetful and uninfluenced. Its strength is the strength of movement. Even "still waters" must "run deep." If they do not, we distrust them and have made a pejorative word for such unnatural behavior—"stagnant," or standing. In New Mexico, the Indians believe that water can die. Mary Austin records the legend:

> At midnight drink no water
> For I have heard said
> That on the stroke of midnight
> All water goes dead.

Water is always now. It demands the present parti- 9 ciple for its description—gushing, flowing, pouring, sprinkling. As every gardener knows, last week's soaking and next week's rain might as well not exist, unless we manage to string them together by constructing tanks and cisterns and reservoirs. Thirst is immediate. Water cannot be an event, it must be a presence. To make it

so must be a primary concern of any stable society, great
or small.

Modern man is astonishingly modest about his   10
achievements. I am not at all sure that this is a healthy
state of mind. Might we not be more confident of our
ability to deal with our future problems if we took a
bit more pride in our successful solutions to problems
of the past? Modesty is all very well for individuals, but
civic pride can give a community a sense of wholeness
and of its obligations to its citizens. We have somehow
lost the knack of celebrating deeds of greatness today,
and are apt to go off to the beach on the Fourth of July,
each family by itself, instead of taking a little time to
remember our heroes and refresh our pride.

I would like to see more holidays, and as one of them   11
I would like to propose a Festival of the Waters. It might
well be held on St. Swithin's Day. I imagine pilgrimages
to the Tennessee Valley, to Grand Coulee and to Boulder
Dam. I think of holiday tours along the St. Lawrence
Seaway, with river steamers full of bands and picnickers
toasting all that good sense, engineering training and
peace between nations have wrought there. The irri-
gated valleys of California could show off their wealth.

Above all, each city should offer thanks to its sani-   12
tary engineers, who might appear with an accompany-
ing guard of master plumbers—for even the grimmest
nature may sweeten a little once it feels itself appreciated. The Mayor might read out the proud statistics
citing the number of years since typhoid or cholera
claimed a victim within his purlieus; and if the statistics
should by any chance not be proud, how quick the
Mayor and the Department of Sanitation would be to
improve them! And each year the ceremony would be
crowned by the dedication of some new Wonder of
Water: a handsome public pool, or a fountain with a bit
of green about it, shining and leaping in the center of
the city where passers-by could refresh their eyes. Or a
boat basin. Or a new wing on the aquarium. Or—

But you see what I mean. Water is a universal symbol 13
because it is a universal need. As we live now, it is
beyond the power of the individual, in the vast majority
of cases, to satisfy this need on his own. Only men
working together can build reservoirs and aqueducts
and dams and hydroelectric stations and sewage conver-
sion plants and, soon no doubt, great structures to
desalt the sea and make the desert blossom like the corn
tassel and the alfalfa.

Our Festival of Waters, then, would be a holiday to 14
celebrate the things that men working together can
achieve. What could be more appropriate? For as we all
know, the just and the unjust both get wet when it rains
and thirsty when it does not. Too often, in the past, the
just and the unjust have preferred to disagree and to
create deserts rather than settle down and share out their
water rights. But now our engineering knowledge is
growing with the world's population, and with its need
for water. Might not, for once, new skills combine with
new deeds? Might not the just and the unjust decide to
work together, literally for dear life? And might not
these projects to control the fluid strength and the eternal changeability of water teach us something about
controlling the fluid strength and eternal changeability
of human nature?

Comment

Elizabeth Janeway begins her reflective essay with an abstract statement, "Water is a universal symbol." She makes this statement
concrete through a wide range of examples drawn from cultural
history, religion, psychology, and personal experience. Her essay is
in fact an exploration of many symbolic meanings, not just one. In
the course of her essay, she states a number of problems associated with water; it is fitting, therefore, that she conclude by
looking at possible solutions.

Questions for Study and Discussion

1. In paragraphs 1 and 2, does Janeway state what water symbolizes? Does she do so in describing the experiences of suburban people in paragraphs 3-5?
2. How do paragraphs 6 and 7 advance the discussion begun in paragraphs 1-5?
3. How did St. John use water to symbolize an abstract idea?
4. In paragraph 8, Janeway introduces another abstract idea: "Water is the present tense." How do the details of the paragraph make this idea concrete? How is this discussion related to the preceding paragraphs?
5. What topic does Janeway introduce in paragraph 10, and how is this topic related to the preceding discussion? How does she lead the reader back to her original thesis, restated in paragraph 13?
6. What problems has Janeway identified in the course of the essay, and what solutions does she propose in her concluding paragraph?

Vocabulary Study

To answer the following questions, you will need to consult dictionaries, encyclopedias, and other reference books in your college library:

1. What was the *Diaspora*, and how is Janeway using the term in paragraph 1? What does she mean in the same paragraph by the word *flotsam*?
2. What is the difference between an aqueduct and an irrigation ditch (paragraph 2)?
3. What kinds of wells and springs does Janeway describe in paragraph 3?
4. To what biblical event is Janeway referring in paragraph 5? To what other biblical events and passages does she refer, and why?
5. In what mythology do the rivers of Lethe and Styx occur (paragraph 6)? What mythological significance did these rivers have?

6. Why might a water festival be fitting on St. Swithin's day (paragraph 11)?

Suggestions for Writing

1. Illustrate an idea about water in Janeway's essay from personal experience and observation, or state and illustrate an idea of your own.
2. Water plays a prominent role in "Dover Beach," "To Marguerite—Continued," and other poems of Matthew Arnold. Analyze one of these poems in a short essay, focusing on Arnold's symbolic use of water.

Figurative Language

Much of our language is *figurative* in departing from the literal meaning of words—as in the following common expressions:

> *blaze of glory*   *drunk with power*
> *hard as nails*   *the angry sea*

"Blaze of glory" is a *metaphor*—a figure of speech in which one thing is talked about as if it were something else. The metaphor does not tell us glory is like a fire: it speaks of glory as if it were. "Drunk with power" is also a metaphor in suggesting that power acts like an intoxicant. "Hard as nails" makes the comparison directly through the word *as*, and we therefore call it a *simile*. *Personification* gives animate or human qualities to something inanimate or inhuman— the churning sea humanized through the word *angry*.

In exposition and argument, figurative language can make an idea or attitude concrete and persuasive. But common expressions may no longer call a picture to mind, and for this reason writers seek original metaphors and other figures that do, as in this description by a surgeon of one of the tools of his art:

> The scalpel is in two parts, the handle and the blade. Joined, it is six inches from tip to tip. At one end of the handle is a narrow notched prong upon which the blade is slid, then snapped into place. Without the blade, the handle has a blind, decapitated look. It is helpless as a trussed maniac. But slide on the blade, click it home, and the knife springs instantly to life. It is headed now, edgy, leaping to mount the fingers for the gallop to its feast.
> —Richard Selzer, *Mortal Lessons*

Metaphor, simile, and personification combine here in a highly dramatic way. The description conveys the excitement of the surgeon in holding the scalpel and preparing to use it.

Annie Dillard

UNTYING THE KNOT

In *Pilgrim at Tinker Creek* Annie Dillard (p. 112) describes her life at Tinker Creek, in the Roanoke Valley in Virginia's Blue Ridge. Dillard tells us in the opening chapter of the book: "It's a good place to live; there's a lot to think about. The creeks—Tinker and Carvin's—are an active mystery, fresh every minute." Later in the book, Dillard comments on the act of seeing: "Seeing is of course very much a matter of verbalization. Unless I call attention to what passes before my eyes, I simply won't see it. It is, as Ruskin says, 'not merely unnoticed, but in the full, clear sense of the word unseen.'" The act of seeing is one of the themes of the following chapter from *Pilgrim at Tinker Creek*.

Yesterday I set out to catch the new season, and instead I found an old snakeskin. I was in the sunny February woods by the quarry; the snakeskin was lying in a heap of leaves right next to an aquarium someone had thrown away. I don't know why that someone hauled the aquarium deep into the woods to get rid of it; it had only one broken glass side. The snake found it handy, I imagine; snakes like to rub against something rigid to help them out of their skins, and the broken aquarium looked like the nearest likely object. Together the snakeskin and the aquarium made an interesting scene on the forest floor. It looked like an exhibit at a trial—circumstantial evidence—of a wild scene, as though a snake had burst through the broken side of the aquarium, burst through his ugly old skin, and disappeared, perhaps straight up in the air, in a rush of freedom and beauty.

The snakeskin had unkeeled scales, so it belonged to a nonpoisonous snake. It was roughly five feet long by the yardstick, but I'm not sure because it was very wrinkled and dry, and every time I tried to stretch it flat it broke. I ended up with seven or eight pieces of it all over the kitchen table in a fine film of forest dust.

The point I want to make about the snakeskin is   3
that, when I found it, it was whole and tied in a knot.
Now there have been stories told, even by reputable
scientists, of snakes that have deliberately tied themselves in a knot to prevent larger snakes from trying to
swallow them—but I couldn't imagine any way that
throwing itself into a half hitch would help a snake
trying to escape its skin. Still, ever cautious, I figured
that one of the neighborhood boys could possibly have
tied it in a knot in the fall, for some whimsical boyish
reason, and left it there, where it dried and gathered
dust. So I carried the skin along thoughtlessly as I walked,
snagging it sure enough on a low branch and ripping
it in two for the first of many times. I saw that thick
ice still lay on the quarry pond and that the skunk
cabbage was already out in the clearings, and then I
came home and looked at the skin and its knot.

The knot had no beginning. Idly I turned it around   4
in my hand, searching for a place to untie; I came to
with a start when I realized I must have turned the thing
around fully ten times. Intently, then, I traced the knot's
lump around with a finger: it was continuous. I couldn't
untie it any more than I could untie a doughnut; it was
a loop without beginning or end. These snakes *are*
magic, I thought for a second, and then of course I
reasoned what must have happened. The skin had been
pulled inside-out like a peeled sock for several inches;
then an inch or so of the inside-out part—a piece whose
length was coincidentally equal to the diameter of the
skin—had somehow been turned right-side out again,
making a thick lump whose edges were lost in wrinkles,
looking exactly like a knot.

So. I have been thinking about the change of seasons.   5
I don't want to miss spring this year. I want to distinguish the last winter frost from the out-of-season one,
the frost of spring. I want to be there on the spot the
moment the grass turns green. I always miss this radical
revolution; I see it the next day from a window, the yard
so suddenly green and lush I could envy Nebuchadnezzar

down on all fours eating grass. This year I want to stick a net into time and say "now," as men plant flags on the ice and snow and say, "here." But it occurred to me that I could no more catch spring by the tip of the tail than I could untie the apparent knot in the snakeskin; there are no edges to grasp. Both are continuous loops.

I wonder how long it would take you to notice the 6 regular recurrence of the seasons if you were the first man on earth. What would it be like to live in open-ended time broken only by days and nights? You could say, "it's cold again; it was cold before," but you couldn't make the key connection and say, "it was cold this time last year," because the notion of "year" is precisely the one you lack. Assuming that you hadn't noticed an orderly progression of heavenly bodies, how long would you have to live on earth before you could feel with any assurance that any one particular long period of cold would, in fact, end? "While the earth remaineth, seedtime and harvest, and cold and heat, and summer and winter, and day and night shall not cease": God makes this guarantee very early in Genesis to a people whose fears on this point had perhaps not been completely allayed.

It must have been fantastically important, at the real 7 beginnings of human culture, to conserve and relay this vital seasonal information, so that the people could anticipate dry or cold seasons, and not huddle on some November rock hoping pathetically that spring was just around the corner. We still very much stress the simple fact of four seasons to school children; even the most modern of modern new teachers, who don't seem to care if their charges can read or write or name two products of Peru, will still muster some seasonal chitchat and set the kids to making paper pumpkins, or tulips, for the walls. "The people," wrote Van Gogh in a letter, "are very sensitive to the changing seasons." That we are "very sensitive to the changing seasons is, incidentally, one of the few good reasons to shun travel. If I stay at home I preserve the illusion that what is happening on Tinker Creek is the very newest thing, that I'm at the

very vanguard and cutting edge of each new season. I
don't want the same season twice in a row; I don't want
to know I'm getting last week's weather, used weather,
weather broadcast up and down the coast, old-hat
weather.

But there's always unseasonable weather. What we   8
think of the weather and behavior of life on the planet
at any given season is really all a matter of statistical
probabilities; at any given point, anything might happen. There is a bit of every season in each season. Green
plants—deciduous green leaves—grow everywhere, all
winter long, and small shoots come up pale and new in
every season. Leaves die on the tree in May, turn brown,
and fall into the creek. The calendar, the weather, and
the behavior of wild creatures have the slimmest of
connections. Everything overlaps smoothly for only a
few weeks each season, and then it all tangles up again.
The temperature, of course, lags far behind the calendar
seasons, since the earth absorbs and releases heat slowly,
like a leviathan breathing. Migrating birds head south
in what appears to be dire panic, leaving mild weather
and fields full of insects and seeds; they reappear as if
in all eagerness in January, and poke about morosely in
the snow. Several years ago our October woods would
have made a dismal colored photograph for a sadist's
calendar: a killing frost came before the leaves had even
begun to brown; they dropped from every tree like
crepe, blackened and limp. It's all a chancy, jumbled
affair at best, as things seem to be below the stars.

Time is the continuous loop, the snakeskin with   9
scales endlessly overlapping without beginning or end,
or time is an ascending spiral if you will, like a child's
toy Slinky. Of course we have no idea which arc on the
loop is our time, let alone where the loop itself is, so
to speak, or down whose lofty flight of stairs the Slinky
so uncannily walks.

The power we seek, too, seems to be a continuous   10
loop. I have always been sympathetic with the early

notion of a divine power that exists in a particular place, or that travels about over the face of the earth as a man might wander—and when he is "there" he is surely not here. You can shake the hand of a man you meet in the woods; but the spirit seems to roll along like the mythical hoop snake with its tail in its mouth. There are no hands to shake or edges to untie. It rolls along the mountain ridges like a fireball, shooting off a spray of sparks at random, and will not be trapped, slowed, grasped, fetched, peeled, or aimed. "As for the wheels, it was cried unto them in my hearing, O wheel." This is the hoop of flame that shoots the rapids in the creek or spins across the dizzy meadows; this is the arsonist of the sunny woods: catch it if you can.

Comment

Metaphor is particularly appropriate to the ideas of this essay. Dillard uses the knotted snakeskin as a metaphor for existence. She makes her point directly: she can no more "catch spring by the tip of the tail" than she can untie the knot—"there are no edges to grasp. Both are continuous loops." She builds carefully to this statement, her full meaning emerging in the details of her account. The open feeling of spring stands for a larger experience: the sense of "open-ended time." Dillard wants to see the world anew at each moment, though she knows that experiences repeat themselves. Having explored these ideas, she can finish her analogy—"Time is the continuous loop"— and she thinks also of a divine power that is everywhere always. It is the oneness and at the same time the variousness of nature that she seeks to express through figurative language.

Questions for Study and Discussion

1.   The power of nature, and its openness, are symbolized in many ways in the essay. Through what metaphor is it symbolized at the end?

2. Dillard moves from ordinary experience to the extraordinary. What words and phrases suggest the extraordinary and mysterious qualities of life as the essay proceeds? Which of these words and phrases are figurative?
3. What use does Dillard make of the Bible (Daniel 4:25) in paragraph 5?
4. In how many ways is the knotted snakeskin used in the essay? That is, how many references do you find to entanglement and overlapping?
5. Why can Dillard not "catch spring by the tip of the tail" (paragraph 5)? What point is she making through this metaphorical statement?
6. How does the author characterize herself through her response to the snakeskin and the world of Tinker Creek?
7. What use does Dillard make of personification?

Vocabulary Study

Write a paraphrase of the final paragraph, translating similes, metaphors, and other figures of speech into literal language.

Suggestions for Writing

1. Write about your feelings and thoughts concerning a season of the year. Focus your discussion on an object you associate with this season. You may want to explore the various qualities of the object and what these tell you about the season.
2. Develop one of the ideas of the essay from your point of view and personal experience.

Tone

The tone of a statement expresses the attitude or feeling of a speaker or writer. The tone of the following statement on zoos is immediately clear:

> Just what sort of instruction do they radiate, and what is its value? I have never been able to find out. The sober truth is that they are no more educational than so many firemen's parades or displays of skyrockets, and that all they actually offer to the public in return for the taxes spent upon them is a form of idle and witless amusement, compared to which a visit to a penitentiary, or even to a State Legislature in session, is informing, stimulating, and ennobling.   —H. L. Mencken, "Zoos"

Mencken's blunt statement expresses his astonishment and exasperation. He says exactly what he means—in contrast to this ironic statement in which the writer implies more in his opening sentence than he actually says:

> Already architectural designers are toiling to find ways out of the technical trap represented by sealed buildings with immovable glass, ways that might let in some of the naturally cool air outside. Some have lately come up with a remarkable discovery: the openable window. Presumably, that represents progress.
> —Frank Trippett, "The Great American Cooling Machine"

The designers of sealed buildings, the writer implies, are not very bright if they are making so obvious a discovery as the openable window. The final comment is openly sarcastic.

Many statements are harder to interpret, particularly in writing. If you heard a person exclaim "What a tragedy!", you would know immediately from the tone of voice whether the person was expressing pain, anger, sarcasm, wonder, or bewilderment. If you came upon the same exclamation in a piece of writing, you would examine its context or setting to discover the writer's tone. Trippett's opening statement seems straightforward when read out of context. Reading the statement in its context, you realize that Trippett has depended on surprise. Ironic statements often say the opposite of what we expect to hear: "He has a great future behind him." Ironic situations surprise us in the same way: "The firehouse burned to the ground."

In writing your own essays, you often adopt a tone without giving it consideration. In looking at your draft, you may need to revise the tone and clarify ambiguous words or statements, as well as your feelings or attitude, perhaps stating them directly rather than implying them.

Hilary de Vries

REAL YUPPIES

Hilary de Vries graduated from Ohio Wesleyan University in 1976 and received her M.A. in creative writing from Boston University in 1981. Her essays and articles have appeared in the *Christian Science Monitor*, *Los Angeles Times*, *New York Times Magazine*, and other periodicals. In 1983 she was named Magazine Writer of the Year by the New England Women's Press Association. The term *Yuppie* became popular in the 1984 presidential election through its association with the primary candidate Senator Gary Hart of Colorado. De Vries writes humorously about her efforts to join the ranks of Yuppies in her article published in the *Christian Science Monitor*, on October 11, 1984.

Yup. I was proud not to be saddled with an acronym, pleased that I nimbly sidestepped the plethora of life-style manuals—"The Official Preppy Handbook," "Real Women Don't Pump Gas," and the rest of that know-thyself paperback pack. I was poised in the face of Woodstock's 15th anniversary; I had spent the Age of Aquarius trying to ace English in a public high school in Illinois.

Yet, despite my best efforts to avoid being pegged to a generational trait, I find the term "Yuppie" not only unwithered but, like so much gourmet wheat germ, still sprouting, even though Gary Hart, the true Yuppie hero, has come and gone.

If I am to believe what I hear during the waning days ₃ of this campaign, I remain a political wooee, an assimilator of food processors, and unbearably upwardly mobile—the latter tips me into yet another socioeconomic category, that of the Yumpie, or "young upwardly mobile professional," in layman's lingo.

Much of this is news to me, not to mention my ₄ parents. As far as I can tell, I still write rent-controlled rent checks every month and coddle along a car that is my college graduation present.

But in a sociological nutshell, it seems that we baby- ₅ boomers have come of age—not by virtue of our achievements, rather by the extent of our style. Make that Style. Brunch has become a rite of passage and an MBA an almost requisite coat of arms.

Apparently we of the Me generation have decided ₆ that, if we can't have it all, we can at least have it all First Class—a sort of "I strive, therefore I am." Our goals lie somewhere in the realm of inputtable data: a six-figure salary, live-in help, and the ability to snare the best tables at the city's top restaurants. All of it apparently reflects our insatiable taste for the good life.

As a newly christened Yuppie—an unutterably pert ₇ term to my way of thinking—I find my native tongue has undergone some rehabbing. "Mesquite" and "dhurrie" are all linguistically right on, at least for the moment, unlike the already déclassé "Fettuccine Alfredo," "networking," and "cash machine." No one has to tell Yuppies the times, they are a-changing. An appetite for affluence is now the unwritten acme of good taste—a far cry from the creeds of beads and flowers hippies.

Hence, as a true YUP, I will never, according to ₈ certain codes of behavior, drink anything instant, cancel reserved tennis court time, or pay cash. I am supposed to be too busy patronizing those restaurants displaying a requisite amount of ferns, brass and marble, where I never eat macaroni and cheese or tuna on white. I am too busy stoking up on sushi, gravlax, and gourmet chocolates.

And there is more to this way of life style.   9

I am supposed to do aerobics in the morning, jog at   10
noon, and meet at the health club after work. I am meant to work—better if I can "bill"—60-plus hours a week. But I must never tire and while away the down time in front of the TV. Excuse me, but I think I hear my arugula calling.

If my furniture doesn't float in my loft, if my cook-   11
ware (and it must be "cookware," not pots and pans) doesn't require copper cleanser or a small loan to finance, if I do not possess multiple vinegars or a particular make of German car, I will be suspected of being out of step. Or, more's the pity, I will miss becoming my own role model.

Yet, in a braver moment, I cannot resist testing the   12
waters. I had successfully brunched in the past, so I picked the yuppiest restaurant I could find and blithely booked a table for four. On the site of a humble eatery where I had previously reveled in plates of meat loaf, mashed potatoes, and brown gravy whenever I felt nostalgic for Mom-type cooking, I picked my way into a stark art deco wonder in order to see if I wore my socioeconomic label well. If I could hold my own with those who knew their way around a wedge of Brie.

I was in for trouble the minute I crossed the polished   13
threshold. Getting a meal here turned out to be as intimidating as applying for a bank loan or country club membership. The menu was as elliptical as a French symbolist poem—perfectly designed to make one feel simple-minded should a particular quail item need explication. Maybe I wasn't a true blue Yuppie after all. Not that I trembled in the face of "lightly oiled pasta," but others in the place seemed so at home, as if they had been weaned on warm lamb salad and not Bosco. My quartet stumbled through the ordering process, selecting

the most familiar dishes with a relief not felt since getting out of grad school. It looked like a long evening.

Ironically, rescue came in the form of our busboy, a 14 pleasant-looking lad who had geometrically shaped hair, wore an earring, and clearly noticed our consternation. As he refilled water glasses and passed out plates of bread and ceramic tubs of pale butter, he murmured without our even asking, "Land o' Lakes served in a ramekin." It was a clear tone of self-mockery totally out of synch with the industrial carpeting and bird-of-paradise flower arrangements. I glanced up. Sure enough, there was a wry twinkle in the busboy's eye not quite obscured by the new-wave coiffure.

Comment

Hilary de Vries defines the Yuppie through a series of humorous examples of the codes Yuppies obey, the games they play, the restaurants they patronize, and the food they eat. But being a Yuppie is more than the sum of what Yuppies do. Being a Yuppie is a state of mind that de Vries must attain. She tries to convey that state of mind and also her anxiety that she is missing the Yuppie style.

Questions for Study and Discussion

1. The Yuppie is materialistic, de Vries shows. But does the Yuppie want to acquire things for their own sake, or does acquisition satisfy other needs?
2. What other attitudes characterize the Yuppie, and how does de Vries illustrate them?
3. What does de Vries mean by the satirical statement, "I will miss becoming my own role model" (paragraph 11)? What other popular phrases like *role model* does she satirize?
4. What words or phrases suggest Yuppie talk? What is the tone of the presentation of these words and phrases?
5. Is de Vries suggesting at the end that she has succeeded in becoming a Yuppie? Or has she failed? What is the tone of

the conclusion? Does her tone change in the course of the essay, or does she maintain the same tone throughout the essay?

Vocabulary Study

1. De Vries depends on the connotations or associations of words to convey the feeling and style that mark the Yuppie. Give the denotative and connotative meanings of the following words—that is, the things the words represent, the feelings and images these words convey. Then discuss what they contribute to the humor or satire of the essay: *brunch, gourmet chocolates, aerobics, arugula, Bosco, cookware, new-wave coiffure.*

2. The phrases *Woodstock's 15th anniversary* and *Age of Aquarius* are references to a rock concert in Woodstock, New York, in 1969, and to a song in the 1960s musical *Hair,* "This is the Dawning of the Age of Aquarius." Use the *New York Times Index* and other reference sources to explain these references in the essay.

Suggestions for Writing

1. Describe your own comical efforts to join the ranks of a fashionable group of people. Choose words that give the reader the sense of what you experienced and felt.

2. Define one of the following or a similar slang or faddish word through the connotations or associations the word has for you. Where possible, illustrate the association through images or brief episodes as de Vries does. Use your discussion to make a point about these associations or uses:

    a. *funky*
    b. *jazzy*
    c. *macho*
    d. *nerdy*

Frank Deford

BEAUTY AND EVERLASTING FAITH— LOCAL LEVEL

The sports writer and novelist Frank Deford attended Princeton University, where he edited *The Daily Princetonian* and the humor magazine *The Tiger*. For many years a senior writer for *Sports Illustrated*, he has written on numerous sports, including tennis, basketball, and roller derbies. His books include *Cut 'n' Run* (1973), *The Owner* (1976), *Alex: The Life of a Child* (1983) and *Casey on the Loose* (1989). In the following section from his book on the Miss America contest, *There She Is (1971)*, Deford describes preliminary interviews in the local contest in Wilson, North Carolina, for the state title. The chapter from which this section is taken focuses on Doris Smith and Judi Brewer, who became finalists for first and second place. The veteran judges of the contest have long-standing memories of earlier winners; one of them mentions Jeanne Swanner, Miss North Carolina of 1963, who sometimes helps to conduct local contests.

The judging formally begins with the Saturday luncheon at the Heart of Wilson Motel. Dr. Vincent Thomas, the head of the judges' committee, welcomes all the judges, and is himself thereafter always introduced as "Dr. Vincent," by Jerry Ball, the well-known "dean of beauty pageant judges." Jerry has sent two state queens on to become Miss America, and judged in states as far away as Alaska. Jerry is joined on the jury by Mrs. Judy Cross, who was Most Photogenic at Miss North Carolina a few years ago, and by Mrs. Marilyn Hull, a former Miss New Jersey. She is married, as so many beauty queens are, to an athlete. Her husband is Bill Hull, a former Kansas City Chief. The other two judges are Jim Church, chairman of the board of the North Carolina Jaycees, and Bob Logan, Charlotte sales manager for Fabergé, the beauty products concern. It is a hot-shot panel for any local Pageant.

The eight contestants keep a wary eye out as they sit down to lunch and make sure to reach for the correct implements. The judges, however, show no interest whatsoever in what eating tools are being utilized. They are genial and pleasant; the girls could be dispensing peas with a knife for all they seem to care about such formalities.

Doris's hat tumbles off. She does not realize it has gone, which is not surprising, since hats are as foreign to these girls as bustles or U.S. Army fatigues would be. Judi has a hat on for exactly the second time in her life. The first time was when she was in another beauty pageant. There are speeches and everyone in attendance is introduced. Then the room is cleared, and a table set up for the judges at the far end. It is time for the serious interviewing. Officially, the girls in any *Miss America* Pageant are not graded on their interviews. Actually, it is the underside of the iceberg that determines the winner. 3

The girls are directed to another room where, one by one, they will be funneled toward the judges. Following an interview, the contestant will proceed on to another room for a sort of debriefing. The judges arrange themselves and pour coffee. The men must concentrate to do their best, for the South Carolina–Duke basketball game is just starting on TV, and their hearts all lie there. Jerry Ball presides in the middle, like a Chief Justice, a leader among equals, and everyone agrees that there will be no set order to the questioning, just "catch as catch can." 4

Dr. Thomas sits at the other end of the room with a stop watch. Jerry says, "All right, Dr. Vincent, bring in the first young lady." The girls have been assigned an order in which they will present their talents in the show; they visit the judges in the same order. Rita Deans is first. Like all the others, she has her little hat on and carries a handbag, and she walks, as she has been taught, in the proper manner. This is an unfamiliar gait for all the girls and makes them resemble the little dogs on the Ed Sullivan Show, who have outfits on, are balanced precariously on their hind feet, and take desperate little steps to keep from pitching forward. 5

Rita, seated, is straightforward and demure. She 6
assures the panel that her fourteen-year Sunday School
record is not in any danger of being jeopardized by a
victory tonight. The judges spring what is considered as
a controversial question: what does Rita think of coed
college dormitories? Rita thinks awhile. "Well, I haven't
formed an opinion about that," she finally says. Mrs.
Butner has instructed the girls to answer that way
whenever they feel that they are unsure of an answer.
The judges nod and agree that Rita would be unwise,
indeed, to venture into unknown philosophical territory.

Sharon Shackleford is next. Talkative anyway, she 7
seems especially garrulous when juxtaposed to Rita.
"You've got to pull the plug on her," a judge says upon
her departure. Wendy Formo, the third contestant, makes
the best approach of all. Over six feet tall, she cannot
help walking like a normal person. Also, she shuffles a
question about Vice President Agnew beautifully, and
the panel is obviously impressed. "It reminds you," Jim
Church says. "I always liked that Jeanne Swanner."

Bob Logan asks, "What time is it?"   8

Jerry answers, "About the end of the first quarter."   9

Peggy Murphy, recovered from the flu, is next, and   10
for her, the judges reach back for a classic old standard
of a question: what kind of person do you think you
are yourself? There is one stock answer to this question,
which every girl ever in a beauty pageant has always
provided. In so many words, it is: that I am naturally
a shy, thoughtful person, but I love a good time on
occasion. Also, I am nuts about people. Peggy is close
enough.

The interviewing is now halfway through, so the   11
judges stand and reach for some coffee. Doris comes in.
She is in yellow, with a matching handbag that she sets
on the rug by the side of her chair. She banters back the
usual polite preliminaries, and then one of the judges
asks her if she believes there is a generation gap. "Yes,
I definitely believe there is one," Doris replies firmly. All
the judges sit up and cock their heads. The regular

answer to this question is that there certainly isn't one around my house, where everyone works to understand each other better. Doris proceeds. "Ours is the first generation brought up with the threat of the hydrogen and atom bombs, and the first generation to have grown up with television as a major force in our lives. I really don't even believe it is surprising that there is a gap. Maybe we should only be surprised that there is not more of one."

The judges nod sagely, and to test her further, pull 12 another old chestnut out of the fire. All right, what about coed dorms? Doris backs down here; she comes out with the company line. "It may be fine for other people," she says, "but I can certainly see enough of the opposite sex on dates and other things." Doris has inserted a proper amount of righteous indignation in her voice by the end of her speech. The judges draw a breath, relieved not to have a genuine revolutionary on their hands. They are spent, though, so they ask her if she has any questions for them.

Gay Butner has informed the girls that they may be 13 faced with this request, and to have a question on standby. "Yes," Doris says, "I'd like to know why you're still interested in judging. Does it keep you closer to our generation and help close the gap for you?" Yes, the judges agree, yes, it certainly works that way for them.

Time is up; the panel smiles and thanks her; and 14 Doris is hardly out of the door when Jerry slams his hand down. "She came through like 'Gangbusters,'" he exclaims. "She took everything we threw at her and came right back."

"A live cookie," Jim Church says. 15

Vince Thomas goes to fetch Judi. She comes in, 16 smiling broadly, wearing her aunt's bright orange sleeveless dress. She talks enthusiastically, almost conversationally, from the moment she deposits herself in the chair before the judges. It is as if she has been doing this all her life. Judi is restrained only by what she keeps reminding herself, to keep her hands anchored in her lap and not to say "you know." She is bright and cheery and carries the judges along with her. "Learn to gain control over the interview," Gay has told all the girls. "Give a brief answer, then lead into another area that you particularly like to talk about."

That advice was like giving Judi a license to steal. [17] She and all the other modern Southern belles are born and bred in this briar patch. In Atlantic City a few months later, Phyllis George, Judi's temperamental and verbal kin, babbled on with such dazzle about her pet crab and her dog that the most serious thing that the judges found time to ask her was whether or not she liked beer—and Phyllis even side-stepped that one, and went rambling right on, absolutely stunning the judges from start to finish of the interview. Judi's footwork is proportionately as good at the Heart of Wilson Motel, but she slows down and twice permits the judges time to reach into the portfolio of controversial questions.

First, they want to know if Judi endorses drugs. Well, [18] she doesn't. Then Marilyn Hull remembers Doris. "Do you think there is a generation gap?" she asks. Judi pauses but for a second, then replies: "I don't think there's any more gap now than there's ever been." The judges nod, and then they want to know if she might have a question for them.

Judi has come loaded for that bear. "What is your [19] idea of a Miss Wilson?" she rips back at them.

A girl with poise, the judges solemnly agree. [20]

"Now, do you have any other question you would [21] like to ask us?" Jerry asks. This is a formality, like drop-over-some-time-and-see-us, but Judi tears into it at face value. "Do you think there is a generation gap?" she asks. Marilyn fields the answer, uneasily, and this time Jerry, does not ask Judi if she has another question to ask. "I'm afraid Dr. Vincent is signaling that our time is up," he informs her. Judi thanks everyone and leaves. As soon as she is out of the room, the judges start marveling about her performance. "Imagine," one says, we asked if she had another question, and she did." There is a first time for everything.

They are still chuckling at Judi's effervescence as   22
Rose Thorne comes in. She expresses a solid opposition to coed dorms, and then Connie Whisenant finishes up by voicing displeasure at those college students who had participated in the Vietnam Moratorium.

Outside the room Doris and Judi are already com-   23
paring notes. It is immediately obvious to each that her rival was not disappointed; at the least, neither felt she had done poorly. Judi is stunned to learn, though, that Doris has actually said that there is a generation gap. Was she right? Was that the correct answer that the judges were fishing for? Anyway, it only reinforces Judi's growing opinion. By the time she goes home to put her hair up in curlers, and to affix false eyelashes for the first time in her life, Judi Brewer is absolutely convinced that Doris Smith is the only thing that stands between her and Miss Wilson 1970.

Comment

Deford's attitude toward Miss America is suggested by his opening comment in the book: "Maligned by one segment of America, adored by another, misunderstood by about all of it, Miss America still flows like the Mississippi, drifts like amber waves of grain, sounds like the crack of a bat on a baseball, tastes like Mom's apple pie, and smells like dollar bills." Deford is obviously concerned with the values the contest represents. In the section reprinted here, he is direct about how the contest affects the participants. "Over six feet tall," he says about Wendy Formo, "she cannot help walking like a normal person." And he has similar things to say about how the young women act on the advice of Mrs. Butner, a woman from Rocky Mount who has been tutoring them. Another important indication of tone is the incongruity he stresses. Deford need not comment directly on the young women. His sympathy for them shapes his attitude and therefore his tone; so does his complex attitude toward the contest and the idea of "Miss America." Tone is revealed unmistakably in exaggeration as in understatement—if the author prefers not to state his or her attitude directly. The details selected for emphasis can be equally revealing.

Questions for Study and Discussion

1. How does Deford's choice of details stress the incongruous? How do his comparisons to army fatigues, bustles, and little dogs make the incongruities vivid to us? What is the tone of these statements and comparisons?
2. Does Deford express or imply the same attitude toward all the girls in the contest? To what extent is his sympathy toward them qualified by his attitude toward the values represented by or implied in the contest?
3. What are those values, and what details best reveal them?
4. How sympathetic is Deford toward the judges? Is it his view that the panel is "hot-shot," or is he giving someone's opinion of it?
5. What does Deford mean by the statement that "it is the underside of the iceberg that determines the winner"? How does he illustrate the statement?
6. Does Deford resort to understatement or irony, or does he depend solely on the details to create tone? Does the essay have an overall tone, or does the tone vary?
7. How does he establish and maintain a consistent point of view in the whole essay?
8. What are your feelings toward the contestants and the judges? How much were they shaped for you by Deford?

Vocabulary Study

Identify words and phrases that you would classify as slang (such as "hot-shot") and determine their use in the essay, in particular their contribution to the overall tone. If this slang is no longer current, suggest how the statements might be reworded to convey the same tone.

Suggestions for Writing

1. Describe a contest in which you participated. Focus on the behavior and attitude of the judges or the participants, and use your discussion to reveal your attitude toward the contest. Choose vivid details that best reveal the values represented by or implied in the contest.

2. Discuss what you think Deford is saying or implying about the contest. Consider his details about the judges as well as about the contestants.

3. Rewrite a part of this essay from the point of view of one of the contestants. Allow her attitude toward the judges and the contest itself to emerge in the details she selects and the feelings she expresses.

Usage

Each of us has a formal and informal vocabulary. We use each vocabulary on different occasions, often without much thought. On formal occasions like weddings, funerals, and job interviews, we use a vocabulary different from that at home or with friends. Though judgments about vocabulary vary from one group of people or one part of the country to another, people usually agree on what is extremely formal and informal—the language of insurance policies and that of television comedy and sports writing, for example.

Consider the following formal and informal statements:

> Increasingly, then, the critical function must be added to the traditional triumvirate of teaching, research, and public service. Criticism must be seen not as the price to be paid for the services of higher education, but as one of the most crucial of these services. As our century progresses, as our society and the world become more complex, as the pace of social change accelerates, higher education that is not eminently critical will be increasingly useless. More and more, our society and the world will need young men and women who have not only assimilated the past and made themselves familiar with the present, but who have become articulate, informed, and thoughtful critics of both.
> —Kenneth Keniston, "Youth and Dissent"

> He sailed up to me, and then cut to my left for the sidelines, with a little grunt, and I could hear the *shu-shu* of his football trousers as he went by, and the creak of his shoulder pads.
> —George Plimpton, *Paper Lion*

The vocabulary of the first passage is formal—abstract words and phrases like *critical function* and *assimilated the past* expressing abstract ideas. In the second passage, the colloquial or everyday

533

conversational phrases like *sailed up* and *cut to my left* contribute to the informality.

Vocabulary and sentence structure work together to make a piece of writing formal or informal. In the first passage the tight parallelisms and the periodic sentence that builds to the core idea (*As our century progresses*) create a highly formal effect. In the second the loose coordination is characteristic of everyday informal conversation. However, formal English is not limited to ideas, nor is informal English limited to concrete experiences. Formal English often deals with specific concrete ideas and experience and uses a simple vocabulary. Informal English often deals with ideas in concrete language and in sentences containing looser parallelism.

Slang and jargon associated with particular jobs or activities are found in informal speech and writing. Slang consists of colorful, usually short-lived expressions peculiar to a group of people. Jargon consists of the technical words specific to a trade or profession. Assembly-line workers and telephone and automobile repairmen have their own special language—in particular, special terms and expressions. So have teenagers, jazz musicians, college professors, and baseball fans. This special language is less common in formal speech and writing, mainly because the audience for that writing is usually a general one. Expressions associated with rock music will be understood by a special audience of rock fans, but a general audience will need an explanation.

As in Art Buchwald's following comic series of letters, awareness of usage often begins when a piece of writing creates an unintended impression or effect. Unless you know your audience will be a special one, you will do best to think of it as general—representing many backgrounds and interests. This advice bears especially on diction, for vocabulary gives readers the most trouble—especially inexact, ambiguous words and phrases and empty, hackneyed expressions or clichés.

Art Buchwald

JOB HUNTING

Art Buchwald was born in Mount Vernon, New York, in 1925, and was educated at the University of Southern California. During the Second World War he served in the Marine Corps. His satirical columns have been collected into many books, including *I Never Danced at the White House* (1973), *I Think I Don't Remember* (1987), and *Whose Rose Garden Is It Anyway?* (1989). His chief target has been the Washington scene but he has also written about contemporary social problems.

Vice President of Development
Glucksville Dynamics
Glucksville, California

Dear Sir,

I am writing in regard to employment with your firm. I have a BS from USC and PhD in physics from the California Institute of Technology.

In my previous position I was in charge of research and development for the Harrington Chemical Company. We did work in thermonuclear energy, laser beam refraction, hydrogen molecule development, and heavy-water computer data.

Several of our research discoveries have been adapted for commercial use, and one particular breakthrough in linear hydraulics is now being used by every oil company in the country.

Because of a cutback in defense orders, the Harrington Company decided to shut down its research and development department. It is for this reason I am available for immediate employment.

Hoping to hear from you in the near future, I remain

Sincerely yours,
Edward Kase

Dear Mr. Kase,

We regret to inform you that we have no positions available for someone of your excellent qualifications. The truth of the matter is that we find you are "overqualified" for any position we might offer you in our organization. Thank you for thinking of us, and if anything comes up in the future, we will be getting in touch with you.

> Yours truly,
> Merriman Haselbald
> Administrative Vice-President

Personnel Director
Jessel International Systems
Crewcut, Mich.

Dear Sir,

I am applying for a position with your company in any responsible capacity. I have had a college education and have fiddled around in research and development. Occasionally we have come up with some moneymaking ideas. I would be willing to start off at a minimal salary to prove my value to your firm.

> Sincerely yours,
> Edward Kase

Dear Mr. Kase,

Thank you for your letter of the 15th. Unfortunately we have no positions at the moment for someone with a college education. Frankly it is the feeling of everyone here that you are "overqualified," and your experience indicates you would be much happier with a company that could make full use of your talents.

It was kind of you to think of us.

> Hardy Landsdowne
> Personnel Dept.

To Whom It May Concern
Geis & Waterman Inc.
Ziegfried, Ill.

DERE SER,

I'd like a job with your outfit. I can do anything you want me to. You name it Kase will do it. I ain't got no education and no experience, but I'm strong and I got moxy an I get along great with people. I'm ready to start any time because I need the bread. Let me know when you want me.

Cheers
EDWARD KASE

DEAR MR. KASE,

You are just the person we have been looking for. We need a truck driver, and your qualifications are perfect for us. You can begin working in our Westminister plant on Monday. Welcome aboard.

CARSON PETERS
Personnel

Comment

Buchwald is not writing in his own person in these letters, but we do hear him indirectly—in the language he has given the correspondents. Buchwald's humor arises in the changes we see in Kase's letters and in the situation itself. Humor must develop out of real problems in the world we know: we will not find humor long in invented qualities and situations. Those problems may be serious—the problem Buchwald deals with is a serious one today. We can laugh with Buchwald because we are laughing not at Kase but at ourselves and at a current social problem.

Questions for Study and Discussion

1. How do Kase's letters change in language? What are the most important changes? What changes do you notice in sentence structure?
2. What situation is the source of Buchwald's humor? Is he satirizing this situation—that is, trying to correct it through ridicule?
3. What do Kase and his correspondents reveal about themselves in the impressions they give of themselves?

Vocabulary Study

Find substitutes for the formal diction in the letters to Kase. Discuss how their substitution would change the humor or point of the letters.

Suggestions for Writing

1. Write three letters of application for the same job. Change your language to give a different impression of yourself. Use these letters to make a satirical point, as Buchwald does.
2. Write an exchange of letters like Buchwald's, satirizing a current social problem through them. Fit the language of each letter to the character and attitude of the writer.

Robert Hendrickson

TALKIN' TEXIAN

Robert Hendrickson is the author of *The Grand Emporiums* (1979), *The Literary Life and Other Curiosities* (1981), *More Cunning Than Man* (1983), and *Human Words: The Words and Ways of American Dialects* (1972), in which this essay on the Texan dialect appears. Hendrickson writes that "almost from the beginning, the language of the nation has been a various language of tongues, beyond number, mixing in the melting pot and turning out a great feast of dialects that have enriched American English. There is no sign that this will cease at any time in the near future, and no reason to fear the process. Dialects, like languages themselves, are simply different ways people have of speaking, and by better understanding our own American dialects we can better understand our fellow Americans who speak them."

"Texian" is another variety of Southern speech, no 1 matter what most Texans may tell you—at least that variety of Texian spoken in the eastern half of the state. Western Texian, featuring the Western drawl, is, like other Southwestern and Far Western speech, more strongly influenced by General American. The Western Texas drawl extends the slight *uh* glide of General American speech (where *uh* is added before *l* and *r* in a stressed syllable, as in *shoo-UHr,* sure) to many more sounds. School, for example, is *skool* in the Middle West but pronounced *SkOOuuhl* in the Western drawl. This same *uh* drawl is added after, among other letters, *a, ow,* and *eh,* examples being *Auhlbert* (Albert), *fowahl* (fowl), and *Eauhlmer* (Elmer). The Western drawl of West Texas is more restrained and not so musical as the Southern drawl of East Texas. While it is an unhurried speech, the Western drawl doesn't suggest "relaxed laziness," suggesting cogitation, or weighing one's words, rather than mere indolence. Many ranching terms enrich this dialect and one hears remarks like "It's such a fur piece you've got to ride a pregnant mare to get back."

Technically, the Southern dialect of East Texas is of ₂ both the twangy lilting South Midland variety of Northeast Texas and the Southern plantation variety heard in Southeast Texas. Of course these two dialects, and that of West Texas, mingle throughout the state, but the East Texas dialect influenced by Southern and Mountain speech, and to a much smaller extent by General American, is the typical speech of Texas. Nowhere in America is there a more effortless speech, one more relaxed in delivery. East Texian is distinctly nasalized with a slow tempo and is intoned almost monotonously. Its vowels are held long, and the first syllables of words are often accented, especially in short words. Speakers are apt to speak rather too loud, for aliens, throughout the great breadth of the Lone Star State.

"There is something good and something bad of ₃ every land" in Texas, as an old saying puts it, for the state was settled by immigrants from many lands, including Mexicans, Germans, Czechs, and Northerners, as well as people from the Southern states, while recently there has been a massive invasion of Yankees. Spanish ways and words are common in a state founded by Spaniards; even something as basic as the famous *ten-gallon hat* that Texas cowboys wore in days past has its roots in the Spanish word for braid, *galón*—because the wide-brimmed hats worn by cowboys were originally decorated with a number of braids at the base of the crown. The nearest thing in Texas today to a ten-gallon hat is called a *Stetson*, every red-blooded male Texan owning at least one of these. This basic Texan hat shows Yankee influence. The *Stetson* was invented by Philadelphian John Batterson Stetson, who had to travel west because of poor health at the time of the Civil War. While out West it occurred to him that no one was manufacturing hats suited to the cowboy, and on his return to Philadelphia in 1865 he went into the hat business, specializing in Western-style headgear. The wide-brimmed, ten-gallon felt hats he manufactured immediately became popular with cowboys. They have been called *Stetsons* or *John Bs* ever since, and the John B. Stetson Company is today one of the world's largest hat manufacturers.

In more recent times Spanglish, a lively combination 4 of Spanish and English, has become so prominent a way of speech throughout Texas that it is also known as Tex-Mex and Texican. From one end of the state to the other there are so many slight variations in ways of speaking that Texans can't even agree on the pronunciation of Texas—the leading contenders are *Tex-siz* and *Tex-sis*, with the Yankee *Tex-suhs* a distant third. Dyed-in-the-wool Texans hold stubbornly to their pronunciations, too. A visiting Britisher told one rancher: "The Hereford bull, who comes originally from my own part of the world, does not pronounce himself Hearford, as you seem to suppose, but Herreford." "Is that right?" the rancher replied. "Wal, he pronounces himself Hearford on my ranch."

Hospitable Texans *do* still say *Y'all all come!* Stetson 5 tipped over his eyes, the typical Texan will say things like *Kin ah carry you home?* for "Can I give you a ride (or lift)?"; *Ah need to visit with you*, when he means he wants to chat with you on the phone; and *Kin ah hep you* for "Can I help you?" One lady who worked for Air France and was taught to say *France* like a Frenchwoman habitually answered the phone, "Air Frawnce, kin ah hep you?"

Texans particularly like to pronounce the *en* sound 6 their own way. They don't cotton to it being pronounced *en*, so when they talk about the *awl bidness* they might mention the innerjy *crunch* or the *free interprise system*. By the same system *ten* becomes *tin*, *twenty* is *twinny*, *cent* is *cint*, *went* is *wint*, *friendship* becomes *frinship*, *tennis* becomes *tinnis*, *temperatures* are *timperatures* *entertainment* is *innertainment*, *Wednesday* is *Winsdy* and—to put an *inding* to this—*Kennedy* Airport is *Kinnidy* Airport.

The rule in Texas is to say *heidi* (howdy) to anyone   7
who says *heidi* to you. *Thank you* is pronounced *thang
cue.* Other *wards* with pronunciation unique to the *airs*
(ears) of most *Markins* (Americans) include *watt* for
while, hem for *him, blond* for *blind, aint* for *aunt, main*
for *mean, day-ins* for *dance, rum* for *room, drouth* for
drought, suede for *sweet, bob wahr* for *barbed wire,
prod* for *proud* and *small* for *smile.* The *Lard* only
knows how many more such specimens there are from
Hico (pronounced *Hy-co*) to Houston.

Many common words with the *ay* vowel sound are   8
pronounced with *eh* in Texian, including *nehkid* (na-
ked) and *eht* (ate). The *aw* sound is heard in words like
dawg (dog) and *cawst* (cost); the long *i* is generally
pronounced as *ah,* as in *fahuh* (fire) and *hahuh* (hire);
and many Texans pronounce the *oo* sound as *oh,* as in
poh (poor) and *shoh* (sure). Among consonant changes
from General American the *d* is often dropped after *n,*
as in *wunner* (wonder); the participial *ing* is generally
pronounced *in,* as in *sittin* (sitting); and the *n* is often
dropped completely, as in *kawfuhdis* (confidence), being
replaced with a distinctly nasalized *aw,* which one speech
teacher calls among "the main reasons for the extreme
nasality in Texas speech." There are, of course, many
exceptions but both vowel and consonant pronunciations in Texian are more similar to those of Southern
speech than any other.

The Southern *yawl* of *you-all* is just as popular in   9
Texian as in Southern speech. *All,* in fact, is also used
after the interrogative pronoun *what* ("What-all did you
do yesterday?") and *who* ("Who-all is coming?"). *Is all,*
a short form of *that's all,* is commonly added to the end
of sentences, as in "He just wants some meat, is all."
Sometimes unheard questions are replied to in Texian
with *Says which?,* a practice similar to the Black English
Say what? Other typical Texian usages are indicated in
these sentences:

- She's the hell-raisingist woman I know.
- I'm about to rustle up some grub (prepare some food or a meal).
- I reckon he's went (gone) to Houston.
- He bought some blinky (sour) milk.
- I might would (I may) do it.
- She put a big pot in a little one (outdid herself entertaining).
- He done went there.
- Did you seed (see) that?
- She give him the gate (divorced him).
- I'll wait on (wait for) you.
- He wouldn't go 'thout (contraction of *without* used in place of "unless") they took the train.
- Don't pay him no nevermind (attention).
- She's about to law (sue) him.
- Ain't nary a one (nobody) coming.
- I might could do that.

Sadly, a lot of Texans feel as embarrassed about their dialect as New Yorkers do about Brooklynese. An amusing article by *New York Times* Houston bureau chief Robert Reinhold, to which I owe several of these examples of Texian, reports Fred Tarpley, a language and literature professor at East Texas State University, as saying, "Unfortunately, Texans have a great inferiority complex about their language [though] this is an honorable dialect that we speak for historical reasons; I feel we need to extend the Texas pride to speech." As Jan Morris has noted, "One feels the pull of metropolitan life" in Texas, as one does all over the world, "like some massive unseen magnet over the horizon." While the rural areas are fighting a strong holding action, the big *innernational cities* in Texas are increasingly becoming merely international, losing a lot of their Texian flavor. Observers have reported that Houstonites, in particular, a breed of archetypal doers, are beginning to sound like everybody else, in both pronunciation and vocabulary, even eliminating such historic Texan redundancies as *cashmoney.* Few people shout *Yahoo!* in Houston anymore, but elsewhere there are still nice euphemisms, like *winter Texans* for senior citizens, places with names like *The Crazy Water Hotel* at Mineral Wells, statues like the one to the cow called *MOO-LAH (42 gallons annually)* at Stephenville, and local football teams with names like the *Itasca Wampus Cats,* the *Mesquite Skeeters,* and the *Hutto Hippos.* The rural rearguard and others proud of their heritage are holding the Alamo and it will be a long time before they surrender, if ever.

Comment

In describing the pronunciation of "Texian," Hendrickson records sounds heard in formal as well as informal speech, though he notes that Houstonites and perhaps other urban Texans "are beginning to sound like everybody else." In contrast to pronunciation, many of the words and phrases he describes probably are heard more in informal than in formal speech; words like *Stetson* are, of course, heard at both levels of speech. Hendrickson makes the point that Texans have no more reason to be embarrassed about their dialect than New Yorkers have reason to be about Brooklynese (described earlier in his book on American speech). Prescriptive standards, based on mistaken ideas on what is grammatical and "correct," often extend to dialect. Some dialects like Black English do, in fact, have different grammatical structures, as the linguist Geneva Smitherman points out. In Black English, the statement "He be tired" means that the person is tired every day, not just occasionally. The speaker would have omitted *be* from the sentence if referring to just a single day. Rules such as this govern the syntax or grammar of dialects, just as rules of pronunciation govern speech. General English, itself a dialect, has leveled or smoothed out many of the differences in regional and other American dialects. Widely written and spoken, it is the favored dialect in the social and political affairs of the country, as well as in its journalism and other public discourse. It is the "edited American English" of the essays in this book. Yet general English is not more "correct" or more expressive than other dialects, as the speakers in Mark Twain's *Huckleberry Finn* and Alice Walker's *The Color Purple* show.

Questions for Study and Discussion

1. Is "Texian" the dialect of all Texans, or only of those in the eastern half of the state?
2. Why does Hendrickson stress that the "Texian" vocabulary has many sources, including Spanish and Yankee speakers?
3. What does "Texian" reveal about the character of some "Texian" speakers?
4. Does your dialect have any of the characteristics of "Texian," if you are from another part of the United States? If you are a Texan, can you cite other words and phrases and features of pronunciation typical of your dialect?

Vocabulary Study

1. What is a *drawl*? Are the drawls of the Western and the Southern speaker necessarily the same?
2. How is a *dialect* different from a *vernacular*, an *argot*, and a *jargon*?
3. Use your college dictionary to find out the source and original meaning, if different from the current meaning, of the following words:

almanac	*poltergeist*	*toboggan*
balcony	*sergeant*	*tornado*
gumbo	*shark (human)*	*tulip*
mosquito	*shibboleth*	*whiskey*
mustang	*slogan*	*woodchuck*

Suggestions for Writing

1. Hendrickson states that "speakers are apt to speak rather too loud, for aliens, throughout the great breadth of the Lone Star State." Discuss different gestures and ways of speaking that you notice among speakers in your college or in your town, city, or state. Show how misunderstandings can arise between people because of these differences.

2. Describe the pronunciation, vocabulary, and syntax or grammar of a friend or relative who speaks a dialect different from
yours. Compare these features with those in your own dialect,
noting similarities as well as differences.

Glossary

allusion: An indirect reference to a presumably well-known literary work or a historical event or figure. The phrase "the Waterloo of his political career" is a reference to Napoleon's disastrous defeat at the Battle of Waterloo in 1815. The allusion implies that the career of the politician under discussion has come to a dramatic end.

analogy: A point-by-point comparison between two unlike things or activities (for example, comparing writing an essay to building a house) for the purpose of illustration or argument. Unlike a comparison (or contrast), in which the things compared are of equal importance, analogy exists for the purpose of illustrating or arguing the nature of one of the compared things, not both.

antithesis: The arrangement of contrasting ideas in grammatically similar phrases and clauses *(The world will little note, nor long remember, what we say here, but it can never forget what they did here.   —Lincoln, Gettysburg Address)*. See *parallelism*.

argument: Proving the truth or falseness of a statement. Arguments are traditionally classified as *inductive* or *deductive*. See *deductive argument* and *inductive argument*. Argument can be used for different purposes in writing. See *purpose*.

autobiography: Writing about one's own experiences, often those of growing up and making one's way in the world. The autobiographical writings of Mary E. Mebane and Maya Angelou describe their childhood in the South.

balanced sentence: A sentence containing parallel phrases and clauses of approximately the same length and wording. *(You can fool all the people some of the time, and some of the people all the time, but you cannot fool all the people all of the time.   —Lincoln)*.

cause and effect: Analysis of the conditions that must be present for an event to occur *(cause)* and of the results or consequences of the event *(effect)*. An essay may deal with causes or with effects only.

classification and division: *Classification* arranges individual objects into groups or classes (Jonathans, Winesaps, Golden Delicious, and Macintoshes are types of apples). *Division* arranges a broad class into subclasses according to various principles (the broad class *apples* can be divided on the basis of their color, use, variety, or taste). There are as many divisions as principles of division or subclassification.

cliché: A once-colorful expression made stale through overuse *(putting on the dog, mad as a wet hen)*.

coherence: The sense, as we read, that the details and ideas of a work connect clearly. A paragraph or essay that does not hold together seems incoherent.

colloquialism: An everyday expression in speech and informal writing. Colloquialisms are not substandard or "illiterate" English. They are common in informal English and occur sometimes in formal English.

comparison and contrast: The analysis of similarities and differences between two or more persons, objects, or events (A and B) for the purpose of a relative estimate. The word *comparison* sometimes refers to the analysis of similarities and differences in both A and B. *Block comparison* presents each thing being compared as a whole (that is, if the comparison is between A and B, then features a, b, c of A are discussed as a block of information, then features a, b, c, of B are

547

compared to A in their own block of information). *Alternating comparison* presents the comparable features one by one (a, a, b, b, c, c).

complex sentence: A sentence consisting of one main or independent clause, and one or more subordinate or dependent clauses. *(The rain began when she stepped outside).*

compound sentence: A sentence consisting of coordinated independent clauses *(She stepped outside and then the rain began).*

compound-complex sentence: A sentence consisting of two or more main or independent clauses and at least one subordinate or dependent clause *(She stepped outside as the rain began, but she did not return to the house).*

concrete and abstract words: Concrete words refer to particular objects, people, and events (Benedict Arnold, Franklin Delano Roosevelt, the Rocky Mountains); abstract words refer to general shared qualities (treason, courage, beauty). Concrete writing makes abstract ideas perceptible to the senses through details and images.

concreteness: Making an idea exist through the senses. Writing can be concrete at all three levels—informal, general, and formal. See *concrete and abstract words.*

connotation: Feelings, images, and ideas associated with a word. Connotations change from reader to reader, though some words probably have the same associations for everybody.

context: The surrounding words or sentences that suggest the meaning of a word or phrase. Writers may dispense with formal definition if the context clarifies the meaning of a word.

coordinate sentence: A sentence that joins clauses of the same weight and importance through the conjunction *and, but, for, or, nor,* or *yet,* or through semicolons; sometimes followed by conjunctive adverbs *(however, therefore, nevertheless, in fact).*

deductive argument: Reasoning from statements assumed to be true or well-established factually. These statements or assumptions are thought sufficient to guarantee the truth of the inferences or conclusions. In formal arguments they are called premises. A valid argument reasons correctly from the premises to the conclusion. A sound argument is true in its premises and valid in its reasoning. See *enthymeme, syllogism.*

definition: Explaining the current meaning of a word through its etymology or derivation, its denotation, or its connotations. Denotative or "real" definitions single out a word from all other words (or things) like it by giving *genus* and specific *difference.* Connotative definitions give the associations people make to the word. See *connotation.*

description: A picture in words of people, objects, and events. Description often combines with narrative and it may serve exposition and persuasion.

division: See *classification and division.*

enthymeme: A deductive argument that does not state the conclusion or one of the premises directly. The following statement is an enthymeme: *Citizens in a democracy, who refuse to register for the draft, are not acting responsibly.* The implied premise is that the responsible citizen obeys all laws, even repugnant ones.

essay: A carefully organized composition that develops a single idea or impression or develops several related ideas or impressions. The word sometimes describes a beginning or trial attempt that explores the central idea or impression instead of developing it completely.

example: A picture or illustration of an idea, or one of many instances or occurrences that is typical of the rest.

exposition: An explanation or unfolding or setting forth of an idea, usually for the purpose of giving information. Exposition is usually an important part of persuasive writing. Example, process analysis, causal analysis, definition, classification and division, and comparison and contrast are forms of exposition.

expressive writing: Essays, diaries, journals, letters, and other kinds of writing that present personal feelings and beliefs for their own sake. The expressive writer is not primarily concerned with informing or persuading readers.

figure of speech: A word or phrase that departs from its usual meaning. Figures of speech make statements vivid and capture the attention of readers. The most common figures are based on similarity between things. See *metaphor personification, simile.* Other figures are based on relationship. See *allusion. Metonymy* refers to a thing by one of its qualities (*the Hill* as a reference to the United States Congress). *Synecdoche* refers to a thing by one of its parts (*wheels* as a reference to racing cars). Other figures are based on contrast between statements and realities. See *irony.* Related to irony is *understatement,* or saying less than is appropriate *(Napoleon's career ended unhappily at Waterloo). Hyperbole* means deliberate exaggeration *(crazy about ice cream). Paradox* states an apparent contradiction *(All great truths begin as blasphemies* —G. B. Shaw). *Oxymoron,* a kind of paradox, joins opposite qualities into a single image *(lake of fire).*

focus: The limitation of subject in an essay. The focus may be broad, as in a panoramic view of the mountains, or it may be narrow, as in a view of a particular peak. For example, a writer may focus broadly on the contribution to scientific thought of scientists from various fields, or focus narrowly on the achievements of astronomers or chemists or medical researchers, or focus even more narrowly on the achievements of Albert Einstein as representative of twentieth-century science.

formal English: Spoken and written English, often abstract in content, with sentences tighter than spoken ones, and an abstract and sometimes technical vocabulary. See *general English* and *informal English.*

general English: A written standard that has features of informal and formal English and avoids the extremes of both. See *formal English* and *informal English.*

image: A picture in words of an object, a scene, or a person. Though visual images are common in writing, they are not the only kind. Images can also be auditory, tactile, gustatory, and olfactory. Keats's line "With beaded bubbles winking at the brim" appeals to our hearing and taste as well as to our sight. His phrase "coming musk-rose" appeals to our sense of smell. Images help to make feelings concrete.

implied thesis: The central idea of the essay, suggested by the details and discussion rather than stated directly. See *thesis.*

inductive argument: Inductive arguments reason from particulars of experience to general ideas—from observation, personal experience, and experimental testing to probable conclusions. Inductive arguments make predictions on the basis of past and present experience. An argumentative analogy is a form of inductive argument because it is based on limited observation and experience and therefore can claim probability only. Analysis of causes and effects, like statistical analysis, is inductive when used in argument.

"inductive leap": Making the decision that sufficient inductive evidence (personal experience, observation, experimental testing) exists to draw a conclusion. Sometimes the writer of the argument makes the leap too quickly and bases his conclusions on insufficient evidence.

informal English: Written English, usually concrete in content, tighter than the loose sentences of spoken English, but looser in sentence construction than formal

English. The word *informal* refers to the occasion of its use. A letter to a friend is usually informal; a letter of application is usually formal. See *formal English* and *general English*.

irony: A term generally descriptive of statements and events. An ironic statement says the opposite of what the speaker or writer means, or implies that something more is meant than is stated, or says the unexpected *(He has a great future behind him)*. An ironic event is unexpected or is so coincidental that it seems impossible *(The firehouse burned to the ground)*.

jargon: The technical words of a trade or profession (in computer jargon, the terms *input* and *word processor*). Unclear, clumsy, or repetitive words or phrasing, sometimes the result of misplaced technical words *(He gave his input into the decision process)*.

loose sentence: A sentence that introduces the main idea close to the beginning and concludes with a series of modifiers *(The car left the expressway, slowing on the ramp and coming to a stop at the crossroad)*. See *periodic sentence*.

metaphor: An implied comparison that attributes the qualities of one thing to another (the word *mainstream* to describe the opinions or activities of most people).

mixed metaphor: The incongruous use of two metaphors in the same context *(The roar of protest was stopped in its tracks)*.

narrative: The chronological presentation of events. Narrative often combines with description and it may serve exposition or persuasion.

order of ideas: The presentation of ideas in a paragraph or an essay according to a plan. The order may be *spatial,* perhaps moving from background to foreground, or from top to bottom, or from side to side; or the order may be *temporal* or chronological (in the order of time). The presentation may be in the order of *importance,* or if the details build intensively, in the order of *climax.* The paragraph or essay may move from *problem to solution* or from the specific to the *general.* Some of these orders may occur together—for example, a chronological presentation of details that build to a climax.

parallelism: Grammatically similar words, phrases, and clauses arranged to highlight similar ideas *(There are neighborhoods of nations. . . . There are streets where, on January nights, fires burn on every floor of every house. . . . There are meadows and fields. . .   —Mark Helprin)*. See *antithesis*.

paraphrase: A rendering of a passage in different words that retain the sense, the tone, and the order of ideas.

periodic sentence: A sentence that builds to the main idea *(Building speed as it curved down the ramp, the car sped into the crowded expressway)*. See *loose sentence*.

personification: Giving animate or human qualities to something inanimate or inhuman (The sun *smiled* at the earth).

persuasion: The use of argument or satire or some other means to change thinking and feeling about an issue.

point of view: The place or vantage point from which an event is seen and described. The term sometimes refers to the mental attitude of the viewer in narrative. Mark Twain's *Huckleberry Finn* narrates the adventures of a boy in slave-owning Missouri from the point of view of the boy, not from that of an adult.

premise: See *syllogism*.

process: An activity or operation containing steps usually performed in the same order. The process may be mechanical (changing a tire), natural (the circulation of the blood), or historical (the rise and spread of a specific epidemic disease such as bubonic plague at various times in history).

purpose: The aim of the essay as distinguished from the means used to develop it. The purposes or aims of writing are many; they include expressing personal feelings and ideas, giving information, persuading readers to change their thinking about an issue, inspiring readers to take action, giving pleasure. These purposes may be achieved through description, narrative, exposition, or argument. These means may be used alone or in combination, and an essay may realize more than one purpose.

reflection: An essay that explores ideas without necessarily bringing the exploration to completion. The reflective essay can take the form of a loosely organized series of musings or tightly organized arguments.

satire: Ridicule of foolish or vicious behavior or ideas for the purpose of correcting them. *Social satire* concerns foolish but not dangerous behavior and ideas— for example, coarse table manners, pretentious talk, harmless gossip. George Bernard Shaw's "Arms and the Man" is a social satire. *Ethical satire* attacks vicious or dangerous behavior or ideas—religious or racial bigotry, greed, political corruption. Mark Twain's *Huckleberry Finn* is an ethical satire.

simile: A direct comparison between two things *(A growing child is like a young tree)*. See *figure of speech, metaphor.*

simple sentence: A sentence consisting of a single main or independent clause and no subordinate or dependent clauses *(The rain started at nightfall).*

slang: Colorful and sometimes short-lived expressions peculiar to a group of people, usually informal in usage and almost always unacceptable in formal usage *(nerd, goof off).*

style: A distinctive manner of speaking or writing. A writing style may be plain in its lack of metaphor and other figures of speech. Another writing style may be highly colorful or ornate.

subordinate clause: A clause that completes a main clause or attaches to it as a modifier (She saw *that the rain had begun; When it rains,* it pours).

syllogism: The formal arrangement of premises and conclusion of a deductive argument. The premises are the general assumptions or truths *(All reptiles are cold-blooded vertebrates, All snakes are reptiles)* from which necessary conclusions are drawn *(All snakes are cold-blooded vertebrates).* This formal arrangement helps to test the validity or correctness of the reasoning from premises to conclusion. See *deductive argument.*

symbol: An object that represents an abstract idea. The features of the symbol (the fifty stars and thirteen horizontal stripes of the American flag) suggest characteristics of the object symbolized (the fifty states of the Union, the original confederation of thirteen states). A sign need not have this representative quality: a green light signals "go," and a red light "stop" by conventional agreement.

thesis: The central idea that organizes the many smaller ideas and details of the essay.

tone: The phrasing or words that express the attitude or feeling of the speaker or writer. The tone of a statement ranges from the angry, exasperated, and sarcastic, to the wondering or approving. An ironic tone suggests that the speaker or writer means more than the words actually state.

topic sentence: Usually the main or central idea of the paragraph that organizes details and subordinate ideas. Though it often opens the paragraph, the topic sentence can appear later—in the middle or at the end of the paragraph.

transition: A word or phrase *(however, thus, in fact)* that connects clauses and sentences. Parallel structure is an important means of transition.

unity: The connection of ideas and details to a central controlling idea of the essay. A unified essay deals with one idea at a time.

Copyrights and Acknowledgments

552

Index

See the Glossary, p. 547, for additional definition of key terms and others not listed above.